Material Christianity

Material Christianity

RELIGION AND
POPULAR CULTURE
IN AMERICA

Colleen McDannell

Yale University Press
New Haven & London · 1995

Set in Garamond Simoncini by SX Composing Ltd, England
Printed and bound in Hong Kong through World Print Ltd

Library of Congress Cataloging-in-Publication Data

McDannell, Colleen.
   Material Christianity: Religion and Popular Culture in America/Colleen McDannell.
   Includes bibliographical references and index.
   ISBN 0–300–06440–3
   1. Religious articles — United States.   2. Christianity — United States.   3. United States — Religious life and customs.   I. Title.
BR515.M35   1995
246'.0973 — dc20   95–18066
                                                                          CIP

A catalogue record of this book is available from the British Library

To my teachers:
Allen F. Davis
William Gravely
Gene Paul Strayer

Contents

Acknowledgments

One of the more enjoyable things about writing a book is publicly thanking some of those friends, colleagues, and institutions who helped in the endeavor. Since I chose to explore several Christian traditions at various periods, I depended on the expertise and kindness of many people. My colleagues and friends at the University of Utah were exceptionally supportive, and I extend my thanks to Russell Belk, Meg Brady, Eric Hinderaker, Rebecca Horn, Dorothee Kocks, Dean May, Peggy Pascoe, and Kathryn Stockton. To help me understand the world of the Latter-day Saints, I appreciate the help of Richard Ouellette, Elbert Peck, George Smith, and Margaret Toscano. For aid in deciphering the world of art, Frank McEntire and David Morgan provided important guidance. Betty DeBerg, Jenny Franchot, Peter Gardella, and Patricia Killen steered me through the intricacies of Christian life in America. A special thank you is extended to Robert Orsi who has always graciously shared his own research and speculations about religion with me and who made conscientious suggestions concerning the direction of several chapters. My "heavenly" co-author, Bernhard Lang, must be thanked for his care in shaping this more materialist solo effort. Robert Baldock, my editor at Yale University Press, London, also encouraged the shift from heaven to earth. Without all of their insights and encouragement, this book could not have been written.

To the anonymous donor who funded my endowed chair, I hope this book is proof that scholars studying religion at a state university can help further the understanding of Christianity in America. Grants from the American Academy of Religion; the Cushwa Center for the Study of American Catholicism, Notre Dame University; the Louisville Institute for the Study of American Protestantism; and the University of Utah Research Committee permitted me to fund research travel and to photograph the objects included in this book. Our university's Undergraduate Research Opportunities Program granted fellowships to several students who enthusiastically and competently helped me with this project. Archivists and librarians guided me through their collections and helped facilitate the reproduction of their Christian material culture. Special thanks go to: Joseph Casino, Philadelphia Archdiocesan Research Center; Ken Rowe, Methodist Archives, Drew University; David Ramsey, Archives of Modern Christian Art, College of Notre Dame; Wendy Schlereth, Notre Dame Archives; and the staff at the Christian Booksellers Association. After finishing the research, a two-quarter Career Development Leave granted by the University of Utah, College of Humanities, enabled me to complete the manuscript. In an age of diminishing resources for scholarly research, I am grateful to these institutions for supporting this study.

I dedicate this book to three of my professors who helped guide me through the turmoil of my undergraduate and graduate study. Their friendship, concern for my intellectual development, and enthusiasm for the humanities proved an excellent model for what it means to be a true teacher. I hope that this book may serve as partial acknowledgment of their support over many years.

Finally, with an abundance of love, I want to credit John Hurdle for seeing yet one more project into print. After twenty-one-plus years of marriage, there is little that he has not done to make it possible for me to write, teach, and live a vibrant life. To my best friend, thank you.

Illustration Credits

1

Material Christianity

In June 1941, Jack Delano took a photograph of the interior of a home built by the Farm Security Administration.[1] The family who lived in this prefabricated house had to leave their original residence because the army wanted the space for military maneuvers. We do not know anything else about this family except what we can see in the photograph. We cannot even be sure how to read the photograph, since we do not know how government photographer Jack Delano influenced the composition of the picture. Did he purposely pose the children under the *Ecce Homo* lithograph? Did he coax the older woman to place her arm spontaneously across the parlor organ?

For all that we do not know, what we can confidently say about this family is that they lived in a house that displayed traditional Christian objects and iconography. On the far left, sitting on a dresser is a reprint of *The Infant Samuel*. The original, painted by Sir Joshua Reynolds in 1776, is owned by the Tate Gallery in London. Above the children is a framed portrait of the head of Christ surrounded by a crown of thorns. It is very similar to an *Ecce Homo* painted by Guido Reni in 1636–7 that hung in the Dresden Gemäldegalerie until it was destroyed during World War II. The suffering Christ is balanced by a calendar with a print of a little girl playing ball with a dog. The dominant object in the photograph is a Victorian parlor organ, festooned with knickknacks and a kerosene lamp. Three books lie on the organ: *Revival Hymns*, *Gospel Hymns*, and one with no cover. Above the *Infant Samuel* may be a chromolithograph of the Holy Family of Jesus, Mary, and Joseph, but the print is overexposed and the images are difficult to make out.

This photograph visually demonstrates an overlooked dimension of American Christianity: the material dimension. This family, as well as other American families, placed in their home pictures and furniture with religious connotations. American Christians, this book argues, want to see, hear, and touch God. It is not enough for Christians to go to church, lead a righteous life, and hope for an eventual place in heaven. People build religion into the landscape, they make and buy pious images for their homes, and they wear special reminders of their faith next to their bodies. Religion is more than a type of knowledge learned through reading holy books and listening to holy men. The physical expressions of religion are not exotic or eccentric elements that can be relegated to a particular community or a specific period of time. Throughout American history, Christians have explored the meaning of the divine, the nature of death, the power of healing, and the experience of the body by interacting with a created world of images and shapes.

People learn the discourses and habits of their religious community through the

1. According to the caption of the photogra[ph] taken by Jack Delano in 1941, this family from Caroline County, Virgin[ia] "had to move out of th[e] area being taken over b[y] the Army for maneuver[s] grounds. They are now living in one of the pre-fabricated houses built [by] the Farm Security Administration for thes[e] people." FSA photographers were expected to document housing improvements accomplished by the agency, and Delano may have tried to indicate th[e] enhanced living conditio[ns] by placing the family nea[r] a symbol of middle-c[lass] respectability.

material dimension of Christianity. By singing Gospel hymns and looking at pictures of the tortured Jesus, this African American family internalized a set of religious ideals.[2] They *practiced* their religion, as one would practice the piano in order to become a competent pianist. The symbol systems of a particular religious language are not merely handed down, they must be learned through doing, seeing, and touching. Christian material culture does not simply reflect an existing reality. Experiencing the physical dimension of religion helps *bring about* religious values, norms, behaviors, and attitudes. Practicing religion sets into play ways of thinking. It is the continual interaction with objects and images that makes one religious in a particular manner. Each of the case studies presented here demonstrates how the material dimension of Christianity may be used to decipher the meanings of religious life in America. Studying material Christianity lets us see how the faithful perpetuate their religion day in and day out.[3]

Material Culture Studies and the Study of Religion

From the 1970s to the 1990s, significant theoretical and practical research has been directed toward understanding what it means to live in a world made up not only of ideas but of things.[4] My exploration of material Christianity extends this research trend. It shares with historians, archeologists, folklorists, art and architecture specialists, and social scientists the goal of understanding American religious practice and thought through a close examination of the physical, sensual, corporeal, and phenomenal world. The non-written text is also a language of expression of American life and culture. Neither utilitarian nor uniquely artistic, the products of human skill and imagination embody and symbolize patterns of beliefs, social needs, and behavior. Unlike historians who generally use visual or artifactual materials only to illustrate themes or topics drawn from written sources, material culture specialists derive meanings from objects themselves by paying attention to the form, distribution, function, and changing character of the objects and their environments. They want to know how people use things and experience spaces. What separates students of material culture from antiquarians is the insistence that objects are not merely interesting forms to be described and collected. The material world of landscapes, tools, buildings, household goods, clothing, and art is not neutral and passive; people interact with the material world thus permitting it to communicate specific messages.

As a body of evidence, material culture may be divided into four categories: artifacts, landscapes, architecture, and art. Artifacts are the objects used in everyday life and on special occasions. The term "artifact" refers to something that has been made by human workmanship. Artifacts are the objects, the stuff, the things that surround us. Sewing machines and grave markers are among the many artifacts that scholars examine to reveal how decorative arts and technological innovations reflect and consolidate American values and behaviors.[5] While the term "artifact" works well to categorize a chair or a dress, the phrase "religious artifact" sounds like something an archeologist digs up rather than something bought in a Christian bookstore or made as a birthday gift. The very lack of an appropriate term to categorize religious objects hints at our reluctance to see that people may give significance to a family Bible, a bottle of Lourdes water, or to a

Mormon priesthood garment. By placing an object in a specific historical context, religious artifacts act as windows onto a particular religious world. Christian goods are not merely the offspring of our growing commercial economy; they constitute a vital aspect of people's religious lives.

Cultivated nature, what may be called "landscape," also comprises part of the material dimension of American life. The natural environment undergoes a transformation when trees are planted, roads paved, houses built, and churches constructed. Like a chair that is made by human hands or a human-designed machine, landscapes are shaped by human intent. People manipulate nature, sometimes subtly and frequently powerfully, to express their communal and personal values. Why, geographers ask, do people put up fences? What structured the vernacular landscape of the antebellum North? Can the American city be read as a text?[6] Religious landscapes have also been, and continue to be, constructed throughout the United States. Christianity is not practiced only in churches. The landscape of a Victorian cemetery, for instance, both expressed the piety of urban Protestants and intensified those sentiments. Laurel Hill Cemetery is one of many religious landscapes. Evangelical Christians build recreational centers, Catholics establish college campuses, and Methodists found camp meetings.[7] Sacred space, as the site for both formal rituals and informal gestures, "anchors a worldview in the world."[8]

Architectural and art historians increasingly study the visual and built environment as a means to understand religious change. The art historical model, that assumes the unique expression of design, is giving way to a cultural approach that uses buildings, paintings, sculpture, and photography as sources to explore topics such as congregational power, the Incarnation, the sexuality of Christ, and the meaning of female nudity.[9] Increasingly, studies of architecture and art are being conducted by scholars outside of the art disciplines. These scholars wonder what social messages we receive as we walk through an art or a natural history museum. Why do people hang prints of landscape paintings in their homes? What does the distinct structure of folk housing mean?[10] Since there have been fine studies of how art and architecture express American religious belief and behavior, I have chosen not to examine a particular church or museum painting.[11] Instead, I shall discuss how the rhetoric describing "tasteful" art and architecture reflects underlying tensions within American Christianity. What connections do Christians make between the body of Christ, the church as the body of Christ, and the individual Christian's body?

The artifacts, landscapes, architecture, and arts that make up material culture are not discrete units. Each of these interacts with the others to produce an array of physical expressions. Material culture is not static; it is constantly changing as people invent, produce, market, gift, or dismantle it. A natural product like water, for example, is transformed into an artifact when Catholics in France bottle it and priests ship it to the devout across the United States. Christian T-shirts do not merely appear on teenagers' bodies. They must be conceptualized, manufactured, advertised, and sold. Changes in technology, fashion, and community composition alter the production and use of material culture. To understand the history of Christian T-shirts or Catholic shrines we must not merely analyze their symbolic qualities; we must also look at how they fit into a system of exchange organized and given meaning by individuals.

Material culture in itself has no intrinsic meaning of its own. Objects or landscapes are understood and gain significance when their "human" elements can be deciphered. Objects become meaningful within specific patterns of relationships. It is only through an examination of the historical and present context of material culture that it can be "read." A Latter-day Saint priesthood garment, for instance, can be recognized as a religious artifact only if one is familiar with Mormon iconography and the history of Mormon rituals. If we want to know more about the garment, we must ask how it was (or is) used in Mormon practice. We also must recognize that different people will use artifacts or experience environments in different ways: meaning is culturally contingent. Sometimes there will be conflicts of meaning and function. People enliven artifacts and landscapes through use but we as scholars are not always privileged to observe that interaction. There are times when we are left alone with the silent object and no documentation. At that point it is even more imperative to place material culture in the society that produced it.

In his review of Thomas Schlereth's *Material Culture: A Research Guide*, Gregg Finley wonders "why so little attention is paid, in this volume and in the literature generally, to the material manifestations of religion. The artifacts of religious belief and practice exist as a compelling category of evidence, long overdue for informed historical and cultural analysis."[12] Unfortunately, the material dimension of Christianity has also been of marginal interest to scholars of religion. Biblical archeologists might be concerned with the pots in which Sarah cooked, and art historians might be fascinated by representations of a naked Eve, but American religionists have only recently discovered the importance of space, objects, art, and architecture. Why has religious material culture been ignored in the study of American Christianity? What can this lacuna in scholarship tell us about the limited way we understand religion?

Scrambling the Sacred and the Profane

One of the reasons why the material dimension of American religious life is not taken seriously is because of how we describe the nature of religion. A dichotomy has been established between the sacred and the profane, spirit and matter, piety and commerce that constrains our ability to understand how religion works in the real world. In spite of the difficulty of defining "religion," scholars and theologians frequently accept a simple division between the sacred and the profane. They also see an evolutionary, modernizing trend that has caused Western societies to become increasingly secular. By looking at material Christianity, we will see little evidence that American Christians experience a radical separation of the sacred from the profane. If we look at what Christians *do* rather than at what they *think*, we cannot help but notice the continual scrambling of the sacred and the profane. Likewise, by focusing on material Christianity we can no longer uncritically accept the secularization model.

Although binary thinking has a long history in the West, we can look to Emile Durkheim's classic study *Elementary Forms of the Religious Life* as perhaps the most influential description of the division of the world into the sacred and the profane. Durkheim wrote in 1912 that all religions classify things, both real and unreal, into the two opposing and distinctive categories of the sacred and the profane. The sacred consists of an ideal and transcendental world that is set apart from ordinary life. Signaled by rites such as anointings, consecrations, fasts, wakes, and seclusion, the sacred is defined primarily by its very opposite, the profane. The profane is the everyday and the utilitarian. While awe, intoxicating frenzy, and a sense of the foreign mark the sacred, the profane is commonplace, frequently boring, and familiar. The space of the church or temple is sacred; the home and workplace are profane. The clergy, privileged leaders, and people who have been initiated into cultic rituals are sacred. Workers, children, women, strangers typically are profane. For Durkheim these two worlds are not merely separate, they are "hostile and jealous rivals of each other . . . The sacred thing is *par excellence* that which the profane should not touch, cannot touch with impunity."[13] In various forms, this dualistic understanding of the nature of religion can also be found in the writings of Max Weber, Gerardus van der Leeuw, and Mircea Eliade. According to these theorists of religion, without this binary division there cannot be authentic religion. "The religious life and the profane life," declared Durkheim, "cannot exist in the same place."[14]

This theoretical construction of religion reflects one aspect of the Jewish understanding of God as developed in classical Christian thought. In this tradition, the God of the Hebrew scriptures is understood as represented as a disembodied voice that interacts with embodied human beings.[15] Humanity and divinity are presented as radically separated; God is uncircumscribable and unmanipulable. The Protestant reformer John Calvin maintained that humanity comes close to God only in our souls because God is a spirit. "Since God has no similarity to those shapes by means of which people attempt to represent him," he wrote in his *Institutes of the Christian Religion*, "then all attempts to depict him are an impudent affront . . . to his majesty and glory."[16] Divinity, the wholly other and sacred, should not be brought into the profane world of bodies and art. The omnipotence and greatness of God, stressed by theologians like Calvin and Zwingli, meant that humanity could not influence the divine.

Built into Christian theology, however, are doctrines that weaken this dualism. The doctrine of the Creation emphasizes both the immanence and transcendence of God. Not only is God majestic and distant; God created and sustains the universe through power and love. The Incarnation also enables the material dimension of Christianity to assume a theological meaning. Through the Incarnation, Christians believe that God becomes intimately associated with humanity because of the divine appropriation of the human body and condition. In Christ, there is a blurring of the material and spiritual; the sacred voice and the profane human body. The longing for the physical presence of God is eliminated in the embodiment of Christ. Jesus of the Gospels is an object of touch and of vision. "The union of God and man in Christ," writes Sarah Beckwith, "affirms the union of soul and flesh, spirit and matter, in humanity."[17] Although Christians hotly debate the nature of the Incarnation, the separation that Durkheim perceived between the ideal and the material was fundamentally overcome, at least this once, in Christ.

For those Christians who emphasize the bodily nature of Christ and his intimate understanding of human longings, the material world no longer could be radically profane and unattached to the sacred. Theologians like the eighth-century Syrian, John of Damascus, closely aligned the embodied Christ not only with matter but with the saving nature of matter. "In former times God who is without form or body, could never be depicted," he wrote in defense of using images in Christian worship. "But now when God is seen in the flesh conversing with men, I make an image of the God whom I see. I do not worship matter; I worship the Creator of matter who became matter for my sake, who willed to take His abode in matter; who worked out my salvation through matter. Never will I cease honoring the matter which wrought my salvation."[18] Throughout the debates over the use of images in Christian communities, whether in the eighth century or sixteenth or twentieth century, some have eagerly accepted the scrambling of the spiritual and the natural, divine and human, sacred and profane. Protestant theologians from the Reformed tradition have generally rejected the possibility that the supernatural could be so frequently manifest on earth. Lutheran and Episcopalian thinkers were more receptive to the visual and sensual world but cautioned against idolatry. As we will see, lay Protestants often ignored such warnings and included material culture in their religious lives. While modern Roman Catholic theologians criticize what they understand as superstitious excesses in devotionalism, typically Roman and Orthodox thought and liturgy have highlighted the divine connection with matter.

The study of American Christianity, however, is not modeled on the Catholic understanding of the frequent fusion of the sacred and the profane. Jon Butler cogently argues that American religious history has been unduly shaped by a Protestant understanding of what defines religious faith, community, and behavior.[19] Butler coins the term "Puritan model" to describe scholarly focus on the themes of Calvinism, evangelicalism, declension, rising secularism, laicization, democracy, and American exceptionalism. While the Puritans themselves may have experienced their lives as "worlds of wonder," this is not how traditional historians have perceived them.[20] The Puritan model is a historiographical construct, not a historical observation. For Butler, Catholicism, Eastern Orthodoxy, Judaism, and Native American religions can only be "authentic" or "real" when they reflect elements of the Puritan or Protestant model. Butler encourages us to consider new models that would take into account the heterogeneity of individual religious experience, the importance of place, and the varieties of institutional authority. In particular, he argues that the Puritan model prevented scholars from seeing that demonstrations of supernatural intervention were (and are) essential to the religious lives of Americans. While the Puritans may have seen the divine everywhere, the Puritan model preferred Christianity separated from home life, sexuality, economic exchange, and fashion.

The assumption that true Christian sentiments can be, must be, set apart from the profane cannot be upheld when we look at how people use material culture in their religious lives. While there are certainly Christians who disdain the material world and strive to eliminate visual representations of it from their communities, there is no compelling reason to hold these groups up as the standard to which all other Christians must be compared. The Puritan model of religious historiography denies the rich complexity of American Christianity and serves as a blindfold to the strong materialist trends in religious culture. If we immediately assume that whenever money is exchanged religion is debased, then we will miss the subtle ways that people create and maintain spiritual ideals *through* the exchange of goods and the construction of spaces.

When Christian activities seem too wedded to the profane, they are typically held up as further signs of secularization and the decline of religious influence in

America. Taking their cues from Durkheim, sociologists report that people need to have an element of enchantment in their lives that mystifies fundamental social relationships. The secularization theory tells us that within Western nations religion no longer speaks to this supernatural longing in humanity.[21] For many scholars, secular popular culture now serves this need. These scholars follow Karl Marx who wrote in *Capital* that in order to understand the relationship between people and commodities we must "take flight into the misty realm of religion." In capitalism, products made by human beings become "autonomous figures endowed with a life of their own" that can interact with their makers, owners, and with each other. Marx described this attitude toward commodities as "the fetishism."[22] Consequently, some scholars conclude that secular objects can provide the magical dimension of life that religious objects once did. For Sut Jhally, advertising is a religion where "the commodity world interacts with the human world at the most fundamental levels: it performs magical feats of transformation and bewitchment, brings instant happiness and gratification, captures the forces of nature, and holds within itself the essence of important social relationships."[23] Ray Browne draws on religious language for his books on material culture, *Objects of Special Devotion* and *Icons of America*.[24] America, for many historians and culture critics, is a non-religious and consumer-oriented country where CB Radios may be interpreted as meaningful icons.[25]

The conclusion that magical mass-produced commodities or spaces substitute for religion in a secular culture can be made only because scholars have disregarded the material dimension of religious life in America. Most historians, folklorists, archeologists, and cultural critics focus on non-religious material culture because they do not recognize the persistent and meaningful continuation of religion in America. While they frequently call things "religious" they rarely discuss religious artifacts. I suspect they share the notion with many scholars and theologians that "real" religion cannot be materialist. It is not surprising that historians and sociologists assume that the American landscape and consumer culture are devoid of religious forms since specialists in religion fail to note the material dimension of explicitly religious culture. If social scientists see only the profane and religionists only the sacred, then both miss the ways Christians combine these concepts. We cannot speculate about the CB radio as "icon" if we have no idea about how religious icons (whether Eastern Orthodox icons or mass-produced Christian images) function in twentieth-century America.

Secularization theory has recently been criticized in light of the spread of "fundamentalism" in America and abroad.[26] Revisionists of secularization frequently postulate that what we are seeing in America is not the continuation of religion but evidence for some totally new religious configuration. At the end of her article on "The Born-Again Telescandals," anthropologist Susan Harding seems surprised to see that now the "religious mingles with secular, churches become businesses, Christ dispenses grace on TV, preachers call themselves CEOs and run for President, faith healers build ultramodern hospitals, AT&T hires New Age consultants, and churches hire religious market analysts." For her we now live in a "new world composed of preposterous categorical hodgepodges." This new world contrasts with the old world where "the things forming these zany amalgamations were kept apart, separated, in their place, properly ordered and moving progressively toward some end."[27] Since religion is not going away, Harding concludes that it must be mutating into something new. In other words, the contemporary religious world in America does not look like a "real" religious world where, in the spirit of Calvin and Durkheim, the sacred is far from the profane. In the "old" world everything religious was in its proper place. Harding has uncritically accepted the notion that at some ill-determined period in the American past "mingling" did not occur. She has, in effect, followed the Puritan model of scholarship by describing the contemporary religious situation as "declension" from a past of theological certainty and fervent piety.

The conclusion that contemporary religions are the creation of something "new" cannot be historically justified. Rather, I show in these case studies that the scrambling of the sacred and the profane is common in American Christianity. Mingling has occurred throughout its history. The categories of sacred and profane are the constructions of scholars and not always a part of the awareness of those involved in practicing religion. What is occurring is that scholars trained in poststructural or critical theories are now finally seeing the "preposterous categorical hodgepodges" of religion. By focusing on the objects, landscapes, and arts that people use to articulate and shape their Christianity, I see complicated and interactive relationships between what has been called the sacred and the profane. To focus exclusively on the binary opposition between sacred and profane prevents us from understanding, rather than enabling us to understand, how Christianity works. The case studies I include provide various angles for understanding how Christians, of assorted types, continuously mix the supernatural, God, miracles, ethical concerns, and prayer together with family, commerce, everyday worries, fashion, and social relationships. The material dimension of Christianity shuttles back and forth so frequently between what scholars call the sacred and the profane that the usefulness of the categories is disputed.

Women, Children, and Other Illiterates

The material dimension of American Christianity has been ignored not merely because a dualist notion of the sacred and profane privileges certain expressions of religion over others. Longstanding theological and intellectual interpretations of art, objects, and places have associated material expressions of religion with certain types of people. Paralleling the assumption that the sacred is separate from the profane is the notion that meaningful Christianity is best defined by specialists in the sacred: people schooled in theology, active in reform movements, or outstanding in church leadership. Buying Bibles, visiting cemeteries, using miraculous water, wearing religious clothing, and owning religious bookstores have been ignored because scholars deem these practices less spiritual or authentic. Those who use non-literary means of expressing ideas about the supernatural and its relationship to the everyday world have not been considered fully "adult" Christians. Christians who use objects or images in their devotional lives or who feel that certain places are imbued with special powers, are seen as needing spiritual helps or crutches. These "weak" Christians who require physical "aids" are separated from "strong" Christians who grasp spiritual truths directly. It is this perception, that only weak Christians express their faith by interacting with material culture, that this book hopes to counter.

The assumption that "strong" Christians do not need material representations of their faith has its origins in Platonic ideas of beauty and Hebraic iconoclasm. Christians who reject the importance of religious images and goods privilege a strand of thought that insists that the divine cannot be represented. Platonic and Neoplatonic philosophy asserted that the highest form of truth and beauty is spiritual and therefore disconnected from the earthly and the material.[28] There is a cosmic hierarchy that proceeds from the mind and soul downward to matter. To turn from spirit toward the bodily realm is to move toward evil, the negation of the spiritual. The phenomenal world of nature and images conceals the ideal world of truth that lies beyond the particulars. The third-century philosopher Plotinus rejected the custom of painting individual portraits because he felt that the pure idea of the person's character would be obscured in the physical matter of art.[29] For those critical of representation, contemplation might initially entail the use of images to assist in reaching a greater insight but the goal was to progress beyond the need for physical aids. As Augustine concluded from his and Monica's vision at Ostia, the soul's goal was to raise itself higher and higher; to have every sign silent, to hear without tongue or voice, and then, eventually, to experience "that eternal wisdom which abides above all things."[30]

To this notion of the hierarchical relationship between spirit and matter we add the Hebraic suspicion of the arts. Biblical iconoclasm served as a continual referent for Christian thinkers. The story of the Golden Calf (Ex. 32) tells Jews and Christians that when people lose their faith in God they construct false images of the divine. The iconoclastic violence that followed the making of the Golden Calf emphasizes the difference between a wayward people looking for a material representation of the divine and their leader to whom God directly speaks without visual mediation. God eventually commands the faithful not to make graven images or a likeness of anything that is in the heaven above or the earth below. Most importantly, they should never bow down to images or serve them (Deut. 5:8–10).

The urge to image, however, is not easily quelled. The iconoclastic controversies in Christianity reveal the persistent desire to create images of God and the saints. Medieval Catholicism produced a rich array of decorative arts and devotional devices to stimulate piety. Among their arguments against the iconoclasts, Catholic theologians developed the idea that it was the illiterate who needed images to enable them to grasp the divine mysteries because they could not read.[31] Our minds, they reminded us, are oriented toward mundane matters and are largely incapable of rising to spiritual things. Images and devotional objects help people contemplate the divine and teach the true faith because not everyone can approach God through the intellect. The uneducated, women, and children were particularly responsive to sacred images, objects, and spaces.[32] For those theologians disposed to see the positive nature of images, the majority of Christians needed to use the visual world to move toward that which cannot be seen. For those who had iconoclastic leanings, such "helps" could be tolerated because illiterate Christians needed them to understand and express their faith.

The Protestant reformers of the sixteenth century reinterpreted the "illiterate argument" for the use of images in liturgy and instruction. While Luther vacillated on the issue of images (prohibiting the adoration of statues or pictures while recognizing their instructive possibilities), Zwingli and Calvin had no such reservations. Images should *not* be placed in churches because Christians were susceptible to confusing the sign with the referent; the representation with what stands *behind* the referent. Art and objects tempted a weak humanity that fell too easily into idolatry. According to the reformers, images were a part of an external cult that tried to manipulate God by placing too much trust in human activities. All Christians must place their faith in God alone and scorn those false activities that implied humanity could magically control the divine. From the Protestant perspective, an all-powerful God controlled humanity and people only fooled themselves if they thought their rosaries and pilgrimages could gain them salvation.

The iconoclastic stream within Christian history has assumed that people who are illiterate or not properly trained in religion frequently mistake the *image* of the divine for the divine itself. This skeptical attitude toward people who use images is not confined to theologians and religious leaders fighting iconoclastic battles. Like Protestants fearful of Catholic images and Catholics fearful of the "excesses" of the uneducated, some modern thinkers have felt that the "weak" easily fall prey to the lure of mass culture. During the first half of the twentieth century, cultural critics observed that a powerful "culture industry" made up of the media, popular arts, entertainment, and fashion controlled the desires and needs of the "masses."[33] The masses, according to theorists like Theodore Adorno and Herbert Marcuse, had weak egos and submissive psyches that were easily pacified. Adorno and his colleagues at the Frankfurt Institute for Social Research remembered how ordinary people were caught up in the fascist movements of the 1930s instead of acting as agents for proletarian revolution. These writers were convinced that the culture industry cheated the consumer of what it promised and turned people into unthinking zombies. American Dwight Macdonald succinctly summarized the Frankfurt School's negative attitude toward the masses and popular culture in his 1944 essay, "A Theory of Popular Culture." He explained that "mass culture is imposed from above. It is fabricated by technicians hired by businessmen; its audiences are passive consumers, their participation limited to the choice between buying and not buying. The Lords of kitsch, in short, exploit the cultural needs of the masses in order to make a profit and/or to maintain their class rule."[34] For the sixteenth-century Protestant reformers, the powerful Catholic church manipulated weak people through images and trinkets; for some mid-twentieth-century critics, the culture industry did the same with jazz and best sellers.

During the mid-twentieth century, the Protestant (and increasingly Catholic) suspicion of images combined with a modernist distrust of popular culture to create an extremely hostile environment for the study of Christian material culture. As we will see in Chapter 6, for a variety of Christian theologians spiritual and cultural growth proceeded from the concrete, visual, and everyday to the abstract, literary, and unique. The more ethically and morally superior the religion, the more it presents an abstract deity who need not be approached through material "helps." The influential German-born theologian Paul Tillich called on Christians to see God as the Ultimate Concern, the "depth dimension" in all experience. He rejected the view that only traditionally religious symbols express the divine and instead believed that Christians could discover an ultimate concern in the secular world. Tillich, unlike Durkheim, saw the sacred in the profane. However, like other cultural critics of the period, he could not see authentic religion in the "Sunday school" art of the masses. "The religious art of capitalist society reduces the traditional religious symbols to the level of middle-class morality and robs them of their transcendence and their sacramental character," he concluded. Tillich preferred modern art, such as Expressionism that "has a mystical, religious character, quite apart from its choice of subjects. It is not an exaggeration to ascribe more of the quality of sacredness to a still-life by Cézanne or a tree by van Gogh than to a picture of Jesus by Uhde."[35] Theologians and scholars of religion ignored the popular "religious art of capitalist society" because expressions of both art and religion that were more intellectual could be found in the achievements of a handful of artists, writers, and thinkers. "The masses crush beneath it everything that is different," summarized Ortega y Gasset, "everything that is excellent, individual, qualified, and select."[36]

It is not surprising that until recently scholars of American religion, following in the steps of the European intelligentsia and Christian iconoclasts, turned away from popular religion and its arts. Historians who embraced the Puritan model of American religions ignored those Christians who used images and objects because they were "less" Christian than evangelical Protestants. If scholars examined the material dimension of American religion, they opted to study either folk customs or utopian communities where religious convictions (like art) were not mass-produced but handcrafted.[37] The material dimension of religion was acknowledged only when it reflected their scholarly preference for the abstract and individual. The fascination with the material culture of the Shakers reflects the scholarly search for an "authentic" religion that was embodied in an "authentic" material culture. According to historian Stephen Stein, popular preoccupation with the details of Shaker material culture and the exclusion of the dynamics of their historical and religious development produced an idealized and frequently Pollyanna-ish view of this community. There is something pathetically revealing in the comment of a 1984 Shaker that "I almost expect to be remembered as a chair or table."[38] We know far more about the material environment of the Shakers – a community that tried to simplify their physical universe – than we do about that of Roman Catholics whose sacramental theology fully exploited the material world.[39] Since American Catholic "arts" were mass-produced and used by unschooled immigrants, they held little interest for scholars looking for the unique and the intangible. In the case of the Shakers, their utopian community life and design preferences marked them off from the "masses" and thus made them fit subjects for study.

In the aftermath of the civil rights movements and student rebellions of the 1960s and 1970s, "the masses" became a more appropriate subject matter. As "the masses" asserted themselves politically, they looked less like a homogeneous lump of people and more like diverse communities of African Americans, students, Native Americans, women, gays, the handicapped, white ethnics, or Hispanics. Historians in America and Europe began to explore the lives of ordinary people. Instead of focusing on politics, the activities of a few "great men," and written sources, historians now construct narratives of social change from the "bottom up." Sociologists are rejecting the Frankfurt School's pessimistic appraisal of the masses and their culture. Scholars at the Birmingham Centre for Contemporary Cultural Studies counter the notion of an undifferentiated "mass" by studying a variety of contemporary sub-cultures. Cultural studies conducted in Britain and the United States challenge the notion of a cohesive "culture industry," diminish the gap between high and low culture, question the idea that mass culture overwhelms the consciousness of the working class, and discuss how small groups of people create their own cultural life style.[40] Mass culture itself is now portrayed as a "contested terrain" where various communities struggle to establish meanings. Recovering the subjective experiences of people and the small details of everyday resistance has become a legitimate scholarly agenda.

As scholars have acknowledged the ability of average people to resist, define, and express themselves through "popular" culture, they have also re-evaluated the ways Christians have used images, objects, and spaces. Historians now explain that Protestants have never been entirely free from using religious images and spiritual "helps" in their lives. Luther, Zwingli, and Calvin, it turns out, made certain exceptions to their distrust of religious images and objects. Luther placed twenty-one woodcuts (including Cranach's series on the Apocalypse) in his 1522 New Testament. The Augsburg Confession of 1530 said that images could be used to encourage people to lead a holy life and to restrain their imaginations.[41] Proper images could direct the mind toward historical scriptural reality and away from religious fantasy. Both Calvin and Zwingli permitted the humanity of Christ to be depicted visually in the home. While it was forbidden to have statues of the saints in church, families could display prints of biblical scenes.[42] In England there was a slow process of eliminating unacceptable images from houses and inns and replacing them with acceptable ones. Painters replaced the saints with Old Testament scenes and allegorical figures.[43] In the space of the home or tavern and in teaching children, images could be used. Historians of early modern Europe and America now entertain the idea that the distinctions between Protestants, Catholics, and "pagans" were less sharp than was originally assumed.[44]

Protestants in the seventeenth and eighteenth century might have been more open to material expressions of Christianity because Europeans were discovering the joys of consumerism. In his work on patterns of modern materialism, Chandra Mukerji revises established sociological and historical explanations of the rise of capitalism by describing the existence of a "hedonistic consumerism" in the early modern period.[45] Mukerji and other scholars have pushed the origin of consumerism back into the sixteenth and seventeenth centuries.[46] Challenging Max Weber's theory that the spirit of modern capitalism finds its sole source in an ascetic, savings-minded ethic of Protestantism, Mukerji contends that early modern Protestants and Catholics indulged in forms of mass consumption that spurred a lively trade in books, art work, chinaware, and furniture. Even poorer Europeans bought "luxuries" such as ribbons and copper pots. Both Catholics and Protestants were exploring new ways to use material goods in their social and economic lives. Colin Campbell arrived at a similar conclusion in *The Romantic Ethic and the Spirit of Modern Consumerism*.[47] He points out that a parallel tradition ran alongside that of the better-known Protestant material asceticism. Not all Protestants, as Weber has led us to believe, lived modestly in order to maximize profits from God's gifts. A more sensual Protestantism promoted free thought, Arminianism, sentiment, romanticism, and consumption. Mukerji and Campbell both conclude that modern consumerism and the sensual needs of the individual did not arise due to the weakening of the Puritan ethic but rather have been a continual part of Protestantism since the sixteenth century.

It is inevitable that a book on material Christianity will include the activities of women, children, and lay men. However, my intention is also to discredit the impression that educated men do not form relationships with pious art, use healing water, or wear religious garments. Lay men and clergy typically hold the key positions in the production and distribution of religious goods and the construction of Christian landscapes. Mormon men wear garments and Catholic men use Lourdes water. Material Christianity is a means by which both elite and non-elite Christians express their relationship to God and the supernatural, articulate ideas about life after death, and form religious communities. To gloss over, ignore, or condemn material Christianity because of its association with "marginal" Christians is to misunderstand who uses the tangible and sensual in religion.

At the risk of perhaps overvaluing the statements of women, children, and other "illiterates," I take seriously their laconic statements on religion. I do not ask: "Is it art? Is it religion?" and then apply an external standard of religiosity to their piety. Too often such questions retard rather than promote inquiry. "What clouds our perception," David Freedberg astutely summarizes, "is exactly the compulsion to establish whether an object is art or not, and whether it belongs in a museum or not."[48] While I am sensitive to the times that Christians accuse other Christians of indulging in unauthentic pious thoughts or superficial religious behavior, I am more interested in what that rhetoric says about their own conceptions of Christianity. Readers may decipher my own religious and artistic prejudices but it is not my intention to evaluate Christian material culture by a set of ethical and theological standards. I am not drawn to criticize Christians who use Lourdes water or who wear "Praise the Lord" T-shirts. I reject, however, the opinions of those who find nothing significant in these religious gestures.

Hearing, Reading, Seeing, Touching

If Jon Butler is correct to conclude that the study of American religions has been hobbled by the indiscriminate application of the Puritan model, then it is not surprising to find an overemphasis on words and "the Word" in religious scholarship. In the iconoclastic controversy of the sixteenth century, the Protestant reformers privileged the ear over the eye, hearing over seeing, the word over the image, and the book over the statue. "A right faith goes right on with its eyes closed," wrote Luther, "it clings to God's Word; if follows that Word; it believes that Word."[49] The reformers attempted to establish a new norm to contrast with what they understood to be a sensual and idolatrous Catholicism. The truth of Christianity was to be conveyed through the Word of God, contained in the words of the scripture, preached from the pulpit, or read from the Bible. For Calvin, it was "by means of words that God descends to the level of the common people."[50] Language was the sword of the spirit that awakened faith. The Reformers trusted words to connect the faithful to God instead of images that were easily confused with the reality behind them.

For sixteenth-century Protestants, material objects and images were more sensual than language. Words not only brought one the Gospel message, they also had an abstract quality that indicated their chaste nature. On the other hand, whatever excited the senses was suspect. For Zwingli in particular, nothing based on corporeal elements could bring the soul to salvation.[51] Zwingli specifically attacked Catholic statues that looked like human beings. "Here stands Magdalene so voluptuously painted that she incites licentiousness," he lamented, "there stand

Sebastian, Maurice and the pious John the Evangelist looking like lords, warriors and pimps."[52] Whatever was given over to the senses took away from the spirit. To indulge in the temptation of the eye was "a kind of illicit visual intercourse."[53] Reading, preaching, singing, and meditating foregrounded the sacred word.

Traditional historians of American Christianity follow the steps of Protestants by valuing words and the Word. Trained in graduate schools that center instruction around books and libraries, it is not surprising that they have neglected non-written expressions of religion. While anthropologists might be attuned to storytelling, dance, gesture, art, and music, historians of American religion have pursued the written word. In spite of hermeneutical theories that assert that language is not as clear and straightforward as we would like it to be, scholarship remains heavily dependent on words to tell understandable stories. While scholars might deny that they avoid material Christianity because of its sensual dimensions, they must accept the observation that material culture has been ignored and that practically nothing has been written on the meaning of the body in American Christianity.[54] Following the lead of Michel Foucault, historians and literary specialists have built up a veritable industry of "discourses" on the body, but historians of American religions have not joined this trend.[55]

Since religion is emotive as well as cognitive, people use their sight, touch, smell, and voice to stimulate pious feelings. To shy away from discussing the role of the body in Christianity is to neglect the primary mediator of religious experience. Human beings seemingly cannot appropriate religious truths or be "grasped by an ultimate concern" without involving their bodies. To the extent that a particular Christian group promotes emotion and feeling as a means to approach the divine, its members will appeal to the senses to activate those special responses. The human body is not only an avenue for expressing and appropriating religious feelings, it also drives people to ask fundamental religious questions. Pain, suffering, death, and decay break down the human world and heighten the focus on the body. Religions provide ways to remake the world by providing pain and death with meaning. In constructing cemeteries, for instance, Victorian Philadelphians both acknowledged the impermanence of the body and asserted the immortality of the spirit. The use of images, objects, and spaces stimulates the senses and orders the threatening reality of the body.

My intention, however, is not to focus exclusively on the body or the sensual elements of religion at the expense of the verbal and the written. What is needed is a more nuanced understanding of the relationship between body and mind; word and image. As "multimedia events," religious practices are areas where speech, vision, gesture, touch, and sound combine. The assumption that Protestantism broke the Word/words away from visual or tactile perception is not correct. A radical division may have been intended but not entirely achieved. Through religious practice, rather than through theological or contemplative reflection, various sensory modes come together. Some nineteenth-century Catholics (often spiritual "illiterates" in the eyes of scholars) made considerable efforts to write down their healing-water experiences. They did not merely drink Lourdes water or put it on their bodies, they picked up pen and paper and wrote "thank you" notes to acknowledge their cures. While they sent the notes to the priest who had mailed them the miraculous water, they intended the message for Christ and his mother. For those Catholics, the religious gesture of using Lourdes water included both the tactile experience of the water and the clarifying medium of language.

If Catholics at times turned water into words, Protestants turned words into objects. During the nineteenth century, family Bibles became so lavish and encyclopedic that they functioned more like religious furniture than biblical texts. Heavily illustrated with copious supplemental essays, they sat majestically on parlor stands and signaled the social respectability of their owners. A highly emotional rhetoric evolved, based on the stimulation of the senses which encouraged Christians to see the book itself (not just its words) as the source of memory and pious feelings. Again, we see the merging of the senses rather than their separation and ordering. Word and image come together in the religious activities of using Lourdes water or displaying a family Bible.

In his essay on the "New History," Peter Burke asks whether the usefulness of the study of material culture can "do anything more than confirm a hypothesis founded in the first instance on literary evidence." He points out the irony that the history of material culture "is based less on the study of the artefacts themselves than on literary sources."[56] Indeed, a few specialists in material culture do believe that it is possible to examine the object itself so carefully that one can derive information from it without recourse to other sources, but typically this is only desirable when written sources are unavailable.[57] While a close description of an object or space or building may help us to understand its latent and manifest functions, to limit ourselves only to the material representation is to eliminate other possible avenues of inquiry. Both the material representation and the ideology that surrounds it must be taken into account. Just as religious practice brings together a variety of sensual modes, so we must be resourceful in gathering sources to understand the interaction between people and objects. Letters, fiction, magazine articles, official pronouncements, and personal narratives are the "words" that are joined with material representations to "cheat the silence" of popular religion.[58]

Let us look again at the photograph taken of the African American family. In this household, the sacred and the profane are not clearly defined as Durkheim would predict. Christian images are placed throughout the room. There is no evidence that any devotional activities take place near the pictures; we see no candles or altars. The religious prints are decorative elements, like the calendar art at the far right. On the other hand, the prints are explicitly Christian in nature; they are not merely representations of the natural order. Their content indicates a privileged supernatural order and its involvement with humankind. The *Ecce Homo* vividly displays the Passion of Christ and his sharing of bodily pain with humanity. *The Infant Samuel*, placed at a level easily seen by children, encourages devotional piety among the young. Framing heightens the prints' special quality and separates them from the calendar art. This family did not make rigid distinctions between religious pictures as ornamentation, devotional focus, or instructional media. They combined religious beliefs with the material culture of everyday life.

The parlor organ also reflects the integration of the church with the home. Prominently displayed on its music stand are hymn books. We do not know if the family ever sang the hymns, but we do know that they did not hide them under the table when the photographer arrived. The organ signals social standing and taste as well as religious sensibilities. As a popular instrument among the Victorian middle class, it came to symbolize family commitment to domestic and cultural values.[59] If the household had the organ since the late nineteenth century (when it was probably built), it testifies, as any antique would, to the family's longevity. If the organ was recently purchased, it demonstrates a substantial financial investment. Christian commitments, musical taste, economic achievement, and domestic stability – none of these elements can be easily separated from the other.

The photograph also complicates our notions about the distinctions between "weak" Christians and "strong" Christians. Are these "weak" Christians who need images because they cannot cope intellectually with biblical truths? Given the social and economic condition of many African Americans in the 1940s, it is not surprising that the woman in the photograph wears a soiled dress and has legs so swollen that she cannot lace her shoes. We might conclude that the woman and her children do not have adequate access to religious education and facilities that would teach them "appropriate" ways to integrate "tasteful" art into their home in order to cultivate "authentic" Christian beliefs. That might explain why they include standard Protestant iconography (*The Infant Samuel*) with Catholic images of Christ (*Ecce Homo*). On the other hand, perhaps these are "strong" Christians who recognize that a picture of Christ is merely a picture and can never have any further meaning. They know that the print of the infant Samuel is only for instructing their children and that the organ is for singing Gospel hymns, not displaying wealth. They might even embrace all of the Victorian values that Kenneth Ames sees embodied in the nineteenth-century parlor organ: the moral superiority of women, the importance of domesticity, the display of material wealth, the maintenance of amiable social relations. The photograph leads us to suspect that there is no simple division between "strong" and "weak" Christians.

While we can speculate on the meaning of organs and chromolithographs based on how they are used in other households past and present, we are limited in what we can say about this family. Without the reports of others who knew the family or their own words, we are left to draw shaky conclusions about the meanings of the prints and the organ. When no words are available, it is too easy for us to read our own words into the material representation. Because this African American family living in Virginia in 1941 may not necessarily have the same set of values as the Victorian Protestants who played parlor organs or as the eighteenth-century Anglican artist who painted *The Infant Samuel*, this photograph cautions us against making unsubstantiated generalizations based on images. While words too must always be questioned, we need them in order to make at least partial sense out of the religious experience of this family. Just as the organ is metaphorically transformed into a producer of words when hymns are sung, so we must find ways to let mute objects speak. Spaces, architecture, and art do not convey information by themselves, they are activated by either their users or the scholars who are trying to interpret their meanings. The image cannot stand alone; it must be a part of a human world of meaning in order to come alive. In Chapter 2 we will examine how people give religious artifacts meanings.

2

Piety, Art, Fashion:
The Religious Object

Shortly after her wedding, Casey Perez was given a statue of Our Lady of Guadalupe by her mother. Casey, however, wanted to live a modern life and put the statue away in her closet. Several years later, during a period of misgivings and depression, Casey took out the statue and carried it everywhere. She even slept with it. Eventually Casey started to feel better. Frank McEntire, an employee of the Church of Jesus Christ of Latter-day Saints, is also an artist. His art installation "Reassemblages" included a plaster model of the Salt Lake City Mormon temple covered with his own hair. By wrapping, burying, altering, and otherwise hiding the form and identity of discarded religious objects, McEntire wanted to investigate "how we, as part of an interrelated biocentric world, can reassess our attitudes towards each other, our use of resources, and our relationship with the environment." Patrick Knight sells T-shirts adorned with pictures of Catholic saints. An Austin, Texas, boutique carries the shirts, along with a $300 shrine featuring prints of Sor Juana de la Cruz (a seventeenth-century Mexican nun), St. George and the Dragon, and St. Jude. Both Knight and the boutique owners insist that the products sell well and that no one has voiced offense at the commercialization of sacred characters.[1]

What meanings do religious objects have for these people? Why do people feel compelled not only to uphold the tenets of their faith but to use objects that reflect and secure their beliefs? As with all quests to discover the meanings of things, I can offer only tentative suggestions. I fully agree with feminist critic Toril Moi that "the attempt to fix meaning is always in part doomed to failure, for it is of the nature of meaning to be always already elsewhere."[2] As we will see, people use religious objects in many different ways. Meanings may be directed and articulated by a controlling institutional body with a long history of custom and tradition. Such meanings, however, do not always help us understand the personal meanings that people find in their daily use of religious objects. Individual meanings do not merely mirror the intentions of a clerical elite or express the idiosyncratic whims of the masses. People construct meanings using a set of theological and cultural "tools" to build responses to their own spiritual, psychological, and social longings. Unfortunately, scholars are rarely privileged to see the "blueprints" of that construction process. People infrequently preserve their feelings for posterity.

This chapter explores the various meanings that people give religious objects. I move from examining how religious authorities endow objects with special powers, to seeing how lay people give artifacts and images meaning. In doing this, I have de-emphasized historical and denominational uniqueness. My concern is to clarify the various functions of material Christianity rather than to explain why a particular thing was used at a particular time. As much as possible, I include the voices of the users and descriptions of the objects they use. In the hope of moving beyond the equation of Christianity with the white, Protestant middle class, I introduce evidence from people of color, from the poor, and from Catholics and Mormons. I do this not only to be inclusive but also to illustrate my view that diverse peoples use religious objects in very similar ways. Ethnicity, class, and religion certainly are important variables, but we can no longer say that only poor Hispanic Catholics build shrines and that only Victorian Protestants put pious pictures up in their homes. The impetus to relate to objects as if they were sacred characters, to use objects to focus memory, or to define community affiliation occurs among all Christians. Protestantism may not have an official, theologically defined way of interacting with objects, but Protestants share with Catholics and Mormons the desire to own, make, manipulate, cherish, sell, and exchange religious goods.

Anthropologist Robert Armstrong has written that "in all cultures certain things exist which, though they may appear to be but ordinary objects, yet are treated in ways quite different from the ways in which objects are usually treated." He explains that the reason for this special and different treatment lies in their "affecting presence."[3] While some objects have only utilitarian functions, others seemingly possess power and energy. I am not saying that power resides naturally in certain objects while not in others. What I want to explore in this chapter is how *people* activate or enliven objects so that an object's influence can be felt. The nature and extent of affecting presence or power may differ, but even commercialized objects that are no longer used in a religious context still have religious associations because their iconography originated within particular Christian communities. By exploring the diverse ways that objects participate in and express changing notions of power, we can chart the various meanings of religious objects. How do religious objects achieve "affecting presence"?

Catholic Sacramentals and the Power of Authority

One way – among many ways – that objects become powerful is by participating in the authority of institutional traditions and organizations. Objects may be powerful because something else powerful has decreed them to be so. Through their writing and preaching, a select group of Christians interprets sacred scriptures and gives meaning to biblical and philosophical statements. A part of the group's theological reflections is an analysis of how and why the sacred can come into contact with the profane. Those interpretations influence the actions and faith of the believers. An official organization presents some objects as special and defines how they should be properly used. The authority of churches and leaders is by no means the final arbiter of what has affective presence, but it does play a significant role in defining not only what is or is not powerful, but how and when an object can effect change.

Christianity is rooted in the mystery of the Incarnation, the infusing of the divine into one man. For orthodox Christians, God enters the world by fully participating in humanity through the character of Jesus Christ. The Gospel of John explains that "In the beginning was the Word, and the Word was with God, and the Word was God. . . . And the Word became flesh and dwelt among us, full of grace and truth. . . ." (John 1: 1, 14). God, as spirit, does not remain as spirit but becomes a part of the material world. Christian theology insists that the Incarnation is a one-time event. God was only fully present in the historical character called Jesus of Nazareth. However, on a more conceptual level, through the Incarnation, the divine and the human worlds are brought together. God became flesh in the body of Christ and in doing so created the possibility that the sacred can be embodied in nature and humanity. "The divine and the human realms are not then discontinuous," summarized James Martin, "the universe is a 'sacramental universe.'"[4] While there would be only one Christ, there could be many repetitions of the fusing, in part if not fully, of the sacred with the profane.

Catholic sacramental theology contends that there are certain ritual gestures, established by Christ himself, that sanctify people and their religious communities. Through "words and objects," these "sacraments" are ways of worshipping God and instructing the faithful. They also nourish, strengthen, and express belief.[5] The sacraments required visible, sensual signs in order to be effective. Christians in general believe that it is through the sacraments that God channels grace into the inner reaches of the soul. To define grace and to explain its power is difficult. Protestant theologian Paul Tillich argued that grace should "always be translated as divine power of being, or power of New Being, which justifies and sanctifies." Through grace the "intellect is driven toward faith . . . the will is driven toward hope; and the whole being is driven toward love."[6] From a theological standpoint, grace is the affective presence that pours through the object or gesture. Though Christians will divide on the exact nature of the sacraments, their number, and their effects, all will agree that at times the gap between human and divine can be bridged. That bridge is at times material.

All Christians recognize to some degree a diffuse and generalized sacramentalism, but Roman Catholicism most clearly delineates how and under what conditions something material can mediate between God and humanity. Catholic theologians uphold the sacraments as the primary way in which the saving power of Christ enters the world. However, "there is hardly any proper use of material things which cannot thus be directed towards the sanctification of men and the praise of God."[7] Evolving out of the concept of the sacrament is the notion of a "sacramental," something that is more than a sign or symbol but less than a sacrament. Sacramentals also channel grace through gestures and objects but not to the same extent as the sacraments. While the concept of sacramentals has existed since the Middle Ages, it was only during the Catholic Reformation of the sixteenth century that theologians carefully delineated the differences between pious acts, sacramentals, and sacraments. Eventually, making the sign of the cross with holy water, praying with a rosary, giving alms, eating food blessed for holiday celebration, or even having a car blessed, all became sacramentals. "If matrimony is a sacrament," explains one modern commentator, "what is more natural than to bless the house, the bridal chamber, the expectant mother."[8] Sacramentals can appear in almost every aspect of daily life and, like sacraments, serve as a doorway between the secular and sacred worlds. The home, fields, workplace, and roads are the appropriate places for sacramentals.

While they are theologically derived from the sacraments, on a popular level sacramentals are often entangled in traditional folk rituals.[9] Catholics use sacramentals in many different ways and accord them a variety of different meanings. However, in this section I focus on how sacramentals derived power from being embedded in an institutional framework. What does official Catholic theology say about religious objects? According to Catholic thinkers and teachers, sacramentals

2. In 1943 Marjory Collins photographed a priest blessing special Easter food prepared by a Polish family living in Buffalo, New York. The original caption noted that "some bring their food in baskets to the church for blessing while others are visited by the priest." While the family has constructed an elaborate shrine with statues of the Virgin Mary and the Infant of Prague, they understand that the priest's ritual gestures are necessary for the proper blessing of the food. Through the priest's visit, the private religion of the home and the public religion of the church are connected.

parallel more complicated, church-bound rites. While a priest might be needed initially to make the sacramental valid, the point of the sacramental is to allow non-ordained men and women to integrate the sacred into their daily lives. Lay people become "priests" and decide when and where the sacramentals will be employed. Unlike a sacrament, that guarantees grace *ex opere operato* (independent of the character of the priest), the efficacy of sacramentals depends on the spirituality of the people who use them. The Eucharist would still be the body and blood of Christ if consecrated by a sinful priest, but holy water would not erase small sins if used by an ill-intentioned individual.[10] Sacramentals also symbolically reflect their position as "little" sacraments because, compared to ecclesiastical objects, sacramentals are often reduced in size. While frequently referring to the same themes and symbols as the sacraments, gestures and prayers using sacramentals are less liturgically complicated. I am not saying that Catholics necessarily believe that sacramentals are less powerful or that they use them in a

3. FSA photographer Russell Lee captured a son of M. LaBlanc building a fire in the fireplace of his Louisiana farm home in 1938. The domestic altar repeats the same themes and symbols as the family sees in their parish church.

simple and uncomplicated manner. I am describing how official Catholic teaching shapes the meanings of one type of religious object.

The role of sacramentals to express a parallel, privatized version of "church" Catholicism may be seen in a photograph taken inside a 1938 Louisiana farm house. On the mantlepiece, someone has created a domestic version of a church altar. The space is set apart by a clean white altar linen, its purity and refinement sharply contrasting with the surrounding rough bricks and floor planks. Just as one would see in church, a large statue of the Sacred Heart dominates the altar while smaller statues of St. Anne, the Immaculate Conception, and St. Joseph accompany the image of Christ. The crucifix stands to the left. Two kerosene lamps flank the sacred figures, like the beeswax candles at church. If we allow our imaginations free rein, the picture of the Capitol might replicate the American flag found on the altar of all U.S. Catholic churches during this period. Only clocks break the liturgical effect and tell us that the family is concerned with time as well

4. Originally part of the monastic habit, the scapular became greatly reduced in size when used as a popular sacramental by both lay men and women. To be effective, the scapular had to be blessed by a priest.

as faith. This family has duplicated what its members see at church. Domestic religious objects may mirror ecclesiastical objects.

Sacramentals may also be condensed versions of the devotional activities of clergy or religious. By analyzing the history of a sacramental called a "scapular" and the indulgences attached to it, we can see how religious authorities define and regulate affective presence through the creation of special objects for lay use. The term "scapular" comes from the Latin word for shoulder blade.[11] Originally it was part of a monastic habit: a long piece of cloth, varying in color according to the order, worn over the monk's gown. Hanging down in front and back, from the shoulders almost to the ground, it was open at the sides and placed over the head by means of a slit. While it originally served as an apron for work, it eventually came to symbolize the burden of monastic life. During the investment ritual of the habit, the scapular was referred to as the "yoke of Christ." In some orders the scapular was never to be removed but was to be worn at night as well as during the day.

The first transformation of the scapular occurred when lay people attached to orders (oblates) wore parts of their monastic habits during the Mass and hoped eventually to be buried in the sacred garb. While these lay people lived in the monastery or convent, they performed only some of the religious rituals. A second change occurred with the establishment of "Third Orders." These were lay people who hoped to follow a condensed monastic discipline outside in the world. Rather than wearing a habit, they wore *under* their clothing a "large scapular"; a square badge of woolen cloth measuring about five inches by two and a half inches. A third reduction followed with the creation of confraternities or societies whose members wanted to participate only through occasional prayer in the merits of monastic orders. At least sixteen different types of scapulars evolved, each connected to a religious order of men or women. The scapular shrank even further. It now consisted of two pieces of woolen cloth about two inches wide, connected by two strings that rested on the shoulders, positioning the badges across the breast and down the back. Each order placed a relevant picture or emblem on the wool swatch (the last remnant of the woolen habit): Our Lady of Mount Carmel for the Carmelites, Our Lady of the Seven Dolors for the Servites, the Immaculate Conception for the Theatine nuns. The scapular had to be worn continuously for any merit to accrue. A final simplification occurred in 1910 when Pope Pius X permitted the faithful to wear a medal instead of the scapular. Catholics, in order to amass multiple benefits, had been wearing several scapulars.

The scapular medal when properly blessed could substitute for all the scapulars.

After the Second Vatican Council (1962–5), the scapular, along with many other sacramentals, fell into disuse. Looking closely at this particular sacramental, however, can help us understand how objects gain power or affecting presence through their association with larger authoritative institutions. The scapular originally was a mundane object, an apron. During the Middle Ages, a tradition arose that the Virgin Mary had presented an English Carmelite, Simon Stock, with a scapular. According to one report, she told him that whoever "dies clothed with it shall be preserved from eternal punishment; that it is a badge of salvation, a shield against danger and a pledge of her protection."[12] It was not the vision, however, that endowed the scapular with power. This "pious and praiseworthy tradition" had to be legitimated and formalized by the appropriate offices of the Catholic church.[13] Over the years, various committees and popes laid down specific details describing the use of the scapular. To be effective, the scapular had to be properly invested by a priest who had been granted the power to invest it. While the investment ritual is simple, it must occur in order for any benefits to accrue. If the scapular was lost or wore out, any new scapular would be "active" if the original investment was done properly. The scapular must also be worn in the prescribed manner. Church authorities explained that if it was not placed across the shoulders and down the back and front, it had no power. While the scapular medal worked in the pocket, the cloth scapular did not. The clergy was to instruct Catholics about the proper use of sacramentals such as the scapular.

The church also defined exactly how many "indulgences" one could gain from wearing a scapular. Although there was some controversy over whether or not wearing a scapular could accord one the "Sabbatine" Indulgence (a release from purgatory following the first Saturday after one's death), other indulgences were routinely attached to scapulars. Until 1967 when Pope Paul VI issued a new apostolic constitution on indulgences, each sacramental act had attached to it a certain number of "days indulgences."[14] Individual recitation of the rosary, for instance, would gain one five years' indulgence while group recitation gained one ten years'. The concept of indulgences has its origins in the early days of the church when public penance – such as shaving one's head or groveling at the feet of church leaders – served as reparation for one's sins. The sinner would spend a specific number of days in pain and humiliation in order to show God and the community that he or she was truly repentant.[15] By the Middle Ages, public penance gave way to private forms. The sacrament of penance was instituted to wash away the guilt (*culpa*) of the sin, but the punishment (*poena*) still remained. The debt of punishment was cleared by the granting of indulgences. Indulgences were thus equivalent to public penance as defined by the early church. Medieval Christians gained partial or total (plenary) remission of the payment for sin by giving alms, saying certain prayers, or going on pilgrimages or crusades.

By the middle of the fifteenth century, indulgences could also be passed on to the dead languishing in purgatory. While some theologians admitted that the church had no direct control over the souls in purgatory, they trusted that God would accept merits from the spiritual treasury of Christ and remit all or part of their pains. In spite of the criticism of Protestant reformers, indulgences became a crucial part of Catholic devotional life because they were a clear and specific way that people on earth could influence divine conduct. Indulgences also reinforced the power of the church as a mediator between the people and God. Only the pope could specify what could be indulged and the character of the indulgence.

All prayers and good works ("pious acts") improved the condition of one's soul in general but indulged activities prescribed specifically how much merit would be gained. Indulgences became a part of Catholic life because they lessened religious insecurity. The church assured the believer that his or her prayers would be effective in specific ways if a set of defined actions was followed.

A particular office of the Catholic church, the Sacred Congregation of Indulgences, regulates how indulgences are attached to gestures or objects. Indulgences, for instance, are to be attached to the object not to the person who uses the object. Blessed objects must be made of sturdy material and not lead, pewter, or blown glass; materials that could be easily marred or broken. Indulgences may be attached to a specific part of the object. On a rosary, indulgences are attached to the beads, not to the crucifix or the medal. Thus, one could still gain the indulgences even if the crucifix was missing (indeed, the earliest rosaries or chaplets had no crucifixes). In 1958 the Congregation determined that indulgences could be gained if one recited the rosary along with a radio broadcast, and in recent years it decided that a papal blessing given over the television was as effective as if the believer was standing in St. Peter's Square in Rome.

The minute details of indulgences and the proper use and investment of sacramental objects must not be seen as trivial or meaningless. Authority is constructed and maintained not merely through overt coercion but also through the micromanagement of power. Meticulous rules and definitions communicate to the believer that the effectiveness of the object is wedded to and dependent on the institutional church. The church asserts that it possesses the knowledge of how to invest an object with life by describing in detail what one must do to achieve spiritual benefits. Michel Foucault is astute in observing that since the seventeenth century religious institutions, in ways similar to prisons and the military, have been preoccupied with "small acts of cunning," "subtle arrangements," "detailed characteristics," and "little things."[16] Social control in the modern world is accomplished by disciplining bodies in modest ways. The Catholic church has also sought to train and discipline bodies not only through education, as Foucault discusses, but also through the sacramental system. I have discussed at some length one specific sacramental, the scapular. This object, however, was only one among a "universe" or "arsenal" of pious objects, all of which were embedded in a detailed discourse of proper use.[17] On one level, sacramentals achieved power by Catholic institutional authority. At the same time, the use of the sacramentals by believers reinforced the power religious authorities claimed to possess.

While I have focused on the Catholic sacramentals, other Christian groups also imbue objects with power through institutional authority. In the Church of Jesus Christ of Latter-day Saints, consecrated oil is used for healing and ritual purposes. In Mormon practice, the oil achieves its unique power through the blessings of a special class of Latter-day Saint men. Currently, only members of the Melchizedek priesthood may consecrate and use the oil. Women might have used the oil in past times to bless and heal, but contemporary Mormon theology stipulates that the power of the oil is transferred through the blessings of only one specific group of men.[18] Mormons, like Catholics, are asked to accept the idea that the authority invested in their leaders is real and that it can be used to channel power into oil, scapulars, statues, rosaries or any word, gesture, or object. God may be understood as the origin of the power, but individuals perceive power as residing in one object and not in another.

5. Nineteenth-century German lithographs of the crucified Christ printed on paper to be swallowed to prevent or cure sickness.

The Power of Relationships: Prints, Shrines, and Art

The kind of power objects achieve through contact with religious authority is formal and impersonal. The Catholic church can report how many days' indulgence a believer will get for properly saying the rosary, but it cannot predict how the believer will feel about the rosary's power. Theologians, however, are well aware that the affective presence of images is closely tied to the emotion generated in the believer. Christian thinkers, such as Gregory the Great, Thomas Aquinas, and Bonaventure held that when one concentrated on a religious image eventually the soul could be inflamed with love for the divine.[19] Through contemplating the signs of God, the mind and spirit of the believer ascend from the visible to the invisible, from the sign to the referant. Devotional pictures and sculptures bridge the gap between the human and divine because they evoke emotion in the viewer. From the emotion comes the desire to live a better life, pray more devotedly, or feel healing comfort.

The Catholic church has a long history of encouraging its members to use images to help maintain and create relationships with Christ and the saints. Images are handled, cherished, prayed to, and even eaten in order to arouse affection and evoke tears. Medieval traditions report pictures of Mary and Christ coming alive, statues seen in visions and dreams later found in trees, and relics mysteriously moving from church to church. In the sixteenth century, the Virgin left her image on a Mexican peasant's cloak, and in the nineteenth century she instructed a nun to design a medal in her honor. Pictures of Christ and the saints were eaten to promote health in spite of clerical condemnation of the practice as late as the 1940s. Even in the skeptical twentieth century, we read in the newspaper that

6. In this embroidery with painting on silk (c. 1830) the infant Moses is being rescued by Pharoah's daughter and her servants (Ex 2:1-10). To avoid cultivating a devotional attitude toward images, sacred characters were portrayed within specific biblical narratives.

icons weep and statues bleed.[20] But surely, isn't it only Catholics who have spiritual relationships with religious prints or statues? Aren't Protestants fully aware that the sign must be separate from the referant, that a picture can only be a picture? Don't Protestants realize that to make an object stand in for a subject is to come perilously close to idolatry? While religious authorities can easily say that an object has no power, I want to argue that Christians have not always listened to church authorities. Protestants, as well as Catholics, cherish religious images to the point that their devotions fuse the sign with the referant. In spite of Protestant concerns about idolatry and image worship, many Protestants have intimate and powerful relationships with objects. Like Catholics, some Protestants treat religious objects as more than inanimate things.

Current scholarship on the history of Protestantism is slowly disproving the notion that the Reformation marked a radical change in the religious mentality of Europeans.[21] The supernatural world of angels and devils, healing waters and demonic witches, did not immediately disappear with Luther and Calvin. This was particularly the case with religious images. Tessa Watt has shown that the Reformation did not eliminate images but rather substituted acceptable images in acceptable places for unacceptable images in unacceptable places.[22] Since, according to Calvin, images could be used for teaching and admonition, images were removed from churches but continued to decorate homes, ale houses, cottages, and inns.[23] Picturing saints was too "papist" but artisans could portray Old Testament figures, characters from the Apocrypha and New Testament parables, and allegorical figures from classical literature. In 1666 color illustrations from Foxe's *Book of the Martyrs* were sold "as a convenient Table for Ornament of every good Christian House, to stir them up to stand to the Faith."[24] To avoid cultivating a devotional attitude toward images, sacred characters were placed in biblical scenes where they were actors in a familiar narrative and not immobile objects of adoration.[25] Women embroidered scenes from the Bible, copying their patterns from Flemish and Dutch artists.[26] By the nineteenth century, lithography and chromolithography enabled the mass production of engraved images. Photomechanical reproduction in the twentieth century meant that cheap copies of religious paintings would be available to Protestant households.

By the end of the nineteenth century, low-church Protestants in the United States had begun to "disobey" some of the regulatory strategies laid down by their European ancestors. Printers were taking paintings by popular artists, reproducing close-ups of the faces of religious characters, and selling the images to evangelical magazines and religious goods firms. The German artist Heinrich Hofmann, for instance, painted two biblical narratives, *Christ and the Rich Young Ruler* (1889) and *Christ in the Temple* (1882). In each painting, Christ stands among other people. His face is one among several. Printers, however, extracted and reproduced only the head of Christ. They put the face on prints, and as we will see in Chapter 8, placed it on books, plaques, lamps, bookends, thermometers, and other everyday goods. While Episcopalians and Lutherans had always welcomed some art into their churches, reproductions of paintings by Hofmann, Bernhard Plockhorst, William-Adophe Bourguereau, and J. James Tissot made their way into Presbyterian, Methodist, and Baptist churches. Many of their paintings were transformed into stained glass.[27]

As part of a study of twentieth-century religious painter Warner Sallman, a professor of art at Valparaiso University, David Morgan, placed a query in Protestant magazines and newspapers: "What does this painting mean to you?" the advertisement asked. "What has the imagery meant for your devotion, worship, prayer, family or friends?" Almost five hundred people sent their response to Sallman's *Head of Christ*.[28] About 10 percent of the letters rejected the

7. In 1889 German artist Heinrich Hofmann painted *Christ and the Rich Young Ruler*, depicting Jesus instructing those who wished to follow him to sell their earthly possessions and give to the poor (Matt 19:20-24). Following Protestant artistic convention, Hofmann portrayed a biblical episode as visual narrative.

8.   Printers later abstracted the head of Christ
from the narrative painting and reproduced it in
order to emphasize the power and emotion of
the divine face. They detached the image from
the biblical story thus making it easier for
Christians to create their own personal
narratives regarding the sacred figure.

popular *Head of Christ* on various aesthetic, theological, and ethical grounds. Most
of the letters revealed that people create intimate relationships with Christ through
Sallman's painting. Protestants empower Sallman's *Head of Christ* in much the
same way that Catholics find an affecting presence in home shrines. In the
following discussion of Protestant usage of Sallman's prints and Catholic
construction of domestic shrines, I emphasize how various people establish a
relationship with Christ and other religious figures via a material Christianity.
While we cannot assume that American Christians have always responded in the
same way to religious lithographs or prints, these letter writers help define the
spectrum of response to images.

Warner Press began marketing Warner Sallman's *Head of Christ* in 1941 and
continues to do a brisk trade with the image. The image emphasizes the humanity
of Christ and responses to it consistently remark upon the personality displayed in
the picture. "There is a warmth and yet an enigmatic intensity about this portrayal
of Christ which has always moved me," wrote a female Lutheran pastor. "This is a
'person' I want to know."[29] Some imagine through the picture a Christ intimately
connected to their bodies: "When I begin my meditation and prayers, I always
like to picture Him holding His hands out to me, I can feel closer to Him in my
Heart, and this is the face I always imagine."[30] The face that they love is a familiar
face, not the face of a first-century Jew. They see a face that could belong to their
uncle, or neighbor, or dad. "My picture hangs on the wall in my living room,"
described a 68-year-old woman, "and as I sit and rock in my favorite chair many

9. Warner Sallman's *Head of Christ*, which eventually replaced the popular portrayal by Heinrich Hofmann, served as the standard representation of Christ until the 1960s.

times I have been blessed with the knowledge that I have a friend looking down at me or perhaps I should say looking up with me with hope and love."[31] According to art historian David Freedberg, "we spontaneously and inexorably seek to invest representation with the marks of the familiar . . . This is why legends about miracle-working images so frequently have at their center images with traits or behavioral predispositions that are self-consciously low-level, intimate, and everyday."[32] The painting reflects a belief in an intimate, friendly savior who cares for Christians personally. This is not the Christ who commands the universe but rather the Jesus who directs everyday life and supports his followers in difficult times.

A critical part of the painting for many of these Christians is the eyes. Writers specifically mention how Warner Sallman got the eyes "right." A Louisiana woman made this association between the eyes and personality of Jesus: "I have studied the face many times," she wrote. "It is the softness of the eyes and the face. I picture what it would be like to talk to this person. I feel he would understand anything you would say to him and would answer in kindness & understanding. He would also be firm. I study this picture many times when I am troubled."[33] The eyes are more than merely friendly. Since Sallman painted the head in profile, the gaze is not directed at the viewer. A Catholic nun commented in her letter that his eyes are fixed on God the Father, while another nun noted that Christ's eyes were on his mission.[34] According to Freedberg, "the images that trouble us most are those in which the gaze of the represented most actively engages our attention."[35] Perhaps Protestant letter writers felt comfortable with Sallman's portrayal in part because their eyes do not meet precisely with the eyes of Christ. The print is less devotional because the believer's gaze does not directly meet the gaze of the divine. Christ's image serves as a mediator between the self and God. The eyes are interpreted as loving; they do not gaze down relentlessly on the believer.

Religious prints have an impact on Christians not merely because they promote personal relationships with Jesus or because the eyes direct the viewer to God the Father. Letter writers explain that the Sallman print hung for many years in their homes or churches. Many remembered it fondly from their childhoods. Prints are treasured because they are associated with significant events in believers' lives. Frequently prints are given as wedding or going away presents. A Methodist minister wrote that his classmates at divinity school gave him and his wife a "framed portrait" for a wedding gift and thus "it has deep sentimental and spiritual significance for me as I associate it with my marriage and my ministry of forty years."[36] Families value their prints and make them spiritual centerpieces of their homes. Furniture may come and go and houses may change but the print stays on the wall, acting as a symbol of stability for mobile Americans. Families pass prints down from generation to generation. An Ohio woman wrote that the picture had hung in her and her son's home for fifty-three years. She also mentioned that on her son's "wall, you will see a picture of his children each in their own frame, and another picture hangs besides them. It's the picture of 'Sallman's Head of Christ!'"[37] This writer wanted to make sure that the reader knew that "we worship the Saviour not his picture." But, as she put it, "how can we express the feeling within our hearts?" That feeling is created through constant and long-term personal interaction with both an image and a spiritual concept.

Sallman prints are able to perform "miracles" because they provide comfort, support, and protection in a stressful world often devoid of love. An elderly

10. FSA photographer John Vachon in 1940 captured the visit of Mrs. Dyson and her daughter-in-law in their home. The sitting room probably doubled as a bedroom. Above the two women is a large, framed print of the *Sorrowful Mother*.

woman was so lonely a week before Christmas that she started crying and could not stop. "I had the television on," she wrote, "but that didn't seem to help matters whatsoever." Instead she looked up at the picture and said, "I need a hug, oh dear Jesus if I could just have a hug I'm so lonely." The request was heard and "all of a sudden" Christmas carolers appeared and at a "magic moment" one little girl gave her a hug. Another woman recalled that as a child she could look out of her bedroom and into the dining room where the Sallman picture hung.[38] "It was a source of hope & peace," she wrote, "in a home of alcoholism & abuse my mother received from a hurting lost alcoholic man: my father."[39] A 38-year-old

11. In 1940 John Vachon took a similar photo of a farmer from Meeker County, Minnesota. Although this home is better appointed than that of the Maryland farmhouse, a religious print still commands an important place in the high-use area near the radio.

12. Russell Lee's 1939 picture of a corner of a living room in a "Spanish-American home" in Taos County, New Mexico, shows *Our Lady of Mount Carmel* presiding over the family's photographs. Religious images are placed where members of the family will see them; they become a part of the household.

Lutheran wrote that her daughter was killed riding her bicycle, and "it helped tremendously to be able to envision her going to heaven on the arm of the Christ I see in my mind, the one from Warner Sallman."[40] A Methodist minister remembered a news story about a robber who saw the Sallman painting and then told his victim, "Lady, I can't do it, not with him behind you."[41] In many less dramatic cases, Protestants reported being comforted, supported, encouraged, and reassured by the picture. In each of these cases, one could imagine that the supporting relationship with Jesus could have been created without the image. Yet, these and other Protestants meld the face as painted by Sallman with the face of Christ. The picture has meaning for them because over the years it has been integrated into their spiritual and domestic lives.

Although the content of the religious print may be different, Catholics also use art to develop relationships with the divine. Consider three interior photographs taken in the 1930s and 1940s by Farm Security Administration photographers. While the locale, class, race, and ethnicity of the Catholics all differ, the domestic presentation of religious prints is similar. In each photograph, the print commands the viewer's attention because of its placement above all other decorations and its large size. Families hang them in high-access areas, where people visit, sleep, and enjoy entertainment. The prints are framed, emphasizing the importance of the displayed sacred scene. All three of the prints depict relationships between the human and the divine. The print hanging in the African American home shows a human Mary mourning over the dead body of the God/man, Christ. The Minnesota farmer tunes in his radio under a depiction of the God/baby, Jesus who affectionately plays with the Italian saint, Anthony of Padua. In the corner of

a home in Taos County, New Mexico, a family displays a scene of Our Lady of Mount Carmel rescuing the dead from the fires of purgatory. The representation of the Virgin Mary presides over a table of family photographs. Christ and the saints are part of the family. During the first half of the twentieth century, such prints were widely distributed and very popular. Photographs from the 1930s and 1940s of an Italian American home in New York City, a Canadian home in Newfoundland, and two other homes in New Mexico, all show this same print of Our Lady of Mount Carmel. As with Warner Sallman's *Head of Christ*, one way that religious prints come alive is through their association with the everyday space, events, and troubles of family life.

Religious prints are also frequently included in domestic shrines. While Catholics are the Christians most noted for their shrine building, Protestants also build shrines. Folklorist Yvonne Milspaw analyzed her Methodist grandmother's home shrine that borrowed freely from Catholic sources.[42] The shrine contained candles, holy cards of the Sacred Heart and the Immaculate Heart of Mary, a framed head of Christ, religious postcards, a holy water container, and blessed palms. Milspaw found that other Methodist women in the area also kept shrines, using Bibles and pious prints to make the space sacred. We see similar items in two FSA photographs from homes separated from each other by class, language, ethnicity, and religion. In the Protestant home of an Iowan farm family (1936), a collection of family photographs and musical instruments is assembled below a

13. While Russell Lee's photographs of Catholic New Mexican homes are particularly rich, this 1936 shot is from the farmhouse of J. E. Herbrandson who lived in the vicinity of Estherville, Iowa. The scripture motto contains a close-up of the young Christ from a biblical narrative painting by Heinrich Hofmann.

scriptural motto. The biblical injunction, "The fear of the Lord is the beginning of Wisdom" is placed next to the young Christ – a detail from Heinrich Hofmann's *Christ in the Temple.* In the second photograph (1943) an old woman from Peñasco, New Mexico, sits underneath a display of family photographs and religious objects. As with the farm family's shrine, pictures of her ancestors are placed next to that of Christ and the saints. Their portraits are approximately the same size as the shrine. Earthly kin and heavenly kin are brought into intimate association with one another.[43] The eyes of the family members, and the eyes of Christ and the saints, all stare out at the family on earth.

Both shrines are informal, eclectic, homemade, and use repetition to emphasize importance and inclusion. Both shrines speak to the social and cultural aspirations of the family, even though their individual styles differ. Domestic shrines, both Protestant and Catholic, condense the religious and social values of the family. The objects and images are not the flotsam of consumer culture but significant pieces of a meaningful whole. The shrine and its objects function in much the same way as artifacts do in domestic novels. Literary historian Jane Tompkins comments that "the measuring out of life in coffee spoons, a modernist metaphor for insignificance and futility, is interpreted in sentimental discourse as a world-building activity."[44] As a collection of meaningful objects, the shrine serves as a detailed and active expression of the power of relationship.

Home altars do not merely demonstrate and cement the relationship between

14. According to the caption on John Collier's 1943 photograph, this was the home of an old couple living in Peñasco, New Mexico. The shrine and the family portraits are approximately the same size. Earthly kin and heavenly kin are brought into intimate association with one another.

divine characters and the family. They also influence the ways in which family members interact with one another. In Kay Turner's study of Mexican American women and their altars, she finds that the intimacy and care that the women express toward Christ and the saints also extend to family members and neighbors.[45] Mothers teach their daughters how to construct and maintain their shrines. Statues and images of the saints are passed down from generation to generation. Women place the photographs of those they pray for on the altar, and portraits of deceased relatives are frequently positioned high on walls to indicate the status of ancestors. Dead children can be remembered at the altar and thus remain a part of the family. Questions about childrearing or other household problems can be addressed to the saints in the intimate and comforting surroundings of home. While the women in Turner's study stress that they express their concern for others at home altars, it is also possible that the darker side of relationships is explored at the altar.[46] If photographs can be placed next to saints' statues, they can also be removed. Mothers can plead for the conformity and submission of their children as well as their protection. Authority can be asserted through not "remembering" people in prayers, just as dissatisfaction with a saint may motivate turning his or her statue to the wall. A home shrine is connected to the patterns of relationships in the lives of family members, and those bonds can both nurture and constrain.

Shrine building has a long tradition in Catholic culture and scholars have discovered domestic shrines throughout the ancient world.[47] In recent years, artists have used the motif of the shrine as a way to convey their own inner sense of spirituality. They draw equally on the religious traditions of altar building and on the artistic traditions of collage and assemblage. Influenced by folk and ethnic arts, artists make three-dimensional sculptures/shrines out of "found objects" which they arrange in provocative and creative ways. Color, humor, ornamentation, texture, layering, glitz, and repetition are all emphasized. Mass-produced religious objects such as statues and holy cards are placed in such a way that they are noticed for their unique qualities. Simultaneously, those individual pieces blend into a whole that conveys the artist's intentions. By placing their shrines in the public spaces of museums and galleries, artists communicate their aesthetic and spiritual visions not only to themselves and their families but to a wider audience.

For many artists, altar building is not merely an artistic endeavor. Some artists come from Catholic backgrounds and seek to rework Catholic images so that the symbols communicate the artist's own political, social, spiritual, and aesthetic goals. Others use Christian images but see themselves as followers of the Great Goddess or explorers of spiritual energy. Chicana Linda Vallejo sees her shrines as "a natural vehicle for expressing my spiritual growth."[48] She and Amalia Mesa Bains are examples of artists who integrate images from their Hispanic culture into their art. For Barbara Ellmann, her shrines elevate "secular ideas to religious importance."[49] Her "Flower altar" mixed pictures and objects associated with the "Little Flower" (St. Theresa of Lisieux) with seeds, bottles, beads, artificial flowers, and seed packets. Through the shrine she examines the life cycle of flowers as a "mirror of human experience." Sharon Smith sees a direct connection between her spirituality and the altars she builds for gallery exhibits.[50] While she was raised in a non-religious home and is not a member of any religious community, she understands her shrines as spiritual explorations of pain, guilt,

15. Sharon Smith, an artist living in Austin, Texas, uses altars containing religious objects to break down the boundaries between art, institutional religion, and individual spirituality.

joy, and laughter. Through her shrines she seeks to break down the common cultural boundaries between art, institutional religion, and individual spirituality. For her, sculpture and altar, kitsch and art, seriousness and frivolity, personal story and collective myth all blend together. Smith seeks to shock the viewer and create conversation. Presenting her own experience is more important than any type of pious communication with the celestial sphere, but her shrine building raises the personal to a higher, more meaningful, level.

In 1992 artist Frank McEntire installed his *Reassemblages* at the Salt Lake City Art Center. *Reassemblages* included shrines, wrapped religious objects mounted on the gallery walls, and burial mounds where visitors could place their own sacred objects. The buried objects were eventually uncovered, taken to places "identified by the community as needing special problem-solving attention" and reburied.[51] The statues, books, models, and prints used in the exhibit had all once been discarded. The plastic model of the Salt Lake City Temple, for instance, is a frequent decoration placed atop wedding cakes. Once found, the objects were eventually reworked to present new meanings. Some of the objects came from McEntire's own Mormon tradition and the rest from various world religions. The installation focused on issues such as spiritual transformation and the environmental consequences of living in a "throw-away society." Like the artist

16. As a part of his 1992 installation called *Reassemblages* Frank McEntire included this plastic model of the Salt Lake City Latter-day Saint Temple (frequently set atop wedding cakes) covered in his own hair.

Christo, McEntire used wrapping to get people to think about objects that they otherwise would ignore. The installation sought to highlight the weak boundaries between art, religion, and politics.

Cultural critic Celeste Olalquiaga perceives a parallel between the art form of the shrine and our current postmodern existence. "In its chaotic juxtaposition of images and times," she writes, "contemporary urban culture is comparable to an altar-like reality, where the logic of organization is anything but homogeneous, visual saturation is obligatory, and the personal is lived as a pastiche of fragmented images from popular culture."[52] If this is the case, we might predict that contemporary audiences will be able to move beyond the religious objects contained in the shrines to see the larger cultural vision of the artist. Olalquiaga's speculations prompt me to ask if people do see their lives mirrored in "gallery shrines." Since artists make shrines for public presentation, do viewers understand that religion can be a symbol for something other than institutionalized religion? In the case of Frank McEntire's *Reassemblages*, written audience responses in a gallery comments book lead me to suspect that gallery goers have a difficult time perceiving the intentions of the artist when religious objects are involved.

Religious goods, even if they are broken, wrapped, and put in an art gallery are still seen as "religious." Comments on *Reassemblages*, while ranging from the negative to the positive, centered on its ability to communicate or distort religious sensibilities. "You missed the whole point of religion," lamented one critic. "I found it offensive because it came across as mocking people's religious views," reported another. "Sacrilegious to a Catholic," stated a third, the "artist does not understand the concepts of Christian faith." Positive responses also focused on the installation's religious, as opposed to political or artistic, merits. "It is very spiritual and mysterious, very peaceful," summarized one viewer. "What a wonderful reminder that all we must do is look *inside* & see God. That we are all one," commented another. At least in this one case, the artist was not able to use religious objects to convey messages about the environment, social disorder, or the relationship between politics, religion, and art. Salt Lake City gallery goers could not transform religious objects into messengers of cultural information. Religious objects covered in hair or decorated with sequins were not seen as tacky kitsch, artistic camp, or harbingers of social decay. For those who took the time to write their observations down, the objects were perceived as still embedded in a system of saints, gods, deities, and religious institutions.

In recent years, considerable effort has been expended in trying to understand the differences between the ways that men think, act, talk, and believe and the ways that women think, act, talk, and believe.[53] When religious objects gain power through their association with the authority of religious institutions, that process is defined and administered by men. When objects are enlivened through the power of relationships, that process is frequently mediated by women. Some men (especially ministers) did respond to David Morgan's request to describe their feelings about Warner Sallman's art, and Frank McEntire does build shrines. However, twice as many letters were written by women as by men, and McEntire recognizes that most contemporary artists who build shrines are women.[54] Why do contemporary women maintain shrines and relate to prints of Jesus?

Since Christian women have traditionally been excluded from public devotional leadership, they developed private religious activities at home. Freed from clerical supervision, women could experience the intensity of their devotions without restriction. In the privacy of their own homes, they were leaders of their domestic altars. As will be discussed in Chapter 3, the home in Victorian America came to be perceived as a sacred space, and women were given control over family religion. As domestic specialists, Protestant women saw to it that their homes presented their Christian commitments in ways that reflected their taste and pocketbook. Catholic women, especially from southern Europe and Latin America, maintained domestic shrines even if they never went to church. Immigrant Catholics, who may have found public church-going a hostile and alienating activity, preserved their ethnic saints and traditions at home.[55] Women purchased, maintained, and displayed religious objects and art in the home because domestic space typically was under their control.

For whatever sociological or biological reasons, women also tend to be concerned with establishing bonds between people. Consequently, it is not surprising that they also maintain the connection between this world and the other world. Folklorist Kay Turner reports that "women draw sacred images into the realm of the social and cultural making them co-partners in a process of nurturing the individual, the family, and the world."[56] Altar makers blur the distinction between the sacred as a distanced other and the sacred as intimate other. The home, rather than the church, becomes the place where power is transferred from one sphere to the other. The home altar becomes the symbolic bridge between heaven and earth. Turner concludes that Mexican American women become ethically, emotionally, and spiritually empowered through their shrine building. Relating to the divine through objects is not merely a private, devotional act. Those who attach themselves emotionally to a print or a shrine find that the relationship gives them strength to cope with the difficulties of real life. Rather than make them passive dependents on the will of God (or family or society) it provides a means for mutual interaction with powerful forces. Although a study comparable to Turner's of Protestant women and religious images has not been conducted, Morgan's correspondence suggests that Protestant women possess similar feelings.

The Power of Memory: Souvenirs and Relics

Religious objects assembled on the top of a piano or tucked in the corner of a room not only serve as a bridge between the human and divine worlds, they can also be objects of memory. Recent writing on memory has emphasized its active, constructive nature.[57] Rather than being a storehouse from which images and feelings can be retrieved at will, it is an imaginative reconstruction of pieces of the past. Through memory we try to recapture an authentic past. However, since the past is changed through remembering, we cannot truly remember it. Instead we look to spaces, gestures, images, and objects to embody memory. While history calls for analysis and criticism, memory is "affective and magical" and bonds us to the "eternal present." Historian Pierre Nora sees memory "in permanent evolution, open to the dialectic of remembering and forgetting, unconscious of its successive deformations, vulnerable to manipulation and appropriation, susceptible of being long dormant and periodically revived."[58] Religious objects frequently serve as the material reminders of significant events, people, moods, and activities by condensing and compressing memory.

We saw in the previous section how Protestants received Warner Sallman's *Head of Christ* as a wedding present. As one woman wrote, "most of all this picture began for us with our marriage & has reminded me each day that God brought us together, & He has led us throughout our entire married life. This picture is such a gentle reminder of all I believe."[59] Since religious gifts are given at rites of passage, when people move from one stage of their lives to another, the gift can come to symbolize that transformation. As we will see in Chapter 6, Mormons receive the sacred underclothing called garments before going on a mission or getting married. As with the Sallman prints, garments become linked to those rites of passage. If the marriage sours or the mission experience provokes a crisis of faith, attitudes toward the garments can also turn negative. For some, memory objects like prints or clothing associated with rites of passage are quickly forgotten. For others, they provide a life-long series of memories.

This capacity of the object to act as a perpetual source of recollection is particularly the case when the memory triggered is of a friend or family member who has died. The giving of memorials to commemorate the dead has a long history culminating in the elaborate mourning rituals of the nineteenth century. On one level, the *mementos mori* were formal and symbolic. Gloves and rings, for instance, were tokens that had no specific reference to the person who had died. On the other hand, embroidered samplers presented information about the deceased and hair art made use of their bodily remains.[60] Photographs were taken of the dead and one early twentieth-century photographer superimposed images of Christ next to the coffin.[61] People use objects to hold on to the image of the dead through memorials, photographs, and hair art. At other times artifacts are used to let go of the dead symbolically. Friends and families of the war dead often leave objects at the Vietnam War Memorial in Washington, D.C. These have been collected and a selection was put on display at the National Museum of American History. Objects are also left on city streets at the site of crimes or on roads where accidents have occurred. They serve not only to remember the dead but to jolt the viewer into recognizing the reality of violence and danger. The impulse to memorialize through objects (whether explicitly religious or not) reflects Susan

17.   Memorial art was extremely popular during the nineteenth century and mass-produced prints like this one might be personalized with a lock of hair and the date of death. In this print, on the left side of the river is the cemetery, a city of the dead. Souls are being ferried to the right side, a heavenly land populated by angels and replete with palm trees.

18.   During the nineteenth century, the dead were often photographed. Children especially were memorialized surrounded by flowers and posed as if they were merely asleep. While this custom fell out of common practice in the twentieth century, some communities continued to take photographs of their dead. Harlem photographer James VanDerZee frequently composed such memorials for his middle-class clientele. In this 1933 photograph, he superimposed an excerpt from Bernhard Plockhorst's late nineteenth-century painting *Christ Blessing the Little Children*.

Stewart's notion of "nostalgic reconstruction" where the present is denied and the past takes on an "authenticity of being."[62] The living seek to recreate the dead through memory activated by objects.

Nostalgia also motivates people to obtain material reminders of places and events. Stewart's comments on souvenirs are applicable for those myriad of cherished religious objects that are brought back from pilgrimages or journeys to religious sites. A traveler to Lourdes not only gathers water from the famous shrine in France, he or she also brings back rosaries, medals, T-shirts, clocks, statues, and countless other trinkets. Some are given as gifts and others capture for their owner traces of the unrepeatable original experience. Through its power to evoke memories, the souvenir begins to replace the event as the focus of attention. Stewart writes that "the function of the souvenir proper is to create a continuous and personal narrative of the past" unique to the possessor of the object.[63] The religious souvenir participates in the power of the original experience. Our modern commercial economy makes it easier to fabricate and purchase religious souvenirs, but the material ephemera of Christian history – amulets, ampullae, pilgrim badges and pennants, woodblock prints, holy cards, medals – attest to the enduring need to re-experience religious memories through objects.

19. Lining the streets that lead to the shrine at Lourdes are many souvenir stores that sell a vast array of goods to pilgrims and tourists. The earliest accounts of Lourdes mention people selling and buying candles and medals. Through remembering, the souvenir helps to evoke the power of the original experience.

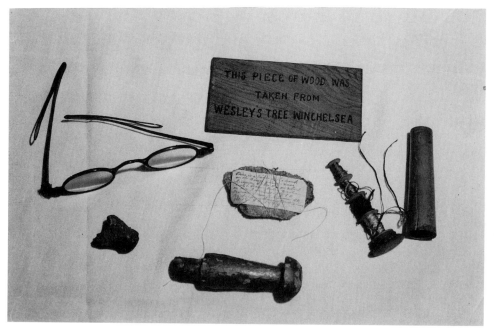

20. The piece of Whitefield's thumb is in the lower left-hand corner. Moving upward from it are Francis Asbury's glasses, a piece of wood taken from Wesley's tree, Asbury's thread case, and a wooden peg from the First Methodist Church in Rahway, New Jersey. In the center is a piece of a rock on which Asbury sat.

Memories of place attached to objects can be negative as well as positive. Many Protestants who commented on Sallman's art associated it with memories of childhood and Sunday school. One minister, however, actively sought to get rid of the *Head of Christ* hung in his church. He had despised Sallman's pictures for fifty years: "They are redolent of mildewed hymn books and 'In The Garden' sung with a nasal twang."[64] For a Texas woman, Sallman's art evoked memories of Sunday school walls painted institutional green and "a tinny-sounding upright piano, a shaky yellow-oak lectern, and stacks of yellowing, outdated Sunday school literature on makeshift wooden shelves." The whole dreary space was presided over by "a succession of prim, stocky, shapeless, middle-aged women, mostly unmarried, who habitually wore dark crepe dresses and black lace-up oxfords with clunky Cuban heels (generally known as 'sensible shoes')."[65] For these two people, Sallman's art triggered rich but unpleasant memories of the religious spaces of childhood.

While the sentimentality of Sallman's art or the hair of a dead relative might evoke powerful personal memories, other objects activate collective memory. Relics are objects of memory which speak to a community's notion of holiness. In the Catholic tradition, relics are remnants of the bodies or effects of Christ and the saints. A relic might be a piece of a bone or a shred of cloth. Catholics venerate relics as physical representatives of people who led exceptionally spiritual lives and who now are in heaven.[66] Relics are meaningful for a whole community of people.

The tradition of "venerating" relics is not unique to Catholics. Along with books and manuscripts in the Methodist Archives at Drew University are a set of Methodist relics. Within the Methodist community, John Wesley, George Whitefield, and other ministers were more than the leaders of the early church. In spite of their reluctance to be turned into charismatic figures, some followers saw them as holy men. In 1775 a group of military officers and ministers, after exhuming and viewing George Whitefield's dead body, "removed the evangelist's clerical collar and wrist bands to pass among their soldiers." The corpse continued to be a focus of attention during the nineteenth century.[67] It was not merely Whitefield's theology or sermonic corpus that fascinated Protestants; his personal power was understood as passing into his own body and possessions. At some point, a piece of Whitefield's thumb made its way to the Methodist Archives where it is preserved in a locked file cabinet. There is no evidence that Whitefield's body parts were used in healing rituals, but Methodists and other Protestants wanted to connect with the sanctity of Whitefield through physically touching and handling his corpse.

While the thumb is the most esoteric relic at the Methodist Archives, other relics are displayed to visitors. Pieces of John Wesley's coat, some plush velvet upholstery from his chair, and the original chair he stood on to preach in 1765 are all carefully preserved. In a 1932 letter to the president of Drew University, Wilbur E. Schoonhoven commented on his donation of Adam Clarke's thread case and silver knee buckle: "I'm grateful to you in consenting to care for these relics which bind the present to the heroic age of Methodism," he acknowledged.[68] The thread case and knee buckle take their place alongside Francis Asbury's spectacles and the wooden peg from the First Methodist Church in Rahway, New Jersey (where Asbury had hung his coat in the early nineteenth century). Wilbur Schoonhoven donated his treasured silver knee buckle of Adam Clarke to an archive where it was cataloged and put in a drawer. We can surmise from the brief letter accompanying his donation that he felt a university could "care" for the relics better than he could. The Methodist Archives care for these objects as if they were historic exotica rather than sacred relics. However, because of the archive's association with the Methodist church the relics remain in a religious context because they were given to a seminary for safe keeping. The Methodist Archives serve as a repository for Methodist memories. The person who carefully wrapped a rock in twine and labeled it "a rock from where Asbury sat" tells us that even Methodists believed that objects somehow shared in the power of people associated with them. The fact that the curators of the Methodist Archives do not throw out the rock as meaningless junk attests to the residual power of the object. While I consider the rock because of what it says about the history of "average" Methodists, the curators keep it because of its association with their collective memory.

Power Through Community

John Wesley is remembered at the Methodist Archives not only through his chairs and coat material. Carefully laid out in a conference room are over a hundred small statues and busts of the Methodist founder. Somewhere around 1780, Enoch Wood made a bust of the aging Wesley and within a few years as many as fifty different busts were produced in England by Staffordshire potters. Between 1825 and the 1880s, potters also made statues of Wesley either holding a Bible or preaching from a pulpit. The statues were either imported to America or brought back as souvenirs from Britain. The commemorative tea and coffee pots produced by Wedgwood in 1775 were copied in 1838 (the centenary of Wesley's conversion), in 1909, and again in the 1960s. Cups, saucers, mugs, teapots, coin

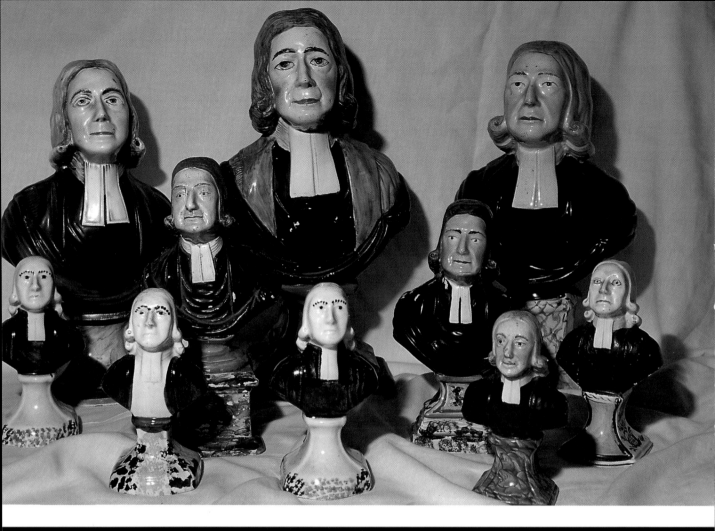

23. Tea pot, c. 1830.

banks, pitchers, and plates also featured Wesley's face and Methodist symbols. A British minister who formed the Wesley Historical Reproduction Association in 1909 advertised "Relics of Wesley Reproduced. Don't Miss a Great Opportunity"; his stated intention was "to introduce to every Methodist home Worthy Memorials of John Wesley."[69] He used the powerful term "relic" as a sales pitch, but what he was really selling were mass-produced medallions, plaques, teapots, and busts that communicated community affiliation. His Wesley memorabilia did not transfer religious power through personal memory or collective feelings about charismatic leaders. Wesley never touched his teapots. What the teapots did was to convey the message that their owners were good Methodists.

Christians use religious goods to tell themselves and the world around them that they are Christians. Like goods in tribal societies, religious objects "are used for paying compliments, for initiating marriages, establishing or ending them, for recognizing relationships, for all celebrations, compensations and affirmations whatever."[70] Religious objects also signal who is in the group and who is not. They teach people how to think and act like Christians. They are used to lure, encourage, and shock non-Christians into considering the truth of Christianity. The social exchange of religious goods can strengthen friendships as well as provide financial support for churches and church organizations. Religious goods not only bind people to the sacred, they bind people to each other.

A young man recalled riding a Chicago subway when, in pulling out his handkerchief, his rosary fell to the floor. Embarrassed, he snatched the rosary off the floor and stuffed it quickly into his pocket. "I don't suppose I was the first Catholic in the world to be embarrassed by an accidental display of a rosary," he confessed. As an adult (and a priest) reflecting on the incident, he admitted, "I was ashamed of the accidental rosary display because 'outsiders' had had a glimpse of my private devotion. . . . I was afraid they would smirk and say to themselves, 'More Catholic superstition! Another dark age Christian.'"[71] In a

21. Staffordshire pottery busts and statues of John Wesley. Placement of the figurines on a fireplace mantel or "what-not" shelf indicated that the family was a part of the community of Methodists.

22. Wesleyan Chapel money box, c. 1845-8.

24. Cup and saucer, c. 1839.

similar manner, journalist Deborah Laake was humiliated when she had to expose her garments to her non-Mormon co-workers.[72] When used in traditional ways, rosaries and garments are embedded in specific religious communities, communities that often have experienced persecution and misunderstanding. To be exposed as a member of such a group is to become vulnerable to ridicule and questioning. In these cases the rosary or garment symbolizes the private, hidden, intimate dimensions of a religious faith that has been unintentionally revealed for outsiders to see and perhaps abuse.

At other times, Christians proudly display their signs of commitment. Catholics place statues of the Blessed Virgin and the saints on their lawns; the tradition of yard shrines is particularly important in Italian and Hispanic cultures.[73] Shops, businesses, and restaurants often display religious shrines or pictures. In the 1960s evangelical Protestants placed religious sayings on car bumper stickers, and in the 1980s many of those sayings also appeared on T-shirts. Christian teenagers and young adults wear shirts and hats that parody American consumer culture, drawing attention to their religious commitments. A Lutheran woman in Independence, Missouri, "purposefully and strategically" positioned a copy of Sallman's *Head of Christ* near her front door so that "those who enter our home . . . know that Christ is the head of our household." It also lets the family witness to the Mormons or Jehovah's Witnesses "who knock at their door."[74] While the law may restrict the use of explicitly Christian symbolism in public spaces, individuals continue to demonstrate their beliefs in the semi-public spaces of yards and workplaces, on car bumpers and bodies.

It is within the home that people feel most comfortable in displaying symbols of their religious community. That demonstration can be explicitly sectarian, as when Methodists display busts of Wesley or Catholics mount holy water fonts in each room. More generalized Christian sentiments may also be promoted. In the 1870s and 1880s, women embroidered in Berlin woolwork pious sayings on perforated cardboard.[75] The perforated cardboard encouraged short, simple designs. Aniline dye introduced between 1856 and 1860 made the scripture mottoes much brighter

25. Catholic lawn ornament of St. Jude displayed in a yard in Malden, Massachusetts. A statue of a saint or the Virgin Mary placed in the semi-public space of a yard indicates the beliefs and values of the family.

26. Evangelical Protestants use both contemporary fashions (like the wearing of baseball caps) and current commercial slogans (like the Coca-Cola slogan, "It's the real thing") to witness to their faith. Rather than totally reject popular culture, they adapt familiar slogans for religious purposes.

27. In 1864 a line from the popular hymn, "Shall We Gather at the River?" was embroidered in Berlin woolwork on perforated cardboard. Families hung such mottoes high on their walls, or over doorways and mirrors, to emphasize that their home was a Christian home.

and more colorful than the older embroidered samplers. Families hung mottoes high· on their walls and over doorways and mirrors to emphasize that their domestic space was Christian space.

When objects function as symbols of community affiliation, they do so in a fairly direct way. Their power to communicate can at times convert the religious object from a reminder of communal solidarity into a focal point of religious contestation. Since the 1970s, Mormon church authorities have encouraged families to include visual statements of their faith in their homes. Pictures of Latter-day Saint temples, portraits of church leaders, biblical scenes, and pious statuary are increasingly popular in Mormon households. Since such objects clearly state the beliefs of the family, at times they can become points of intrafamily conflict over religion. A young Mormon couple had been given a print of a *Head of Christ* (not Sallman's) as a wedding present.[76] The print is sold in Latter-day Saint bookstores and distributed by the church so it carries strong Mormon associations. While the wife intended to put the print up in the living room, the husband felt that such a display of church affiliation made his house look like "a religious shrine." Although he goes to church each Sunday, he did not want to be equated with those Mormons ("goody goody types") who put up such art in their homes. As a compromise, his wife put the print on a shelf in a room where he works. She placed it so that he must see "Christ's" face, but he turns the print around so that the face is toward the wall. The couple do not talk about their attitudes toward religious art or the "game" that they play. They both seek to avoid overt conflict and tension and use the print as a means to act out their differing religious perspectives.

Whoever gave the print to this Mormon couple was probably unaware of the problems the gift created. In other cases, giving religious goods as presents can help affirm communal ties and maintain balanced social relationships.[77] Up until the 1960s, Catholics commonly exchanged holy cards and medals as gestures of affection. Some bought fancy lace cards and tied medals to them; other cards were hand-decorated with flowers and designs. Small pictures of Christ and the saints were assembled on velvet. These intimate gifts were exchanged between Catholic women, nuns, and children as signs of mutual friendship. Such gifts frequently

28. Up until the 1960s, Catholics exchanged medals and holy cards as tokens of friendship and esteem. Children were given holy cards as souvenirs for their First Holy Communion. Cards were given out at funerals as memorials for the dead. Colorful and in keeping with the fashions of the times, holy cards were collected and placed in prayer books and Bibles. Catholics learned the iconography of the saints and devotions through the exchange of holy cards.

S. Mary Magdalen
of Pazzi,
Divine Charity.

29. While this medal was mass produced, someone has attached the medal to a card, hand-drawn flowers, and added a bow. The gift has thus become personalized and unique. Catholics wore medals around their necks, attached them to wrist watches, and pinned them on children's clothing. As they were small and inexpensive, medals became convenient tokens of friendship.

were mass-produced religious objects or prints personalized by the giver with handmade embroidery, crochet, or coloring. The objects themselves combined commercial art with unique designs. Even post-Vatican II Catholics who might see such objects as tasteless religious kitsch sometimes give them as gifts to provoke laughter or remind each other of childhood sentiments.[78]

Protestants have also used small religious goods with little economic, but high symbolic, value. From the mid-nineteenth century onwards, Protestants used bookmarks and decorative cards in the same ways that Catholics used holy cards. Rather than having pictures of the saints, Protestants preferred biblical scenes, picturesque scenery, and innocent children. Catholics put their cards in their Sunday missals, Protestants in their Bibles. Both groups shared a fondness for the colorful and the sentimental. While Catholics no longer give holy cards with the enthusiasm they once did, evangelical Protestants frequently distribute religious presents on holidays and special occasions. The intensity of small-group relations is maintained through the exchange of religious gifts. Trust and affection were,

30. St. Theresa, the Little Flower, was a popular saint in the 1930s and 1940s. A small print of her has been carefully fashioned with velvet and satin into a miniature prayer book that could be folded and secured with a clasp. The handmade object is small enough to fit in the palm of the hand and was probably placed in a purse or drawer as an intimate reminder of human and divine love.

31. From the mid-nineteenth century onwards, Protestants used religious bookmarks and decorative cards in ways similar to Catholics. Rather than having pictures of the saints and popular devotions, Protestants preferred scriptural texts or inspirational mottoes. As with Catholic holy cards, Protestant prayer cards reflected the current fashion in greeting cards. In this case a stern verbal message is accompanied by a sentimental visual message.

32. While embroidered samplers with pious sayings often graced the walls of Protestant homes, this small prayer card follows the same form as the Catholic miniature prayer book. The card folds into a "book" and can be secured by clasps. It might have been made by "Jane Barron" to be given as a gift symbolizing her faith, domestic skills, and affection.

33. Contemporary Protestant prayer cards are made of updated materials and display contemporary themes but they are used in traditional ways. In this card, adolescents dressed in jeans are comforted by Jesus, who still wears his biblical robes but looks like a modern American male.

and are, cultivated through the making, buying, and giving of material expressions of Christianity.

Toys also are used to socialize children into their Christian communities and to allow them imaginatively to integrate religion into their play worlds. In early America, Puritan children were not permitted to play on the Sabbath. They could, however, enjoy games that taught them biblical principles. Families carved or purchased wooden Noah's Ark sets so children could play with the boat and animals. The first board game, "Mansions of Glory," was a game where the player's goal was to reach heaven. Christian toys developed alongside secular toys and games. Biblical stories became the source for creating puzzles, card games, magic lantern slides, and dolls. The development of the Sunday school meant that children would have to be entertained in church as well as at home. As we will see in Chapter 8, the character of Protestant material culture was deeply affected by the needs and attitudes of Sunday school teachers. Now, contemporary Christians can buy their children everything from "prayer clothes" to Bible games played on Nintendo. Mormons buy "Book of Mormon" paper dolls and Lutherans statues of Martin Luther. Even when adults may be reluctant to use religious objects or display religious art themselves, they feel that children need to be socialized in tactile and imaginative ways into their religious communities.

Unlike Protestant children who had their own special Bible toys, Catholic children typically "played" with adult statues, medals, scapulars, and holy cards.

34. Toys socialize children into specific Christian communities and allow them to integrate religion imaginatively into their play worlds. Families who did not permit children to forget God on the Sabbath gave them toys like "Noah's Ark" to entertain them without neglecting their religious instruction.

GRANDMAMA'S SUNDAY GAME

of BIBLE QUESTIONS

McLOUGHLIN BROS N.Y.

NEW TESTAMENT.

35. While the first board game, "Mansions of Glory," had the pursuit of a Godly life as its main theme, by the turn of the century nonreligious games and toys dominated the marketplace. Secular companies like McLoughlin Brothers, however, also produced games with Christian themes.

36. This set of twelve wooden blocks (c. 1880) could be arranged to show six scriptural scenes. Puzzles taught Bible stories and could be used at home and at Sunday school.

37. Cartoonist Calvin Grondahl in *Marketing Precedes the Miracle* underscores the modern use of "Sunday games" for Mormon children.

"Six days of the week it's G.I. Joe, Transformers, and Masters of the Universe.
But on the seventh day it's Heroes of the Book of Mormon."

LEARNING THAT EXCITES THE MIND
WISDOM TREE... FOR PLAY ON NINTENDO

Catch the spirit that is spreading across the nation! For the first time parents are encouraging their children to play Nintendo. Why? Because Wisdom Tree is producing Bible-based video games with God's ministry at heart. Only God *"can choose the foolish things of the world to confound the wise."*

1st Corinthians 1:27

WISDOM Tree

FOR INFORMATION
PLEASE CALL
1-800-77-BIBLE (USA)
1-800-88-BIBLE (CANADA)
TEL.: (714) 528-3456

38. Contemporary children can play with Bible games made out of a variety of materials or which run on their home computers or VCR.

Just What The Doctor Ordered!

Kids' everyday clothes with God's everyday messages.

Pray Clothes' artwork is designed to encourage values such as sharing, caring, loving and helping others, all from a biblical perspective.

Items such as boys and girls bibs, tees, short and long pant outfits, playsuits, and rompers are included in Pray Clothes line of popular kids clothes.

Kids like Pray Clothes because they're stylish and comfortable. Parents appreciate the quality garments and messages.

PRAY CLOTHES™
Clothes fit for a Child of the King.

ORDER TOLL FREE 1-800-333-3722 or
dial 615/833-9465, FAX 615/832-0785

Exclusive licensed agent: Design Impressions, Inc.
P.O. Box 111389, Nashville, TN 37222-1389
Net terms available with approved credit. No minimum order.

39. "Pray clothes," a product of Design Impressions from Nashville, Tennessee, markets "kids' everyday clothes with God's everyday messages." The artwork on the outfits is "designed to encourage values such as sharing, caring, loving and helping others, all from a biblical perspective." Note that in this advertisement, run in the April 1991 issue of the *Bookstore Journal*, it is the little girl who is playing the doctor and the little boy who is her patient. Contemporary gender roles reinforce the modern and "stylish" nature of the clothing.

No. 425G   No. 426G.   No. 427G   No. 428G

No. 429G   No. 430G   No. 431G   No. 432G

OUTLINE PICTURES FOR COLORING

Black line prints on heavy white vellum paper. Will take either water color or colored crayon. Designed for use by children in schools.

Size of prints, 8 x 6 inches.

Single Subjects or Assorted .... 90c per Hundred

40. Foley & Dugan, a Catholic goods company from Providence, Rhode Island, advertised many toys and games in their 1943-4 wholesale catalog. Note that two of the illustrations in the coloring book are of Protestant origin: No. 426G *Christ Knocking at Heart's Door* originally painted by Holman Hunt in 1811 and No. 428G *Christ in the Garden of Gethsemane* painted by Heinrich Hofmann in 1890.

They built altars in their bedrooms and imitated the actions of priests and nuns. Specialized goods for children were a later development and may have followed the rise of the Catholic school and the move of Catholics out of ethnic urban enclaves into the suburbs. A 1943 religious goods catalog included photo buttons of various saints, puzzles, "double view pictures" where a different religious figure appeared when viewed through special spectacles, religious stamp albums (with stamps), and coloring books that included drawings of the Infant of Prague and St. Anthony.[79] In 1957 a popular Catholic magazine contained an advertisement

41. This advertisement for "little nun" and "little priest" costumes appeared in a popular Catholic magazine, *Sign* in April 1957. While it seems to be addressed to parents, the note "Suitable for Mission Sunday Exhibits" implies that parishes might have also ordered the costumes for special occasions.

selling miniature nun and priest outfits for children. "Watch how they will assume the quiet dignity of those who have dedicated their lives to the Church," the advertisement confidently stated. The producer of the costumes, "Nanette Studios," assumed what most producers of toys and games assumed: "This fine imaginative play will help them plan their lives . . . the Catholic way."[80] Through "imaginative play" children would learn the stories and traditions of their family's religion. Toys and games served as instructional tools and as the means by which children entered into the creative world of religion.

Commercial Power: Decoration and Fashion

Religious objects function within complicated networks of beliefs, values, myths, and social structures. Clerical elites articulate the proper use of objects based on their understanding of scripture and religious traditions. People relate to objects as if they were sacred characters, in spite of warnings against idolatry. Religious artifacts may also function like tools: they help Christians to acknowledge common commitments, delineate differences, express affection, or socialize children. In all of these cases, seriousness and sincerity are taken for granted. The user of the object is embedded, at least to a certain extent, in the same system of meaning that produced the object. While their relationship to their religion may be complicated, and while they may break certain "rules" of practice, users still see themselves as a part of a larger religious community. For these Christians, objects speak to sincere religious needs and sentiments.

However, religious objects can also be used for other purposes. We have seen how prints, statues, scripture mottoes, and even teapots are displayed in the home to express religious commitment. At the same time, these goods are a part of a fashion aesthetic that has no connection with Christianity. They help communicate the taste and status of the family, irrespective of personal beliefs and commitments. In America, the use of Christian art and objects as home decorations had its beginning in the mid-nineteenth century when Gothic Revival architecture and design became popular. At the same time, Protestants elaborated a domestic ideology describing the sacred quality of home and family life.[81] Manufacturers accommodated the Protestant desire simultaneously to sanctify and decorate their homes. They sold and marketed religious goods alongside secular images. Victorian Protestants did not find the commercial marketing of religious images distasteful or profane. Fashion and faith co-existed.

In the 1840s, for example, statuary made of hard porcelain called Parian ware was developed at the Copeland factory in Staffordshire, England, and by the early 1850s Bennington Pottery in the United States was making secular and religious statues.[82] Parian models of praying children were particularly popular before the Civil War. C. Hennecke's Florentine Statuary, established in 1865 with offices in Milwaukee and Chicago, imported and sold statues to meet every taste.[83] Their 1887 catalog illustrates the enduring fashion for including religious statuary among mythological, patriotic, sentimental, and allegorical pieces. The company served both Protestant and Catholic customers. Protestants could buy an alabaster statue of *Dr. M. Luther*, a fifteen-inch high figurine version of *Praying Samuel*, or the familiar *Rock of Ages* complete with clinging woman. According to an 1878

No. 821.
ST. JOSEPH AND CHILD.

Height, 22 in.; base, 8 in. $ 6 00
Alabaster..............12 00

No. 541.—HOPE.

Height, 13 in.; base, 6x5½ in.
$2 50.

No. 607.
BLESSED VIRGIN.

Height, 15 in.; base, 4½ in.
$1 75.

No. 543.
BLESSED VIRGIN.

A—Height, 13 in.; base, 4 in.
$1 50.
Alabaster................ $3 00
B—Height, 33 in.; base, 11 in.
$9 00.

No. 553.
THE CHILD JESUS.

Height, 41 in.; base, 13x9½
in., $14 00.

No. 729.
ROCK OF AGES.

Height, 17½ in.; base, 11x6½
in., $3 50.
Alabaster........... $7 00

No. 549.
HOLY WATER FONT.

Height, 10 in.; diam. 7 in...... $2 50
Alabaster.................... 5 00

No. 552.
PRAYING SAMUEL.

Height, 15 in.; base, 7x6 in.
$3 00.

43. Jack Delano captured the refined lifestyle of Harold Lamb, owner of the Union Point hosiery mill in Georgia. Murillo's *Immaculate Conception* is on the back wall, over the set of bookcases on the left.

decorating guide, such ornaments should be placed "upon the bracket, or shelf above the bed."[84] Catholics had their choice of St. Joseph, a variety of Virgin Marys, and the Sacred Heart. Guardian angels in various poses, allegories of Hope, and biblical characters might appeal to those of either religious tradition. Families indulged in whatever was currently in vogue for interior design while simultaneously stating their intention to create a Christian home through material goods.

In 1852 the Louvre Museum bought a painting by Murillo of the Immaculate Conception, originally painted in 1678 for a Seville hospital. The purchase made the news because the museum officials' bid was the highest price ever paid for a single painting. Although Murillo was a prominent Catholic painter and the Immaculate Conception a controversial doctrine, prints of the painting were widely reproduced and became standard decoration in both Protestant and Catholic households.[85] While other Victorian religious objects such as wax crosses or embroidered mottoes fell out of fashion, the Murillo *Immaculate Conception* remained popular. While the subject of the print, the Virgin Mary, had obvious religious associations, the print frequently was placed in a non-devotional context. Christians used it not to stimulate religious piety but to demonstrate fashionable taste or provide visual excitement. This is not to say that the print may not simultaneously have had both religious and aesthetic meaning, but rather that families displayed it in ways that stressed its decorative capacity. At times, fashion overshadows faith.

In 1941 Jack Delano photographed the interior of Harold Lamb's home in Georgia. Lamb owned the Union Point hosiery mill, and his house reflected the refined life style of the Southern upper middle class. Positioned over a set of bookcases at one end of the living room was a copy of Murillo's *Immaculate Conception*. The print is part of an overall decorating scheme of harmony, symmetry, restraint, permanence, and balance. No effort has been made to make

42. C. Hennecke & Company, with offices in Milwaukee and Chicago, produced a variety of statuary and alabaster objects for both Protestants and Catholics. In this page of their 1887 catalog, a Catholic holy water font is set next to the quintessential icon of Victorian Protestantism, a woman clinging to the cross as memorialized in the hymn, "Rock of Ages."

44. In 1939 Russell Lee photographed this "Mexican home" in San Antonio, Texas. The Murillo print is above and to the immediate right of the large vase.

the print stand out from the other household effects by making it bigger, placing it higher on the wall, or surrounding it with other religious objects or family photographs. The Murillo print is presented as a framed piece of autonomous "art," displayed as the original might be in a 1940s museum. The carefully chosen reproductions, vases, statuary, and busts communicate to the viewer that this is a family that respects and understands fine art. The display reflects what Pierre Bourdieu calls "aesthetic distancing." For those possessing "educational capital," art is experienced as something detached and autonomous from the observer.[86] The content is less important than the form. The presentation of the Immaculate Conception does not necessarily signify that this is a family that believes that Mary was conceived without original sin. As "art" the print can be used without reference to its religious roots.

Two years earlier, Russell Lee, another FSA photographer, captured another interior displaying Murillo's *Immaculate Conception*. This home was described as being in the "Mexican section" of San Antonio, Texas. Since only a part of the room was photographed, and no further description was given, it is difficult to surmise the social class of the family. We can, however, make some observations about their aesthetic taste. The Murillo print is placed among a myriad of prints, calendars, holy cards, Valentines, drawings, and postcards. All of the decorations function like wall paper – to give the wall color and keep the eye busy. As in the Georgia home, no effort is made to privilege the religious print. The San Antonio family's aesthetic is an open-ended eclecticism that encourages sequential growth and accumulation of decorations. Things are spontaneously added to the wall as they find their way into the home. There is always room for one more. Decorations are polychromatic and of varied sizes and textures. Nothing is balanced; the asymmetry of the decorations communicates energy rather than repose. Studies of poor and working-class people emphasize that this eclectic and dense visual environment is used to contradict the constrained narrowness of the conditions of everyday life.[87]

Neither household uses the print as a devotional object: the Georgia family displays it as art and the San Antonio family treats it as a commercial product no different from a calendar or postcard. In the mill owner's home the religious print is placed within an aesthetic of restraint; in the Mexican home it is placed within an aesthetic of excess. In both cases, the religious connotation of the print fades into the background because of the way it is displayed within the home. While the families may be Christian and recognize the significance of the Virgin Mary, neither family singles this print out for special reverence. The religious print has been transformed from an object of devotion into a decoration.

While many religious images are used as decorative elements in American homes, the presence of the Virgin in a Protestant household leads us to ask the question, why do Protestants display Catholic art? For the Georgia family, the painting most likely has little Catholic reference because it was used so extensively in Protestant households during the nineteenth century. The Catholic Madonna and Child, pictured in Medieval and Renaissance art, were reinterpreted to be any mother and her child. The Mary was emblematic of all mothers and not merely the mother of Jesus.[88] Protestants could include Mary among their visual images by emphasizing her maternal qualities and downplaying her mediating capacities.

In recent years American retailing has been more active in appropriating Christian symbols for commercial use. As institutional religion no longer promotes certain symbols, they become more available to the fashion industry. The beginning of the 1990s, for instance, saw an introduction of religious symbols into clothing design. "Designers are giving us that old-time religion," writes a fashion editor in 1993, "today's well-dressed woman, so they say, looks divine when shrouded in a rope-belted monk's robe and decorated with a slew of heavy crosses."[89] Laurence Moore pithily observes that "if you do not commodify your religion yourself, someone will do it for you."[90] The commercial appropriation of Catholic symbols began after the Second Vatican Council when the institutional church simplified public worship. Catholic material culture began to disappear rapidly from churches and more slowly from homes. The once flourishing religious goods industry found that Catholics were no longer buying statues, rosaries, and religious prints at the rate they once did. Thirty years later, the secular marketplace has found that Catholic images have an exotic and erotic quality. Antique stores, boutiques, mail order houses, as well as traditional religious goods stores are finding that people will buy Catholic objects for their "camp" and fashion value. Detached from any devotional overtones, Catholic material culture can communicate "style" just like Murillo's *Immaculate Conception* once did.

In the 1980s, the "southwestern" style exploited the ethnic colors and designs of Hispanic culture. Just as religious statues became integrated into the revival styles of the nineteenth century, manufacturers detached Catholic folk art from its devotional function and marketed it as household decoration. Importers carried

45. With the T-shirt becoming a fashionable part of the American wardrobe, designers struggled to find new and unusual designs for their shirts. Religious prints, such as this one of St. Gerard, patron saint of expectant mothers, provide a rich source of images.

shrines of the saints or Our Lady of Guadalupe cut out of beer cans or batteries. The same shrines might also contain the ubiquitous face of Mexican artist Frieda Kahlo. Bleeding crucifixes and hand-carved "bulto" statues fetched high prices. The commercialization of Hispanic arts is part of a fashion trend that has encouraged the "revalorization of Catholic iconography and the accentuation of those traits that make its aesthetics unique: figurativeness, dramatization, eclecticism, visual saturation – all those attributes for which kitsch was banned from the realm of art."[91] In the same way that Protestants once bought reproductions of works by Raphael and Murillo to hang in their parlors, fashionable Americans now buy mass-produced Hispanic Catholic "folk" art.

The commercial fascination with the material culture of Catholicism is currently widespread in the United States. In Austin, Texas, an entrepreneur uses a sophisticated laser transfer machine to reproduce chromolithographs on to T-shirts. Patrick Knight buys from a local Mexican-American bodega prints of the Sacred Heart, the Virgin Mary, and the saints. The images he reproduces on T-shirts are exactly the same sentimental, sado-masochistic, and theologically suspect art despised by reform-minded Catholics. The saints have large eyes and Christ's heart bleeds in profusion. The same print of Our Lady of Mount Carmel popular in the 1930s and 1940s is now sold on a T-shirt with a boutique's name printed underneath. Knight sells the shirts to Catholics, ex-Catholics, and non-Catholics. In Austin the church of San Jose bought four hundred Sacred Heart T-shirts, and a lacrosse team ordered a set with St. Martha and the dragon. The team manager asked that the torch she holds be replaced with a lacrosse racket.

Why do people who are not Catholic buy T-shirts with explicitly Catholic themes? The reasons are varied: T-shirts have become fashionable and producers constantly try to find new graphics to entice customers. Religious representations provide a rich source for the T-shirt industry and are exploited as any artistic image might be. Producers recognize that the Catholic images they use are no longer embedded in mainstream Catholicism. Since young Catholics no longer learn the iconography of the saints, the representations have lost their connection to the institutional church. Many Catholic images have been freed from their ideological context. Wearing a St. Gerard T-shirt, for instance, does not mark one as a Catholic, in the same sense that wearing a "University of Heaven" T-shirt marks one as an evangelical Protestant. Few people have enough of a devotional relationship with St. Gerard (patron saint of expectant mothers) to recognize his image or be offended when his representation is displayed on a T-shirt. Instead, such Catholic images, because they have never been commonplace in American culture, carry with them the aura of the exotic. They are easily transformed into camp.[92] Nostalgia, exaggeration, otherness, artificiality – all of these traits are appreciated by those non-Catholics who buy Patrick Knight's T-shirts. For T-shirt wearers the images only retain a trace of their religious context.

Catholic images also embody a sensuality that has been successfully exploited in recent years by the rock star Madonna. Protestants in the United States have a history of seeing in Catholics an uncontrollable sexuality that continually threatens the harmony and restraint of WASP culture. In the mid-nineteenth century, Protestant writers produced polemical novels and "exposés" filled with lurid stories of sexual misbehavior by nuns and priests. Maria Monk's *The Awful Disclosures of the Hotel Dieu Nunnery* sold an astonishing 300,000 copies between 1836 and the Civil War.[93] Ironically, at the same time that poor Catholics were being blamed for populating urban slums with Irish and Italian babies, they were condemned for their prudish attitudes toward simple bodily pleasures. In the mid-twentieth century, the Catholic nun of the movies became a symbol of virginal innocence and sensual beauty. American culture placed Catholics in a double bind. They were simultaneously seen as both sexually promiscuous and sexually repressed.

It is within the cultural context of sensual/inhibited Catholicism that Madonna plies her trade. Beginning in the 1980s, Catholic sacramentals served as props in Madonna's rock videos. In the video *Like a Virgin*, Madonna popularized a new role for the rosary by wearing several as costume jewelry.[94] In 1985 she established a line of commercial products (under the "Boy Toy" label) to sell crucifix earrings along with finger-less gloves and lacy black garments to those who desired a "Madonna" look. Her characters in *La Isla Bonita* performed/prayed in front of home shrines, one ablaze with candles. Madonna used Catholic objects to assert the meanings that she gave them; mocking, rejecting, or modifying the meanings given by the institutional church. For her, the objects were beautiful and sexy ornamentations that did not need to be connected to an established religious tradition.

It was in the video *Like a Prayer* that Madonna fully utilized Catholic material culture to achieve her commercial and artistic goals. In pop postmodern fashion, the dream-like narrative revolves around a black man falsely accused of murder. While the video includes an African American church choir, its focus is on a voluptuous Madonna "turning on" a statue in a Catholic church. The statue is of a black saint who comes alive after being gazed on, prayed to, and humbly kissed by the devoted Madonna. Although the statue-as-saint only chastely returns the attention, he eventually becomes the accused black man who more romantically kisses a reclining Madonna. At the end of the fantasy, the saint goes back on to his pedestal behind the altar grate, the black man is released from the bars of his prison, and Madonna with her cast takes a final bow before the curtain drops.

Like a Prayer is a commercial product. Like the T-shirts and boutique shrines, it takes provocative religious images and sells them. The video works on one level because Madonna plays with long-standing attitudes toward images. According to David Freedberg, throughout Western culture there are stories of individuals becoming so aroused by a statue or painting that "the image gives rise to more or less sexual feelings and so it can only be construed as living . . . the image seems to be or simply comes alive; and more or less overt sexual relations ensue."[95] Thus in the myth of Pygmalion, a king of Cyprus falls in love with the beautiful statue he has created and the sculpture comes to life. In the commercialized version of this myth, it is the body of the rock star that brings the saint to life. The role of the beauty has been reversed: Madonna is not aroused by the black statue, rather the black statue cannot remain inert after being confronted by the intensity of Madonna. In the commercialized myth, the power (the affective presence) remains in the hands of the one profiting from the video. It is Madonna who begins the transformation of the statue (by opening up the altar grate), and it is Madonna who goes to the police to convince them to set the black man free (and opens his jail cell door). Madonna's saint, probably modeled on the Afro-Peruvian St. Martin de Porres, does not hold his rosary in his hand in a gesture of prayer; instead he wears it fashionably around his neck as Madonna does in her other videos. Madonna exploits the same themes that prompt people to buy T-shirts of Our Lady of Mount Carmel and St. Gerard. Contemporary Americans see pre-Vatican II Catholic material culture as sensual, exotic, sentimental, exaggerated, artificial, and other.

Meanings and Religious Objects

In 1936 James Agee traveled through the South gathering information for a magazine article on white tenant farmers. While the article was never published, his work *Let Us Now Praise Famous Men* became a noted poetic reflection on American life during the Depression. Agee's minute descriptions of the material culture of the poor provide a catalog of what tenant farmers found meaningful, and his own observations reflect the attitudes of a 27-year-old writer fleeing New York intellectual society. Raised as an Anglican, Agee at times projects his own theological orientation on to the religious lives of those he sought to represent. While staying at the home of George and Annie Mae Gudger, Agee imagined that a table, fireplace, and mantle made up a shrine and an altar. Vases, a photograph, a white china swan, a cut-out paper valance, and a calendar were placed with care. Next to the calendar hung a locket containing pictures of the Sacred Heart of Jesus and the Immaculate Heart of Mary. In a footnote, Agee commented, "If the Gudgers realized that this is Roman Catholic, they would be surprised and shocked and would almost certainly remove it. It is interesting and mysterious to me that they should have found it anywhere in their country, which is as solidly anti-Catholic as the Province of Quebec is roman."[96] Agee leads us to conclude that while shrine-making may not be limited to Catholics, certain images are and they should not be tolerated by Protestants.

There is no question that the Sacred Heart and the Immaculate Heart of Mary are Catholic images shunned in Protestant church worship. However, the simple assumption that Agee made about the Gudgers' attitude toward their locket may not be true. Agee relied on his educated Anglican background to tell him that each Christian denomination has its own unique symbols and images. If a community distrusted Catholics and had an ideology that considered Catholicism aberrant, then a family living in that area would not knowingly display Catholic items. Agee mistakenly saw religious objects functioning only to communicate the community affiliation of their owners. Given that assumption, the Gudgers' placement of the locket on their "altar" obviously pointed to their cultural ignorance.

This line of reasoning neglects the subtle variations in meaning that religious objects may have. Folklorist Yvonne Milspaw's Methodist grandmother had a shrine with what sounds like the same pictures as the Gudger family. The Gudgers, like Milspaw's grandmother, might have received the locket as a gift and cherished it for its role as a memory object. We have seen that middle-class Protestants display prints of the Virgin Mary as "art." Perhaps the Gudgers were making an aesthetic statement by enhancing their living space with whatever colorful and evocative items they could find. If Agee had told them of the locket's origin, they might have responded, "It's only decoration." Or perhaps, if the Gudgers went to church, they might have felt that while the church was not the place for religious images, the home was. For them, the locket might have represented only Jesus and his mother, not the Sacred Heart and the Immaculate Heart of Mary. Why would they not have wanted to show respect and affection for these sacred characters? They might have insisted that this was how children learn about God. Since Agee did not ask the Gudgers where they got these pictures and why they put them on their "altar," we can only speculate as to the diverse meanings that the locket had for this family.

Agee made the mistake of assuming that religious objects function primarily as signs of denominational commitment. Displaying denominational affiliation is only one of several meanings objects may have. The object itself, and the memories and emotions it elicits, may supersede whatever its "official" theological meaning might be. People frequently use objects to ease, or even to erase, the boundaries between sacred and profane; divine and human; art and religion; profit and piety. When we look at how Christians *use* objects, rather than merely what they *say* about them, we find that the similarities between groups outweigh the differences. Religious objects can serve to unify or confuse as much as they separate groups. They can blur boundaries as well as strengthen them. They can cause conflict and struggle, as well as defuse tensions.

Likewise, artists also use religious objects to loosen the boundaries between religion and other realms of life. The very use of holy cards or plastic temples in sculpture/shrines emphasizes that mass-produced objects can be presented in ways that question both their devotional and their commercial quality. Artists force religious objects to communicate meanings other than their obviously religious ones. By confusing meanings, artists encourage viewers to think again about the relationship between art, religion, and politics. Even the use of religious images as decoration or fashion statements blurs the distinction between sacred and profane. We cannot say that a Victorian woman who embroidered "Shall We Gather at the River" on perforated cardboard and mounted it high on a room wall was unconcerned about fashion or taste. Even if we seriously doubt that much motivates Madonna other than profit, we must still consider the possibility that her videos reflect her own struggles with her Catholic past. It is not simply that objects used in different contexts have different meanings, it is that within one context the same object may have many different meanings.

In their book *The Meaning of Things*, Mihaly Csikszentmihalyi and Eugene Rochberg-Halton reflect that "the material environment that surrounds us is rarely neutral; it either helps the forces of chaos that make life random and disorganized or it helps to give purpose and direction to one's life."[97] Objects function both to shape and to reflect religious beliefs and values. The realistic portrait painted by Warner Sallman, for instance, helps reinforce the theological position that Christ is a personal savior available to everyone. At the same time, the ways that people treat the print parallel their ideas about the person of Jesus. The print of Warner Sallman can convey those meanings because of its own inherent qualities; an abstract portrayal of Christ would not evoke the same sentiments. The material make-up imposes certain limits but by pushing the limits of the physical object people impose their own meanings. Thus, religious prints get eaten by the devout and rosaries get worn by the avant-garde. Religious objects may be effective either because of their physical character or in spite of their physical character. It is this very ability to combine opposing elements and to have diverse meanings that makes the religious object a powerful part of Christianity.

In this chapter I have de-emphasized the historical context of various religious objects. I have pointed out how people from diverse classes, ethnic groups, and religious traditions use religious artifacts in similar ways. At the same time, the iconographic content of particular artifacts and the type of aesthetic preferred by their users may significantly differ from community to community. While such generalities help us better understand the meanings that objects may have, Christian material culture must be placed in an historical context to see how a specific object, landscape, building, or piece of art works for a particular group of people. In Chapter 3 I focus exclusively on one artifact – the Bible, and one specific place – the home, to understand how a set of sacred words became transformed into a holy object.

3

The Bible in the Victorian Home

"We had a big family Bible," Anne Ellis wrote in her memoir, "it must have been made to sell, certainly not made to read; it was too heavy unless one laid it on the floor." Growing up in the 1880s, the eldest daughter in a Colorado pioneer family, Anne remembered reading the family Bible along with many other books. Even though the family never went to church, she read from it to herself and "once or twice" to her illiterate mother who cried at relevant passages. Anne also used the Bible for fortune-telling, "if the passage sounded good, I believed it, and if bad, I didn't think it would come true anyway." The Bible sat in the room that doubled as "the best room" and her mother's bedroom. The family tried to present the room as a proper parlor by taking a "round poker table" and covering it with "a checked tablecloth." In true Victorian fashion, they placed their family Bible on the table and hung a brass lamp above it. The family Bible had "designs all around the leaves, places for photographs, [and] places for births, deaths and marriages." Her mother and step-father's marriage and "the births of one or two of the first children were recorded." The other births "came too fast" to be inscribed, and Anne "always resented it that I wasn't there." Resting between the leaves of the Bible were "a lady's slipper and some ferns from Mama's old home, and some taken from a dead baby's coffin – there was a lock of hair twined with this bunch." When Anne wanted to place some of her own flowers along with those tokens that "had a divine right [to be] there," her mother told her they would leave rust marks on the pages. Mother scolded that the Bible should not "be spoiled, it cost ten dollars." At a time when a local restaurant charged twenty-five cents for a meal and the family cow cost $75, the Bible had real financial value.[1]

Anne Ellis was an avid reader who bought dime novels and borrowed copies of books such as *Don Quixote*.[2] While she listed many of her favorite books in her memoirs, she only discussed reading her family's Bible. How or where she read Dickens or Kipling did not merit attention, but there was something special about the ten-dollar Bible that contained flowers from a dead baby's coffin. If Anne Ellis remembered correctly, the family Bible was a distinctive domestic object in her pioneer home. While it may have reminded the household of the importance of Christianity in their lives, Anne remembered it more as a repository for family memories and a resource for fortune-telling than as a moral guide. For many Americans like Anne Ellis, the Bible was not only a text telling of eternal salvation, it was a revered object.

Scholars have argued that Bible reading made the United States into a "Biblical Nation" by providing the country with a common set of morals, myths, and rhetorical language. They have shown how Catholics promoted their translation of the Bible within a Protestant milieu. Even the traveling Bible salesman has been studied.[3] No attention has been given, however, to how or why the Bible became not only a revered text but a sacred object in the American home. While the written words clarified moral or ethical categories, supported denominational doctrine, and provided a standard for "great literature," the physical book itself also conveyed messages. In their determination to see the Bible as a sacred scripture, scholars have ignored its role as a sacred book.

For most of America's history, the Christian Bible was not merely the writings from the Old and New Testaments. During the nineteenth century, the Bible became the center of a material Protestantism that depended on the physical senses to produce religious emotion. American printers and publishers created a book that was more than a compilation of canonical scriptures. Biblical commentaries, illustrations, family records, essays on biblical life, picture albums, temperance pledges, and theological treatises were added to "clarify" the basic biblical text and satisfy family needs. Bound in leather and fastened with a golden clasp, family Bibles were displayed on parlor tables as signs of domestic piety and taste. Mothers sewed scriptural passages in needlepoint, children played with puzzles of biblical stories, and fathers entertained their households with magic lantern slides of Bible characters. Protestants explored the connection between faith, sensation, and emotion through the Bible. They touched the pages of the Holy Writ, cried over its injunctions, saw the faces of their mothers in the memories evoked by Scripture reading, and heard the voices of their fathers. This biblical material culture provided a physical and sensual dimension to American Protestant life. The redemptive power of the spirit, through the sacred words of the Bible, became matter. The "Word" literally became "Flesh" and "dwelled among us" (John 1:14). Nineteenth-century Protestants, in spite of their fear of idolatry, understood that deep religious feelings could be bound up in a book.

The creation of a material Protestantism centered on the Bible depended on three European developments that spread to America. First, sentimentalism and romanticism cultivated throughout Western Europe beginning in the eighteenth century encouraged Christians to understand faith as an element of feeling rather than rationality. Provoking the emotions by engaging the senses was believed to be one way people could encourage each other to move toward God. The Bible as a text and an object acted to stimulate religious sentiments and memories. Second, European Protestants argued that the place to develop feeling and emotion was in the home. While church services, revival meetings, and reform organizations were essential for the promotion of religion, the family increasingly was seen as the foundation of all true faith. Domesticity was imbued with a sacred character and the clergy promoted the Bible's role in family worship and prayer. Third, industrialization in Europe made material goods increasingly available to households who wanted to use objects to awaken religious feelings. American publishers readily borrowed printing and marketing techniques from the Old World. They reproduced and modified European engravings, printing them in Bibles. While the American market was uniquely vigorous and expanding, American producers closely followed the trends set by more established European firms. The Bible became embedded in a commodity system dependent on changing notions of fashion. Affectionate religion, domesticity, and improvements in printing and marketing, all served to imbue the Bible with a unique character. During the nineteenth century, the Bible and other artifacts that referred back to the Bible, linked scriptural religion to the senses.

Bibles in America

Since before the Protestant Reformation, the Bible served as a source of Christian salvation to those who would "search the scriptures." According to Patricia Anderson, by the late eighteenth century few English Protestant households lacked a Bible.[4] Both the Geneva Bible (1560) and the King James Bible (1611) were used throughout the English-speaking world by clergy and lay people. The Geneva Bible, oriented to the common reader, included marginal commentary on every page. Normally published in quarto format, it was compact and portable. The King James Bible had no marginal commentary to help explain difficult passages and was used in the seventeenth century by Puritan clergy. As the Bible of the meetinghouse, it oftentimes was printed in the large, folio dimension. Seventeenth- and eighteenth-century Protestants frequently had two Bibles, a large folio Bible (sometimes referred to as a "great" Bible in wills) and one in smaller format.[5] In 1782 Robert Aitken first printed the complete English-language Bible in the newly formed United States. The independence of the colonies from England enabled American printers to disregard the monopoly the British Crown had given to select publishers. Slowly Bible printing became a part of American book publication. Although Matthew Carey first published the Catholic Douay edition in 1790, Catholics would not express the same concern for the domestic use of the Bible as Protestants until the late nineteenth century.[6]

During the eighteenth century, Bible making was no easy task. Each individual letter of a book of almost eight hundred thousand words had to be separately laid out. Errors abounded. In America, paper was a rare commodity. However, at the beginning of the nineteenth century Bible making became much easier. Not only did paper and leather become more readily available with the development of a local American economy, "stereotyping" made it simpler to produce error-free Bibles quickly and cheaply. A process invented in England, the British Bible societies had popularized stereotyping in the early nineteenth century. Rather than lay each letter by hand, stereotyping was a process by which pages of type were cast into metal plates so that the plates could then be used many times over. Printers no longer had to reset type each time the book was reprinted. Plates could also be easily transferred from printer to printer. In 1812 the Bible Society of Philadelphia printed the first stereotyped Bible in the United States from plates imported from London. The printing was subsidized by the British and Foreign Bible Society, and the U.S. government allowed the plates to enter the country free of duty. Three years later, in 1815, the first set of stereotype Bible plates was made in the United States by Philadelphia printer David Bruce.

During the nineteenth century, Bible publishing followed the same commercial patterns as general book publishing. For the first half of the century, printers took advantage of the increasing number of roads and canal systems to purchase book-making materials and distribute their products. Cooperstown, New York, Brattleboro, Vermont, Concord, New Hampshire, and towns in the Connecticut Valley, all produced editions of the Bible. Bible production, like book production, was decentralized. With the expansion of a railroad system, however, local book publishing came to an end. Printing materials and books followed the lines of the railroad, emanating from the large East-coast cities. By the 1860s, Bibles were made almost exclusively in New York and Philadelphia. Stores in large cities carried Bibles, and traveling salesmen peddled the scriptures to families in rural

AN ENTIRELY NEW EDITION OF LARGE TYPE
❧ ❧ HOLMAN ❧ FAMILY ❧ BIBLES ❧ ❧

The Original and First Impression from a New Set of Electrotype
❧ Plates just Received from the Foundry ❧

Containing the Authorized Version Old and New Testaments; Marginal References; Illuminated
Title; Marriage Certificate; Family Record; Temperance Pledge; Full-page Maps in
Colors; Pronouncing Dictionary of Nearly 4,000 Scripture Proper Names; Chronological Index; Full-page Dore Cuts; Full-page Illustrations
..........in Colors, etc., etc...........

Nos. 2, 2G.

Nos. 12N, 305.

Nos. 24, 317, 317*.

Nos. 299, 299g, 7½, 7½g.

Large Quarto.
Size, 10½ x 12½ inches.

No.		Price.
0	Imitation of Leather, arabesque, paneled, gilt side and back titles, comb edges.....	$1 80
00	Same Bible, with gilt edges..	2 25

areas. Bible publication, like print culture in general, became a national rather than a local industry.[7]

Commercial publishers competed in the Bible market with non-profit Bible societies. The idea of distributing Bibles as a religious rather than a commercial enterprise originated in Britain as an aspect of evangelical reform. In 1804 an interdenominational group of elite Englishmen formed the British and Foreign Bible Society. They eventually oversaw the mass production and marketing of cheap Bibles, spurred foreign translations, and placed the Bible in the hands of the working class and the poor. The profits from Bible sales went to finance the distribution of religious books and Bibles abroad. In 1808 a similar Bible society was established in Philadelphia. By 1816 some one hundred and thirty Bible societies had sprung up prompting the formation of a national organization, the American Bible Society (ABS). The Bible Society supplied and sold the King James Bible (the "Authorized Version") without supplements through its auxiliary societies and individual agents. It was not enough for each home or church to have a copy of the scriptures. The goal of Bible societies was for each individual to own his or her own Bible. In the year 1827–8, 74,428 Bibles were distributed. A year later the number had more than doubled to 171,967. During the Civil War, almost a million and a half Bibles were sent to Northern soldiers and 300,000 to Southern forces. Although the number of Bibles distributed in the United States declined in the later part of the century, Bibles sent throughout the world increased. In 1896 alone an astonishing 630,000 Bibles were sent overseas.[8]

While we do not know the number of commercial Bibles sold or imported, the increase in the number of new editions printed each year indicates that by the mid-nineteenth century, America was awash in a sea of Bibles. Between 1777 and 1799 sixty-eight different English *editions* of either full Bibles or New Testaments were published.[9] In the next thirty years (1800–29) the number had increased almost ten fold to 622 different editions. The peak years for new editions occurred between 1830 and 1860 when over one thousand different editions were published. In the 1840s alone, 345 new English editions of the Bible or New Testament were available to Americans. After the Civil War, the number of separate editions slowly declined (the 1860s saw 131; the 1870s, 93; the 1880s, 92; the 1890s, 73). By 1910 only fifty-five new editions were introduced. Cost, limits on distribution, and perceived doctrinal slant limited purchase of these Bibles but the sheer number of editions – of supposedly the same sacred scriptures – indicated that nineteenth-century Americans wanted Bibles.

Probate records from the eighteenth and nineteenth centuries also tell us that families owned Bibles. The Parker family farmed a 135-acre homestead in Vermont, and Joseph Parker did carpentry and house building. When Parker died in 1830 his estate included a "Great Bible" and a small Bible. Vermont lawyer Ebenezer Fisk also left behind a large and a small Bible.[10] In William Gilmore's study of the Upper Connecticut River Valley (1780–1835), 89 percent of estates with identifiable books mentioned a Bible. He concluded that "no other book approached this range of readership."[11] Court records from areas outside of New England also show that until the mid-nineteenth century probate documents frequently mentioned Bibles.[12] Estate surveys in the late nineteenth century, however, seem particularly negligent in mentioning books or Bibles. In 1885 Henry Rothgeb had a parlor organ, sewing machine, a series of pictures, and a marble top washstand. He owned a story book about China and Japan. Could it

46. With the expansion of a railroad system, local Bible publishing slowly came to an end. The Holman company, for instance, printed and distributed their Bibles from Philadelphia. Advertisements for Holman Bibles appeared in newspapers, magazines, books, and religious goods catalogs throughout the United States. This one is from Gospel Trumpet Company's *Catalogue of Holiness Literature* for 1900.

be possible that this Illinois farmer did not own a Bible? Or that his neighbor Henry Root, who died in 1895 and owned two small "B stands" (Bible stands?), did not own a Bible?[13] Most likely both of these families owned Bibles, but the Bibles did not stay in the house after the death of the head of the household. They were either passed on to relatives or overlooked in the inventory of possessions. As middle-class Americans increased the number of goods they owned and counties ceased to mandate detailed estate inventories, Bibles were no longer listed in probate records.

Estate records and descriptions in diaries, letters, and memoirs tell us that people who were not white and middle-class also owned Bibles. Aaron Burdow, a free African American tenant farmer, had $195 worth of goods at his death in 1830. He owned a six-volume Scott's *Family Bible* that was valued at $6.[14] While such goods would certainly have been more readily available to a free black Vermont farmer than a Southern slave, some slaves had access to Bibles. The Southern policy of restricting slaves to oral instruction in religion limited their access to the printed word of the Bible. Consequently, a "Bible politics of literacy" developed that associated reading and memorizing the scriptures with acts of rebellion. In addition to spiritual and emotional uplift, reading became a subversive act against a dehumanizing system that commanded slaves to obey the injunctions of a text they were not permitted to read.[15] Given what Albert Raboteau called the "biblical orientation of slave religion," Bibles became cherished objects bought from peddlers or eagerly received from slave masters. Slaves memorized long passages from the Bible and attributed power to the book itself. One illiterate slave carried a "big Bible" with her through the woods and swamps. She had her mistress read her verses which she memorized and later recited over the open book. Another slave opened the book at random and searched for the one word she knew how to spell, "Jesus."[16]

There can be no doubt that during the nineteenth century, Protestants, black and white, rich and poor, owned Bibles. The peak years (1810–70) of both ABS Bible distribution and commercial Bible publishing paralleled the extraordinary growth of Protestant denominational institutions. Churches were built throughout the country, sacralizing the landscape. Cross-denominational religious reform societies were formed and religious publishing concerns proliferated. Sunday schools, seminaries, and Christian colleges were founded. At the same time, mid-nineteenth-century America also became an "environment of abundance" permitting people of every social rank to consume information at a voracious rate.[17] Innovations in printing technology enabled the Bible to be published quickly. Improvements in transportation and the mail system provided for efficient and centralized distribution systems. If Christians wanted Bibles, their needs could easily be met.

Affectionate Religion, Domesticity, and the Iconography of Bible Reading

Why did Christians want Bibles? Bible publication and the creation of a material Protestantism would not have occurred during this period if there had not also been a parallel rise in America of affectionate religion and domestic sentimentality. Bible reading would have developed as an exclusively private religious activity.

47. *Père de Famille* by Jean-Baptist Greuze. The painting was widely reproduced (this is a nineteenth-century engraving) and served as the model for portraits of family Bible reading.

Bibles would have been like those produced by Bible societies: small, simple, and with no commentary. What prompted the extraordinary growth in the Bible industry was the development of an ideology that stressed the importance of the Bible in the home. ABS Bibles were perfectly satisfactory for prayer and meditation, but they did not satisfy other religious and cultural needs. A plain Bible made up of the Old and New Testaments had a "use value" that was exclusively religious. Such a Bible was, in effect, a tool that produced spiritual insights, moral instruction, and doctrinal justifications. However, large numbers of Bibles were sold during the nineteenth century because Christians used the Bible in additional ways. No longer merely a religious tool, the Bible became a revered possession that activated sentiment and memory. Bibles assumed qualities that transformed them from acting as a saving text to functioning as a saving object.

To understand how this transformation took place, we must explore how the family Bible became a part of affectionate religion and domesticity. Visual representations give us some clues about how the Bible's association with both feeling and authority helped imbue the sacred book with its special quality. In 1755 Jean-Baptist Greuze began a career as a fashionable genre artist by exhibiting a series of paintings in a French salon. One of the pieces, *Père de Famille*, captured what Greuze imagined was a scene of Bible reading among peasant Catholics. In *Père de Famille* the father reads from a large Bible to his assembled household. Only the father has a book and rapt attention is given to his reading of the Bible. The household is made up of a diverse group of people who assemble around a wooden table. Babies and even pets are included in the tableau. Symbols of domestic activity, such as a basket of wash and dishes, emphasize the working nature of the home. This is not a mother who gives her clothes over to servants to wash and her children to wet nurses to be fed. Even though the Greuze painting depicts Bible reading in a Catholic family, the viewer is not visually informed that this is a Catholic home. There is neither crucifix nor statues of the saints and so the scene looks decidedly Protestant.

Rather than depicting mythological heroes or powerful rulers, Greuze's painting reflected a sentimental version of everyday life. *Sensibilité* – an attitude of mind that stressed emotionally charged feeling at the expense of reason, valued goodness of heart more highly than noble deeds, and used a highly moralized rhetoric – was the key element in Greuze's painting. In the mid-eighteenth century when Greuze depicted Bible reading, the sentimental nature of the painting encouraged viewers to feel the emotional intensity of the scene. A contemporary, l'Abbé de La Porte, imagined that the father, "moved by what he has just read . . . is himself imbued with the moral he is imparting to them; his eyes are almost moist with tears."[18]

In France, late seventeenth-century Catholicism had encouraged a more emotional devotionalism, and in Britain evangelical revivals in the 1730s and 1740s challenged Enlightenment rationality. The heart and the affections, rather than the mind and the will, were to be the controlling force in religion. It became acceptable for men to cry. Ministerial writers like Isaac Watts encouraged pastors to address the passions of their congregations and to awaken feelings that would motivate appropriate Christian action. Reformers of Calvinism wanted to direct it away from intensive learning, politeness, the written word, coolness, generality and toward plainness, the speaking voice, warmth, liveliness, immediacy, and intimacy.[20] Feeling in itself was not enough; sentiment must move Christians to rectify behavior, act charitably, and refine moral awareness. Isabel Rivers, in her study of English religion and ethics, calls this type of Christianity "affectionate religion."[19] In keeping with eighteenth-century notions of *sensibilité*, this domestic vignette was not a rational exercise in biblical analysis but an expression of sympathetic feelings. Greuze's painting depicted the power of religious sentiment directed by the head of the household.

The idea of a paternal *sensibilité* accompanied a long-standing tradition of patriarchal authority.[21] In theory, a father exercised absolute authority over his household which included wife and children as well as servants and apprentices. He was to support his family and rule over them with a firm but just hand. Fathers negotiated for their families in the public world and women and children had few legal rights. Because of Eve's sin, women were to be submissive to their husbands. Although good wives were praised as virtuous women, the notion that women were temptresses like Eve lingered. As wives submitted to and cherished their husbands, so children were to honor and obey their parents. Bible reading was a serious effort to shape and discipline children so they would be concerned about the state of their souls. It was believed that children were not born innocent and sinless but, as Jonathan Edwards preached, were "young vipers . . . in a most miserable condition . . . and they are naturally very senseless and stupid . . . and need much to awaken them."[22] Children's wills needed to be broken because unless they were obedient to their parents the young would never understand what it meant to be obedient to God or to secular rulers. Affections had to be controlled because human depravity made it difficult to steer love in the proper direction and moderate its desires.

Consequently, there was a tension in the eighteenth century between the patriarchal household based on a hierarchy of authority and obedience and the notion that the home was a place for mutual expression of affection and support. The Enlightenment and the Great Awakening moved Christians toward recognizing the autonomous will, self-assertiveness, and the moral authority of the individual. This conflicted with traditional ideas of a communal order designed by God and dictated by men in authority. The romantic promotion of affections contrasted with Calvinist suspicion of emotion. In the patriarchal family, children waited for their inheritance and assumed the burden of caring for ill parents. By the eighteenth century in America, the declining ability of fathers to transmit land to their sons meant that boys moved off the land and out of the range of parental authority. Children negotiated their own marriages with considerations of love frequently taking precedence over property. The patriarchal family did not disappear but it increasingly had a rival in the evolving companionate family.

The tension between the patriarchal and the companionate family can be seen in the eighteenth-century painting *Père de Famille* and those engravings based on its themes. Diderot, who was quite fond of Greuze's art, reported that "there is no man of taste who does not possess [a copy of] this print."[23] Rustic simplicity, domestic virtues, and uncomplicated piety drew the accolades of the Parisian bourgeois who also enjoyed the Romantic writings of Rousseau. A similar illustration appeared as the engraved frontispiece for the second volume of Restif de la Bretonne's popular 1778 memoir *La vie de mon père*. Greuze established an iconographic tradition of father-led Bible reading that would be extensively duplicated in America and Britain. The popular American magazine for women, *Godey's Lady's Book*, published in Philadelphia by Louis Godey and Sarah Hale, reproduced several variations of Greuze's painting.

According to art historian Michael Fried, Greuze's popularity stemmed from his ability to render "an emotionally charged, highly moralized, and dramatically unified situation that alone was capable of embodying with sufficient perspicaciousness the absorptive states of suspension of activity and fixing of attention."[24] The engraving's visual message is not one of variety and multiplicity of individual responses but of the unity of the group. Sentiment is provoked through social homogeneity. For Fried even the distracted children and grandmother serve to heighten the absorption and unification of the scene through their contrast with the other figures. Greuze seems to be saying that through domestic Bible reading, class, age, and sex differences become irrelevant. Just as in Christ there is no distinction between Jew or Greek, slave or freeman, male or female (Gal. 3:28), so in hearing the word of Christ (in the home) there is no distinction to be made between old and young, servant and master, mother and father. The Christian ideal is stipulated in the engraving: although the body of Christ has many members, through the Spirit all become one body (I Cor. 12:12). The Bible acts as the trigger to produce the feeling of spiritual unity and equality.

Greuze's painting became the model for visual representations of family Bible reading in the nineteenth century because it illustrated sentiment, domesticity, and authority. By the mid-nineteenth century, affectionate religion had been fully enveloped in an emerging Victorian domesticity. Feeling and emotion, while still important, were conditioned by a domestic religion that emphasized disciplined moral instruction in the home. Since the early decades of the nineteenth century, ministers and domestic reformers had promoted the family as a religious institution. In 1840 Presbyterian Erastus Hopkins looked hopefully to a future when "we can look upon every abode of man as the house of God – upon each family as a little church, in the bosom of which, immortals are reared, secure from the more destructive snares of a wicked world."[25] For many Protestants, salvation no longer required a radical, emotional experience of God as Calvinism once required. A true Christian could slowly be made over the course of an individual lifetime. Victorian Americans, just as their British counterparts, believed that every task served a moral purpose and could be defined by absolute standards of right and wrong. Through the virtues of industry, self-control, hard work, modesty, and temperate behavior, civic-minded men and domestically minded women would create a civilized, Christian world. The goal of the true Christian was to pursue the good and to develop the benefits of civilization.

One learned how to be both a Christian and a civilized person at home. Family worship led by the father was a hallmark of evangelical devotion in Britain and America. Emotion in itself lacked direction and refinement and so had to be controlled by disciplined, daily religious worship. Here we see the lingering effects of patriarchal Calvinism. Affectionate religion needed to be tempered by domestic order. In Hannah Moore's influential *Colebs in Search of a Wife* (1804) the model of Christian manliness, Colebs Stanley, conducted daily religious services at home. Rather than hunt, fish, and drink with other members of the English aristocracy, Mr. Stanley was serious about his familial duties. He sought to guide members of his household in their religious explorations; to shape and deepen their emotions. While men obviously had responsibilities in the public world, evangelicals in Britain and America emphasized that their domestic duties were equally important. Clergy and women writers told men to act as ministers in their homes, assembling their domestic congregation to listen to the Bible being read.[26] Children and wife might take turns reading from the Bible, singing hymns, and praying out loud, but advice books told the father to provide the spiritual leadership for his family. Domestic worship – with the Bible as focus – was a reduced and condensed version of evangelical liturgy.

In 1842, to accompany a poem by Sarah Hale, *Godey's Lady's Book* published an engraving of a father reading from the Bible to his family.[27] The engraving looks similar to *Père de Famille* and helps us see how Bible reading did not merely symbolize equalized social relationships but rather promoted the authority of God and father. In the engraving a genteel parlour is the site for evening devotions by the whole household. A basket of pots and clothes does not sit in front of the mother as it did in the original Greuze, but instead a basket of wash is placed in front of a maid. Through this illustration, *Godey's* encouraged readers to relate daily Bible reading to their middle-class lives rather than to an imagined peasant past. In 1855 the peasant motif was evoked in another *Godey's* engraving, *Cottage Devotions*. Rather than a genteel household, *Godey's* shows a rural family gathered around a rustic table to listen to the head of the family read from a folio Bible. As with the Greuze, children play with pets, and the others, old and young, listen attentively. A spinning wheel tells us this is a working household. The standing woman, indicating her lower status, may be a maid but the intentions of the engraver are unclear.

Looking again at the American variations of Greuze's theme, another image of Bible reading emerges. Emotion and sentiment are not merely expressed, they are directed and controlled by a paternal authority figure. The traditional patriarchal family is recalled in the engravings. The presence of the Bible as a revered object breaks the homogeneity of the scene, challenging the illusion of a harmonious, all-

48. "Evening Devotions," a poem by Sarah Hale, was accompanied by this engraving and published in *Godey's Lady's Book* in 1842. The illustration not only encouraged family prayer, it promoted the authority of the father as the spiritual and temporal leader of his household – in spite of the increasingly feminized nature of Protestantism and the rise of companionate marriages.

49. This engraving entitled "Cottage Devotions" was published in *Godey's Lady's Book* in 1855. The similarity to the Greuze painting of one hundred years earlier is striking, although the scene is more subdued and the dogs more numerous.

absorbing, unifying experience. At a time when Bible societies wanted everyone to have his or her own Bible and printers hoped to sell many versions of the sacred book, these artists show only the father with a Bible. An environment is created where Bibles are still rare objects and the father functions as the sole domestic explicator of the sacred text. The other people in the illustrations have no books and so must rely on the father for the message of salvation. They turn toward the father and the book, two traditional symbols of religious and secular authority. When Bible reading includes younger and older males, the reading is done by the senior male. Pets might be present, but they either disrupt the mood or rest obliviously under the table. Servants stand or sit outside of the family circle in recognition of their lower position in the household. Age, sex, and status are reinforced rather than eliminated through representations of domestic worship.

The portrayal of family Bible reading thus underscores the hierarchical nature of Christianity. Emotion and sentiment in themselves cannot eliminate the power of the father because he controls access to the Bible. Rather than attesting to the fact that all bodies come together in the one body of Christ, the representations echo the biblical insistence that Christ is the head of his church and that social arrangements must duplicate that power relationship. Authority and obedience accompany divine love. While the intention of the artist might have been to reconcile differences under the auspices of religion, what simultaneously occurred was the legitimation and clarification of difference. Both social homogeneity and social hierarchy were explored in such art. The family Bible sanctified both opposing tendencies. Because it was the focus of domestic worship it became associated both with the religious sentiment gained from the ritual and from its association with patriarchal authority. The Bible participated in the power of the father and was the catalyst for the father's ability to provoke emotional response in his household.

It is always difficult to move from cultural representations to real life. Paintings and engravings are preserved in museums, books, and archives lending more credence to their portrayals than perhaps they merit. To what extent did real families have family worship and thus help endow the family Bible with spiritual and cultural meaning? For early American Methodists, family worship paralleled the emotional effervescence of revival meetings and love feasts. Both conversions and spiritual support were accompanied by shouts, cries, music, and Bible reading in the Methodist homes of the antebellum period.[28] Anecdotal evidence leads us to suspect that families did try to have Bible-centered domestic worship. In 1827 Fanny Lamson wrote to her father in Ipswich, Massachusetts, asking for "a copy of your evening & morning prayers."[29] Presbyterian minister and father of Alexander Campbell assumed that it was both his ministerial duty and "the dictate of his parental affection" to have daily worship that included Bible reading, singing, catechizing, and prayer.[30] Southern Baptist Kathleen Mallory announced in 1889 her intention to be baptized after her father had finished reading a Bible chapter to his family at morning devotions.[31] A photograph from the 1860s shows the influence of engravings of family Bible reading. The family sits around a table listening to the eldest male read while the servants linger in the background. Even Christians who had only tangential connections to evangelicalism participated in family devotions. The biographer of Episcopalian Phillips Brooks emphasized that his was a religious family where "the usage of family prayer was rigidly observed, in the morning before going forth to the work

50. A posed photograph of an unknown family from the 1860s in which the household has assembled for Bible reading in a way that reflects the popular engravings of the time.

of the day, and again in the evening at nine o'clock."[32] Even Mormon Brigham Young wrote to British followers in 1841 not to let missionaries take over family worship but to "let the head of the family dictate, I mean the man, not the woman."[33]

The Bible became a focus of attention not only because it reflected church rituals led by a male minister. Family Bible reading also reflected traditional ways of reading that were in decline by the Victorian period. Historians of reading have argued that in early modern Europe and America, group reading was a common and significant practice.[34] Memory and recitation were valued cultural accomplishments cultivated in children and revered in adults. Since books were expensive and rare, reading from them accorded readers special status. The close relationship between oral performance and reading continued into the nineteenth century. Reading out loud to families may not have been as prevalent in France and Germany as it was in Britain and America where the Protestant emphasis on household religious instruction encouraged group reading. A visitor to Boston in 1845–6 reported seeing fathers of the middle and lower classes reading novels to their families.[35] These men participated in a social world in which the male masters of the house took on the responsibility to provide intellectual and cultural leadership for their families. Bible reading within the context of domestic worship gained in importance not only because of its connection with religion but also because it reflected secular cultural activities that lent authority to male readers.

In 1755 a painting depicting a Bible-reading father could become popular and a model for other representations of domestic religious sentiment. Sentimentality and masculinity were not yet opposing cultural traits. However, rationality had long been associated with men and emotion with women. As Isaac Watts recognized, "we are often told, that this warm and affectionate religion belongs only to the weaker parts of mankind, and is not strong and manly enough for persons of sense and good reasoning."[36] In the nineteenth century, the warmth, immediacy, and intimacy of affectionate religion was more often represented by mothers than fathers. The sentimental aspect of father-led Bible worship cultivated in the eighteenth and early nineteenth century could no longer be felt by Victorian Americans. Historians Barbara Welter and Ann Douglas have argued that antebellum American culture created a "cult" of "True Womanhood" that promoted piety, purity, submissiveness, and domesticity as the cardinal feminine virtues.[37] Sentiment increasingly was gendered feminine. Religion acted as a foundation for the other virtues, enabling women to function as spiritual authorities in their homes. Maternal love, rather than paternal sentiment, came to be associated with religion of the heart.

The cult of True Womanhood promoted the association between domesticity and Christianity to the extent that mothers were considered to hold the key to the salvation of their children. "You have a child on your knee," wrote Samuel Goodrich to mothers in 1838. "Do you know what that child is? It is an immortal being; destined to live forever! It is destined to be happy or miserable! And who is to make it happy or miserable? You – the mother!"[38] No longer depraved, sinful creatures with wills that needed to be broken, children were portrayed as tender flowers requiring the care of mothers. Children shared with women spiritual purity and possessed redemptive qualities as the popular character of Eva in *Uncle Tom's Cabin* (1850) so clearly illustrates.[39] As seen from the perspective of Victorian culture, the relationship that the child had with his or her mother was based less on authority and more on love. Mothers understood their children's psychology and could adapt moral and religious concepts to a child's personality.

51. Lydia Sigourney included this engraving entitled, "Teaching the Scriptures" in her *Religious Souvenir of 1840*. The engraving stresses the intimate and non-hierarchical nature of maternal instruction. The mother rests her hand on her child's shoulder, drawing her daughter near. The tilt of the mother's head and the angle of her child's eyes emphasize the connection between the two.

Ministers, writers, artists, and reformers created a parallel between the Madonna nursing the divine child Jesus and the human mother feeding her child the words of salvation. The Puritan image of the Bible as spiritual milk resonated throughout literature and art. Mothers needed to give their children religious instruction as they gave them food. In 1869 Davis Newton commended all Christian mothers who "had poured, drop by drop, into [their child's] half-open mouth the pure milk of the gospel."[40] Just as breast milk gave nurture and pleasure to children, so the mother's use of the Bible fed, comforted, and delighted her progeny. Just as breast milk could only be given to one or two babies at a time, so mothers would read from the Bible only to one or two children at a time. Bible reading, like breast feeding, should be intimate, emotional, and all-encompassing.

Engravings of mothers reading from the Bible present an intimate glimpse of a mother and her child that resembles nursing. There are no bookcases or bird cages to divert the viewers' attention. The space is enclosed, restricted, and limited. The mother holds the book, but the distance between reader and listener is reduced. In an 1869 illustration, the son rests his hand on the Bible while in a 1840 engraving, the Bible is positioned in such a way as almost to touch the daughter. The artists also reduce the size difference between mothers and children thus stressing the equality between reader and listener. Tables do not accentuate the ordered hierarchy of the social group but act as an extension of the mother's lap. Not bound by the physical presence of the table, sons or daughters snuggle close to their mothers. Artists then blend the clothing of one into the other, and the bodies of the two fuse into one. No one is excluded; no one (or thing) is present without fully participating. We can easily imagine that mother has the child read to her and that she listens attentively. In Victorian America, intimacy, intensity, and affectionate religion were best represented when mother and children were evoked. The Bible became one way that the spiritual exchange between the pious mother and the receptive child could be represented.

The importance of the mother in the spiritual upbringing of her children was so rooted in the Victorian imagination that no respectable Christian would deny the connection. Autobiographies, biographies, and memoirs frequently mention the mother's role in educating her children. Baptist Adoniram Judson Gordon expressed a typical thought when he wrote that for his mother, "her family was her parish; to them she ministered, and for them she ceased not to pray until the end."[41] The corporeality that shaped cultural representations of maternal instruction also echoed in biography and memoir. Writers connected the physical presence of women with prayer and Bible reading. Presbyterian David Coulter wrote that "the look and the tones" of his mother and her voice "are still vividly present with me." Her religious instructions and admonitions "sometimes with a tearful eye," were "drawn from the word of divine truth, are yet fresh in my memory."[42] Episcopalian Arthur Selden Lloyd recalled that "a little boy looks up into the face of his mother, and what he sees there he becomes."[43] Another Episcopalian, James Hall, recalled that "grandmother always prayed with me at her knee and it was one of the pleasures of my life to lean down and bury my face in her lap."[44] Henry Ward Beecher (b. 1813), whose mother died when he was three, wrote that "no devout Catholic ever saw so much in the Virgin Mary as I have seen in my mother, who has been a presence to me ever since I can remember."[45] If we can trust ministerial biographies and memoirs justly to represent childhood memories, then women played a significant role in literally embodying religious sentiment.

Representations of mothers with Bibles also reflected the ways that secular books were increasingly being read. Historian Roger Chartier notes that reading in eighteenth-century urban France was primarily a private endeavor. Reading involved the intimate self and required the "investment of intense emotional, intellectual, and spiritual efforts."[46] When Chartier looked at how reading was portrayed in art, he noticed a shift from reading as a male act demonstrating status and social condition to a female act of emotional abandonment. Even when men were portrayed reading, the book served as a "companion in solitude."[47] Rather than being an oral performance for a group, the act of reading presupposed an intimate relationship between the reader and a book. The individualization of reading also became the feminization of reading. As reading materials became more widely available and cheaper, the act of reading no longer symbolized intellectual accomplishment or wealth. American women avidly consumed fiction, popular magazines, and advice literature.[48] No longer a communal performance orchestrated by men, reading involved elements associated with women. Sitting down with a book was seen to be emotional and uplifting – just like Victorian evangelical Protestantism. As with feminized Protestantism, feminized reading

THE MOTHER IMPARTING HEAVENLY WISDOM.

52. From Davis F. Newton's 1869 *Apples of Gold in Pictures of Silver*. The biblical wisdom is conveyed through motherly love rather than paternal authority.

revered the heart over the mind. Women, as specialists in emotion and feeling, were seen to be naturally drawn to both. The image of the mother reading the Bible to her child reflected individualized religion and private reading.

Family Bibles achieved importance in the Victorian home because they were a critical element in domestic worship and maternal instruction. As the home became a place for Christian nurture, Bibles increasingly were seen as the cornerstone of the Christian home. Reading a Bible in solitude, while understood as a worthy activity, did not help instill religious sentiments in the household's children or servants. Religious sentiments were activated by either the father, or increasingly the mother, reading from the scriptures. The Bible could either be associated with the loving authority of the father or the nurturing affection of the mother, and Bible reading in the home, organized by either father or mother, served as the source of spiritual strength and moral instruction. Church services, revival meetings, reform societies, and Sunday schools were important in Protestant lives, but they were not praised as consistently as the sacred nature of the home. Preaching sermons from the revival pulpit could spark religious sentiments but only regular use of the Bible at home could maintain those attitudes. While the Victorians insisted that the presence of the Bible in the home made the home holy, I propose that the emphasis on family worship and sacred domesticity provided an ideology which enabled the Bible to be seen as a special object.

Memories of My Mother's Bible

Bibles served not only as religious tools used in family rituals, they were special objects that activated family memories. Historian Michael Kammen concludes in *Mystic Chords of Memory* that the period between 1875 and 1915 was an "age of memory and ancestor worship by design and by desire."[49] During this period, symbolic expressions of patriotism were created and enacted in the public sphere. Americans participated in Memorial Day celebrations. They built libraries to hold rare books and constructed pioneer memorials. Women joined the Daughters of the American Revolution, and history writing became a source of inspiration for readers. While Kammen traces the development of national collective memory, the same fascination and nostalgia for the past also developed in the private space of the home. Victorian Americans not only traced their genealogies and went to annual family reunions, they prized the Bible as symbolic of the unification of family and religion. The creation of national memories and family memories paralleled each other and both were critical to the Victorians' search for order and rootedness in an increasingly pluralistic and industrial America.

The Bible's participation in the "mystic chords of memory" that echoed between 1875 and 1915 can clearly be discerned in a series of hymns extolling the Bible's merits. As with visual representations, hymns express cultural ideals and establish acceptable interpretive norms. Sometime prior to 1841, George P. Morris penned a poem called "My Mother's Bible" that served as a model for several popular hymns. The poem was put to music by Henry Russell, another Englishman who claimed credit for writing over eight hundred songs, most not of a religious nature. During the 1840s the Hutchinson Family, a singing group from New Hampshire, popularized the song. It appeared in their song collections and some hymnals reprinted it as "The Family Bible."[50] An 1860 variation, "The Old-Fashioned Bible," was published in a Methodist hymnal and in 1893 a Southern musician, Charlie D. Tillman, wrote still another version of the hymn. Tillman's "My Mother's Bible" became a part of a growing tradition of Gospel music emanating from the South. From his headquarters in Atlanta, Tillman published his own song books; some sold over a quarter of a million copies. In 1925 "My Mother's Bible" was one of the first Gospel hymns to be electronically recorded. By then its Victorian sentiments seemed out of date and the song never became a best seller.[51] The original Morris and Russell version captures the Victorian tendency to personify objects by imbuing them with the ability to evoke memory:

This book is all that's left me now! –
    Tears will unbidden start –
With faltering lip and throbbing brow,
    I press it to my heart.
For many generations passed,
    Here is our family tree;
My mother's hands this Bible clasped –
    She, dying, gave it [to] me.

Ah! well do I remember those
    Whose names these records bear;
Who round the hearth-stone used to close,
    After the evening prayer,
And speak of what these pages said,
    In terms my heart would thrill! –
Though they are with the silent dead,
    Here are they living still!

My father read this holy book
    To brothers, sisters dear –
How calm was my poor mother's look,
    Who leaned God's word to hear!
Her angel face – I see it yet!
    What thronging memories come!
Again that little group is met
    Within the halls of home!

Thou truest friend man ever knew,
    Thy constancy I've tried;
When all were false, I found thee true,
    My counsellor and guide.
The mines of earth no treasures give
    That could this volume buy;
In teaching me the way to live,
    It taught me how to die.[52]

Family Bible hymns used tactile memory as the primary means to evoke spiritual emotions. Memory was aroused through looking at and touching a Bible that had been in the family for many generations. Singers told of "pressing" the Bible to their hearts, of mothers having "clasped" the book, of the pages "speaking." In Tillman's "My Mother's Bible," the singer loved the "dear and precious book, Tho' it's worn and faded now" with its "tear-stained leaves." It is not merely the Bible's scriptural wisdom, but the book itself that generates the sentiments. In the hymns, the physical body of the mother is also associated with the Bible. Singers see her "angel face" and remember her "calm" look through their family Bible. The mother in the Tillman version placed "her hand upon my brow," dried "flowing tears with her kisses," and spoke "in gentle tones and low." While in the 1841 original "father read this holy book to brothers, sisters dear," his voice remained disembodied. We never see father, we only hear his voice. Likewise in

"The Old-Fashioned Bible" (1860) it was "our sire" who recited the prayer of "sweet invocation," but the singer does not mention his face or the feel of his touch. By 1893 "My Mother's Bible" contained no mention of father at all. The memory of mother's body – her tears, voice, and touch – lingered through the generations.

Memories of mother, but not of father, provided the comfort "oft when battles sore oppress me."[53] Fathers, associated in Victorian culture with politics and economics – divisive social activities in flux – could not provide a sense of meaningful security. Representations of motherhood reflected the eternal, reliable, unchanging truth of the Bible. The hymns encourage Christians nostalgically to equate the stability of biblical truths with the joys of their own childhoods. Victorians frequently used childhood as a symbol of a personal utopia. The childhood sung about in hymns is consistently portrayed as an ordered, past time that contrasts with the troubled, disordered present. Hymns invite the singer to see the Bible as a conduit for returning to an imagined security experienced before difficult moral questions challenged one's inner peace. Rather than promote independent thought in religion, hymns ask Christians to gain strength through recalling their childhood dependence on simple biblical truths. The Bible, like the parent, could be trusted to be the "truest friend" or a "counsellor and guide."

As with most sentimental literature, Bible hymns mixed nostalgia with melancholy to produce pleasure. The first line of "The Old-Fashioned Bible" recalls, "how painfully pleasing the fond recollections of youthful connections and innocent joy." Pain and pleasure were experienced simultaneously through the trigger of the family Bible. Unlike the advice books on family worship that told families immediately to establish Bible reading in their households, Victorian hymns portray the family Bible as a source of memories of past religious activities. Although we might live "broken-hearted" in "sorrow and sadness," the "dear Savior's protection" remains ever available through the memory of the family Bible, if not actual family worship. Pleasure is achieved not as the result of a routine of daily rituals, but through the *memory* of those rituals. Even in 1860, hymnists represent the family Bible "which lay on the stand" as "old-fashioned." Perhaps more than any other Protestant object the family Bible embodied the imaginative reconstruction of a utopian past.

The family Bible imagined by the hymnists was not a commodity bought and sold in the marketplace. In order for the book to achieve an affecting presence for Victorian Protestants, it had to be removed from the profaning influence of the commercial economy. Just as men were tainted by their interaction with the world of business and women freed from such stain, Bibles had to stay independent from mercantile exchange. The hymn, "Holy Bible, Book Divine," explains that the Bible is a "precious treasure" owned by the singer. According to Victorian rhetoric, what makes the family Bible priceless is not its binding or gilded pages. True worth is determined by God and family, not the market. Bibles, like other material objects cherished by the Victorians, were treasured possessions not commodities.[54] "The mines of earth no treasures give," states the Morris/Russell hymn, "That could this volume buy." The sacred book, so prized for its intense associations with mother, had to be bestowed as a gift or inherited.

By transforming certain commodities into treasured possessions, Victorians created symbolic avenues for Christians to experience a meaningful, idealized past. The value given to the family Bible in the nineteenth century served to clothe the relatively new idea of the sacred character of the home with an aura of permanence. Victorian ministers told their congregations, and writers told their readers, that family worship was as old as Eden, and that Mary had taught Jesus the Torah in the same way that contemporary mothers instructed their children.[55] Continually presented as "old," the family Bible possessed the quality of connecting adult Christians to an imagined childhood. The physical presence of the Bible with its elaborate covers and emotive associations assured Protestants that the "simple" truths of the Bible were substantial and enduring. To treat the Bible as a commodity, something routinely bought and sold, equated eternal truths with the fleeting and imprecise nature of everyday life. Victorian ministers and writers promoted the family Bible as unchanging and invariant in a constantly shifting modern world.

The Bible as Fashion Statement

It would be incorrect to assume that the ideological promotion of the family Bible as a source of religious emotion and memory was the only way that Bibles became endowed with affective presence. Ministers, engravers, hymnists, and writers most likely would have been perfectly happy if each family had owned one large family Bible and passed it down from generation to generation. However, in spite of such anti-commercial sentiments, Bibles were commodities in nineteenth-century America. They were designed and marketed by secular companies who knew that Americans wanted nostalgia and fashion, the old and the new. Consequently, Bible publishers realized that if they were to sell Bibles, they would need to counter the notion that Bibles only contained the eternal truths of the Old and New Testaments. An unchanging Bible never became obsolete and therefore never needed to be replaced. The "use" value of the Bible as a religious tool had to be augmented. Publishers revamped the Bible, moving it out of the "unchanging" realm of religion and into the "ever new" realm of fashion. In doing so they designed Bibles significantly different from those mass distributed by the American Bible Society. Publishers made their Bibles convey messages about status and taste, in addition to spiritual uplift.

Victorian producers, of all goods not just Bibles, sought to convince the consumer that their tasteful objects could evoke purified emotions. Taste should not be a fashion statement dependent on individual whims. For the Victorian producer and consumer alike, taste had a distinctly ethical dimension. In her study of nineteenth-century domestic literature, Lori Merish finds that as early as the 1830s writers and ministers emphasized the importance of proper consumption. "According to this ideal," she writes, "a synthesis of pietistic Protestant and neoclassical aesthetic categories, refined domestic artifacts would civilize and socialize persons and awaken higher sentiments; such objects would seduce wayward individuals into the regenerative sociability of the domestic sphere and, by inspiring purified sentiments, could draw individuals to God."[56] Obviously the Victorians saw the Bible as the direct way to draw individuals to God, but in order to sell many Bibles producers had to transform it into a domestic commodity that could inspire purified sentiments even if it was never read.

Families had to be convinced to buy Bibles not only because they were the Word of God but because the book as object could civilize and socialize persons.

British printers and publishers were the first to recognize that they could sell more Bibles if they distinguished home Bibles from church Bibles. With the idealization of the middle-class home, printers found that they could sell Bibles to families if they emphasized the unique character of their "domestic" Bibles. As early as 1788, British publishers exported to the United States Bibles that were specifically called "family Bibles." Publishers labeled their Bibles "Domestic Bibles" or "Cottage Bibles" or "Home Bibles" in order to encourage households to purchase their particular edition of the scriptures. In 1788, for instance, *The Christian's New and Complete Family Bible* was printed in England and sold in Philadelphia. Two years later, William Woodhouse printed the text in Philadelphia and advertised it in local newspapers. The *Cottage Bible, and Family Expositor* was first printed in London in 1825–7 and the stereotype plates later sold to a Hartford printer who continued to publish it into the 1860s. Although the translation of the scriptures used in church and at home was exactly the same, printers sought to erase that similarity by inventing the "family" Bible.

Bibles that were printed for families contained supplemental material that would not have been needed for church worship. In 1791 American printer Isaiah Thomas included additional religious material to help lay people better understand the biblical text. His Bible included not only the scriptures but also a topical index, an explanation of scriptural measures, weights and coins, a chronological table, lists of offices and conditions of men, kindred and affinity, proper names, and a concordance.[57] Intended to help the lay reader, the addition of such materials also provided a text that could be easily changed. Traveling Bible salesmen could point out the contemporary nature of these supplemental materials to their customers, indicating that their previously purchased Bibles were now out-of-date. In 1846 Harper Brothers published their lavishly illustrated *Illuminated and New Pictorial Bible* that grossed over $1.5 million during its first twelve years of publication. Confident that its modern equipment could produce elaborate Bibles cheaply, Harper Brothers even made a bid to publish Bibles "at one half the present prices" for the American Bible Society, but the Society rejected the suggestion.[58]

Following the Civil War, publishers increased the number of additional features placed in family Bibles. Along with family records, they added photograph albums, temperance pledges, wedding certificates, and copious color illustrations. The actual text of the scriptures became almost secondary to the illustrated Bible dictionaries, treatises on ancient coins (and gems, trees, plants, flowers, manners, and customs), illuminated parables and The Lord's Prayer, and chronologies. While Isaiah Thomas's Bible had eight such additions, the Hubbard *Complete Domestic Bible* (1873) had forty-one, and by 1882 A. J. Holman's *The Holy Bible* could boast an overwhelming 190 supplemental entries. It is not surprising that pioneer Anne Ellis remembered her family Bible as something to sell rather than as something to read.

American printers also included family record pages in their Bibles to chronicle births and deaths. Printing family records within the Bible ordered and tidied the seventeenth-century tradition of covering the Bible's blank pages with the dates and births of family members. British printers noted this custom and began providing printed record pages. As with other design and technological

53. This frontispiece from the *Pictorial Family Bible* (Philadelphia: A. J. Holman, 1872) was designed to capture and hold the attention of lay people.

54. This essay on "Ancient Coins and Gems" from the *Pictorial Family Bible* illustrates one of many supplementary entries included to explain the biblical text more fully. It was these entries, rather than the scriptures themselves, that made Victorian Bibles so large and encyclopedic.

55. In the seventeenth century, families covered the blank pages of their Bibles with information about the family. Printers in the eighteenth century saw this habit and began to print separate pages for recording birth, marriage, and death dates. This family record included in a 1856 Bible published by Jesper Harding of Philadelphia, has separate columns for family names, place and date of births, marriages, and deaths.

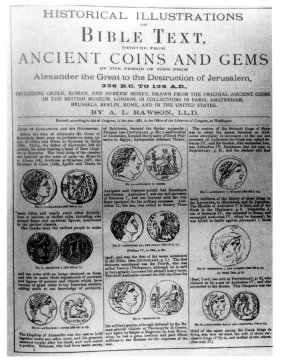

innovations, American printers copied British techniques. By the late nineteenth century, Bibles also included illustrated pages for recording when family members took temperance pledges, got married, or joined fraternal societies. Printers inserted pages for families to include photographs of their kin and friends. Families, their names, activities, and even faces were literally contained within the Bible.

The large family Bible with its family records functioned as a domestic equivalent of the "Book of Life" mentioned in the biblical Book of Revelation. In one of the visions of John of Patmos, the dead stood in front of the divine throne as the sacred books were being opened. "And the dead were judged out of those things which were written in the books, according to their works" (Rev. 20:12). If one's name was not inscribed in the Book of Life the soul would be "cast into the lake of fire" (Rev. 20:15). Anne Ellis, as we have seen, resented the fact that she was left out of the records in the family Bible. The Bible enabled families not only to catalog whom to remember but also whom to forget. When Mary Lee Bland Ewell converted to Mormonism, her family disowned her. "My brother wrote that my portrait was thrown into the attic," she entered in her diary, "and my name was taken from the family record in the Bible."[59] Bible salesmen promoted the Bible's ability to act as a legal record of births, marriages, and deaths. Especially for rural families, through the family Bible one came "officially" into existence.[60]

The large size of family Bibles encouraged people to store not only written information about their lives but physical reminders as well. As a book that symbolized truth, eternity, and stability the Bible was a convenient place to house everything from a will, to a church membership note, to pressed flowers. Families frequently kept special objects within the Bible. Sentimental poetry, clippings of hair, homemade bookmarks, bills and receipts, insurance policies – any object that needed to be remembered and small enough to be easily forgotten, could end up in the Bible. Victorian Protestants sought to preserve and make sacred the minutiae of everyday life by placing special objects in their Bibles. The Bible not only stored the names of the family members, it stored the mementos of family life.

While families could purchase inexpensive Bibles from the growing number of Bible societies, Bibles with family records, illustrations, and supplementary materials were expensive. In order to sell their Bibles, American publishers copied the British system of installment purchases. This method was particularly prominent in early nineteenth-century America when families owned few books and Bibles were difficult to print. In 1816 Dodge and Sayer of New York sold Scott's *Family Bible* in fascicles that cost seventy-five cents for each installment.[61] Families could buy one fascicle at a time and eventually have the whole Bible bound when they completed their set. They could finance the purchase of the Bible over several months, or even years, making it easier to subscribe to a particular edition. After completing their set, they could pick out a leather cover and metal clasp to suit their taste and pocketbook.

Since ministers and writers consistently promoted the spiritual and moral power of the Bible, and poets and musicians sang its praise as a source for family memory, publishers did not have to advertise its religious or cultural meaning. Instead, producers focused on championing their Bibles' physical quality. Traveling Bible salesmen carried samples of the leather bindings and metal clasps so families could see the caliber of their goods. In 1878 Nelson & Phillips boasted in newspaper advertisements that their *Pictorial Family Bible* had the largest and finest engravings, the richest and most durable bindings, was printed on the finest paper, and was the cheapest and fastest selling of all Bibles. Other Bibles printed

56.   Bibles were promoted both as containing an eternal, unchanging set of sacred scriptures and as new, fashionable, up-to-date books. This family register from the *Complete Family Bible* was printed in 1822 by Joseph Teal of Boston. Although the pelican feeding her young from her own flesh is a traditional Christian symbol, the columns and robed figures reflect the early Republic's fascination with classical design.

57.   Printers freely reprinted illustrations from a variety of sources in their Bibles. This Noah's Ark was originally published in Diderot's *Encyclopédie*. Its order, balance and symmetry were appropriate both for the Age of Enlightenment of the *philosophes* and the readers of the 1822 *Complete Family Bible*.

from worn-out plates on flimsy paper "fall to pieces before they have been in use one year." People might as well "throw their money in the fire as to buy" these inferior Bibles.[62] The physical quality of the book itself made the family Bible stand out from the increasing number of cheaply produced books and magazines. After the Civil War, most Americans could afford books, newspapers, and almanacs but a large family Bible showed that the household appreciated the finer things of life.

Publishers advertised the enduring and durable quality of the materials, implying that their Bible would be long-lived. Consumers, however, wanted both the eternity of a priceless possession and the fashionable newness of a commodity. To accommodate that desire, publishers included illustrations and designs that were susceptible to changing artistic styles. The Bible itself might last for generation after generation, but the images contained within it changed with the times. Although eighteenth-century secular books could be highly illustrated, initially American printers respected the wishes of their patrons and limited the number of engravings.[63] By the beginning of the nineteenth century, however, family Bibles began to reflect changes in attitudes toward religious art. In 1807 Collins, Perkins and Company bragged in their advertisements that they paid a great price for their engravings, even winning a gold medal for the best engraved plates, but since "some persons may prefer their Bibles without plates copies may be had without them."[64] These early nineteenth-century Bible engravings show a reserve both in their level of artistic design and in their subject matter. Illustrations never vie with the text for dramatic appeal. As the Calvinist suspicion of images declined, however, publishers felt free to include illustrations of biblical passages and to decorate their family records. Not surprisingly they followed design styles fashionable for their time. In the 1820s, biblical characters sported togas, Grecian columns graced the interior of Hebrew temples and homes, and family records reflected a fascination with the Greco-Roman world. Order,

58. This Bible located in the rare books room of the Free Library of Philadelphia, illustrates how designs changed as the nineteenth century progressed. The records on the left are the original ones in the 1807 *The Holy Bible*, published by Collins, Perkins and Company of New York. At some point the family who owned the Bible ran out of register pages and so had the newer ones on the right inserted. Those pages reflect the preference for Gothic design popular after the 1840s.

balance, and symmetry as seen in Noah's Ark or a stylized family record illustrated the preference for neoclassical designs. Bibles, like houses and banks, reflected contemporary aesthetic taste.

The preference for classical Bible decoration would be short lived. Beginning in the 1840s, Gothic Revival architecture and Romanticism arrived from Europe. The pointed arch increasingly framed family registers, medieval characters replaced cupids, and illustrations took on a more decidedly dramatic character. Just as some families updated their neoclassical houses with Gothic trim, families modernized their family records. One Philadelphia family added to their plain, 1807 family records colored Gothic-style plates copyrighted in 1873 by the Hubbard Brothers.[65] The contrast between the two styles is striking. By the 1870s publishers utilized an electrotype process developed in the 1860s that allowed the once expensive woodblock engravings to be duplicated almost indefinitely without significant loss of quality. Not only did the illustrations become more emotional and dramatic, they appeared more often within the text.

While publishers might print biblical scenes created by any European or American artists, the work of one engraver became almost synonymous with family Bibles. The art of French illustrator Gustave Doré (1832–83) first appeared in an expensive English Bible in 1866. Throughout the late nineteenth-century, Doré's engravings drew the reader into a fairytale land of mighty pharaohs, seductive women, and powerful redeemers. The illustrations' drama, pathos, and detailed character engaged the viewer emotionally and permitted the opening up of the religious imagination. Biblical figures came alive and helped readers remember the stories of the scriptures, if not their messages. The exotic character of Doré's art resonated in turn-of-the-century America when Orientalism became an appropriate design style. Japanese vases, Persian rugs, and Moorish ornaments entered the homes of the upper middle class as their owners hoped that such eclectic decorations would create a fantasy environment for relaxation and delight.

59. The biblical illustrations of Gustave Doré. In this illustration from the *Pictorial Family Bible*, Jesus drives the money changers out of the temple. Full of emotion, pathos, and drama, Doré's engravings engaged the viewer emotionally.

The biblical world represented by Doré's illustrations harmonized well with the late nineteenth-century fascination with the sensuous and mysterious East. Even as color lithographs threatened to replace black-and-white engravings, publishers continued to include Doré prints in family Bibles.

Publishers took advantage of modern developments in photography, printing, and anthropology to update their Bibles continually. Ethnographic surveys of Middle Eastern peoples enriched essays like the "Domestic Life of the Israelites" and photography provided readers with glimpses into the "ancient" world.[66] Ethnography and photography – while both new ways of understanding the world – actually helped readers return to the mythical time of the biblical past. Victorians felt that they could understand scripture better through the available "facts" provided by the natural and social sciences. Publishers exploited the Victorian fondness for collecting and cataloging by packing Bibles with detailed information. Bibles evolved into religious encyclopedias where there was an easy mix between sacred text, biblical commentary, and informative essays.

The **Ostrich** was reckoned as an unclean bird. It is mentioned several times in Scripture, but nowhere is it described so fully as in the splendid poem of Job. There the description is wellnigh perfect, even to the beauty of its feathers, its enormous strength, and its great velocity. The feathers of the ostrich have in all ages and countries been used as evidences of rank and fashion. They appear on the monuments of Egypt cut in stone.

The ostrich is careless of its eggs, leaving the sun to do the work of incubation. The young are able to care for themselves as soon as hatched. Voracity is inseparable from the ostrich nature. It makes food of everything, even metals, and its power of digestion is without bounds. Its stupidity is proverbial, and it is constantly the subject of metaphor, as seeking safety by hiding its head in the sand while its vital parts are exposed.

Job says of the ostrich "What time she lifteth up herself on high, she scorneth the horse and rider." Few horses can catch it in a fair chase. Its short wings come to the assistance of its long legs, and together an immense speed is secured. The Arabs call the ostrich the "camel bird," because it resembles the camel in shape, is peculiarly an animal of the desert, and can do a long time without water. Its cry resembles the roar of the lion.

THE OSTRICH.

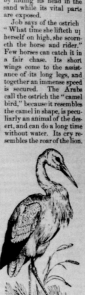

Scripture mention of the **Crane** alludes to its noisy cry and habit of migration. The crane is gregarious. When swarming at evening toward its roost its trumpet cry can be heard afar. It builds in secluded spots and watches with great caution. It is a fisher like the heron, but equally fond of worms and insects. Parts of the plumage of the crane are very beautiful, and it vies with that of the ostrich for fashionable wear. The bird lays but two eggs, and manifests the greatest solicitude for its young.

The **Stork** of Scripture is almost a reverenced, always a protected, animal in the East. This is not more on account of the notion that it is a pious bird than because it is the destroyer of snakes, insects, and garbage. In many cities of the East the stork walks freely in the streets and gathers offal without molestation.

When storks settle on a tract of land, each bird seems to appropriate a section, and its first duty is to cleanse it of every reptile, worm, and insect its keen eyes and knowing beak can discover. Storks have a small, light body, but great expanse of wings. They resemble mankind in choosing a single habitation, which they adhere to for years.

The **Heron** was classed as an unclean bird. The heron species abounds in the East, and it is a frequent object in Egyptian monuments. Herons are natural fishers. They wade into the water, assume an attitude of perfect quiet, and suddenly pounce on their prey, which consists of frogs and small fishes. Their beaks are very powerful, very long, and pointed. If their capture should be larger and stronger than they can handle, they leave the water and dash it against a stone till it is subdued.

The **Pelican** was prohibited food. Says David; "I am like a pelican of the wilderness." The pelican is fond of resorts far removed from man. It is a silent, meditative bird, careful of its young, and a great gourmand. While the Hebrew word for pelican signifies "to vomit," it comports with the now better-known structure of the bird, which is armed with a capacious pouch into which it takes its catch of fish. On its return to its nest it disgorges its catch as food for its young by pressing its breast with the red tip of its beak. This red in contrast with the white led to the legend that it fed its young with its own blood.

THE CRANE.

THE STORK.

THE HERON.

THE PELICAN.

60. The family Bible served not only as a repository for moral vision and artistic fantasy, it also provided essays on the natural and social sciences. Victorian readers could learn about "Birds of the Bible" from the *Pictorial Family Bible.*

Even as late nineteenth-century scholars busied themselves in restricting the scope of the Bible through higher criticism, publishers advanced the popular notion that the Bible contained all of the world's wisdom. Family Bibles included copious historical materials but not of a critical nature. Rather than implying that parts of the Bible may have been culturally conditioned and thus irrelevant to modern Americans, family Bibles demonstrated how historical scholarship fully supported every text in the Bible. The purpose of biblical scholarship as used by publishers in family Bibles was not to limit the scope of the Bible but to expand it. Scholarship helped Christians to connect with the biblical past, not to be critical of it. Photography, ethnography, and historical studies provided "scientific facts" that encouraged the literal interpretation of biblical texts.

If a Bible was to make a statement about a family's religious knowledge and

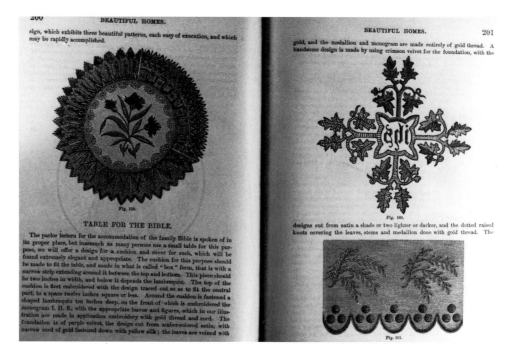

61. Tablecloths for a Bible table from Henry T. Williams and Mrs. C. S. Jones, *Beautiful Homes* (New York, 1878).

taste, it had to be displayed. Domestic art manuals gave instructions on how to construct a proper parlor lectern for formal Bible reading. Women learned how to embroider tableclothes to place under the Bible. Marble and wood brackets could be made to hold the Bible. *Household Elegancies* displayed one bracket shaped like a Gothic window, eighteen inches high and carved out of walnut.[67] In a children's story, *Jennie Prindle's Home*, a new Bible stand and grandpa's Bible (now, after his death, owned by grandma) changed not only the religious attitude of the family but also gave "a look of taste to the room."[68] A slave-owning Southern woman patronizingly approved of one of her white neighbors because she "lives very neatly – keeps a cow, a horse and garden & poultry – A large bible lay on her stand."[69] We have seen that family Bible hymns praised the memory of domestic worship rather than domestic worship itself. Likewise, when the family Bible entered the realms of fashion, its size, presentation, and elegance were relished. The display of the Bible was the crucial act.

During the nineteenth century, Victorians accepted the Bible so unquestioningly as a household decoration that fragments of its text and illustrations appeared throughout the home. Embroidered on perforated cardboard and placed in elaborately carved frames, Victorians hung biblical mottoes over doorways or high on walls. Kenneth Ames's study of more than a hundred and fifty such texts indicated that about 60 percent of the mottoes were drawn from the Bible.[70] Print companies like Currier and Ives or Prang, mass produced chromolithographs and families displayed them in similar ways.[71] Biblical themes appeared on American pottery. The U.S. Pottery Company, for instance, copied the relief mold jug of the Good Samaritan made in 1841 by Jones & Walley of Cobridge, Staffordshire. Other firms produced pottery with relief molds of Naomi and her daughter-in-law, Samuel and Eli, the death of Abel, Moses striking the rock, Ruth, Daniel in the lions' den, and St. Peter. A British firm registered a tea set with the twelve apostles in Gothic Revival style that a series of American companies copied. Produced in

62. Cross and Gothic Window bracket for a Bible from Henry T. Williams and Mrs. C. S. Jones, *Household Elegancies* (New York, 1875).

63. Cross bracket for a Bible from Henry T. Williams and Mrs. C. S. Jones, *Househod Elegancies* (New York, 1875).

large quantities, it set the standard for relief mold jugs.[72] Children played with Bible puzzles and games. Parian statues of biblical characters like the boy David or praying Samuel were placed in their rooms. Magic lantern slides entertained families with biblical stories.[73] Victorian Protestants made, bought, and displayed a biblical material culture that spoke to their religious convictions and fashionable taste.

Historian Katherine Grier has noted that the fashionable Victorian parlor functioned as a "memory palace" enabling families to retrieve personal memories

64. This salt glaze pottery tea pot was made around 1840 by the Jersey City Pottery Company. A matching milk pitcher, creamer, and sugar holder also display biblical figures.

65. Parian statues of biblical characters, like the boy David playing his lyre, brought the Bible to life through their three-dimensionality.

and communal information. Photographs, handiwork, carte de visite albums, paintings of relatives, parlor tables where family members could sit together and read, all emphasized the importance of domesticity. Parlors also reflected genteel social life and the cosmopolitan atmosphere of learning and high culture to which Victorian families aspired. Filled with globes, mineral specimens, busts of famous orators, and special books, parlors allowed families to make statements about their interests in the natural and social world around them.[74] The parlor was not merely a private world of family concerns. Through the display of cultural objects it linked the family to the world outside of the home and made unusual cultures or natural phenomena more familiar. Even modest families tried to have rooms in their homes that spoke to their domestic and cosmopolitan commitments.

The family Bible, like the parlor, also spoke to the family and cultural concerns of the Victorians. The sacred book and the special room were both intended to elicit memories and emotions from those who came in contact with them. At the same time, the Bible and the parlor contained elements of worldly learning. Neither was presented as a neutral commodity and each was highly susceptible to changes in design and fashion. As powerful symbols, the Victorians used the Bible and the parlor to recall specific ideas to the mind. The Bible and the parlor both evoked domesticity, piety, social propriety, wealth, learning, and refined sensuality. It is not surprising that the room and the book became so closely associated that the term "parlor Bible" came to mean a large Bible that demonstrated cultural sophistication rather than personal piety.

The Decline of the Family Bible

Late in 1850, in time for the Christmas season, a domestic novel called *The Wide, Wide World* appeared in American bookstores. The speed and volume of its sales far exceeded the dreams of its author, Susan Warner. This now relatively unknown novel may qualify as the first American "best seller" and only *Uncle Tom's Cabin* would rival it in sales.[75] Early in the novel, the protagonist Ellen Montgomery goes with her mother to purchase her first Bible. The shopping expedition is not merely an exercise in consumerism. Ellen's mother is deathly ill and soon will be separated from her devoted daughter. Prior to the outing, Ellen reads to her mother biblical passages that "speak of heaven and its enjoyments." Then the invalid and her daughter venture out to a jewelry store to sell a favorite ring in order to have enough money to buy the Bible and a few other supplies. Once in the bookstore, Ellen is shown dozens of Bibles. "Such beautiful Bibles she had never seen," wrote Warner, "she pored in ecstasy over their varieties of type and binding, and was very evidently in love with them all." There are large, small, and middle-sized Bibles. Black, blue, purple, and red-covered Bibles. Bibles with gilt and no gilt; clasp and no clasp. Entranced by the variety and sensuality of the books, Ellen throws "off her light bonnet, and with flushed cheek and sparkling eye, and a brow grave with unusual care" weighs the comparative advantage of her upcoming purchase. Mrs. Montgomery gazes on her daughter "with rising emotions of pleasure and pain" and eventually sheds bitter tears. Only the thought of the morning's biblical verse, "Not my will, but Thine be done," calms the worried mother. After careful discussion with her mother, Ellen decides to buy a moderately sized red one, "because it will put me in mind of yours."[76]

This scene in an extremely popular Victorian novel aptly summarizes how at mid-century the Bible brought together faith, family, and fashion. Warner depicted Bible reading between mother and daughter not exclusively as an instructive exercise but instead as an intimate exchange of earthly and divine love. The emotion that existed in the morning devotion did not remain in the home but the women extended it into the commercial environment of the bookstore. There Ellen became ecstatic not because of the words contained in the Bibles but because of their material characteristics. Susan Warner did not chide her heroine for her enthusiasm; she allowed her to relish the textures and colors of the sacred books. While the scriptures held an unchanging truth, the Bible as commodity came in a myriad of forms. Knowing that she would soon be leaving her daughter, Mrs. Montgomery experienced a combination of pleasure and pain watching her daughter with the Bibles. Tears could be shed because Ellen intended to buy not just any book. The Bible symbolized the spiritual and domestic heritage being purchased for Ellen. While Ellen and her mother were fully enmeshed in a Christian world view, we cannot overlook the fact that Susan Warner represented Bibles as being bought rather than inherited. Ellen's purchase would combine eternal truth, stylish covers, and family memories.

In the decade that *The Wide, Wide World* was published, almost three hundred *new* editions of the Bible and New Testament were published. Sixty years later, during the decade of the 1910s, that number had declined to 55 new editions. What had happened to the Bible? Why were Christians of 1910 not buying as many Bibles as they did in 1850?

Beginning in 1870, a steady decline in the publication of new editions of the Bible occurred. This was partially a result of the centralization of Bible printing in a few East coast cities and the decline of local presses. Competition with larger publishing houses forced regional printers to relinquish printing large, complex texts like the Bible. While we know that the number of editions declined, we do not know if the absolute number of Bibles printed declined. Perhaps a few large publishing houses printed as many copies of the Bible as many smaller companies. However, certain social and cultural changes lead us to suspect that the decline in Bibles paralleled a slow decline in the importance of the family Bible to many Protestants.

As Victorian sentimental culture declined after World War I, the people and ideology that had provided a context for family Bibles changed. Victorianism, basically the culture of Protestants of British-American origin, had been partially adopted by a variety of immigrants and African Americans as they tried to integrate into American life. By the 1920s that conceptual framework had been erased for many middle-class Americans. Intellectuals had questioned Victorian assumptions about race, women's nature, the economic order, and politics.[77] Realism in literature, from newspapers to novels, forced Americans to think in different ways about social and personal problems.

Nostalgia and tradition continued to be a part of the American imagination but increasingly modernist concepts of culture caught the attention of middle-class Protestants. Individual domestic objects, like Bibles or arm chairs, continued to hold personal meaning for their owners but they were now infrequently glorified in hymns, ladies' magazines, and decorating advice books. Decorators encouraged their readers and clients to take a realistic attitude toward their possessions and to relegate "objects of sentimental associations, of affected culture . . . certain heirlooms and souvenirs" to "a memory chest where the viewing of them at intervals provides a source of interest and amusement."[78] Designers no longer understood houses to be places where social, cultural and religious rituals were acted out. Instead, homes facilitated an increasingly casual and informal American life style. With the advent of electric power in the 1880s, the whole family did not need to gather around one central light source. People could read (Bibles or dime novels) throughout the house. In 1884 George Eastman patented the roll film of paper paving the way for the development of amateur photography. By the early twentieth century, photograph albums rather than the Bible contained family memories in snapshots. Americans came to prize casual and active photographs of their relatives, more appropriate for "living room" walls than for the parlor. Memory ceased to be a formal category and, as Michael Kammen neatly summarizes, "critics of a myth-making society acknowledged that its memory had been highly selective."[79]

As will be discussed in Chapter 8, not all Protestants rushed to embrace modernist views of society and the arts. For the middle-class heirs of Victorianism, however, the demise of domestic ideology meant a change in attitude toward the family Bible. By the late nineteenth century, upper middle-class Americans treated their homes like shrines to art rather than to faith or domesticity. Interior decorators enjoined their clients to create spaces for fantasy rather than faith. For the less wealthy, advice books and ladies' magazines advocated replacing the parlors with more informal "living rooms." According to Katherine Grier, by 1920 the term "living room" had replaced "parlor" in a prominent furniture trade periodical. While the displacement of the parlor by the living room was gradual and uneven, the overall cultural change was quite clear. Americans wanted their homes to be more informal and multipurpose. They wanted rooms both guests and family could use. With the decline of the servant class, middle-class women needed utilitarian homes. Houses decreased in size and included more open spaces. Rather than spend money on rooms which expressed social achievements and aesthetic taste, families wanted heating, plumbing, and electricity.[80] Automobiles rather than rooms became symbols of economic presence and cultural sophistication. The decline of the parlor as a fashionable domestic space for serious contemplation and interaction meant that the Bible had no place to be displayed. The "parlor Bible" may have continued to be passed from generation to generation but its role as a cultural signifier diminished.

Even though Bibles were tightly enmeshed in Victorian commercial and fashion economy, cultural rhetoric typically downplayed their commercial nature in order to exaggerate their sacred character. By the early decades of the twentieth century, advertising increasingly sought to promote *all* material culture as numinous and inspiring. Truly valuable objects did not have to be inherited or created through the shedding of tears; they could be easily bought at a store or ordered through a catalog. Advertisers promoted a consumer ethic based on purchasing rather than possession. Emotion still survived as a key element in promoting material culture, but advertisers cultivated it for everything they hoped to sell. As Roland Marchand relates, even a new Hoover vacuum cleaner could, according to one advertisement, elicit a "worshipful expression and posture" from stylishly dressed ladies.[81] As all commodities became marketed as sacred objects, the "original" sacred object became less special.

As Bibles lost their place in the American fashion system, publishers simplified their content and form. Biblical commentaries, histories of Palestine, and ethnographic surveys of the Middle East continued to be printed but not in family Bibles. As photography became more available and photographic reproduction cheaper, the romantic engravings of Doré were replaced by black-and-white depictions of the Holy Land. Publishers exchanged the imaginary and sensuous Middle East for realistic scenes of Palestine. Color printing of popular religious art works continued to be included in Bibles, but their drama had been diminished with the reduction of size and reproductive quality. Family records became simple and stark. As publishers eliminated supplemental material and engravings, Bibles contained only the essential Old and New Testaments. The Bible returned to being a compilation of sacred scriptures, a source for spiritual uplift and doctrinal justification. The controversies over biblical interpretation that flourished during the first third of the twentieth century were over the meaning of the sacred text, not the object.

Protestants in the nineteenth century developed a material Christianity that was aligned to the growth of sentimentality, domesticity, and industrialization. Domestic religion became associated with material Christianity because people could visually display their piety at home. Family Bibles became symbols of family stability and continuity. At the same time as Protestants stated their commitment to God and home, they could make statements about their sense of style and fashion. Material Christianity developed because lay men and women controlled what they made, bought, and displayed in their homes. The home was not the only space that lay people controlled. Domestic sentiments extended into certain public

spaces as well. With the advent of the garden cemetery, lay people became the·
creators and maintainers of sacred environments unattached to specific denominations. In Chapter 4 we shall explore how the Victorian cemetery as a Protestant
landscape reinforced the optimistic attitudes of Christians sure of their salvation.

4

The Religious Symbolism
of Laurel Hill Cemetery

In the autumn of 1835 a distraught father returned home from the grave of his five-year-old daughter. She had died that year of scarlet fever and was buried in the Philadelphia Quaker graveyard at Fourth and Arch Street. John Jay Smith, Jr. (1798–1881) was not comforted by his visit. He was alarmed instead since he was not absolutely certain he had found the grave of his daughter. Following Quaker tradition no markers were permitted on the graves. Smith also recalled that when he buried his daughter the coffin had been lowered not into the dry earth but into clay soil that acted like a cup holding accumulated water.[1] In his *Recollections* Smith accused the Quakers of "greatly neglecting the last resting-place of the people who were not without sensibility when alive. The friends of those buried long deplored this want of proper feeling."[2] For Smith the final insult to the dead would come when the Quakers built the Arch Street Meeting House on top of the old graveyard. "There is no deep cellar, it is true," Smith explained, "but the foundations displaced many bones, skulls, etc."[3]

In spite of his Quaker upbringing John Jay Smith displayed a feeling for the dead that, while contrasting with earlier Quaker traditions, reflected the sentiments of many Philadelphians. While the Society of Friends tried to guard against the excesses of mourning, expensive funeral processions, and elaborate grave markers, new attitudes toward death rituals increasingly prevailed. Unable to change the theological outlook of his denomination, as a private citizen Smith did take steps to remedy what he understood to be a serious moral problem: how to care for the dead. He also saw the possibility for a good investment. In November of 1835 Smith called together five of his friends and formed a cemetery company. Land was purchased. A year later the first burial was conducted at Laurel Hill Cemetery. Smith and the other investors struggled through the economic depression of 1837 and by the 1840s had firmly established their cemetery. According to Philadelphia's influential *Godey's Lady's Book*, Laurel Hill now served as the resting place "of our most responsible families in every walk of life."[4]

By interpreting the Christian landscape of Laurel Hill Cemetery from its founding to 1890, we can better understand how elite Philadelphians sought to elicit, control, and display their religious sensibilities. During this period the managers of the cemetery, the poet-author contributors to the Laurel Hill guidebooks, and the families who purchased funeral sculpture asserted the inherent sacredness of the cemetery. By excluding the clergy from controlling Laurel Hill, John Jay Smith and the other managers opened the cemetery to lay expressions of the meaning of death. In spite of the religious pluralism of nineteenth-century Philadelphia, the cemetery environment taught the

inconsequential nature of religious differences and contentions. The creation of
Laurel Hill Cemetery was another way that Protestants ignored denominational
boundaries and assured themselves of the existence of one single, eternal, over-
arching truth. The reverential atmosphere of the cemetery, its placement in a
timeless environment, and the creation of family shrines to the dead were all
aspects of the lay piety that flourished alongside church-bound rituals.

I hesitate to use the term "popular" piety to describe the religious sentiments
reflected in Laurel Hill. Laborers, Catholics, African Americans, the poor – a large
portion of Philadelphia's population – were excluded from being buried in the
cemetery. While many Philadelphians did not purchase graves there, they did
come to visit the cemetery once it became a major attraction in the city. The
"popular" piety expressed in the cemetery was not attacked by Philadelphia's
clergy as somehow being out of step with their own theology. Both clergy and laity
were buried in Laurel Hill. The symbols used in the cemetery were not subversive
images that spoke of an alternative Christianity attune to working-class needs. For
the most part, they had long histories in Christian iconography or were emblems
familiar from home or church. The piety expressed in Laurel Hill was "popular"
because, in the words of Jon Butler, it reflected the sentiments of "real people in
real places."[5]

While historians note that liberalizing trends in American Protestantism facilitated the spread of the rural cemetery movement, the role of the cemetery as a
repository for Christian sentiments and values has yet to be explored.[6] The
prevailing assumption is that as cemeteries moved out of the control of the clergy
they lost their religious character. Since cemeteries were not connected to a
church or denominational body, death had been secularized. Kenneth Ames in his
article on the meaning of nineteenth-century gravestones observes that "the
erosion of faith made death a phenomenon that could not be understood or
confronted in traditional terms."[7] While acknowledging that crosses (once only
used in Catholic cemeteries) were increasingly becoming popular at Mount
Auburn Cemetery, Boston, Stanley French concludes that "symbols of Christianity
were infrequently used" there.[8] For John Sears, the popularity of Victorian
cemeteries could be attributed to "the way they intensified and reflected back the
emerging fashion-conscious, status-oriented, property-owning culture of the
time."[9] What these scholars of the rural cemetery movement overlook among the
obelisks and funeral urns is the persistent use of traditionally Christian themes and
symbols. For the Victorians, Christianity was not antithetical to ostentatious
display. In the rush to define the cemetery as a secularized space free from
Protestant denominational control, historians neglect to take into account the
fundamentally religious outlook of middle-class Americans during the nineteenth
century. Christianity was not a minor theme in the rural cemetery movement; it
was the reason Victorians could assert their right to immortality.

The Victorian cemetery played an important function in the religious lives of
urban Protestants. As Jon Butler perceptively recognizes, the Puritan model of
American religious historiography assumes only Catholics have sacred places. The
traditional scholarly assumption has been that "Protestantism centers itself on
grace, not place."[10] While the lack of substantial primary documentation limits our
interpretation of Laurel Hill, there is no question but that the cemetery functioned
as a sacred place for nineteenth-century Philadelphians.[11] We cannot be certain
why Philadelphians wanted to be buried in Laurel Hill, although we know that it

was *the* fashionable city cemetery. Likewise we know that during the mid-nineteenth century thousands of people visited the cemetery, but we do not know what conflicts arose as different people used the cemetery for different purposes. Since the feelings of the people who used the cemetery have not been preserved, we are left with the religious landscape of the cemetery itself to help us decipher Victorian attitudes about death and after death. This chapter argues that Laurel Hill was not only a sacred place, it was a Christian (qua Protestant) place. The Victorian cemetery, as much as the church or the revival meeting campground, was a Protestant landscape.

The Rural Cemetery Movement

John Jay Smith's disgust at Quaker burial practices reminds us that by 1835 traditional Christian burial customs were no longer accepted by urban Protestants. What unnerved Smith was the idea that individual grave sites could not be recognized and that dead bones were being dug up. Smith rejected the long-standing Christian attitude that "normal" dead bodies should not be accorded special treatment. While the ancient Greeks and Romans often carved portraits on tombs or painted images of the dead on wooden markers, Christians turned away from the pretentious tomb as a symbol of worldly concern.[12] Only the remains of holy men and women deserved special respect and these might be buried in the church. The more well-to-do were buried along an outer wall of the churchyard under a covered arcade. For most people, however, gravediggers dug holes and placed corpses in communal, unmarked graves in the ground around the church. Bodies were piled on top of each other and eventually decomposed. The dried bones could then be removed (perhaps to an ossuary) if more space was required. For medieval Catholics, it was important to be buried near the relics of a saint preserved in the church and to pay for masses to be said to hasten the soul's journey to heaven. Communal burials stressed the importance of group membership over individual autonomy. Prayers, not place, tied the living to the dead.

Until the nineteenth century, most people did not put their dead in individual tombs or construct permanent graves. It was only in the twelfth century that funerary monuments began to be constructed for notable clergy and leaders that included their names, dates of birth and death, and a summary of their accomplishments.[13] Eventually the very wealthy built family chapels called chantries within churches. Here masses and prayers could be continually said for the dead. By the end of the eighteenth century, artisans were making wooden crosses for individuals who were not nobles, clergy, or wealthy. Many of these markers decayed over time and the grave sites eventually were indistinguishable from the rest of the land. Permanent graves were not commonplace in early modern Europe.

With the coming of the Reformation some customs began to change. Because the Reformers rejected the existence of purgatory and prayers for the dead, families no longer attended to their dead through masses or prayers. In 1517 Martin Luther called his colleagues in Wittenberg to consider the thesis that: "They preach only human doctrines who say that as soon as the money clinks into the money chest, the soul flies out of purgatory" (Thesis No. 28). Hiring a priest to say prayers only made the clergy rich and the soul no better off. According to Protestant theologians, each individual was responsible for the fate of his or her own soul. The living could have no impact on the dead.[14] Protestantism stripped death rites of any religious significance, and so the clergy lost power in defining what families could do to ease their grief. Since families did not need priests to say masses, households made statements about the memory of their dead free from clerical control. Wealthy Protestants did not save their money by burying their dead in the common grave. They constructed family funerary chapels and individual grave plots. Physical monuments replaced verbal prayers as the way that the living connected with the dead.

By the eighteenth century, Humanist notions of the importance of the individual combined with the Protestant belief in personal salvation to make the communal grave seem repugnant, even for the unwashed masses.[15] Concerns for clean air and open spaces motivated enlightened Europeans to condemn the churchyard as a spawning place for disease and a danger to public health. Burial grounds were taken out of the control of the clergy and given over to civil officials. In France Napoleonic reform conferred on citizens the right to their own individual graves. The wealthy could make these graves permanent by obtaining a "concession" described as "a distinct and separate place where people can establish graves for themselves, their relatives, and heirs, and where they can construct vaults, monuments, or tombs."[16] As the middle class became more financially powerful, they imitated the aristocratic penchant for constructing family funerary chapels and monuments. By the nineteenth century, it was generally assumed in Europe and America that everyone had the right to his or her own grave.

The rural cemetery movement resulted from changing attitudes toward death that emphasized the importance of individual and permanent graves. With the opening in 1804 of the Parisian cemetery Père Lachaise, a new standard was set for the creation of burial parks separated from religious control. Landscaped with elegant trees and luxuriant vegetation, Père Lachaise's winding paths encouraged the visitor to meditate not on the finality of death but on the glories of heaven. By the height of its popularity in 1825, visitors to Père Lachaise could pause at the tomb of the lovers Abelard and Héloïse, marvel at the view of Paris, and derive moral uplift from the aesthetic sculpture placed throughout the cemetery. Gone were the epitaphs and grave markers warning of the unpredictable character of death. In spite of the over twenty-six thousand monuments, irregularities of the terrain, and dense forestation that necessitated the use of a guidebook, Père Lachaise's prominence went unchallenged until the development of similar cemeteries in Britain and America.

During the 1820s and 1830s reform movements in the English-speaking world echoed the desire of the French to place cemeteries under private control, situate them in a natural environment free from urban blight, and display gravestones that promoted civic and domestic values.[17] The rural cemetery movement culminated in the establishment of modified versions of Père Lachaise in most British and American cities: Low Hill General (Liverpool, 1825); Mount Auburn (Boston, 1831); Kensal Green (London, 1833); Laurel Hill (Philadelphia, 1836); Greenwood (Brooklyn, 1838); Highgate (London, 1839); Allegheny (Pittsburgh, 1844); Spring Grove (Cincinnati, 1845); and Hollywood (Richmond, Virginia, 1849). These cemeteries and many others established throughout the century sought to tame the pain of death by providing comfort and moral instruction. Picturesque landscapes purified the sentiments of visitors while monuments to the dead evoked a sense of history, continuity, and patriotism. Cemetery founders expressed very practical, hygienic reasons for the establishment of cemeteries outside of the city limits, but Stanley French justifiably notes that "the rural cemetery through its intended capacity as cultivator of the finer emotions was another facet of the conservative cultural uplift movement during the Age of the Common Man."[18]

The Landscape of Life after Death

Laurel Hill was not the first cemetery in Philadelphia free from clerical control. As early as 1825, private citizens ran six cemeteries in the city. Ronaldson's cemetery, an elegantly landscaped downtown cemetery founded in 1827, served for many years as the city's model burial place. Its symmetry and parallel lines of graves reflected the popular fascination with classical architecture and design. Prominent Philadelphia churches like Christ Church could not offer much more to their parishioners. Because of urban growth, congregations had to buy land away from the church in order to bury their dead. Private cemeteries such as Ronaldson's assumed that Philadelphians preferred to be buried not with their fellow Episcopalians, Presbyterians, or Quakers but with others of similar social and philosophical outlook. John Jay Smith's idea of a private, for-profit cemetery was not novel. He followed a pattern already established in the city.

A year after their initial November meeting, Smith purchased thirty-two acres of land that had been a country estate and later a failed Catholic boarding school.

66. "Central View of Laurel Hill Cemetery" from *Guide to Laurel Hill Cemetery Near Philadelphia with Numerous Illustrations* (Philadelphia, 1844).

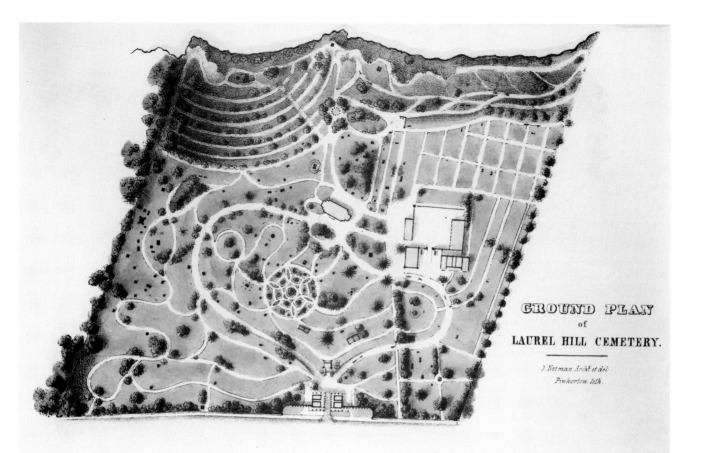

GROUND PLAN
of
LAUREL HILL CEMETERY.

J. Notman Arch.t et del.
Pinkerton lith.

67.   Like the other "garden" cemeteries of Britain and France, Laurel Hill was a planned cemetery. Its managers took particular pride in its designed buildings and the horticultural specimens planted throughout its grounds. "Ground Plan of Laurel Hill Cemetery" from *Guide to Laurel Hill Cemetery Near Philadelphia with Numerous Illustrations* (Philadelphia, 1844).

Situated high on a hill four miles out of town and three miles down the picturesque Schuylkill River, the land had already been partially landscaped. In 1837 the legislature of the state of Pennsylvania approved the establishment of the Laurel Hill Cemetery Company made up of: John J. Smith, Nathan Dunn, Benjamin W. Richards, Frederick Brown, William M. Meredith, Edward Coleman, George N. Baker, Henry Toland, and Nicholas Biddle. Four men, Smith, Dunn, Richards, and Brown, were named as "Managers." They accepted the responsibility to lay out the grounds, construct and alter buildings, arrange burial lots, and set up cemetery rules and regulations. They also oversaw the publication of guides to the cemetery.[19] Sometime in the 1840s, Lloyd P. Smith was added as manager after the death of Nathan Dunn. From then on those four men (or their sons) ran the cemetery as a business into the twentieth century.

John Jay Smith, the main force behind the founding of Laurel Hill, was a member of the Philadelphia Quaker elite. His entrepreneurial activities included serving as secretary of a company that organized Conestoga wagon trains from Philadelphia to Pittsburgh and arranging the meeting that resulted in the formation of the Girard Life Insurance Company. He combined an astute business acumen with an interest in the arts and sciences. For over twenty years he was director of the Philadelphia Library Company where he worked each morning before attending to Laurel Hill business. A member of the Academy of Natural Sciences, Smith edited Downing's *Horticulturist*. He also acted as the treasurer of the Athenian Institute. Like many Philadelphia gentlemen, Smith moved easily between the business world and the world of arts and sciences. His connections

Jno Jay Smith

68. John Jay Smith Jr. from J. Thomas Scharf and Thomas Westcott, *History of Philadelphia, 1609–1884* (Philadelphia, 1884).

throughout the city were substantial and mutually supportive. It is not surprising that the creation and management of Laurel Hill Cemetery allowed Smith to combine his interests in horticulture and the arts as well as develop a sound financial investment. Smith most likely also had personal reasons for building Laurel Hill. Altogether three of his seven children died while young.

During the nineteenth century it was not easy to get to the cemetery. It took between an hour and a half and two hours to get to Laurel Hill from Philadelphia. By building the cemetery far from town, Smith avoided any hint that his cemetery was in competition with cemeteries still sponsored by churches. Some clergy

69. The distance between Laurel Hill and central Philadelphia helped create the idea that the river excursion was symbolic of life's journey and that the visitor was on a pilgrimage to a sacred place. "Landing at Laurel Hill" from *Smith's Illustrated Guide To and Through Laurel Hill Cemetery* (Philadelphia, 1852).

complained that "the time for attendance [at Laurel Hill funerals] was too long to suit their other duties."[20] The cemetery was not constructed with the clergy in mind. However, by the 1830s Protestant ministers (even the Methodists) were promoting the importance of "pious consumption." Lori Merish argues that Protestant writers and clergy, even the frontier preacher Peter Cartwright, acknowledged the "civilizing" influence of luxury and tasteful surroundings. While ministers might have grumbled about the long trip to Laurel Hill, they supported the idea that a tasteful environment spiritualized the self and animated economic and moral progress.[21] Laurel Hill, as we will see, became the resting place for pious preachers as well as for Philadelphia's Protestant elite.

Smith and his colleagues not only snapped up cheap land outside of the city, they also tapped into traditional Christian notions of pilgrimage. To go to the cemetery entailed thought and planning. While the professional clergy might have found the distance inconvenient, for the person who was accompanying a funeral or visiting the dead the distance heightened the meaning of the cemetery. Cemetery guidebooks poetically suggested visitors see themselves as "pilgrims" and the river excursion as symbolic of life's journey. As the pilgrim boarded the hourly steamboat up the Schuylkill River, he or she duplicated the journey of the soul to its resting place. Like the soul itself, the pilgrim journeyed on the ferry of Christianity as it steered the soul across the currents and eddies of life to an arrival at the other side, the haven of heaven. Once safely on the shore, the pilgrim looked back on the now conquered river:

"Through the green vista see the tranquil river,"

mused Mrs. Barton Stout,

"Bathed in the rosy sunset's richest glow!
The sparkling waves lift up their voices ever,
And murmur music in their onward flow!"[22]

Even with the establishment by 1865 of a road along the river, the building of Fairmount Park adjacent to the cemetery, and its eventual access by the Philadelphia & Reading Railroad, the guidebooks insisted that Laurel Hill was "peculiarly and perfectly protected from encroachments by its surroundings."[23] The journey from life to death, in spite of the realities of improved transportation, must not be too easy. The traveler to Laurel Hill became a pilgrim to a sacred place.

Sacred spaces are marked off from profane space, carved out of the ordinary environment. Rituals, ceremonies, and religious gestures can be conducted there because the area itself is special. According to *Godey's Lady's Book* there "was something in the atmosphere of the place which comes over the spirit like echoed music or remembered affection, soothing even the most worldly minded into religious awe and the desire of a happy immortality."[24] The owners and managers of Laurel Hill consciously tried to create an atmosphere in the cemetery that was different from that in Philadelphia. They wanted the cemetery to be like a church and exude a reverential atmosphere. "Let no man tread with levity or profaneness the mazes of the cemetery grounds," explained the 1844 guide, "it [the cemetery] is the Christian's commentary on the truths and hopes he holds most sacred."[25] By purchasing the land in front of the cemetery, the owners believed they had prevented "the proximity of taverns, or objectionable buildings" from impinging on the sacred space of Laurel Hill.[26] The environment surrounding Laurel Hill needed to reflect its special status.

It was not only the space that needed to be purified through separation. By limiting who could gain access to its precincts, the cemetery became an exclusive and sacred place. Beginning with the 1837 rules and regulations, and continuing throughout the nineteenth century, the managers restricted families to burying only "white persons."[27] Marginal Philadelphians such as African Americans or the poor were excluded entirely. The managers primarily sold plots to families. Single interments, "either for strangers or others," were separated from the family plots.[28] Only socially "significant" families were welcome in the cemetery. As with all sacred places, those in power define who can and cannot approach sanctified ground. The space itself acts as a means to categorize people. To encourage the proper respectful attitude, no dogs, saddle horses, or picnics were permitted in the grounds. Even visitors were restricted. Sundays at the cemetery, the day which most Philadelphians had free from work, were limited to "funerals, and the relations and friends accompanying them; or to lot-holders on foot with their tickets, (which are in no case transferable) with members of their families, or friends in company."[29] Visitors on other days had to secure tickets from John Jay Smith or one of his associates so as "to prevent the admission of improper persons."[30] By restricting who could be buried in the cemetery and who could visit it, the managers of the cemeteries set apart the space as special and

70. The owners and managers of Laurel Hill cemetery restricted burials in the cemetery and attempted to control visitation. "The Grave of David W. Gihon" from *Smith's Illustrated Guide To and Through Laurel Hill Cemetery* (Philadelphia, 1852).

privileged. Just as only an ordained clergyman could mount the pulpit at church so only the "proper" people could be buried at Laurel Hill. Laurel Hill served as one more reminder of class divisions in urban Philadelphia.

In 1840 the corpse of Revolutionary War general Hugh Mercer was removed from the Episcopalian Christ Church burial ground by the St. Andrew's Thistle Society, eulogized at the Presbyterian Church on Washington Square, and reinterred at Laurel Hill. Mr. William B. Reed who delivered the eulogy remarked that when the first funeral rite was performed "over the body of Mercer, with its death-wounds fresh and bloody, [it] taught to a struggling people the lesson of patriotic martyrdom. When we, their children, assemble for these new obsequies, the blood which has poured from those wounds has long since mingled with the earth – the blessings which it earned have been enjoyed by generation after generation."[31] Mercer's removal to Laurel Hill was not merely a step in recognizing the merits of a dead war hero. It was an effort by Philadelphians to claim and to create sacred characters. The space of the cemetery was made religious not merely by limiting who could enter the grounds; the burial of national heroes and martyrs heightened the sanctity of the area.

Large sections of the Laurel Hill guidebooks commented on both the public and private virtues of the people buried in the cemetery. Philadelphia notables such as Commodore Isaac Hull and Commodore Alexander Murray, both originally buried at the First Presbyterian Church, were reinterred in Laurel Hill. The guidebooks always included the names of interred clergy at the front of the list of plot-holders, and one late nineteenth-century history of the city included all the names of clergy from the Presbyterian, Episcopal, Methodist, Lutheran, and

71. In this engraving of "Old Mortality, His Pony, and Sir Walter Scott" a well-dressed couple leave the cemetery ground, ignoring a beggar and her baby. Beggars often assembled outside of churches to plead for charity from the attending congregation. That they would also beg for alms outside of Laurel Hill underscores the cemetery's function both as sacred space and a gathering place for Philadelphia's elite. "Old Mortality" from R. A. Smith, *Philadelphia As It Is* (Philadelphia, 1852).

Baptist churches buried in Laurel Hill.[32] The guidebooks assumed that visitors should admire the achievements of these sacred characters. Protestants who did not have a formal cult of the saints developed the equivalent through their popular piety. More than moral guides, the noted dead of Laurel Hill were mythical ancestors who through their presence helped maintain the sanctity of the site. Early Christians and medieval Catholics wanted to touch relics of the saints and be buried near the graves of holy people. The promoters of Laurel Hill also cultivated this traditional Christian behavior.

John Jay Smith estimated that during the year 1860 almost a hundred and forty thousand visitors entered the cemetery.[33] With so many people wandering the cemetery grounds, there was probably a certain level of noise and confusion that reflected the business of Philadelphia streets more than the quiet of a church. As I discussed in Chapter 1, the distinction between the sacred and the profane cannot be as radical as Emile Durkheim and other religious scholars would lead us to believe. We can speculate that some "improper" people entered and enjoyed the cemetery. An engraving from *Philadelphia As It Is* (1852) shows a woman and her baby begging in front of one of the cemetery's main monuments. R. A. Smith, the author of the book, made no mention of the beggars. When in that same year he again published the engraving in *Smith's Illustrated Guide To and Through Laurel Hill Cemetery*, the beggars were eliminated. We can assume that the cemetery

72. During the nineteenth century, an elaborate mourning and burial cult evolved in the United States. Social custom dictated that after funerals families would maintain their graves as if they were shrines complete with flowers, plants, and neatly painted iron fencing. Burial rituals, such as those at Laurel Hill and other Victorian cemeteries, assured families that the memory of their loved ones would not die, thus binding the living to the dead.

managers did not want anything to compromise the idea of Laurel Hill as a place for well-dressed strolling couples. Just as the cemetery managers sought to eliminate the fear of death by evoking the Christian promise of eternity, so they strove to present Laurel Hill as a place of "saints" and not "sinners." Beggars, laborers, and people with picnics probably entered the grounds and enjoyed the environment in their own ways. Unfortunately, their stories have not been preserved.

Laurel Hill was designed and promoted as a sacred space where it was appropriate for proper people to express refined sentiments. As we have seen in Chapter 3, affectionate religion permitted the expression of emotions as a way of stimulating piety. During the nineteenth century, an elaborate mourning and burial cult evolved.[34] Social custom dictated that after the funeral families maintain their burial shrines with flowers, plants, and neatly painted iron fencing. *Smith's Illustrated Guide* recalled "with melancholy pleasure, the visitors to these and kindred spots trimming the shrubbery and flowers that sprout up from the graves of their kindred, and, as they handled the yielding branches, we also imagined that the dead stretched forth their leafy arms from the earth, to embrace once more those whom they had so fondly loved."[35] Since Protestants typically did not believe that their prayers influenced the state of the dead, visiting graves and taking care of grave plots tied the living to the dead. Like the placement of a lock of a dead baby's hair in a Bible, cemetery rituals assured families that the memory of loved ones would not die. Laurel Hill was not constructed to separate the living from the dead but rather to allow the living to control their communications with the dead.

The cemetery managers urged visitors to let their higher sentiments be touched by the natural beauty of Laurel Hill. John Jay Smith especially sought to combine the best of landscape gardening with the wild beauty of a hilly river front to provoke refined sensibilities. Guidebooks hailed the rugged beauty of the cemetery: "Every mind capable of appreciating the beautiful in nature," one instructed, "must admire its gentle declivities, its expansive lawns, its hill beetling over the picturesque stream, its rugged ascents, its flowery dells, its rocky ravines, and its river-washed borders."[36] On the one hand, wild nature invoked feelings of the sublime. The sublimity of nature lifted the emotions by stimulating feelings of awe, admiration, and astonishment. On the other hand, the cultivated nature of Laurel Hill moved its visitors to feel the beauty of the picturesque. Wild nature could be savage and unmanageable, but when controlled by the human hand nature became the servant of humanity. Laurel Hill was a means by which urban Philadelphians could experience what historian Catherine Albanese calls "nature religion."[37] They felt both the awesome and intimate character of the divine through the natural environment. According to the literature provided by the cemetery company, planted and wild nature never conflicted with one another. All forms of nature existed to help pilgrims evoke, purify, and preserve their sentiments for the dead. Philadelphians did not have to journey into the wilderness. To experience the feelings romantic poets and novelists described, they could travel to Laurel Hill and participate in a landscape of sentiment.

The emphasis on the natural beauty of Laurel Hill was not merely a selling point during a time before public parks. By stressing the cultivated character of nature, the creators of the cemetery illustrated the Christian promise of life after death. In spite of its ubiquitous character, death's unpredictability challenges the orderliness of everyday existence. Death forces us to face the chaotic, alienating side of nature. Christianity denied the permanence of death and thus transformed death from being the natural end of life to being a passageway into a new life. Just as humanity triumphed over nature by cultivating it into a garden, so did the Christian defeat death through his or her belief in Christ. Through the Christian message, one controlled and cheated death. Laurel Hill provided a developed environment that symbolically allowed the visitor to experience death not as uncontrollable and alienating but as the beginning of an ordered eternal life with Christ.

As with the Victorian parlor, the cemetery was not merely a place for exploring emotions and cultivating religious sentiment. High-minded Protestants expected their feelings to be closely linked to their intellects. Laurel Hill was more than a garden with dramatic vistas. It also was a walk-through textbook where one could learn about nature as well as experience it. John Jay Smith, an amateur botanist, saw to it that the names of the trees planted in the cemetery were all listed in the guidebooks. Andrew Jackson Downing remarked that Laurel Hill was especially rich in rare trees and that "it is a better arboretum than can easily be found elsewhere in the country."[38] Laurel Hill's landscape entranced Philadelphians on a variety of levels. Education of the mind was not separated from education of the heart.

In the mid-1830s when Smith and his company purchased the land of Laurel Hill, the area was rural and unpopulated. By the 1850s industrial Philadelphia had intruded on the bucolic. "The occasional sound of the boatman's horn, borne from the passing canal boat on the opposite side of the river," observed an 1852 guidebook, "or the whistle of locomotives, which ever and anon are seen whirling

73. Illustrations of the vistas seen from Laurel Hill clearly depict factories and smokestacks nestled in the landscape. Factories and commercial establishments were not to be avoided, rather they were positive signs of social progress. "View from South Laurel Hill of the Village at the Falls of the Schuylkill" from *Smith's Illustrated Guide To and Through Laurel Hill Cemetery* (Philadelphia, 1852).

their immense trains across the distant bridge, comes wafted on the breeze." It quickly concluded: "they interrupt not ... but rather enhance, by contrast, the repose of the scene."[39] The same book took great pride in noting the commercial buildings one could see on a trip to Laurel Hill: the Merchants' Exchange, the Jayne Building, and even the 984 ft. long Reading Railroad bridge that brought a "shrill whistle and tumultuous noise" into the cemetery.[40] Illustrations of the vistas seen from Laurel Hill frankly depicted factories and smokestacks nestled in the landscape. In contrast with the erasure of the beggar from cemetery illustrations, signs of commercial life frequently were found in guidebooks. Beggars, perceived as non-productive members of society, had no place in a perfected landscape. However, for mid-century urban dwellers industrialization was not despised. Factories and commercial establishments were positive signs of progress. Progress belonged on earth and existed in heaven.[41] Change and movement were essential for physical and spiritual growth.

Laurel Hill was not a retreat from industrialization but a place to view the factories, railroads, and commercial buildings while not feeling overwhelmed by them. The cemetery, both physically and metaphorically, gave Philadelphians distance from the city while encouraging them to reflect upon the "contrasts" of this vision. When viewed from the sacred groves of the cemetery, the industrializing world looked ordered and harmonious. Laurel Hill's promoters encouraged Philadelphians to stand back from the profane elements of the city, not to ignore them. Commercial life did not require the rejection of religion. High religious thoughts did not have to conflict with everyday life. Laurel Hill blessed and refined commercial and industrial life.

That John Jay Smith moved easily between seeing Laurel Hill as an experiment in landscape gardening, a profit-making endeavor, and as a sentimental and religious outlet underlines the integrative nature of popular piety. Rather than separate religious experience from the worlds of money, art, science, or even entertainment, middle-class Philadelphians linked together these diverse strains of nineteenth-century life. Unlike a revival meeting or church sermon where clergymen elicited religious response through manipulating verbal images, lay men created a non-verbal Protestant landscape at Laurel Hill. The everyday and the extraordinary merged. The everyday was raised to a higher, more significant level and the extraordinary was brought down into the realm of the human. It is exactly this integrative nature of popular piety that makes it popular. In 1849 Andrew Jackson Downing complained that people go to cemeteries "to enjoy themselves, and not to indulge in any serious recollections or regrets."[42] Downing hoped that the creation of public parks would remedy this problem. He did not understand that it was precisely the unification of entertainment, leisure, sentiment, and piety that motivated people to flock to the cemeteries. As urban living became more specialized and fragmented, Philadelphians sought the reassurance of a cemetery where an apparent harmony existed between science, art, religion, social status, and business. Just as John Jay Smith perceived no apparent contradiction between the profit-making status of the cemetery and its spiritual nature, so the visitors to Laurel Hill could be uplifted and entertained at the same time.

Christian Immortality in Stone

One element of Laurel Hill's popularity at mid-century was its ability physically to articulate the Christian promise of eternal life. Philadelphian Protestants were not secularized Americans who strolled in the cemetery because they appreciated the outdoors. The cemetery reinforced the belief that by following Christ's message they would be assured a place in heaven. For the Christian, death was only a brief pause in the continuation of life. Cemeteries like Laurel Hill were not places of death, they were environments of resurrection and immortality. Protestants who were helpless to secure their loved ones a place in heaven after their death needed physical reminders that death was not the end of life. Since they could not buy masses to hasten their family's travel to paradise, they built physical landscapes of eternal life. Laurel Hill Cemetery utilized a constellation of symbols to assure Philadelphians of immortality.

In 1836 a young Scot, John Notman, won the design competition for the construction of Laurel Hill. His Grecian design for the entrance gateway was chosen over two more daring Egyptian Revival designs by architects William Strickland and T. U. Walters. Although Egyptian Revival architecture evoked the memory of immortal pharaohs buried beneath massive pyramids and was used for the gateway at Boston's famous Mount Auburn Cemetery, Greek Revival seemed more in keeping with Philadelphia's architectural outlook. In 1836 the three major buildings in Philadelphia, the United States Bank, the Mint, and the Merchants' Exchange, were all designed in some variety of Greek Revival architecture. When describing the Doric design of the U.S. Bank (the same design Notman chose for Laurel Hill's entrance) one critic called it a "defiance to the elements and to time

74. "Entrance to Laurel Hill Cemetery, Philadelphia." John Notman's 1836 design for Laurel Hill's gateway reflected the popularity for Greek revival architecture. The stability, duration, and eternal quality of classical designs suited a cemetery whose owners and users assumed the immortality of the soul.

itself."[43] The stability, duration, and eternal quality of Greek designs eminently suited a cemetery whose owners and users assumed the immortality of the soul.

Just as Greek architecture was timeless and eternal, so the grounds of Laurel Hill reflected that eternity. Laurel Hill's "dry soil" and "undulating surface" would not be transformed into mud and washed away like the clay-earth of the city.[44] Unlike the graveyard of Philadelphia's First Presbyterian Church, "the site of which is now occupied by extensive storehouses," Laurel Hill's managers guaranteed to plot-owners perpetual maintenance of the grounds.[45] Quaker Mercy Carlisle, the first person buried (or rather reinterred) in Laurel Hill, might rest assured that no Quaker meeting house would be built on top of her grave as once had happened at Fourth and Arch Street. According to the guidebooks, Laurel Hill was not a city cemetery soon forgotten, nor a family-farm burial ground where in one case "the new occupants ceased to reverence the graves of the family, and a cart-lane was opened over the spot."[46] The dead of Laurel Hill would never be forgotten.

To erase the feeling of time from the cemetery, Laurel Hill's owners and managers encouraged plot-owners to use materials that resisted the aging process. The 1844 guidebook asked plot-owners to use granite for monuments since marble, although beautiful at first, too soon wore away. Iron railings that rusted were condemned. Hedges of holly should be planted because of "its slowness of growth, patience of the shears, and length of life."[47] Certainly practical, economic, and stylistic concerns also dictated the choice of those materials but to overlook their symbolic importance denies the full impact of Laurel Hill. The cemetery stood as a monument to memory and any sign of decay weakened its ability to assure Philadelphians of their immortality. There was, in effect, no real death.

After entering through the Doric gateway, the visitor faced a group of sculptures in an "ornamental temple" that acted as the cemetery's chief shrine and main symbol.[48] James Thom's sculptured group *Old Mortality, his Pony, and Sir Walter Scott*, reflected the popular view of immortality promoted by Laurel Hill (see Illustration 71). The statues retell the tale, popularized by Sir Walter Scott, of an old man in Scotland who traveled across the land with his pony restoring the gravestone epitaphs of martyred Presbyterians. The old man, whom Scott called a "religious itinerant," was known as "Old Mortality."[49] Old Mortality, a timeless character, brought the dead back to life by enabling the memories of their righteousness to survive. The owners of Laurel Hill frequently recalled how the statue group itself had been broken and through its purchase and display at the cemetery brought back to life. "As Old Mortality loved to repair defaced tombstones," the guidebooks recounted, "so the originators of the plan of the Cemetery hope it may be the study of their successors to keep the place in perpetual repair, and to transmit it undefaced to a distant date."[50] The resurrection motif thus appeared in four layers: Old Mortality brought the memory of the righteous back to life; the noted Sir Walter Scott revived the story of the forgotten religious itinerant; the owners of the cemetery reassembled the broken statue; and the future caretakers assured the eternal continuation of Laurel Hill.

Inside of the cemetery families constructed shrines to their dead that also emphasized timelessness and eternity. Confronted with the traditional Protestant suspicion of images, Philadelphians initially faced the problem of how to assemble a set of symbols that spoke to their Christian belief in everlasting life. In the early years of the cemetery, gravestone carvers remedied this problem by appropriating neoclassical designs that symbolized the durable character of republican virtues. Non-Christian symbols gathered from the ancient cultures of Greece, Rome, Egypt, and the Orient became available to funerary designers via reference volumes such as J. N. B. Durand's *Recueil et parallèle des édifices de tout genre, anciens et modernes* (1800). Designers of grave markers borrowed ideas from eighteenth-century Italian artist Giovanni Battista Piranesi whose engravings and etchings of ancient ruins profoundly influenced nineteenth-century neoclassical architecture. By the 1830s, the cemetery of Père Lachaise was a model for all garden cemeteries, and guides such as *Promenade aux cimitières de Paris* (1823) were popular souvenirs.[51] I do not want to argue that Laurel Hill's non-Christian symbols were insignificant. As in similar cemeteries, pyramids, obelisks, funeral urns, broken columns, and upside-down torches proliferated. What I do insist is that we recognize how traditional Christian symbols linked Victorians to past religious stories, behaviors, and values that centered around immortality. What they saw in the cemetery reflected what they heard in church and experienced at home.

By the 1850s Philadelphians had weathered a series of religious revivals that fired up their enthusiasm for evangelical Protestantism. Starting in the 1820s, businessmen were caught up in revivals that made them add prayer meetings and Bible study groups to their commercial activities.[52] Anti-slavery movements, tract societies, benevolent associations, and missionary activities flourished. Revival ministers preached personal piety and business integrity. In 1854 the young John

Wanamaker, who would become famous for his department store, was hired to run the YMCA. His evangelical fervor accompanied his growing commercial successes. By 1876 he was wealthy enough to rent and furnish a Pennsylvania Railroad freight warehouse for Dwight Moody's two-month evangelical crusade.[53] In Philadelphia religion went hand-in-hand with business and commerce. Just as factories were included in cemetery illustrations and beggars were not, mid-century Protestantism accommodated wealth better than poverty.

Romanticism, which had spread from Europe to the New World, gave Protestants a means to express their Christian piety visually. Gothic Revival became an acceptable mode of church design in the 1840s, and throughout the nineteenth century Protestants reinterpreted medieval styles to suit their theological and cultural orientation.[54] Philadelphia's Episcopal churches built in Gothic design include St. Mark's (1849) and St. Clement's (1857) as well as several designed by architect Napoleon Le Brun. John Notman, who designed Laurel Hill's front entrance, designed Calvary Presbyterian Church (1851) in Gothic style. In 1856 even the Moravians built a Gothic style church. If a new church could not be built, a steeple could be added to make the building look more classically Christian. St. Peter's Episcopal Church built in 1758 added a steeple in 1842, the Seventh Presbyterian Church (Tabernacle) added a steeple around 1860, and the Fifth Baptist Church added one in 1863. According to Philadelphian Gideon Burton, Episcopalians frequently put crosses on their steeples.[55] *Godey's Lady's Book* printed engravings of Gothic-styled household goods. Issues included illustrations of a pin cushion built like a church, a prie-dieu with a crown of thorns stitched on the kneeler, and a paperweight with a chapel inside.[56] Revivalism in Philadelphia stirred up Christian piety and fashionable Gothic designs made it acceptable to place Christian symbols on almost any object.

As Christian images came into vogue, Philadelphians turned a skeptical eye on their past fascination for classical pagan designs. In 1852 R. A. Smith's guide criticized the monuments of a "dial of a clock and the goddess of Liberty" assembled west of the grave of "Little Willie." Such allegories were "in exceeding bad taste" because people did not understand their meanings. Appropriate symbols were "intelligible" but classical allegories were "a sealed language." Smith condemned "the intruding of anachronisms and mythology into such sacred places as Christian cemeteries." To help remedy the problem of pagan images that were incomprehensible, Smith pointed out the Christian meaning of a carved fountain and broken pitcher by quoting a biblical passage referring to death as a pitcher "broken at the fountain" (Eccles. 11:6–7). Smith apparently felt compelled to distinguish between the "intelligible" Christian symbols of Laurel Hill and the "sealed language" of republican allegory too often found in the cemetery.[57] We cannot determine how many families utilized classical or Christian images because of the steady deterioration of the cemetery. However, many of the enduring grave markers constructed between 1838 and 1890 display explicitly Christian themes of resurrection and hope.

During the second half of the nineteenth century three major Christian symbols were employed in the cemetery: the cross, the book, and the angel. Because of its direct connection with the Resurrection, the cross was the most widespread symbol. The empty cross, like the empty tomb, was a sign of the resurrected Christ. Unlike Catholics who meditated on the suffering body of Christ, Protestants preferred the cross without reference to bodily pain. Christ who had

triumphed over death was the key to immortal existence. "For in Adam all die," Philadelphians read in their Bibles, "even so in Christ shall all be made alive" (I Cor. 15:22). The iconography and landscape of the cemetery assured Philadelphians that true believers (at least those buried in Laurel Hill) would live forever. The issues of possible damnation or spiritual oblivion were not articulated or reinforced. Laurel Hill preached immortality through Christ, not judgment.

A popular rendition of the cross was to sculpt it with leaves and flowers at its base or "growing" around the structure. Guides to the cemetery also illustrated real foliage climbing up a simple cross. The foliage softened the impact of the cross by adding the appearance of life on to the barren "wood." Although the cross was the place where Christ died, the growing ivy or flowers indicated that from death came life. "I am the vine, you are the branches," Jesus said, "He who lives in me and I in him, will produce abundantly, for apart from me you can do nothing" (John 15:5). The flowering cross was also a variation on the Tree of Life, one of the trees in the Garden of Eden (Gen. 2:9). The fruit that Adam and Eve ate from the Tree of Knowledge caused their expulsion from paradise and eventual death. That Eden tree (made of living matter) served only to condemn humankind to suffering and mortality. As an antitype to the Tree of Knowledge, the cross (made of dead wood) enabled the Christian to live eternally. From apparent death sprang forth life. Thus the cross came to be equated with the Tree of Life. Through Christ's sacrifice on the cross, humanity finally had access to the fruit of eternal life. The flowering cross symbolized the Tree of Life that Christians could now eat from and live forever (Gen. 3:22).

75. The empty cross, like the empty tomb, was a sign of the resurrection of Christ. It proclaimed the Christian promise of immortality from *Guide to Laurel Hill Cemetery Near Philadelphia with Numerous Illustrations* (Philadelphia, 1844).

76. Crosses placed on graves frequently had carved foliage symbolizing the life that would come from death; that the cross of Christ was the source of eternal life.

77. The home and the cemetery were places where a Protestant iconography developed. Design books showed how to make crosses and either train plant vines to climb up the cross or carve wax leaves. This illustration is from Mrs. C. S. Jones and Henry T. Williams, *Household Elegancies* (New York, 1875).

78. Crosses could also be made to hang on walls and hold Bibles, prayer books, or hymnals. Here the grapes and grapevines refer both to the wine that Christ offered at the Last Supper and to John 15:5: "I am the vine, you are the branches. He who abides in me, and I in him, bears much fruit for without me you can do nothing". This illustration is from Mrs. C. S. Jones and Henry T. Williams, *Household Elegancies* (New York, 1875).

79. The eighteenth-century poem, "Rock of Ages," became the most popular Victorian hymn and a source for grave markers, home decorations, and church stained glass.

Crosses similar to those found in Victorian cemeteries were also found in mid-century Christian homes. Ladies fancy work books showed women how to make crosses to train real plants on them or to festoon them with wax leaves or shells. The frontispiece for an 1875 book on "household art" shows a woman making such a cross for her home. The instructions explain that the cross should look as if it was made of marble or granite.[58] Like the cemetery crosses, it resided on a three-tiered platform, perhaps symbolizing the traditional three times Jesus fell on his way to Calvary or the Trinity. Crosses with carved foliage could be made into wall brackets to hold a Bible or prayer book. Some were sculpted out of wood but others were made to look like marble by clever applications of plaster of Paris.[59] Ladies' handiwork books also included patterns for crosses made out of perforated cardboard. By cutting out pieces of paper of increasing size and pasting them together, women could achieve a three-dimensional effect.[60] Protestants used the same group of symbols in both funerary art and domestic decorating. The home and the cemetery, places not controlled by a clerical elite, became the spaces where a Protestant iconographic tradition developed.

A popular marker for graves at Laurel Hill and other Victorian cemeteries was a statue of a robed woman draping her arm around a cross or mournfully leaning against it. The image is not biblical. It comes from the hymn, "Rock of Ages."[61] In 1776 Augustus Montague Toplady, a Church of England clergyman, composed a poem for *Gospel Magazine*. A contentious and peculiar man, Toplady appended the poem to his calculation of how many sins an individual could commit in one lifetime (2,522,880,000 by the age of eighty). "Rock of Ages" was the poetic response to the conviction that Christ would forgive the debt not merely of one individual's sins but of all the sins of the world. In 1815 the Englishman Thomas Cotterill altered and condensed the poem, publishing it as a hymn in *Psalms and Hymns*. Cotterill, for instance, changed Toplady's line "When my eye-strings break in death" to "When my eyelids close in death." In 1830 Thomas Hasting composed the music with which we are now familiar. The hymn quickly became popular and was reprinted throughout the nineteenth century in the hymn books of every Christian denomination, including a Catholic one (1876). Prince Albert asked that it be sung at his deathbed and British Prime Minister William Gladstone translated it into Latin.

The representation of a woman holding on to or reaching for a cross was frequently used in domestic designs and funerary sculpture. The image comes from the stanza:

> "In my hand no price I bring
> Simply to Thy cross I cling."

Enthusiasts of the hymn or sentiment could buy lithographs of the cross printed by Currier and Ives, bread dishes depicting a woman pulling another one up toward a cross, glasses etched with the verses of the hymn, and bookmarks or postcards inscribed with simple crosses and the verse.[62] Parian ware statues were made to set on tables or fireplace mantles.[63] While churches did present the "Simply to Thy Cross I Cling" motifs in stained glass, the image was primarily displayed in places where lay people controlled the iconography.

Like *Père de Famille*, Toplady's poem expressed an eighteenth-century *sensibilité* that was adopted and reinterpreted by Victorian Christians. While the

80. Sarah Newbold's grave at Laurel Hill.

81. Angels at Laurel Hill Cemetery suggest the resurrection and eternal life. In cemeteries they frequently point a finger upward to heaven.

82. Like the cross, angels were a part of Victorian home decoration. This illustration is from Mrs. C. S. Jones and Henry T. Williams, *Beautiful Homes* (New York, 1876).

original poem is written in the first person so the "clinger" could be male or female, nineteenth-century representations show a woman supported by the cross. The religious spirit, the "soul," is depicted as female. The soul is represented as female not only because the Latin word *anima* is gendered feminine. A major theme in Victorian Christianity was that life was difficult and unpredictable; men and women were incapable of standing up against all of its trials and tribulations. Humanity was weak and only God was fundamentally strong. Within Victorian culture the woman was seen as "weak" in contrast to the "strong" male. The soul was passive, just as a woman was meant to be passive. God supported the weak soul just as a husband supported his delicate wife. In their relationship to God, all Christians were women: frail and in need of support.

The "Simply to Thy Cross I Cling" motif reverses the biblical sentiment of Matthew 16:24 where Christ asks his followers to deny themselves, take up their crosses, and follow him. In the biblical passage, Christ calls upon his people to be strong. Weakness is not recognized as a virtue. "Rock of Ages" and the illustrations that spun off from it became popular because it encouraged Christians to admit that life was disorienting and painful. It then reversed the image of the cross as a place of pain, transforming it into a physical support. Christians (men and women) may lean, cling, or rest on the cross. The Christianity created and learned at Philadelphia's Laurel Hill and other Victorian cemeteries emphasized the supportive, non-judgmental character of Christ. Although death was real and the singer would "soar through tracts unknown," the end result was seeing Christ "on Thy judgment-throne." For Victorian Protestants, Christ *sat* on

the judgment throne, he did not judge. The "Rock of Ages" motif visually asserted the feminine nature of the religious person, the supportive nature of Christ's message, and the promise of immortality.

We have seen in Chapter 3 that the family Bible was also used by Victorians in ways that both expressed and strengthened their convictions about women's spiritual character, the nurturing ability of Christianity, and the importance of family continuity. Considering the importance of the Bible in the Protestant home and church, we should not be surprised to see the sacred book made into grave markers. On the grave of Moses Reed, the Bible is placed in a Middle Eastern-style niche where a Catholic might have placed a statue of Mary. Margaret Smith's family inscribed "At home with Jesus" on the marble book placed at her grave. Again we see the continuity of symbols between the home, the church, and the cemetery. On Sarah Newbold's grave, a wide-open Bible sits on a carved altar cloth. Above her epitaph is a flowery wreath. A variation of the crown of victory, the wreath is the positive parallel to the crown of thorns. Like a cross that has ivy growing around it, the wreath stresses the Christian victory over death. Philadelphians buried in Laurel Hill appeared sure that they would be awarded heavenly citizenship and so they boldly opened the books of their lives for God to read. The biblical warning that "whosoever was not found written in the book of life was cast into the lake of fire" (Rev. 20:15) did not enter into the theological imagination cultivated at Laurel Hill.

In early Christian and medieval art, artists used angels to suggest the Resurrection: an angel told the women that Christ was not in the tomb but had

83. Female images appeared throughout Laurel Hill and other Victorian cemeteries. Here a woman, with her robe sensuously falling off her shoulder, appears to be letting the spirit out of a coffin. Her bodily presence contrasts sharply with the ethereal nature of the escaping soul.

84. J. Lacmer's masculine angel for the grave of Lawrence S. Pepper.

85. "No cross no crown". This perforated cardboard motto is mounted on a velvet backing.

86. Everyday objects, like this 1898 paperweight, brought symbols into the home, linking home, church, and cemetery.

risen (Matt. 28: 1–7) and angels carried the dead Lazarus to rest in Abraham's bosom (Luke. 16:22). Genesis mentions that God stationed angels outside of Eden (Gen. 3:24) and therefore Christian tradition assumed that angels guarded the gates of heaven, the new paradise. Philadelphians wealthy enough to commission the sculpting of an angel asserted their conviction that one of these holy helpers would assist their soul in its journey to heaven. With a finger pointing upwards the angels of Laurel Hill asked rhetorically: "Why do you seek the living among the dead?" (Luke 24:5). In the Middle Ages angels were portrayed as sexless, bodiless characters. Ever since the Renaissance, however, artists had painted angels with more feminine characteristics. In the nineteenth century the belief that women were angels and angels were women was quite common. Like a mother, the angel gently guided the soul to heaven. The female angel joined an active female cast at the cemetery: women clinging to crosses, long-haired allegories of faith holding their anchors of hope, and feminine characters letting out the soul from the coffin.

On the other hand, one of the most striking angels in Laurel Hill is a very masculine angel who presides over the grave of Lawrence S. Pepper (d. 1886). Designed by J. Lacmer, the sculpture recalls the archangel Michael who defeated Satan, casting him out of heaven (Rev. 12:7). The masculine angel in medieval folklore was a warrior who fought for the souls of the dead against equally aggressive devils. The weapons of Lacmer's angel, the cross and the book, reminded the viewer of the inevitable crown of victory of eternal life. To emphasize the point, Lacmer engraved the motto: "No Cross, No Crown." Philadelphians were well acquainted with the title and symbols of William Penn's popular book *No Cross, No Crown*, even if they had never read the text. The cross and crown appeared on embroidered mottoes, paperweights, and Sunday school attendance pins. The difference between Penn's eighteenth-century theology and this nineteenth-century version was the elimination of the act of final judgment. Suffering on earth *itself* was enough of a "cross" to win one a place in heaven.

Victorian Cemeteries and Victorian Christianity

From its founding in 1836 until the late nineteenth century, Laurel Hill served as a place of pilgrimage where Protestants set their own standards of behavior and created their own religious art. While theologians controlled doctrine and ministers the sermon, lay Christians voiced their religious sentiments in the material world. Families and fashions, not denominational commitments, determined what visual statements would be made. Businessmen, architects, artists, gravestone makers, and prosperous Philadelphians replaced the clergy as the experts on how to house and properly commemorate the dead. The shift from clergy control to lay control did not mean that the cemetery was secularized. Perhaps even more than the clergy, lay people believed that a literal heaven was theirs after their death. While this chapter has looked exclusively at one rural cemetery, comparable cemeteries built throughout the country in the nineteenth century taught similar values and behaviors.

The Victorian cemetery did not ask Protestants to consider their spiritual lives and then struggle to make themselves more holy. If Philadelphians felt anxious about what happened after death, they did not express this fear in either their cemeteries or their homes. Cemeteries taught the urban elite that they already were saved and that as a privileged people they would quickly pass through death and into eternal life in heaven. "The shorter life the longer immortality," reflected Lewis Copper's (d. 1874) epitaph, "the less of this brief world the more of heaven." Although those beliefs might appear shallow or self-righteous to our twentieth-century eyes, they centered around the longstanding Christian guarantee of immortality. Walking through the cemetery provided security, not a sense of dread. Victorian landscapes were visited by many people because they emphasized that Christianity was about immortality and not judgment. Like the cross to which one could "simply cling" for support, the cemetery was a physical treatise on the certainty of everlasting life. Just as the cross was about resurrection and not about pain, the cemetery was about heaven and not death. Life itself provided enough tests and judgments; the cemetery reinforced the idea that in spite of setbacks, eternal success would be accomplished. The space of the revival meetings might have asked Protestants to accept their sinfulness, but the cemetery preached their righteousness.

The longing for heaven did not mean that the Victorians turned from this world and longed for the next. Heaven was not the opposite of this life; it was the continuation and perfection of what made this life good. Love, family, friendship, work, progress, conversation – all these familiar earthly involvements continued in the next life. Laurel Hill (and, I suspect, other Victorian cemeteries) was not a retreat from urban ills or a means to avoid the anomic quality of death. Just as heaven perfected the ideas of family and progress, so Victorian cemeteries allowed for the symbolic control of disorienting conditions. For Protestants the cemetery provided a sanctuary where "the heart can forget the cares and sorrows of busy

87. The vacant grave "bed," like the empty cross, indicated its inhabitant had departed to heaven. While the earthly family might mourn, the soul would awaken into a new life. These 1883 markers at Laurel Hill were designed by J. Lacmer.

life, and muse upon the future with calmness, looking up to heaven for happiness and consolation."[64] As a foretaste of heaven, Christian belief could not cause anxiety and despair. Like much of the popular iconography of the nineteenth century, the cemetery stressed religion's role in helping people deal with the inevitable disappointments and pains of life.

If the cemetery asserted the Christian promise of immortality, then we must correct our contemporary understanding of the Victorian cemetery as a place of numbing sleep. In the religious thought of sixteenth-century Anabaptists and Lutherans, the soul slept between the time of death and the Last Judgment. Everyone who has died is in a state of sleep. They are free both from pain and from consciousness while awaiting the end of time. In this Protestant notion, no one is in heaven meeting friends and living in mansions. Calvin, however, refuted the idea of a sleeping soul. "By 'rest' we understand, not sloth, or lethargy, or anything like the drowsiness of ebriety which they attribute to the soul," countered Calvin, "but tranquility of conscience and security, which always accompanies faith but is never complete in all its parts till after death." Rest meant peace, not an unconscious sleep. Although the dead cannot experience full bliss because they lack a spiritual body (attained only after the Last Judgment), they can experience the glory of salvation.[65] Throughout the eighteenth century the tendency was to reject the view of theologians like Thomas Burnet who thought the state of death, for both good and bad souls, was one of silence and inaction.[66] The more popular sentiment was that expressed in a 1707 hymn by Isaac Watts: "Death like a narrow sea divides this heavenly land from ours."[67]

It is the understanding of "sleep" as rest that became popular in the nineteenth century. While Victorians endlessly wrote epitaphs that declared, "Asleep in Jesus," they did not mean that the soul was unaware of what was happening to it – as we would be if we were asleep. The popularity of novels such as Elizabeth

Stuart Phelps's *The Gates Ajar* (1868) that described heavenly society, or the countless ministerial discussions of eternal life could not have been written if Victorians believed that after death they would literally sleep until the Last Judgment.[68] Nothing truly slept – the body decayed and the soul lived in heaven. To sleep meant to participate in immortality as far as was possible without a spiritual body. Sleeping implied that the sleeper would awake. Just as the empty tomb represented Christ's resurrection, the empty bed often memorialized in Victorian cemeteries symbolized the departure of the person to heaven.[69] While the family on earth might mourn because of the empty cradle or bed, the soul awakened into a new life. If Victorians had actually equated death with sleep, then we might conclude that they were losing their belief in the Christian promise of immortality and were caught up in the process of secularization. Cemeteries were material proof of the Christian heaven, not modern statements of the finality of death.

Symbols like books or beds may look to our modern eyes like secular symbols but they actually referred to Christian objects or ideas. Walking through Laurel Hill, a nineteenth-century man or woman carried in his or her memory countless Bible stories and texts. The proper Christian, according to Victorian values, knew the scriptures and could recognize common religious symbols like the sacred book or the anchor. They knew these symbols because they played with them as toys, wore them as jewelry, used them in paperweights, placed them on their walls, and perhaps saw them at church. Even if someone never went to church, the visual language of Christian symbolism and the verbal language of the Bible were everywhere in the culture.

Laurel Hill survives as the physical manifestation of a lay Victorian piety that freely combined facets of Christianity, domesticity, and social prestige. The families who expressed their religious sentiments in the cemetery refused to separate piety from leisure or belief from display of social position. Laurel Hill held meaning for them precisely because, there, they simultaneously experienced religious satisfaction and aesthetic uplift. Lay people tolerated the mixing of the commercial and spiritual aspects of life. Fashionable display in the cemetery taught Christians that religion was not irrelevant and detached from "important" things in life. For Victorians, their Christianity was "in style." As Laurence Moore aptly describes in *Selling God*, ministers who accepted their congregation's need to link leisure and entertainment with religion prospered. "Americans remained a religious people," he reminds us, "because religious leaders, and sometimes their opponents, found ways to make religion competitive with other cultural products."[70] Victorian cemeteries not only taught that immortality could be gained without judgment, they reassured Americans that material goods, commercial life, and fashion should be linked with faith.

By using multivocal symbols families connected religion at home to the public space of the cemetery. In spite of Protestantism's assertion that families could not help their dead after death, families believed that memorializing the memory of their loved ones was a Christian duty. Laurel Hill was a cemetery for families. Individual interments were not encouraged and were segregated within the grounds. The dead were grouped not by denominational commitments but by family. Victorian cemeteries were the material expressions of the common ideal that heaven was home and home was heaven. Just as there was no radical division between what was religious and what was mere entertainment or fashion, there was a fluidity between the public space of the cemetery and the private space of the home. The cemetery was not considered a public, profane place in comparison with the private, sacred space of the home. Public and private, profane and sacred, mixed together. In both places, an effort was made to control who was permitted into sacred space. Cemetery managers did this through regulations and the cost of burial plots. Families did it by requiring servants to use back staircases. Homes and cemeteries, as much as churches, were places for Christian expression and fashionable display.

By searching for the eternal and the enduring in Christian thought, Philadelphians ignored denominational differences that tended to fragment and question belief. Crosses, broken pitchers, open Bibles, angels, wreaths, and crowns were symbols accepted by Quakers, Presbyterians, and Episcopalians. The pious memories and biblical sayings of the epitaphs voiced the common sentiments of the day. "The rural and ornate cemetery," reflected a guidebook, "is the common ground upon which all parties can meet in forgiveness and harmony; it is the lap of the common mother which receives at last, in no unkind embrace, all her children, however widely sundered in their lives by the jarring controversies of their day."[71] By emphasizing the natural, eternal, and harmonious qualities of the cemetery, Philadelphians sought a spiritual wholeness increasingly difficult to achieve in a growing industrial and urban center. In the next chapter we will see how nineteenth-century Catholics also sought spiritual and physical wholeness through material objects, landscapes, and rituals.

5

Lourdes Water and American Catholicism

By her own description, Mary Hayes was poor, consumptive, and had been keeping company with a man addicted to drink. She suffered from pains in her head so severe that she thought she would become insane. In 1879 she wrote to Father Alexis Granger, pastor of the Church of Our Lady of the Sacred Heart on the campus of Notre Dame thanking him for sending her some Lourdes water. "After I used the blessed water," she wrote in a rambling stream of explanation, "the headaches ceased and I gave some of it to a lady that had an abscess in her face she tried everything and nothing seemed to relieve her so I told her about the holy water and gave her what I had left so she said some prayers and used the holy water at night and the next morning all the swelling had disappeared and in three days she was as well as ever." Mary Hayes thanked Father Granger for his advice on her personal relationships, regretting that she did not have a father or mother to whom she could tell her troubles. She did, however, "have a mother in heaven and I hope she will always keep me in the path of virtue." In ending her letter, Mary asked for more Lourdes water, "for I have more faith in that than in all the doctors in the whole world."[1]

Mary Hayes was one of many Catholics who wrote to Alexis Granger during the last third of the nineteenth century. Letters from over one hundred Catholics who discussed the miraculous water of Lourdes survive in the archives of the University of Notre Dame. These Catholics are only a handful of the tens of thousands of Americans who in the past century have used water from the shrine in Lourdes, France. Images of Lourdes are ubiquitous in Catholic life. Not only do American Catholics bring water back from trips to Lourdes, gallons are still shipped from France to devotional centers such as those in Boston and Notre Dame.[2] Catholic goods stores sell statues of Our Lady of Lourdes and replicas of the grotto adjoin Catholic churches. In the Bronx, a multi-ethnic group of devotees claims that water from St. Lucy's Lourdes shrine built in the 1930s has healing powers. Although the Second Vatican Council encouraged Catholics to focus their piety more fully on the biblical Christ and the sacraments, devotions to the Blessed Virgin Mary and the saints continue to be an important part in the spiritual lives of many Catholics.

The period between 1870 and 1896 represents a distinct pocket in American Catholic history. Irish and German immigrants who arrived during the first half of the century were beginning to gain economic and political stability. Internal conflicts over who would run the parish had ended with the supremacy of the priest. While anti-Catholic cartoons still appeared in newspapers and journals, disputes with Protestants no longer erupted into riots. Clergy were successful in their bid to have parishioners join pious associations, send their children to parochial schools, contribute to the building of elaborate churches, and support an extensive Catholic social welfare system. Religious orders conducted missions that stirred pious sentiments, fortifying Catholic commitments. The Irish, new arrivals and those born in America, were more active in the church than during the antebellum period. Italians and Eastern Europeans had not yet arrived in enough numbers to provide alternative expressions of Catholicism to those of the Irish, Germans, and French. Catholic life in the United States had never been as vital.

One way that Catholics successfully claimed a part of the American religious landscape was by creating a devotional life that spoke to their concepts of the supernatural. The religious community at Notre Dame devised specific methods to spread the veneration of the Virgin Mary throughout the United States. By producing a Marian devotional journal, organizing a national Association of Our Lady of the Sacred Heart, and distributing Lourdes water, the Holy Cross community created an institutional focus on the Virgin Mary. As shrines were built on the campus, Notre Dame became a pilgrimage spot for local Catholics. Notre Dame's outreach program touched Catholics throughout the United States and forged a national Marian piety. Widely distributed Lourdes water and constructed grotto replicas became material reminders of the power and influence of Mary.

People who are caught up in the holy rarely notice the institutional and cultural structures that construct, define, and even distribute the sacred. This chapter explores the "economy of the holy." How did Lourdes water become a part of a spiritual exchange between priests, lay people, import agents, and the divine? How was spring water "manufactured" into a miraculous object? The spiritual economy of the sacred took place between those on earth and those in heaven, as well as between Catholics living in the United States and in France. It originated in a cult that centered on two saintly women and yet was co-ordinated exclusively by ordained men. The letters sent by Catholics to Father Granger clearly show that in the nineteenth century both lay people and the clergy articulated a discourse of the miraculous.

Marian piety with its Lourdes water and replica grottoes flourished in the United States because its themes resonated not only with Catholic traditions but also with Victorian culture. Protestants and Catholics both acknowledged the healing capacities of water and sought to articulate religious and aesthetic values by creating Christian landscapes. Like the Philadelphia Protestants who rejected the notion that a cemetery should be a place to reflect on the fragility and mortality of the human body, Catholics sought release from pain, not the mortification of the flesh. Although Catholics understood their Marian piety to be truly "Catholic," the expressions of that piety drew from the culture of the time. Christians who drank Lourdes water or sang "Simply to Thy cross I cling," hoped for the miraculous end to suffering. Religion concerned the body as well as the soul.

The Visions at Lourdes

In the early spring of 1858, a young peasant girl was gathering wood near her home in the Pyrenees mountains in southern France. Bernadette Soubirous, illiterate and poor, eventually reported that she had seen something white, in the

THE CHURCH AND SHRINE OF OUR LADY OF LOURDES.

88. Bernadette Soubiros and the visions of the Blessed Virgin Mary near Lourdes from the *Catholic Herald*, 24 April 1880. The water which flowed from the vision site has been used in healing rituals throughout the Catholic world.

shape of a woman, at the grotto of Massabielle. Using the local dialect of the area, Bernadette called the lady *aquerò*, meaning "that one." Between February 11 and July 16, she saw the same person eighteen times. The lady gave Bernadette messages: she asked for prayers, penance, and the conversion of sinners. She also asked for a chapel to be built at the grotto. On February 25 the crowd that had gathered watched as Bernadette scrambled over to one side of the grotto and began to eat the tufts of a local herb called *la dorine*. She then dug in the ground, uncovered some muddy water, and began to drink from the newly formed spring. Bernadette explained that the lady had asked her to "go and drink from, and wash yourself in the fountain, and eat of the herb which is growing at its side."[3] The next day the first healing miracle occurred. A quarryman who had injured his right eye in a mine accident regained his sight after bathing the eye in the muddy spring water. Although Bernadette had asked *aquerò* several times who she was, it was not until March 25 that the lady responded, "I am the Immaculate Conception."

The visions stopped as quickly as they had begun, but the number of people who came to the grotto in hopes of a glimpse of the lady increased. Bernadette remained in the village for eight years. While local and episcopal authorities debated the authenticity of the visions, Bernadette struggled with her asthma and the increasing number of pilgrims who came to Lourdes to see her and the grotto. Church authorities concluded that the visions were worthy of the concern of the faithful, and in 1862 the church sanctioned the cult of the "Immaculate Mother of God" at the Lourdes grotto. The vision of Our Lady of Lourdes helped to popularize the newly established Catholic dogma that Mary was conceived without stain of original sin. While the purity of the Virgin had a long tradition in Western Christianity, the official Catholic dogma had only been promulgated in 1854, four years before the vision. In 1866 Bernadette joined the Sisters of Charity at Nevers, performing the humble tasks of a nun until her death in 1879. Both the number of pilgrims visiting the shrine and the amount of water issuing from the spring increased over the years. Currently Lourdes authorities estimate that each year 5 million people visit the shrine. The once muddy spring, that lies near the River Gave, developed into a flow of 32,000 gallons of water per day.[4]

The Virgin Mary told Bernadette both to wash in the water from the newly found spring and to eat an herb growing nearby. While healing by eating herbs is standard in folk medicine, Lourdes did not become famous for its greenery. It was the *water* flowing from the spring that healed and that would be shipped all over the world. Water as a symbol of sustenance and regeneration has a long history in Western religious traditions. Spring water frequently appears in biblical stories to represent the nurturance of God and his ability to grant life from nothing. When the thirsty Israelites asked for water in the wilderness, God permitted a stream to gush forth from the rock Moses struck (Ex. 17). To the prophet Jeremiah, God defined himself as "a fountain of living water" (Jer. 2:13). In the New Testament, Jesus characterized his message as a spring "always welling up for eternal life" (John 4:13–14). God explained in the Book of Revelation that "to the thirsty I will give water without price from the fountain of the water of life" (21:6). Not only did water symbolize self-renewal and spiritual regeneration, biblical stories connected it with healing miracles. In Jerusalem certain pools were known for their healing powers (John 5:2), and Jesus commanded a blind man to wash off in the pool of Siloam the clay and spittle placed in his eyes, enabling him to see again. Healing, both spiritual and physical, came from God through the medium of water.

Biblical water symbolism became an essential aspect not only of church ritual but of individual Christian behavior. Baptismal waters specifically represented the regenerative passage from sin to life. Catholics used specially blessed water, called holy water, to ward off evil and to insure the good will of God. In the second century apocryphal Acts of Peter (19), a Christian purified his home by sprinkling it with water and invoking the name of Jesus. By the ninth century, not only did priests use holy water to bless their parishioners, people took such water home and scattered it over their fields, vineyards, cattle, and food. Thomas Aquinas suggested that small sins could be remitted by the sprinkling of holy water. Even Bernadette, when she first encountered *aquerò*, decided to bring holy water with her the next day in order to ascertain if the apparition was of God or of the devil.[5] Although pre-Christian attitudes toward holy wells certainly shaped the attitudes of peasants like Bernadette, the notion of water as a source of spiritual renewal and protection is deeply embedded in the Catholic imagination.[6]

Consequently, it is not surprising that the *water* of Lourdes, and not the herb, materially represented the apparition. For the devout, water was not merely a symbol of a spiritual growth; it could actually link the natural to the supernatural. Those who traveled to Lourdes believed that the water had affective presence; they felt the physical presence of the holy. From the very beginning of

Christianity, followers of Jesus left their homes and traveled to places imbued with the power of the sacred. As early as the second century, the study of the Hebrew Bible motivated Christians to visit Palestine. The desire to be in the presence of holy people, who embodied the sacred in their persons, evolved in late antiquity into the cult of the saints. As we have seen, even nineteenth-century Protestants sought the experience of sacred places and people at Philadelphia's Laurel Hill Cemetery.

Longing for the sacred did not always have to be satisfied through pilgrimage. Historians tend to emphasize the "rootedness" of the holy to the detriment of its mobility. The holy can also be reduced and transferred from one place to another. In the sixth century, pilgrims brought back vestiges of the sacred by collecting oil, earth, or water from holy sites. Holy oil, for instance, bubbling from the grave of St. John the Evangelist "like a spring of sanctification" was collected and said to have healing powers even far away from the shrine.[7] Archeologists have found collections of small, round ampullae called *eulogiae* ("blessings") made of clay, lead, or glass that held sacred substances like earth, oil, or water. On the *eulogiae* were schematic representations of the place, building, or holy person the Christian had visited. The representation, the sacred substance, and the memory of the journey helped duplicate the sanctity of the original site at a distance. The ampulla itself also assumed a spiritual power as it became a reminder of the experience of the pilgrim. The holy did not reside in a fixed place. It could be de-localized, moved from place to place, and still retain its ability to heal or work other miracles.[8] Pilgrimage (the movement of people to relics) shaped Christian behavior, and the concept of translation (the movement of relics to people) legitimized the distribution of Lourdes water.

Because of the prominence of Lourdes as a Catholic pilgrimage place, the translation aspect of the devotion has been overlooked. Historians, sociologists, and pious writers describe journeys to Lourdes and the activities within the locality, but they ignore the importance of exporting water and other religious objects from the site. The first healing miracle of Lourdes was accomplished when someone brought the spring water to the quarryman in the village. Like the oil from St. John's grave, Lourdes water could be packed in containers and moved away from the site. Catholics believed that the intrusion of the divine into the human world happened not exclusively at the grotto but also away from the shrine. Because water functions as a dominant symbol in Catholic devotional life, water and not an herb was exported. Lourdes infused conventional Christian water symbolism with a newly revealed supernatural power. In some regards the water became like the Word of God contained in the scriptures. Like the Bible, it could be packaged and exported. Just as the words of the scriptures had healing powers, so did the water.

Notre Dame and American Marian Devotions

The visions of Bernadette at Lourdes, while perhaps the best known of the Marian apparitions of the nineteenth century, were not the only ones. Mary told a Parisian nun to make a special medal in her honor (1830), children heard the Virgin deliver apocalyptic messages at La Salette (1846) and ask for prayers at Pontmain (1871), and St. Joseph and St. John appeared with Mary at Knock, Ireland (1879). Apparitions were reported by children in Austria (1849) and Bavaria (1876), as well as by a French winegrower in Saint-Bauzille-de-la-Syylve (1873), but these were not approved by the church.[9] Marian visions comprised only one aspect of a general Catholic nineteenth-century fascination with the Blessed Virgin. The American Catholic hierarchy in 1846 declared Mary Immaculate the patroness of the United States. In 1900 Our Lady of Guadalupe became patroness of the Americas. In addition to the promotion of the dogma of the Immaculate Conception, Pope Leo XIII (1878–1903) actively promoted the saying of the rosary. Catholics named churches, schools, and seminaries after the various titles of Mary. Marian associations flourished.

The reasons for this flurry of Marian devotions in Europe and the Americas have been debated among scholars. Barbara Corrado Pope postulates that nineteenth-century secularism forced the Catholic hierarchy to identify with Mary's purity and power.[10] Michael Carroll discusses the psychological reasons for the promotion of Mary as the Great Mother, and Thomas Kselman reflects on the political implications of the cult's popularity.[11] By ignoring her role as Queen of Heaven, Victorian Protestants could easily adapt the biblical Mary – who dutifully bore and reared the divine child – into the cult of True Womanhood. Men and women were equally attracted to Mary's non-judgmental and accepting nature. Protestants and Catholics both used Mary to articulate their belief that a central characteristic of Christianity was its ability to nurture and support humanity.

Much of the renewed enthusiasm for Catholic devotion to the Virgin Mary came from France. According to Thomas Kselman, the French Revolution had shaken Catholicism to its core.[12] External persecution by the state, internal conflict, and the attempt to establish a humanistic "Cult of the Supreme Being" challenged Catholic hegemony. After the Revolution, the church tried to re-establish itself in a changing political and social environment. The miracles, prophecies, and supernaturalism of nineteenth-century France reassured Catholics that their world was indeed blessed by God and would continue in spite of war and social change. The French clergy looked increasingly to Rome for ways to fight rationalism and liberalism through more emotional devotions, a strong religious press, and the encouragement of vocations. The devotion to Our Lady of Lourdes in France shored up a fragile French faith and promoted conservative church/state relationships.

Consequently, it was not surprising that when French missionaries established a school in the wilderness of Indiana they called it "Notre Dame du Lac." While the community of Notre Dame would eventually be known as the "Fighting Irish" because of the ethnicity of most of its students and faculty, its origins lie not in Ireland but in France. The founder of Notre Dame, Edward Sorin (1814–93), was born in Anhuillé, France, and in 1840 joined the newly formed French religious order of the Congregation of the Holy Cross. After being sent to America to establish a community, the bishop of Vincennes, Indiana, gave Sorin a parcel of land. In 1842 he founded a college for boys, and in 1855 Holy Cross Sisters began St. Mary's College for girls. Throughout his tenure as college president and superior general of his order, Sorin evinced a devotion to the Virgin Mary under various titles. Notre Dame became a leading Catholic educational institution and a critical force behind the American promotion of Marian devotions.

The key to the spread of Marian devotions from Notre Dame was the founding

89. Father Edward Sorin and Native Americans. While Notre Dame University would later be associated with Irish Catholicism, its origins are distinctly French.

in 1865 of the journal *Ave Maria*. Edward Sorin sought to publish a journal geared toward the spiritual life of Catholics. Unlike the *Catholic World* (founded the same year) that had an intellectual orientation that might appeal to Protestants, *Ave Maria* was to "speak exclusively to our own family affairs." Catholic newspapers reported on local and ethnic concerns, and *Ave Maria* promoted spirituality. Sorin expected the readers of *Ave Maria* to range from the "the grey-haired grandsire who tells his beads at eventide, to the prattling child who kisses his medal as he falls asleep in his down cradle, with rosy dreams in which the loved images of his mother on earth and his Mother in heaven are sweetly blended."[13] Rosary beads, medals, and Mother Mary defined the Catholic, and *Ave Maria* was to be an unashamedly Catholic journal. Through *Ave Maria* American Catholics were exposed to Catholic news and doctrine, read approved Catholic fiction, ordered devotional objects such as scapulars and medals, and learned about new institutions that needed financial support. Two long-term editors ran this multifaceted journal: Father Neal Henry Gillespie (1866–74) and Father Daniel Hudson (1875–1928). They not only provided stability to the publishing endeavor but corresponded with hundreds of Catholics who wrote to the journal.[14] By 1897 *Ave Maria* had achieved a circulation of 22,000, ten times the circulation of the erudite *Catholic World* and had become one of the most popular Catholic weeklies.[15]

In addition to the journal, Edward Sorin decided in the early 1860s to build a church dedicated to Our Lady of the Sacred Heart on the Notre Dame campus. No mere student chapel, Sorin imaged a magnificent edifice of Gothic design. The appellation "Our Lady of the Sacred Heart" was a new Marian title devised by a

90. Sorin's Gothic-style church, later known as Sacred Heart Church, was raised to the status of basilica in 1992.

group of French priests, the Missionaries of the Sacred Heart of Jesus. Its iconography included the Virgin Mary as the Immaculate Conception reaching out with extended arms that encompass the standing child Jesus. Beneath Mary's feet lies a crushed serpent. With one hand the child points to his inflamed heart and with the other to his mother. The image combined the icons of three popular devotions: the Miraculous Medal, the Sacred Heart, and the Infant Jesus.[16] Our Lady of the Sacred Heart was understood to be "one of the most perfect unions of devotions to Jesus and to Mary which has ever yet been suggested." Through Mary, the devout reached her son: "We know that the Heart of Jesus is all-powerful, but He obeys His Mother, and thus we ask Mary to speak to the Heart of Jesus for us, knowing that what she asks we shall surely obtain."[17] Although the title, "Our Lady of the Sacred Heart," is no longer well known, it was one of the many titles that evolved during the nineteenth century in connection with the Immaculate Conception.

In 1867 the Holy Cross Sisters at St. Mary's College organized an association to honor the Virgin Mary under this title. At first the Association of Our Lady of the Sacred Heart was a part of the larger French group that in 1868 numbered two million members worldwide. According to *Ave Maria* the association formed "to meet the wants of this age that bears within its heart the moral gangrene of materialism and unbelief."[18] The association's publicity explained that its objective was to obtain both spiritual and temporal favors through the intercession of Our Lady of the Sacred Heart. Masses would be said in France and at Notre Dame for the intentions of both the living and dead members. Members were required to say in the morning and evening the invocation: "Our Lady of the Sacred Heart,

91. Our Lady of the Sacred Heart was the appellation for Mary invented by a group of French priests during the mid-nineteenth century. The image combined the iconography of several popular Catholic devotions.

pray for us"; offer their prayers and good works for the intentions of the members; carry a medal of Our Lady of the Sacred Heart; receive communion on May 31 (the principal feast day); and make a small offering to meet the expenses of the association.

In 1869 Edward Sorin gave over the task of building Our Lady of the Sacred Heart church to Father Alexis Granger. Granger, like Sorin, was born in France. He served as the church's pastor until his death in 1893. Granger immediately took over the Association of Our Lady of the Sacred Heart, transferred it from the auspices of the sisters, and publicized its existence through *Ave Maria*.[19] During its first three months of operation, he reported that ten thousand new names had been added to the register and hundreds of letters had been sent asking for the associates to pray for temporal and spiritual favors.[20] That same year, Granger organized a series of masses to be said at Notre Dame for members of the association. For those who sent $50 for the erection of the church, masses would be said for their intentions for fifty years. Those who could not donate the full amount would receive ten years of masses for $10, five years for $5, and so on. Priests said masses not only for the donors but for any of their relatives, friends, or dead for whom they wished to have prayers said. In 1871 the cornerstone for the church of Our Lady of the Sacred Heart was laid, and over the next ten years contributions from grateful users of Lourdes water financed the church building. In 1888 the church became free from all debt.

American Catholics engaged in an ancient system of relating to the divine at the same time as they pragmatically built up their churches and charitable institutions. Catholics participated in an "economy of salvation" that provided a "temple of interest" accessible to all people.[21] Beseeched by the prayers of the faithful, Mary and the saints would be influenced to ask Christ to grant favors to those who petitioned. Historian Joseph Chinnici sees distinct contractual features in how Catholics articulated the individual's relationship with God, Christ, and the saints. The economy of salvation set up a series of required obligations between those on earth and those in heaven. The institution of the church was necessary to facilitate

92. Father Alexis Granger.

that interaction. Through the power and authority of the church, the contract was carried out. Catholics learned the details of the negotiation while recognizing the importance of the institutional church to broker the negotiation. God and the saints did not act only out of love, they also acted out of obligation.

The contractual model was not the only model Catholics used in their devotional life. A more informal, less institutional model also shaped the ways Catholics experienced the other world. Historian Ann Taves, for instance, describes a "household of faith" of familial relationships established between nineteenth-century Catholics and their supernatural "relatives."[22] She argues that the clergy and devotional literature urged Catholics to converse through prayer in an intimate and friendly manner with God, their father, and Mary, their mother. Care, communication, and concern structured the interaction between those on earth and those in heaven. Through their petitioning prayers, Catholics sought spiritual and material favors. Devotional practices, such as prayers to the Virgin Mary, defined Catholic spiritual life. Catholics experienced their relationship with those in heaven as both a type of supernatural contract and as a supernatural family. In both cases the bonds between the human and the divine were strong.

The Association of Our Lady of the Sacred Heart as promoted through *Ave Maria* reached a widespread Catholic readership. Unlike other sodalities or confraternities, association members were not merely asked to form bonds with members of the same parish or community. They were not neighbors sharing ethnic and economic ties. Members were connected to fellow associates in France, across the United States, and, most importantly, to the community of saints in heaven. It was, in the words of anthropologist Victor Turner, the "reciprocal action of soul on soul in a corporate circulation of blessings."[23] American

Catholics participated in communities made up of saints and strangers as well as in parish-based communities made up of neighbors and family. Catholics learned and accepted the reality of a supernatural community because they were taught how to interact with it through their devotional practices.

In 1868 *Ave Maria* began reprinting extracts from letters sent to the association that described the favors received by members. *Ave Maria* frequently printed accounts of miraculous cures, but these new accounts were unique because they happened to individual members of the association. In one letter, a member wrote that after making a novena (a nine-day series of prayers) and joining the association "my eyes commenced to get better and ever since the 31st of May they seem to be really well and strong."[24] In another case, a man who had been severely injured when a house fell on him was told by "our Sisters" to say special prayers each day "and place the [association's] medal on the parts affected, and that our dear Mother would cure him." The next day "he met us at the door saying he was *cured*."[25] Catholics anticipated that by joining the association they would gain benefits for themselves and their families. By printing descriptions of the favors granted by Our Lady of the Sacred Heart, Granger encouraged more readers of *Ave Maria* to join the association. Miracles proved that Mary was particularly attentive to those who addressed her by this title.

Lourdes Water and Those Who Used It

The devotion to our Lady of Lourdes and the miraculous cures attributed to the water followed the pattern established by the Association of Our Lady of the Sacred Heart. In January of 1870, the first mention of Our Lady of Lourdes (in an extract from the *London Lamp*) appeared in *Ave Maria*. The following month, *Ave Maria* serialized an English translation of Henri Lasserre's, *Notre Dame de Lourdes* that Edward Sorin had sent from France. Lasserre, a "French literary man," had failing eyesight. After receiving some Lourdes water, he applied it to his eyes: "Scarcely had I touched my eyes and my forehead with this miraculous water than I felt that I was suddenly cured, instantaneously, without transition, with a suddenness which in my imperfect language I can compare only to that of lightning."[26] Thankful for the cure, he traveled to Lourdes and wrote a popular exposition of the shrine's history. In 1869, its first year of publication, the French book ran to fifteen editions. In 1870 *Ave Maria*, D. & J. Sadlier, and Peter Cunningham all published English translations in the United States.[27] The *Catholic World* also serialized the Lourdes history. The English publication of *Notre Dame de Lourdes* marks the beginning of the devotion in the United States. That same year of 1870, students recited a poem about Lourdes at the Notre Dame graduation and an extension made to a hall at St. Mary's became known as "Lourdes Hall."[28] Our Lady of Lourdes had made her arrival on the Notre Dame campus, and Catholics throughout the United States became interested in obtaining the miraculous water.

The years between 1870 and 1872 were difficult ones for the shrine in France. The Franco-Prussian War made it dangerous to travel or to transport Lourdes water. After the end of the war, the Assumptionist fathers held a series of pilgrimages and celebrations to assert the prominence of Our Lady of Lourdes, bolster the mood of the French after their losses to the Germans, and promote conservative political causes.[29] The popular American Catholic newspapers, the *Boston Pilot* and the *New York Herald*, summarized the activities at Lourdes. In the August 1872 issue of *Ave Maria*, a letter was printed that had been sent to Edward Sorin from France on June 24, 1872. The letter reported on a miraculous cure effected by the Lourdes water. In a postscript to the published letter, Sorin wrote: "We expect the writer at Notre Dame on or about the 5th of August, at which time through his kindness we shall receive a supply of the water of Lourdes, and be able to comply to the many demands which for some time past we could not fulfill."[30] In the next issue Sorin acknowledged, "I have received the medals and the water of Lourdes, for which I am grateful."[31] The first Lourdes water had been shipped to Notre Dame for distribution. Letters immediately came into *Ave Maria* requesting water and describing cures. Granger may have placed advertisements in the New York *Freeman's Journal* mentioning that he possessed quantities of Lourdes water.[32] Cures by Lourdes water, rather than from membership of the Association of Our Lady of the Sacred Heart, began to be published.

The demand for Lourdes water far exceeded its availability. Although Sorin returned frequently to France to attend meetings of the Holy Cross congregation, he and Granger failed to establish an effective way of shipping the water. In 1873 Sorin wrote from Paris that he was having a difficult time getting Lourdes water. He explained that the Holy Cross fathers in France had written three times to the shrine at Lourdes with no success. Then they actually contacted the Nevers convent where Bernadette lived and had been promised a barrel. "Should it fail to come," Sorin reported, "I am determined to start myself on Monday morning for the spot, and to ship you from there one or two casks of the precious water."[33] Without a steady supply of Lourdes water, Sorin must have known that the devotion could not endure.

By 1877 the shipping problem had been solved. A customs house agent in New York, John A. McSorley, who imported medals, statues, and other religious articles, served as the importer of the Lourdes water from France. Sorin and Granger used the same process to distribute Lourdes water as they did other pious goods. The water (medal, scapular, or statue) was produced in France, shipped via a middle-man to New York, stored in a warehouse, and eventually shipped to Notre Dame. In 1881 McSorley wrote to Sorin that his expenses were $13.50 per case of water. This cost most likely included a donation to the French shrine and a fee for shipping. McSorley imported between ten and twenty cases at a time and each case contained thirty bottles of water.[34] When the water arrived at Notre Dame, Granger divided it into small vials and mailed it to his correspondents.

John McSorley maintained a longterm relationship with Sorin and Granger. On his birthday McSorley made donations to the Church of Our Lady of the Sacred Heart and asked for prayers for his wayward brother who lived in California. He told Granger of the deaths of his infant daughter and eldest son. McSorley also participated in the Lourdes devotion. In 1877 he wrote that he and his family said the rosary for Sorin's intentions in front of a statue of Our Lady of Lourdes and that he had received a "leaf of the wild rose that grows in the *very spot* where the Blessed Virgin appeared to Bernadette."[35] McSorley did not only import Lourdes water and other religious goods for financial gain. He believed he and his family benefited spiritually from his exchanges with Notre Dame clergy. Commerce and devotion were not in conflict.

Some of the letters written to Alexis Granger requesting Lourdes water and describing cures have been preserved in the Notre Dame University Archives. Granger explained that he saved the letters because "to us they present undoubted evidences of sincerity."[36] Granger probably did not save all the letters. We do not know, for instance, how people reacted when the water failed. While the letters span the period between 1872 and 1893, all but three were written between 1872 and 1879. It is unclear why Granger stopped saving the letters or why fewer of them came in the last decades of the century. Of 118 letters, fifty could be identified as coming from men, sixty-six from women, and two could not be identified by sex. Most were written by lay people; only twelve came from priests or sisters. The letter writers lived where Catholics then lived: nearly half each in the East and the Midwest and a smattering in the South and West. While it is difficult to get a sense of the age of the correspondents, most appear to be at the childrearing age when worries about young children and spouses predominate. Some of the letters contained misspellings and poor grammar indicating that the writers had little education, but other letters showed the careful penmanship and language of the educated Victorian. Other than such cursory observations, it is difficult to ascertain the class of the writers.[37] We can only speculate that like most American Catholics of the time the writers were of the working class. Most had Irish surnames although a few were of German descent. This also reflects the ethnic origins of Catholics in the United States during the 1870s. Although Sorin and Granger were French, none of the letters came from French-surnamed Catholics.

The letters shared a common narrative. First the writer discussed an illness, one as dramatic as consumption or as commonplace as a nose bleed. Children's illnesses were often reported. Some writers described difficult pregnancies. Eye disorders were the most frequently named malady, with pains in the limbs cited second. Then, the writer usually mentioned receiving the water, commonly giving it to other family members or friends. The water was either drunk or placed on the injured part of the body. Recovery came immediately. The letters generally concluded by thanking God and the Blessed Virgin for the cure and asking for more Lourdes water. Typically, correspondents included a contribution for the building of Our Lady of the Sacred Heart Church or for masses to be said. Letters were brief and rarely varied from this pattern.

Robert Orsi, who has written about how devotion to the saints functions in the lives of contemporary Catholics, explains that the "space of sickness" is constricted and closed. Mailing a letter to a shrine in a faraway place "parallels going on pilgrimage: it creates an opening in the bounded world of one's sickness."[38] Illness disrupts the everyday flow of life by introducing pain, uncertainty, and worry. It affects not only the individual who is ill but family and friends as well. Parents who are sick cannot work and support their families. Children who are ill drain their families' financial and psychological resources. In the nineteenth century, a sick child's income might also be lost. Even minor pains could be of major concern. Mary Sullivan from Chicago wrote in 1873 that she was suffering from a toothache and neuralgia. "I was almost crazy with pain," she explained, but "I put a few drops of the miraculous water where the pain was, and I was instantly cured."[39] Whether the illness was life-threatening and disabling or of limited duration, sickness disrupted the ordinary flow of life and introduced chaos and uncertainty where order once was.

Letter writers did not discuss their illnesses in any great detail. However, in the very act of writing anything about their pain, they broke apart the dreadful isolation of sickness. In her meditation on the meaning of pain and torture, Elaine Scarry describes how pain is not only resistant to language but actually destroys it. "As the content of one's world disintegrates," she writes regarding pain, "so the content of one's language disintegrates; as the self disintegrates, so that which would express and project the self is robbed of its source and its subject."[40] In the process of finding paper and pen, sitting down, and composing even the briefest of letters, the sick objectify their pain. By verbally expressing suffering, those in pain recapture their disintegrating language. At that point they begin to externalize and share what was an interior and unsharable experience.[41] By telling of their illness to Granger they simultaneously express their suffering to the Virgin Mary and Christ. What cannot be truly known by anyone else, the reality of an individual's pain, can be known and felt by the divine. In writing letters, an intercessory structure was constructed that was the psychological and linguistic opposite to the voiceless immediacy of illness.

Given the state of medicine in the 1870s, letter writers had little information about what was making them sick. Doctors informed one man that "water on [the] brain" would cause his death and another was told that his wife had a "disease in her head."[42] The writers also did not elaborate on what other treatments they were taking for their illness or what types of cures doctors had tried. Doctors, in general, did not figure prominently in their narratives. Physicians were shown as having given up in their attempts to cure the patient but were not chided for being ineffectual, incompetent, or skeptical. "My wife was on the point of death," wrote Harman Griese from West Virginia, "the doctor had given her up and expecting to here of hir death the nex morning."[43] An attorney, C. A. Korby, recounted that his sister was very ill with "cerebral-spinal meningitis or spotted fever" and "her doctor pronounced the case hopeless and said her blood was poisoned by the intensity of the fever." The doctor did agree to inject a drop of the Lourdes water "subdermically" into her circulation.[44] Doctors mentioned in the letters did not resist the use of Lourdes water.

The letters are devoid of details about illnesses, treatments, and doctors because the world of the late nineteenth-century Catholic did not include what we now think of as the "medical establishment." Theirs was a world without widespread hospital care, emergency rooms, ambulances, pharmacies, and self-help books. Medical jargon, which peppers our modern language, did not structure the thoughts of these Americans. Diverse and competing theories comprised American medicine during this period. "Regular" allopathic doctors were slowly moving away from the theory that bleeding and purging cured the imbalances in the body to thinking that drug and alcohol-based medications enacted healing changes. Homeopathy was popular among the upper classes and faith healing occurred among Protestants as well as Catholics.[45] Mesmerism, phrenology, and water cures had all been ways in which Americans sought to heal themselves. "Nineteenth-century medical theory and treatment," summarized one historian, "were an extremely uncertain business for all practitioners."[46] Physicians had not yet established themselves as sole authority figures over the sick body. Using Lourdes water did not serve as an oppositional gesture against the modern medical establishment because that establishment had not yet been born.

The way that Catholics used Lourdes water reflects the fluctuating state of

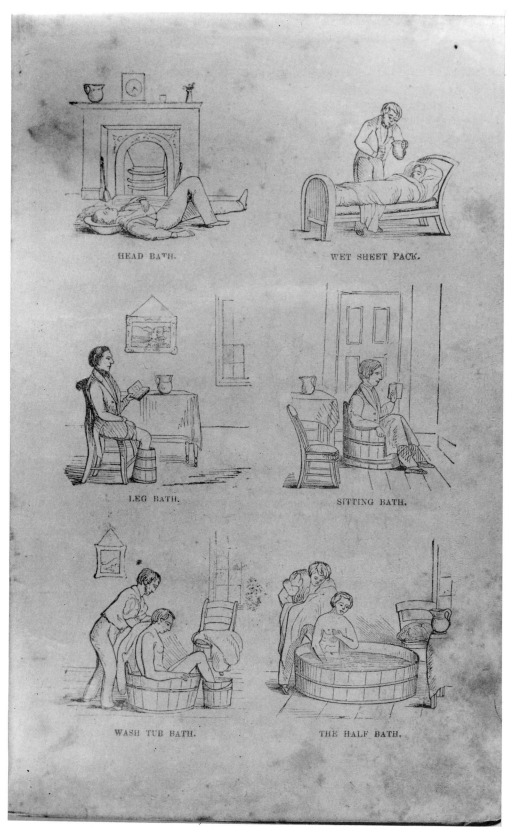

HEAD BATH.   WET SHEET PACK.

LEG BATH.   SITTING BATH.

WASH TUB BATH.   THE HALF BATH.

medicine in the 1870s. The fascination with Lourdes water was part of a larger trend in American health care that accepted water as a curative force. Between 1843 and 1900 Americans established 213 water cure centers to help a predominately female clientele cope with illness. Through bathing, wet compresses, steam, massage, exercise, drinking cold water, and Spartan diet, cure center owners predicted gradual improvements in health. Water cure centers focused on bodily sensation and physical exertion, provided a supportive communal atmosphere, and stressed the curative power of outdoor exercise.[47] Spas were more rowdy than water cure centers, but "taking the waters" comprised another popular nineteenth-century health activity (especially in Europe). At spas people took hot baths and imbibed the local mineral water as well as also enjoying champagne dinners, gambling, and romance. For those who could not afford days or months at spas or water cure centers, special waters could be drunk. In 1878 the Methodist newspaper, *The Christian Advocate*, ran a series of advertisements for "Buffalo Lithia Water." The advertisements heralded the Virginia water as taking "the place of the surgeon's knife" and being particularly useful "in all the affections [sic] peculiar to women." In nineteenth-century America, water – whether bathed in as part of an overall life style change at a water cure center, drunk along with other spirits at a spa, or consumed in the privacy of the home – was believed to have healing powers. A comment from Henry Maguire, a former Notre Dame student, could easily have been an advertisement for the Victorian water mania: "The water of Lourdes makes me feel better every time I take it."[48]

The consumption of Lourdes water also resonated with another nineteenth-century health practice: homeopathy. Introduced by German doctor Samuel Hahnemann in 1825, homeopathy was well received in the United States by 1850. Homeopathic healers used minute doses of tinctures and powders to return the body to a harmonious state. Violent emetics, bleeding, and purging were replaced by the ingestion of drugs sometimes diluted to the thirteenth degree. Homeopathy also emphasized self-care, a moderate living regimen of fresh air, pure foods and water, and avoidance of overstimulation.[49] Those who used Lourdes water took it in small doses as if they were using homeopathic medicines. They did not ask for large quantities of water from Father Granger, and he sent only small vials through the mails. Mary Garrigan described how a young lady, "troubled with a smothered feeling of the breast," took "about one drop of the water of Our Lady of Lourdes when she was relieved."[50] Mr. C. A. Korby recalled how a lady far advanced in pregnancy, "troubled with violent headaches, and fearing the intense pain might produce pre-mature labor, used a drop of the water and said a Hail Mary or two." The headaches left her the next morning.[51] Several letter writers took the water a few drops at a time over a period of several days. Gertrude Sevey from Rome, New York, began a novena and took a "few drops every day and in nine days I was entirely relived."[52] As with homeopathy, Catholics understood the water of Lourdes to be intensely powerful and so only a small amount was needed to accomplish a cure.

The similarity of water cures, homeopathy, and using miraculous water was not lost on some of those using Lourdes water. In 1875 an Ohio priest wrote to Granger about one of his parishioners who had a painful "neuralgic" in his face. The parishioner, "a man not overcredulous," rubbed his face with the water and the pain was relieved. To the priest's astonishment, however, "he suggested that the *mineral* qualities of the water might have produced [the cure] but I knocked

93. Between 1843 and 1900 213 water cure centers were established in the United States. The use of Lourdes water by nineteenth-century Catholics accords with the general understanding of the curative power of water. This illustration is from Joel Shew, *The Hydropathic Family Physician* (New York, 1854).

that out of his brain & told him that if he wanted any of it as a mineral-agent for cure, I would not send for it."[53] For the water of Lourdes to be miraculous, it had to be understood as having supernatural not natural powers. In this particular letter the priest as religious authority chided his parishioner, and the users of Lourdes water would agree with his clerical sentiments. Health came not from mineral properties but from the Virgin Mary asking Christ to act on her behalf. Consequently, no evidence survives showing that users of Lourdes water ever followed the lifestyle changes promoted in homeopathy or water cures. Improvement of health came from God, not from fresh air, exercise, and proper diet. Prayer alone accompanied the ingestion or application of the blessed water. In the nineteenth century, clergy, laity, and even at times doctors accepted the discourse of the miraculous. Doctors supported patients using Lourdes water because their own medical models were in flux. Clergy facilitated the use of the water because miraculous cures emphasized the strength of the one, true church.

Only a few correspondents included discussions of the types of prayers they offered in connection with using Lourdes water. The most common prayer associated with the water was a nine-day novena that Granger sent along with the vials. Father Kelly from St. Bridget's Church in Cleveland saw to it that the young man to whom he gave the water performed a novena "as ordered," but the priest sent no details about which novena was said.[54] Joseph Mukawtz from Chicago described how a consumptive girl recovered during a novena, "that her strength returned and that within nine days she could walk up and down stairs."[55] For a Pennsylvanian man, who had his daughter write to Granger, the novena instructions were problematic. "I cannot either read or write, and I used the water before I made the novena," he explained. "My parish priest has told me that I should not use the water until after the novena."[56] Since his pains were not entirely relieved, he asked for more water to be sent so that he could perform the ritual properly. Saying a novena fitted into traditional Catholic devotional practice and cures frequently occurred during that special period of time. The sick felt that Jesus and Mary were particularly attentive to their pleas during these nine days.[57]

While Granger might have requested that the sick say a novena, letter writers wanted their thanks to be returned to Mary and Jesus via *Granger's* position as priest. Father Granger not only was the person from whom one obtained the miraculous water, correspondents also expected him to offer prayers on behalf of those who received divine favors. John Nalsh from Baton Rouge, Louisiana, mentioned that his wife was improving and that she "most humbly requests of you, Rev. Father, to help us in returning thanks to our Blessed Mother, for the favors obtained thro. the use of the Blessed water of Lourdes."[58] Michael Kelly wanted to be remembered to the Sacred Heart of Mary so that he would have not only his appetite and health back but "the strength to serve her on earth and enjoy her in heaven."[59] It was not enough that people offered their own prayers, it was expected that a priest amplify their intentions and thanks. Through him people publicly acknowledged the healing power of the water.

Granger comprised one link in a long chain of intercessors. A sick wife might ask her husband to write for the water, the husband would correspond with Granger, her family and the Associates of Our Lady of the Sacred heart would pray to Mary, then Mary would obtain the favors of her son. Catholics did not forget the order in the chain of intercessors. They acknowledged that Mary had to petition Christ, just as they asked friends and family for help in times of sickness.

Neither Bernadette, nor the story of Lourdes were discussed in the letters saved by Father Granger. The letter writers focused on connecting "real" divine characters with "real" earthly individuals. Catholics participated in a complicated ethos of spiritual exchange that emphasized the social, mediated nature of the divine. They placed themselves within a community of the concerned: those residing in heaven and on earth.

Letter writers formalized the relationship between human and divine by recognizing Granger's request for donations to Our Lady of the Sacred Heart Church. In almost every letter, individuals enclosed a contribution for the building of the church or to pay for masses to be said. The money was enclosed as a thank-you for favors received, not as payment for the Lourdes water. Writers explicitly mentioned that money was an offering for the new church, for masses offered for the souls in purgatory, or for the prayers of the association. Typically, letter writers enclosed $5, but some writers sent as much as $50. When a female office clerk in 1870 earned $6 a week and an unskilled male laborer $7 a week, such contributions were not trivial.[60] Martha Conaty from Philadelphia sent a small donation but "if I remain able to work I will send you a donation once and awhile."[61] Money donated for masses assured the writer that his or her family and friends received the blessings generated from the priest's prayers. While Lourdes water usually brought instantaneous relief, donations ensured continued divine intercession.

Sending money for church construction or for masses for the dead tied the individual to a world beyond his or her immediate circle. In the same way, using the water itself also cemented social bonds. In spite of the fact that Granger only sent small amounts of Lourdes water, the letters indicate that the people who received the water went out of their way to share it with friends, families, and even Protestants. A common pattern was for one person to write on behalf of someone else. Mrs. Lancaster wrote for the water because of neuralgia, but before mentioning her own ills she wrote, "Mrs. Gibbs who is a friend of mine was taken sick with the spine disease. She is the mother of a large family and took it [the illness] from a child of hers." Mrs. Lancaster used the water sent to her to enable Mrs. Gibbs to gain "instant relief."[62] Emma Gorman, from Galena, Illinois, asked for "some more of the precious water of Lourdes" because she had distributed it to six persons.[63] From Minnesota, Michael McDonnell wrote to thank Granger for sending the water and included a dollar from Daniel Day. McDonnell had given Day the water, and Day had successfully used it on his son.[64] People wrote on behalf of others who either were too sick or unable to write. Granger mailed water to one person, and that person then carefully distributed it to others in need.

This is not to say that the clergy did not try to control sacred power. While the availability of Lourdes water made it easier for lay people to heal, the example of Notre Dame demonstrates that clergymen like Sorin and Granger managed the flow of Lourdes water into the United States. They determined to whom it would be sent, how much would be sent, and how the devout should properly use the water. At the same time, the Notre Dame letters show that people who received the water gently pushed against this authority by apportioning the water once they got it, giving it to whosoever they pleased, asking for more water as soon as they received what they were given, and using the water however they wanted. What is crucial to note is that when lay Catholics used Lourdes water the gesture was not interpreted by the clergy or physicians as a challenge to religious or medical authority. Lay Catholics had acquired authority without confronting the power of experts because most professionals did not perceive their behavior as aberrant.

The response of nineteenth-century Catholics to Lourdes water resonates with traditional attitudes toward the "translation" of relics. Peter Brown's research on the development of the cult of the saints in late antiquity reveals that the movement of relics and other holy objects reduced social distance between people. "Those who possessed the holy, in the form of portable relics," Brown explains, "could show *gratia* by sharing these good things with others."[65] Distributing relics, or, in the nineteenth century, Lourdes water, created gestures of good will and solidarity. Translation secured intricate systems of patronage, alliance, and gift-giving. While the sharing of Lourdes water was more informal than the transfer of relics, it still allowed people to create bonds of friendship and concern. Unlike possessing a relic, once a patron used the miraculous water it was gone. In the spiritual economy of the sacred, restricting the supply increased the value. Getting more water entailed negotiating with more people. Consequently, the water was a more precious gift to give away than sharing a relic. Catholics used Lourdes water not as a solitary gesture of piety but as a communal ritual.

In his work on devotion to St. Jude, Robert Orsi has indicated that most of the people who pray to that saint for help in difficult times are women. Through their devotion to St. Jude, women "were learning by an intimate pedagogy the religiously consecrated cultural grammar of gender."[66] There is no question but that the twentieth-century devotion to St. Jude is a woman's devotion. Nineteenth-century devotion to Our Lady of Lourdes, however, was not dominated by women. Men wrote to Granger almost as frequently as women. Male narratives differed from those of women in understandable ways. Illnesses that affected employment, for instance, figured in men's letters. James Doughtery wanted the blessed water as his eyes were weak because he had worked seven years with chemicals used in a mill.[67] John Sullivan was grateful because "I can use my fingers better and lift more thanks be to God and his Blessed Mother."[68] Father Thilban of Portland, Oregon, who suffered from "bronchitis and weakness of the lungs" reported that he was much improved and "able to give nine instructions during a retreat" at the convent.[69] Concerned about their own health and well-being, men willingly wrote to Granger for the water. Their letters expressed faith in the curative power of the water and in the benefits gained by having masses said for their intentions.

Men also asked for Lourdes water for their friends and family. The letters indicate that men frequently took responsibility for the health and welfare of their loved ones. James McGeogh, a conveyancer from Philadelphia, asked for water to ensure his wife would have a safe delivery.[70] Men referred to their sick children as "my little pet" or "my little girl" and asked for water for them. Patrick Early sent money for the new church and for *Ave Maria*'s publication of Lasserre's *Our Lady of Lourdes*. He mentioned that both his wife and two children had been helped.[71] When John Nalsh's wife was cured, he requested that Granger enroll them both in the Association of Our Lady of the Sacred Heart.[72] Mark Foote of Mt. Pleasant, Iowa, asked for water for his mother since "her friends seem to consider her headquarters [for Lourdes water] and fly to her whenever they are in need of any."[73] John Kirmane sought to enroll several people in the association and mentioned that John Flynn, who had a pain in his ear, sent fifty cents for a medal.[74] Priests and brothers sent for water for their parishioners.[75] Men both used the water and wrote to ask for water for others. The letters which were sent to Granger during the 1870s indicate that at that point Catholic devotional life was not strictly in the domain of women. Like women, men nourished their relationships with those they cared about as well as with the supernatural by using and distributing Lourdes water.

Since we do not know how "feminized" Catholicism was in the late nineteenth century, we cannot speculate about whether the letters were unique or not.[76] The letters raise more questions about male participation in Catholic devotions than can be answered here. What we can conclude is that men recognized that Lourdes water had curative power, and that they sought it for those they cared about. Nurturing, at least for these Irish American men, was something they took seriously. Since the state of medicine was in flux, there was no dominant medical model. Consequently, alternative healing systems were not devalued or solely in the domain of women. Pragmatic men might try Lourdes water as they would experiment with other healing methods. Because the focus was on the water and not on a relationship with a specific saint, men did not have to become involved in complicated devotions. They could obtain Lourdes water just as they would have obtained any medicine for their family and friends. On the other hand, the letters show men who seem sincere in their willingness to have masses said for their intentions and to join the Association of Our Lady of the Sacred Heart. Perhaps devotion to Mary, with its attention directed toward a woman, was easier for men to express.[77]

In 1883 Louise Ifams from Omaha, Nebraska, wrote to Father Granger that she had been suffering for years from a sickness that defied medical skill. She had been praying to the blessed Virgin "for her intercession promising to love her very dearly" and would start a novena. "I beg you will join your prayers with mine," she wrote, "and do tell me how to use the water."[78] The only unique characteristic of this particular letter was that Louise Ifams was a Protestant. The circle of concern that men and women created through their distribution of Lourdes water included Protestants as well as Catholics. When George Thompson asked if he could give the water to a Protestant, Granger penned "yes" on his letter. Edward Robinson, a dealer in lumber from Millview, Florida, asked that his name be placed in the Association of Our Lady of the Sacred Heart even though he was not a Catholic. Since he did not have any money, he promised to send $5 at a later date.[79] Laurence Corcoran enrolled three friends in the association who were non-Catholics.[80] James Neil from Chicago gave some of the water to a Protestant friend who "has great faith in it and it has done him more good than the doctors."[81] Certain Protestants responded in the same way as Catholics to the possibility that water could heal. Some were probably sympathetic to Catholic devotions prior to their use of the water, while others might have used the water because trusted friends had suggested it might help. Catholics may have enrolled Protestants in the association without their knowledge, but Protestants appeared willing to try the water. In spite of public Protestant skepticism about Catholicism, it appears that some Protestants availed themselves of Catholic healing and devotional activities.

Catholics did not always give Lourdes water to Protestants without strings attached. It was assumed that a miraculous healing would turn the Protestant toward the proper religious path. Sister Eusebia from Cincinnati asked for Lourdes water to use on one of the young ladies in her boarding school who had poor hearing. The sisters believed that, "if she were cured, she would become a fervent convert; she is at present a very prejudiced protestant."[82] Sometimes the cures did motivate conversion. Sara Trainer Smith wrote from Cape May, New Jersey, that her "child at heart who has been a helpless cripple for two years, has been entirely cured by the help of Our dear Lady of Lourdes and is now a Catholic."[83] Catholics assumed that cures accomplished with Lourdes water would inevitably lead to conversion, and so they readily gave Protestants the water. By using the water, Protestants were drawn into the Catholic world of spiritual exchange.

Letters as "*Ex Votos*"

The letters sent to Alexis Granger were nineteenth-century American versions of "*ex votos*," physical expressions of thanks for a cure or divine help. Found in the ancient world, *ex votos* became popular throughout Christian Europe. As early as the sixth century, synods and councils placed restrictions on offerings made in thanks for, or in hopes of, a cure because of lingering pagan associations. Votive images could be elaborate paintings depicting the saving act or cure. They could also be simple representations in wax, silver, or wood of the part of the body that was healed. Sometimes they were marble plaques with a simple "Merci" engraved on it. The *ex votos* were hung in churches, placed at pilgrimage sites, and left at shrines. According to David Freedberg, votive images are realistic because "we see the sound replica of the body, or of part of it; we respond to it as if it were real; and its soundness (or sometimes its sheer preciousness) reassures us of the fact of healing and of deliverance into safety."[84] The *ex votos* were placed in the church *after* miraculous healing and are material reminders of the possibility of the sacred breaking into the world of nature.

The linkage of representation, mediation, and gratitude which Freedberg sees in the traditional *ex votos* can also be seen in the written *ex votos* of late nineteenth-century American Catholics.[85] The letters follow the same pattern as the *ex voto* paintings: they describe the event which has necessitated the intervention, illustrate the role the divine played in the intervention, and they offer thanks. Like the visual *ex voto*, they connect the past disordering event with the now ordered present. They also connect individuals in very specific ways to the divine and to each other. Both types of *ex votos* differ from sincere prayer of thanks because they are public gestures. The *ex voto* is placed at a shrine or in the church for all to see. It publicly testifies to the intercession of Christ, Mary, and the saints in the lives of the devout. So too with the letters sent to Father Granger. Since excerpts were printed in *Ave Maria*, letter writers realized that their correspondence would be used as evidence for the intervention of the divine in the lives of average people. Catholics acknowledged the divine through a public ritual linking together the institutional church, the individual, and the supernatural.

Ex votos, as they appear in parts of Europe and Latin America, are intensely visual. They graphically depict the sick body or the accident through art and craft. While the letters are descriptive, they are not visual. Granger replaced the traditional setting – the shrine with the *ex votos* – with one more appropriate to the age of mass communications. The journal *Ave Maria* supplanted the shrine as the site where the exchange of thanks took place. By the late nineteenth century,

94. Votive images frequently depicted the saving act or cure by supernatural characters. In this 1787 Austrian *ex voto*, Our Lady of Mount Carmel, through the intercession of St. Simon Stock, has saved a boy from falling down a well. Photograph taken by Wulf Brackrock.

95. In lieu of an elaborate and costly painting, *ex voto*s may also be simple representations of the healed part of the body, bought and laid in the church or on the domestic altar. Photograph taken by Wulf Brackrock.

Americans enjoyed an efficient and inexpensive postal system. Newspapers and journals could be easily produced and distributed. Reading *Ave Maria* helped reduce the distances between American and European Catholics and between Catholics within the United States. In a modern society dominated by the written word, a letter might more easily express the sentiments of the votive object or painting. Rather than place silver eyes or wax limbs in their churches, American Catholics described their weak eyes and abscessed limbs in letters. Letter writing was a means to recapture the language, self, and humanity that sickness and pain destroy. Catholics who wrote to Granger and who used Lourdes water united the image and the word.

This is not to say, however, that the nineteenth-century Catholic had a modern, critical understanding of Lourdes water. Contemporary Catholic thought tries to deflect the desire for miraculous cures by affirming the meaning of physical suffering. From a modern, theological perspective, expecting Lourdes water to accomplish a cure borders on superstitious magic. What the contemporary Christian at Lourdes should do is to accept suffering as Christ did, strive to eliminate sin, and use the pilgrimage experience as a means to revive his or her religious commitments. Sending and receiving Lourdes water through the mail, from a modern outlook, does nothing to improve the overall spiritual character of the individual.

For the nineteenth-century Catholic, however, the discourse of the miraculous was still dominant. The letters infrequently mentioned that suffering should be endured. The closest any of these Catholics comes to voicing such sentiments was by saying: "Maybe it is not God's holy will that I am to be cured. May his holy will be done."[86] Terms like sin, suffering, offering it up, forgiveness, and fortitude do not appear in the letters. Nineteenth-century Catholics employ a discourse of the miraculous and prefer terms like power, precious water, miraculous water, eased her immediately, entirely cured. While the format of a letter sent through the mail reflected modern technology and efficiency, the focus on the miraculous reflected traditional religious attitudes. The "truest" contact with the sacred for these Catholics did not permit them to endure suffering; it eliminated it. Nineteenth-century Catholics would probably agree with anthropologist Victor Turner when he wrote that, "indeed, a mark of the true Church is that it is electrically charged, so to speak, with the potential of miracles."[87]

Authentically Unauthentic: Lourdes Shrines

American Catholics carefully imported Lourdes water because they believed that the water itself was charged with "the potential of miracles." Like the medieval Catholic pilgrim who brought back holy oil from the grave of St. John the Evangelist or dirt from the Holy Land, Lourdes water mailed by Father Granger participated in the sacredness of the original source. For the user, it was important that the water *really* came from Lourdes and not from one of the lakes at Notre Dame. The authenticity of the water ensured its spiritual properties. Authenticity itself, however, does not make something sacred. The water from Lourdes is sacred because it is a part of a sacred context, a larger religious story: the original story of Bernadette's vision, the tradition of water symbolism, the clerical support of the Lourdes shrine for various political and ecclesiastical reasons, the reports of miracles by people who had been healed both at the shrine and at a distance, the association of Lourdes water with specific church needs such as Father Granger's desire to finance the building of Our Lady of the Sacred Heart Church. The water became sacred because its meaning was embedded in a complicated layering of religious meaning. The Virgin Mary also told Bernadette to eat the herb growing at the grotto. Eating Lourdes herbs might be real and authentic, but it has little religious meaning. Authenticity, to be meaningful in a religious sense, must be culturally constructed.

Through using Lourdes water, Catholics could experience the power of the French shrine at a distance. The water served as a link between the miraculous events which happened to Bernadette, the Virgin and her son in heaven, and the needs of people living throughout the world. Likewise, the construction of replicas of the Lourdes grotto also served to connect these various historical and temporal realms. Like the water, duplicate grottoes were translations: they permitted the sacred to be de-localized and moved about. The construction of facsimiles of the Lourdes grotto was completely an exercise in creating authenticity. Catholics did not ship rocks and dirt from Lourdes to be used in the building of new grottoes. Duplicate shrines became sacred because they participated in the story of Lourdes and allowed Catholics to express dramatically their sentiments about the miraculous and the supernatural. Catholics extended their piety outside of the church through Lourdes shrines. Just as the water's miraculous cures ordered the internal space of the individual by eliminating sickness, so the shrines gave religious meaning to the outside space of the community. As with the spiritual power of water, the construction of replica shrines enjoys a long tradition in Catholic history.

Edward Sorin's vision included both providing education for Catholics on the western frontier of Indiana and promoting Marian piety throughout the United States. He also intended to claim the land on which Notre Dame sat; transforming it from the wilderness into an ordered, sacred space. Catholics would be nurtured not only through proper education but also through living in a Catholic "natural" environment. Toward this end, a series of shrines was built at Notre Dame to promote visitation not only by students but also by Catholics from the surrounding area. Notre Dame leaders engaged in "religious replication," an exercise common in the processes of claiming sacred space. The eventual construction of the now well-known replica of the Lourdes grotto in 1896 capped off a past tradition of shrine building at Notre Dame.

Sorin oversaw the construction of at least two major replica shrines prior to building the first grotto to Our Lady of Lourdes in 1877. The first replica was built at St. Mary's College, probably at the behest of Father Neal Henry Gillespie. In 1856 Gillespie had completed his theological studies in Rome, was ordained a priest, and appointed vice president of Notre Dame College. His sister, Eliza Maria Gillespie (Sister Angela), supervised the nuns who taught at St. Mary's. According to one account, Gillespie brought back from a trip to Italy the plans to build a replica of "Sacra Casa di Loreto" at St Mary's.[88] The replica was completed in 1859. Since the fifteenth century, Sacra Casa di Loreto has been one of the most famous shrines in Italy, and its history is certainly curious. Tradition has it that, in 1291, angels carried the home of Jesus, Mary, and Joseph from

96. The replica of the "holy house of Nazareth," built on the grounds of St. Mary's College for Women at Notre Dame. The replica still stands, although it is now encased in another building.

Nazareth to Tresato, Italy. Evidently, the threat of Muslim desecration of the home of the Holy Family and the birthplace of Mary had motivated the divine move. Three years later, angels moved the house to woods near the village of Recanati. Still not at rest, the house moved three more times during one year, finally settling down forty miles from Rome in Loreto. It was alleged that the bricks and mortar of Sacra Casa were "chemically identical" with materials commonly found in Nazareth and that miraculous cures took place at the shrine.[89] The replica built at St. Mary's reportedly followed the exact measurements of the Italian shrine: thirty-one feet by thirteen feet.

A year later in 1860, another replica shrine was constructed. This time Sorin directly oversaw the building of a copy of the Portiuncula chapel of the Church of St. Mary of the Angels in Assisi. The original Portiuncula chapel was where, in 1208, St. Francis of Assisi recognized his vocation. Sorin built the replica Portiuncula for the noviate chapel of the Holy Cross Brothers. He was interested in more than the informal influence that a replica of the Portiuncula would have on the Notre Dame community. In 1862 he obtained for the Notre Dame Portiuncula all of the indulgences granted for the Portiuncula in Assisi.[90] The Portiuncula Indulgence was originally granted to those who on August 2 (the Feast of Our Lady of the Angels) visited the Assisi chapel. Prior to the visit the devout had to receive the sacraments of Penance and the Eucharist. For each visit they gained a plenary indulgence – total remission of the temporal punishment due to their sins. The Portiuncula Indulgence was *toties quoties*, that is, one could receive it as many times as one visited the church. It also could be applied to the souls in purgatory. In the late fifteenth century, Pope Sixtus IV extended the indulgence to all churches run by the Franciscans. Later popes extended the privilege to any church, not near a Franciscan church, that wanted to grant the indulgence.

97. The 1860 replica shrine of the chapel where St. Francis recognized his vocation. The House of Loreto and Portiuncula were the most important replicas built prior to the 1896 construction of the now-famous Lourdes grotto.

By securing the Portiuncula Indulgence for the Notre Dame replica, Sorin assured the community that once a year the spiritual power of the brothers' chapel would be heightened. One could always mystically connect with the religious commitment of St. Francis by praying in the chapel, but once a year the devout could receive the same indulgences as if they had traveled to Italy and entered the original chapel. Sorin then petitioned the local bishop to permit the Notre Dame

Portiuncula to become a place for pilgrimage. If one could receive the same indulgence at Notre Dame as in Assisi, why make the pilgrimage to Italy? Why not just develop pilgrimages to Notre Dame?

In 1873 the *Notre Dame Scholastic* first mentions pilgrims coming to the chapel from local parishes.[91] By 1875 the annual pilgrimage had changed to October, perhaps so it could coincide with St. Francis of Assisi's feast day and Rosary Sunday. Five hundred pilgrims from the nearby town of Mishawaka walked four miles to Notre Dame where they received the sacraments at the main church and then went in and out of the Portiuncula to gain the plenary indulgences for themselves and the dead.[92] Masses, said in succession from half past four until nine o'clock in the morning concluded with a solemn high mass. Religious instruction was given in both English and German; the Italian origin of the Portiuncula was superfluous to these German-American Catholics.[93] A mutual interaction between clergy and lay people was needed to imbue the shrines with affective presence. The clergy had to construct the buildings and secure the proper indulgences and the people needed to come and find spiritual solace at the shrine.

The tradition of religious replication had been firmly established by the time that Sorin built the first shrine to Our Lady of Lourdes. Lourdes water had been distributed from Notre Dame since 1872, Sorin had visited Lourdes for the first time in 1873, and in 1874 he helped lead the first American pilgrimage to Lourdes and other religious sites in Europe.[94] According to the college newspaper, when Sorin decided to build the grotto only three other Lourdes replicas existed in the United States, all associated with Catholic sisters. One of the replicas had been built at St. Mary's College at Notre Dame.[95] The success of the other Notre Dame shrines, and Sorin's increasing attention to Our Lady of Lourdes, motivated him in 1877 to build his own shrine to Our Lady of Lourdes. As with the other shrines, Sorin wished "to reproduce with scrupulous exactness as regards height, length, depth, etc."[96] In April 1877, building commenced to the northwest of the church, but it is unlikely that the shrine was a replica grotto, like the one the sisters had built, since later descriptions called it a "tower-like niche."[97]

Pilgrims to Notre Dame added the Lourdes grotto and shrine to their religious itinerary. In 1878 "fully two thousand people" came on the pilgrimage, this time in September for the Feast of the Seven Dolors, the seven sorrows of the Virgin Mary. The date of the pilgrimage continued to change and the places the pilgrims visited reflected the increasing number of sacred spots at Notre Dame. When the pilgrims came for the Feast of the Holy Rosary in 1879, they devoutly visited "the Holy Sepulchre, Grotto of Lourdes, Tomb of the Blessed Virgin, House of Loreto, and other facsimiles and representations of holy places which are so numerous here and at St. Mary's."[98] By the late 1880s, twelve hundred pilgrims took the train to Notre Dame, wore special badges, and carried lit candles. They enjoyed the "happy day spent in venerating 'Our Lady' at her greatest shrine in the United States and one of the greatest in the world."[99]

The proliferation of sacred places at Notre Dame ended in 1896 with the construction of a second grotto of Lourdes. This grotto, the existing one on campus, became so well known that it overshadowed the other shrines. Edward Sorin died in 1893 and his concern for Lourdes shrines was taken up by Father William Corby, a former Notre Dame president. In 1894 Corby traveled to Europe on a fund raising trip and said mass at Lourdes. When he returned to Notre Dame, he decided to build a larger and more authentic replica Lourdes

grotto on the men's side of the campus. On June 8, 1896, Father Corby contacted Father Thomas Carroll, a former Holy Cross priest living in Pennsylvania and noted for his philanthropy. In the letter Corby related a story about a Frenchman who, although born a Catholic, did not go to mass but did pick flowers for his wife's shrine to Mary. When the man died, a priest told the grieving widow that her husband was in purgatory and that "we can pray him out." Corby then delivered his plea for money to build a new Lourdes grotto:

> now such an act as that of procuring a few flowers for the B. V. Mary secured salvation to this poor French man can there be any doubt that our dear Lady of Lourdes will refuse your request for the grace of a happy death after what you are doing to build her a Grotto? You have made many good investments; but likely this [is] the best you ever made. With the prayers of the com'ity and the maternal care of Mary, you, I hope will be richly rewarded in time and in eternity.[100]

Father Carroll paid in full for the construction of a new grotto.[101]

In the spring of 1896 the grotto was begun. According to one recollection, it was built at the site of "an old midden where everything from old shoes and tin cans or what have you were thrown – just a dump heap." During the construction a spring appeared but, "wiser people closed it up so as to prevent wild rumors regarding it."[102] Because the grotto was built in order to make the space holy, it did not have to be placed in a romantic or spiritual locale. The clergy at Notre Dame already mailed out authentic Lourdes water; there was no need for a competitor source. If water had been available, it would have been difficult for the Notre Dame authorities to control how it would be used. Lighting candles at the

98. Father Sorin's shrine to Our Lady of Lourdes, of 1877, erected northwest of the church. Although he intended to create a replica grotto, what was finally built was only a small enclosed shrine.

99. The large replica Lourdes grotto built in 1896. This grotto would eventually evolve into the most sacred place on the Notre Dame campus, rivaling even the football field.

shrine for special intentions, rather than seeking miraculous cures, better reflected standard Catholic devotions. The Carroll grotto soon became *the* shrine on campus, so much so that the Portiuncula chapel would be torn down in 1898 and its bricks used to build a new college gymnasium. Because people no longer saw it as a sacred spot, the Portiuncula chapel lost its affective presence. None of the other sacred places on campus would garner as much attention as the Lourdes grotto.[103]

Religious Replication

Religious replication is a critical aspect of Catholic culture. What Sorin and other Notre Dame leaders were doing was assembling a material world to mark off a sacred domain as ordered and meaningful. On the one hand, they built schoolrooms and dormitories. On the other hand, they reproduced shrines. Although Catholics had their own local ethnic traditions that defined them as Irish or French or German, to be Catholic also meant to embrace the universality of the supernatural. It meant to participate in a worldwide community that did not recognize the limits of time and space. Houses could be miraculously moved by angels from their original site in the Middle East to various places in Italy and then reproduced in Indiana. The divine was not anchored to one place. The construction of the shrines and the distribution of miraculous water made a physical statement that the divine, and Catholicism in general transcended national boundaries. Reproducing shrines told the Catholics of northern Indiana that they were not living in an undefined, wild space but that they were directly connected to the spiritual centers of Catholicity.

The production of religious replicas was, curiously enough, the production of authenticity. While we might think that building copies of European shrines is merely an exercise in fakery, what actually happens is just the opposite. For the religious person, the real is achieved *not* by appealing to a natural experience but rather to an experience associated with the sacred. As we saw with Laurel Hill Cemetery, nature was augmented by human design and interpretation. Since the sacred can transcend place, it can be established in a variety of locales. There is no reason why the house of the Holy Family cannot be transported to Italy and then reproduced in Indiana. The granting of the same indulgences to both the original Portiuncula and the one at Notre Dame formally legitimized what informally had taken place. By visiting the various shrines, Catholics emotionally engaged with the sacred past. They entered into a series of Catholic stories. It was the engagement with the material object and the religious narrative that made the shrine "real."

The religious replicas at Notre Dame belong to a Catholic tradition of building shrines with realistic portrayals of sacred places and characters.[104] David Freedberg argues that accurate reproductions ensure that the thing being presented as the substitution for something real can be treated as real, and thus becomes real. When images are perceived as being realistic, they achieve a living presence. For Freedberg, reproduction, verisimilitude, and representation enable people to imagine relationships creatively. The shrines at Notre Dame enabled the Catholic to learn the devotion easily because the duplicates resembled traditional religious centers. At the shrines, Catholics participated in what Freedberg describes as the "automatic transition from seeing to empathy and involvement."[105] Time and distance conflate when the visitor emphatically participates in the religious replication. While an outsider might not see the resemblance between the original and the replica, for the devout even the barest hint provides an imaginative orientation toward the sacred. The site or object becomes authentic in the desire of the spectator, not in the precision of the details.

Nineteenth-century popular culture was also filled with reproductions and replication. Technological innovations allowed for artistic duplication through methods such as chromolithography. By the nineteenth century, everyone could have a copy of Murillo's *Madonna* or Da Vinci's *Last Supper*. Middle-class Americans imitated European aristocratic tastes for "objects rich in narrative signs suggesting allegorical fantasy and far-off places – leaves, claw feet, embellished figures."[106] They delighted in making one variety of object look like another: wax was made into flowers, one type of wood was painted to look like another, metal furniture was twisted to look like tree branches, plaster of Paris was applied to look like marble. Shrines resembling those at Loreto, Assisi, or Lourdes, made sense to Victorian Catholics who accepted reproduction and facsimile as a part of their aesthetic lives.

While mid-nineteenth century reformers like A. J. Downing disparaged those who wanted simple homes to look like European mansions, and late nineteenth-century critics hailed the Arts and Crafts Movement's authenticity, most Victorians felt comfortable in a material world filled with the real and the fake. "And indeed it was often precisely the purpose of the Victorians," explains historian Miles Orvell, "to confuse the realms of artifice and nature as part of an over-all aesthetic in which the imitation became a central category, not merely endured, but exulted in." Late nineteenth-century culture may be described as one of imitation.[107] Catholic culture in Indiana reflected both the traditions of baroque Catholicism which built religious replicas throughout Europe and of Victorian culture which reveled in artifice. For the Catholics of the late nineteenth century, reproduction did not diminish sacred reality but made reality available for all.

Scholars of American Catholicism have paid particular attention to the "American" quality of Catholicism: lay Catholics asked for decision-making power in the parish, Catholic sisters deserted the cloister and became more task-oriented, and parochial schools were to "Americanize" their students. While the American environment certainly made an indelible mark on Catholics living in the United States, we need not overlook the continuing presence of Europe in shaping American Catholicism. Understanding the devotion to Our Lady of Lourdes reveals a strong impulse within American Catholic devotional life to reach beyond the ethnic neighborhood and pragmatic American ideology to the transtemporal and transnational. Catholics embraced this universalizing trend not merely because it was being forced upon them by a church increasingly directed from Rome. They embraced it because it allowed them to transcend restrictions set up by nature, history, and society. By using Lourdes water, Catholics in America denied the debilitating necessity of illness, the restriction of the miraculous to the time of Christ, and the limits of national boundaries. At the same time that Catholics enjoyed the warmth of their ethnic communities and the liberties of American society, they could participate in devotions that challenged the reality of everyday life. In late nineteenth-century America, Catholics simultaneously enjoyed the familiarity of ethnic traditions, the freedoms of democratic ideology, and the universality of the supernatural.

The shrines Catholics built at Notre Dame and the Protestant landscape created at Laurel Hill Cemetery, were both public displays of religious sentiment tempered by private concerns. In both cases, clergymen did not perceive the activities of lay people as going against the general sentiments of their religious traditions. Although Protestant ministers would not have approved of overtly costly funerals or grave markers that seemed to speak more of the wealth of the dead than of their piety, they themselves chose to be buried at Laurel Hill. Catholic priests of the nineteenth century would not have approved of the use of Lourdes water that did not recognize the healing power of God, but they did use and distribute the miraculous substance. During the nineteenth century, clergy and lay people shared many common attitudes toward Christian practices. However, by the mid-twentieth century that mutuality had broken down. In Chapter 6 we move into the twentieth century and briefly away from describing how lay people experience religious objects, landscapes, and art. Instead, we look at the language Catholic and Protestant art critics used to attack the previous generation of Christian arts. In doing this, these "professional" Christians unintentionally expressed their fears of an overly sensuous and feminized Christianity.

6

Christian Kitsch and the Rhetoric of Bad Taste

In 1939 *Partisan Review* published an article by a young writer who worked in the customs service at the port of New York. A literary magazine, *Partisan Review* sought to disseminate creative and critical essays from the view point of the "revolutionary working class." If Clement Greenberg was trying to position himself within the Marxist intelligentsia of New York City through his article, he succeeded.[1] "Avant-Garde and Kitsch" had an immediate impact. Four issues later, Greenberg published another essay on modern art, "Towards a New Laocoon," that secured him a place in art circles. For the first time in America, the word "kitsch" entered the vocabulary of literary and art critics.

Greenberg argued in "Avant-Garde and Kitsch" that Western culture simultaneously produces both the abstract art of the avant-garde and the popular commercial kitsch of the "rearguard."[2] Abstract art, he wrote, takes its inspiration from the medium in which the artist works and has little interest in the external world of ideas or nature. Its opposite, kitsch, is a debased copy of genuine culture that operates through formula, vicarious experience, and faked sensations. Greenberg explained that art is produced by individual artists like Picasso, Braque, Miró, and Kandinsky. Culture is then "looted" and "watered down" only to be "served up as kitsch." While art asks much of its viewers, kitsch provokes immediate emotions that are vividly recognizable. For Greenberg, abstract art is produced by an avant-garde culture with revolutionary and critical attitudes toward society and history. Kitsch is consumed by peasants who have settled in cities as proletariat and petty bourgeoisie. Genuine folk traditions were wiped out after kitsch "flowed out over the country side." It would be up to socialism not only to produce a new culture but *simply* to preserve whatever living culture managed to survive. "Superior culture," Greenberg concluded, "is one of the most artificial of all human creations, and the peasant finds no 'natural' urgency within himself that will drive him towards Picasso in spite of all difficulties." With Greenberg's assault on kitsch, the debate over the "culture" of the people had reached a new rhetorical high.

Greenberg joins a group of Western thinkers who since the eighteenth century have tried to clarify the notion of taste. The same desire to promote abstract art as tasteful that motivated Greenberg's writing also moved Catholics and Protestants to discuss what kind of art was appropriate for Christian worship. Like Greenberg, a collection of Christian teachers and artists wrote critical essays defending their artistic preferences. While they rarely employed the term kitsch, their disdain for certain types of art paralleled Greenberg's antipathy to kitsch. In the other chapters of this book my intention has been to understand how objects and landscapes fit into the religious lives of average people and how commercial culture promoted the material dimension of Christianity. During the nineteenth century, there were critics of material Christianity, just as there were critics of the popular culture of the time.[3] However, it is not until the advent of modernist art in the twentieth century that a rigorous and well-articulated criticism of Christian material culture occurred. This chapter explores how certain Christians during the second half of the twentieth century defined the difference between good religious "art" and what they perceived as bad religious "kitsch." What in the nineteenth century was considered tasteful and pious, in the twentieth century came to be seen as tacky and irreligious. In this chapter I shift my focus from how the people in the pews practiced their religion to how certain priests, artists, and educators articulated what "good" religious art should look like.

Art criticism conducted by secularists or by Christians is not an objective, disinterested study free from historical influences.[4] Embedded within the arguments about appropriate Christian art are other debates that have little to do with aesthetics *per se*. We could, for instance, explore the question of commercialization and commodification of religious sentiments in a capitalist society via changing styles of art. However, here I explore how categories of gender are used to distinguish art from kitsch and to masculinize Christianity. Like Greenberg, Christian art critics used a vivid, picturesque language to persuade their readers. Art was given characteristics that Western culture defines as masculine: strength, power, nobility. Kitsch became associated with stereotypical feminine qualities: sentimentality, superficiality, and intimacy. The debate over bad taste is more than a question of whether or not Christians should modernize their arts and eliminate mass-produced, sentimental kitsch. The aesthetic debate in the twentieth century has as much to do with the roles of men and women in Christianity as it does with art.

Gender does not merely identify certain biological or social traits of male and female. It is a symbolic system of social location that signifies established power relationships within a society. Masculine and feminine are contextually defined and repeatedly constructed. Along with historian Joan Scott, I ask "what is at stake in proclamations or debates that invoke gender to explain or justify their positions?"[5] By focusing on Catholic and Protestant art criticism of the 1950s and its echo in the 1980s, I argue that these Christians were concerned with gender, as much as aesthetics. To create a particular identity of "art" there must be a reference to some other that is non-art. The discussion of art and kitsch is also a discussion of where men and women, masculinity and femininity, fit into twentieth-century Christianity. Is the church – the body of Christ – to look like a "man" or a "woman"?

Three Responses to Kitsch

The word "kitsch" has an unclear etymology. While it achieved international usage in the 1930s, it may have been used by German painters during the mid-nineteenth century. They used the English word "sketch" to deride the cheap tourist art bought by British and American visitors to Munich. The German word *kitschen* has the sense of "to collect rubbish from the street" and in the Mecklenburg dialect *verkitchen* meant "to make cheap."[6] Kitsch may have originated in the Russian word *keetcheetsya*, meaning "to be haughty and puffed up."[7] Perhaps the word became popular in America because English, unlike other European languages, lacked a single word to describe trivial literature (Gr. *Trivialliteratur*); shoddy goods (Fr. *pacotille*); low quality materials (Yid. *schlock*); sentimental arts (Yid. *schmaltz*) or vulgar merchandise (Rus. *poshlust*). Trying to find an appropriate word to describe religious objects and devotional arts, with or without the derogatory sense of kitsch, is difficult. English lacks an equivalent of the French word *bondieuserie* that refers both to religious knickknacks and to a notion of the conformingly banal. The unknown origin and the imprecise meaning of the word kitsch leaves it open to multiple meanings and manipulations by its users.

There are three basic responses to the type of goods or art that might be labeled kitsch. These responses help clarify the meaning of the term and provide a sense of how scholars and critics feel about the usefulness of the concept. In the first response, kitsch is a pejorative term and reflects cultural bias. Kitsch, as such, does not exist. In the second response, kitsch is described as mass-produced, inferior art. Kitsch may communicate cultural information but it fails aesthetically. In the third response, kitsch is perceived as anti-art. Kitsch is not merely a cultural artifact or a piece of bad art. Kitsch contains a negative moral dimension. I call these three categories the cultural, aesthetic, and ethical responses to kitsch.

Those who present a cultural response to kitsch argue that the term is unnecessarily pejorative and derogatory. This attitude – typically taken by sociologists, anthropologists, and specialists in cultural studies – implies that kitsch is merely what one particular group does not appreciate in another group's culture.[8] The writings of French sociologist Pierre Bourdieu perhaps best typify this cultural response. In his book, *Distinction: A Social Critique of the Judgement of Taste*, Bourdieu analyzes the responses to a survey carried out in 1963 and 1967–8 on a sample of 1,217 French people. His explanations of taste are discussed with an eye to class, power, authority, and economics. Kitsch for Bourdieu has no intrinsic value or meaning of its own. Taste reflects various educational and economic levels. "Art and cultural consumption," Bourdieu concludes, "are predisposed, consciously and deliberately or not, to fulfil a social function of legitimating social differences."[9] Referring to religious objects ridiculed as kitsch, Jean Pirotte echoes Bourdieu's position: "In an indirect way, the *kitsch* object will fulfill a new pedagogical function by giving an enlightened elite the opportunity to exercise its purifying and normative function through it."[10] The cultural response to kitsch insists that every group of people has its own artistic expressions that include a system of aesthetics with its own internal logic. Although that system may be influenced by other groups, it is incorrect to judge one group's notion of taste by the standard of another group. Calling something kitsch immediately devalues it and so the term must be used carefully.

Artists and cultural critics, however, frequently hold less relativistic views. For those who express an aesthetic response to kitsch, kitsch is an imitation of something else.[11] While cultural critic Stuart Ewen displays an awareness of how kitsch is coded by class in *All Consuming Images*, he does not analyze kitsch as a self-contained cultural product of a particular group. Instead, he defines kitsch as "cheap, mass-produced imitations of elite style." Ewen argues that middle-class Americans in the nineteenth century made and used copies of elite goods in order to identify with the upper class.[12] While Ewen's historical analysis is primarily cultural, his understanding of kitsch is aesthetic. Unlike the cultural response that places kitsch within a social order, the aesthetic response considers kitsch as a sub-set of art. Kitsch tries to be art but it fails. Kitsch lacks creativity, style, imagination, and nuance.

Clement Greenberg's attitude toward kitsch was primarily an aesthetic response. Kitsch required the existence of "a fully matured cultural tradition" from which it could make inferior copies. Kitsch "draws its life blood, so to speak, from the reservoir of accumulated experience."[13] By employing such imagery, kitsch was accorded the negative character of a vampire. We can see in Greenberg's essay how difficult it is to maintain a purely aesthetic critique of kitsch. Those who express an aesthetic response to kitsch tend eventually to move either toward the cultural response or toward the ethical response. When Greenberg called kitsch "deceptive," he implied that its failing is more substantial than merely being poor or overly reproduced art.[14] Whereas Ewen moves toward a cultural response in his analysis, Greenberg moved toward an ethical response.

"The producer of kitsch does not produce 'bad' art," wrote the German critic Hermann Broch in 1933, "he is not an artist endowed with inferior creative faculties or no creative faculties at all. It is quite impossible to assess him according to aesthetic criteria; rather he should be judged as an ethically base being, a malefactor who profoundly desires evil."[15] Hermann Broch did not see kitsch as bad art. For Broch and others who respond to art ethically, kitsch is the anti-system of art.[16] The ethical response to kitsch is derived from the classical associations of art with the True, the Good, and the Beautiful. Art, in this way of thinking, is not merely a visual expression. Art possesses moral capacities. Immanuel Kant articulated the ethical nature of art in the *Critique of Judgment*, and the notion was expanded by nineteenth-century art critics. For Kant, art should have no connections to sensuality. Art expresses disinterested pleasure and it should not be practical. Art is unique but of universal import.[17] By 1905 James Lindsay concluded that "art, then, is, in its own way – no less than theology – a revelation of the Divine." Art is no mere creative endeavor, "art aims – as religion itself does – to teach and elevate, not merely to amuse, bewilder, and fascinate."[18] While Kant never argued that art had a pedagogical moral function, later promoters of art frequently praised its ability to civilize and uplift.[19]

Given this notion of the spiritual nature of art, it is not surprising that non-art could be accorded a demonic quality. For Broch, kitsch's ability to "sentimentalize" the infinite has ethical connotations because kitsch portrays beauty rather than truth. Kitsch does not reflect the true, real world but instead leads people to believe that kitsch alone could satisfy fundamental needs. "And as it is this radical evil that is portrayed in kitsch," Broch insisted that it "should be considered 'evil' not only by art but by every system of values that is not a system of imitation."[20] The ethical response, classically stated by Hermann Broch, sees kitsch not as the art of the "people" or as some inferior copy of real art. "Kitsch is," Broch concluded, "the element of evil in the value system of art."[21]

Proponents of the aesthetic and ethical response to kitsch employ a binary logic that structures visual representations into oppositional poles. Within this formal system, one of the pair is privileged over its opposite. Art is idealized and kitsch is devalued. Art is progressive, it pushes the consumer/viewer to respond in new and creative ways to the world. Rather than being progressive and challenging, kitsch is conservative in form and content. Kitsch is based on fixed structures, clichés, and conventional subjects. While kitsch indulges in the sentimental, art cannot be enjoyed in an immediate way. There is a distance between art and the observer, an "estrangement of the represented object," explains Avishai Margalit.[22] The viewer can only be purified and uplifted by art if he or she "works" to appreciate that art. Within this binary system, the enjoyment of kitsch is easy, immediate, and familiar. Lurking behind the notion that art is not immediately accessible (while kitsch is) is the belief that art must not "fall" into the sensual. Art should not arouse or eroticize. Art, even if it portrays ecstasy or sexuality, must still remain chaste. With kitsch, on the other hand, sensuality may reign.

The easy dualism that Greenberg and Broch set up between kitsch and art has been sufficiently scuttled by recent developments in artistic and philosophical circles. In the early twentieth century, Surrealism contradicted the modernist distrust of ornamentation, irrationality, and disorder. Camp, Pop Art, Hyperrealism, and Kitsch Art all blur the distinction between art and kitsch. Poststructuralist and feminist criticism challenge the Cartesian dualism that shapes much of Western thought and culture. Artists use kitsch as deliberate rhetorical devices, as we have seen in the shrine/sculptures described in Chapter 2.[23] Artist Jeff Koons, for instance, had his assistants in Italy make a series of sculptures based on a greeting card he bought at an airport gift shop. The sculptures sold for $367,000. However, in 1991 Koons was sued by the photographer who shot the original picture of two people holding eight cuddly puppies.[24] The Pop Art of Andy Warhol that once shocked and amused now appears tame. Artists routinely invert established values and assail elitism by exploring the relationship between people and consumerism. Irony, social criticism, and playfulness are firmly rooted in the worlds of postmodern art and philosophy.

During the 1950s and 1960s, at the same time that secular artists were rejecting Greenberg's and Broch's admonitions by creating Pop Art, critics of the religious arts were defining the struggle between Christian art and Christian kitsch. Protestants and Catholics who reflected on the importance of art in the church assumed an ethical response to kitsch. In order to justify what they saw as necessary adjustments to worship and art, clear boundaries were established between what was tasteful and what was not. Catholic art critics were the most active in creating and promoting a binary system of aesthetics that promoted one type of art over another. Even after the success of liturgical and artistic changes in the 1960s, Catholics continued to maintain an art/non-art dualism. When Protestants reflected on their art with an eye to reform, they too set up a binary opposition between good and bad arts. Whatever postmodern playfulness art was accorded in the secular world, this was not brought into the churches. There is no equivalent of Jeff Koons's placement of a Hoover vacuum cleaner in a Plexiglass vitrine in the liturgical art world. Artists use religious objects and images in their work, but clergy do not place art in their churches that blurs the boundaries between seriousness and humor, consumerism and Christianity, art and kitsch. Irony is not a religious value. Religious art, even more than secular art, has to be aesthetically pure and theologically proper.

Catholics as Art Critics

As early as 1863, a Catholic congress in Belgium castigated those "sensual and spineless representations which are a perversion of good taste and emasculate

100. In this shop, mass-produced statues are being hand-painted. "Le Paradis" from *L'illustration*, 1894.

piety."[25] The "representations" the congress referred to were the outpourings of French companies producing what would become known as *l'art Saint-Sulpice*. In 1862 Paris had at least a hundred and twenty-one firms that made and marketed the material culture of Catholicism: holy water fonts, medals, statues, crucifixes, rosaries, holy cards, *ex voto*s, religious jewelry, candles, scapulars, crêches, wax *Agnus Dei*, lace pictures, and novena cards.[26] Since the 1840s, Paris's Left Bank had become the worldwide center for the sale of liturgical arts (chalices, vestments, monstrances) and sacred arts (stained-glass windows, statues, church murals). The area around the rue Saint-Jacques and the church of Saint-Sulpice became synonymous with the *objects de religion* used in domestic worship and church art. What concerns me here is not the small objects which Catholics put in their pockets or placed on their home shrines. Rather, it is the debate over what was kitsch and what was art which originated with the domination of *l'art Saint-Sulpice* in church decoration.

The shops in the Saint-Sulpice quarter sold statues and other church furnishing made in factories outside Paris. In the 1840s and 1850s white plaster statues were mass produced and sold primarily to urban French churches. By the 1860s, the white statues had fallen out of fashion and painted statues had become popular, especially in rural areas. While the white statues were perceived by clergy and parishioners as cold and lifeless, the realistically colored statues were thought to bring sacred figures to life. French producers encouraged the clergy to equate their painted statues with medieval polychrome statuary. Like the wax sacred figures of the sixteenth and seventeenth centuries, plaster could be molded and

BERNARDINI STATUARY CO.

Established 1849.

SCULPTORS and MANUFACTURERS of

High Grade Ecclesiastical Statuary and Stations of the Cross.

| Sacred Heart | Immaculate Conception | St. Joseph |

Models of all styles and sizes carried in stock.

Special statues of any Saint sculptured on short notice.

3 and 5 Barclay St. :-: **NEW YORK.**

101. This advertisement from the 1908 *Official Catholic Directory* illustrates "Barclay Street art," the American equivalent of *l'art Saint-Sulpice* which was eventually derided by art critics in spite of its popularity.

easily carved to achieve realistic images of Christ, Mary, the saints, and angels.[27] Unlike the realistic statues of the baroque period, *l'art Saint-Sulpice* avoided the bloody and pained images of Christ and the martyrs. There was almost no decay or decomposition in *l'art Saint-Sulpice*. Clergy, for the most part, found that the plaster statues were cheaper and more attractive than the traditional statues made of wood or marble. Most nineteenth-century Catholics did not deride their mass-produced art but rather saw it as modern and technologically sophisticated. Religious goods bought from the catalogs of mass producers reflected standard Catholic iconography and were assured of being free from any local heresies. Since firms in Paris could quickly produce large quantities of the same item, they could easily respond to the needs of religious orders who promoted new devotions.

By the end of the nineteenth century, *l'art Saint-Sulpice* became the international style of Catholic church art. From Ireland to Mexico to India to the United States, local art was replaced by goods either imported from France or copied from French standards.[28] In the United States, the area around Barclay Street in Manhattan housed import firms that dealt with French-produced religious arts and companies that made Catholic devotional goods. The clustering around Barclay Street began as early as 1865 when a branch of the largest German religious publishing house, F. Pustet & Co., settled there. Other firms quickly followed and the term "Barclay Street art," like the phrase *l'art Saint-Sulpice*, became a derogatory term for books and objects that were cheap, vulgar, and pretentiously pious.[29] The proliferation of Barclay Street art (also known as catalog art) increased in the latter part of the century. Prior to 1884 the federal government levied a hefty 40 percent value added tax on all imported statues that were not made of marble or stone and carved by hand. After that date even colored, plaster statues were imported free of duty, thus lowering their overall cost and making them more affordable to the growing number of Catholic churches in America.[30]

Imported art and statuary, ornate altars, fine wooden pews, and grand organs were purchased or built whenever a congregation could afford it. Statues took their place on and around altars laden with candles, flowers, potted plants, lace linens, paintings, and brass-work. Catholics gave their time, money, and energy to build palaces where the "Real Presence" of God would dwell. The church functioned as a place where God and his sacred entourage were treated as royalty.[31] *L'art Saint-Sulpice* made it possible for even small congregations to imitate what they assumed would be the glories of heaven. The dazzling delights of the church were to lift the soul into the realm of the divine.

The proliferation of art and objects within the church paralleled the growing number of Catholic paraliturgical devotions. Catholics not only heard mass, they recited the rosary, made novenas to various saints, went to "missions" at church to hear charismatic preachers, attended Benediction and Forty Hours devotion to the Eucharist, and became members of religious societies. With each new devotion, the symbols of that devotion were made into statuary, medals, pendants, and pictures. If Catholics could not manage to get their special saint or Virgin into the church, they could place visual reminders of their devotions in church meeting rooms, hallways, hospitals, or homes. For at least a hundred years, from 1840 to 1940, Catholic devotionalism and *l'art Saint-Sulpice* were closely aligned.

Criticism of *l'art Saint-Sulpice* began in the last third of the nineteenth century. In 1872, *La Société de Saint-Jean pour l'Encouragement de l'Art Chrétien* was founded in Paris to protest against *l'art Saint-Sulpice*. French scholars and clergy made sporadic attacks on the commercialization of religion and the tastelessness of the art. It was not, however, until the twentieth century that a sustained effort was made to turn Catholics away from *l'art Saint-Sulpice* and toward what became known as *l'art sacré*. In 1919 Maurice Denis and George Desvallière founded the Sacred Art Studios in Paris to promote modern religious art. One of their students, the Dominican Marie-Alain Couturier, went on to edit the influential journal *L'Art Sacré* (founded in 1935). In 1930 Catholics in America established their own society for the promotion of modern church arts: the Liturgical Arts Society.

102. Although this 1893 photograph of St. Mary's Church in Philadelphia is faded, there is a sense of the opulence of Victorian Catholic churches. Note that the statuary (at least on the front altar) is not painted in keeping with the overall classical design of the church. The array of candles, plants, and larger-than-life mosaics, however, contradict any notion of federal style simplicity.

Catholic bishops and clergy in France, the United States, and Rome were initially skeptical of contemporary arts. By the late 1940s the mood had changed and authorities in Rome started to listen to the Catholic artistic avant-garde. In 1947 Pope Pius XII issued an encyclical "On the Sacred Liturgy" ("Mediator Dei"). For the first time in the history of Catholicism, Rome commented on style and taste in religious arts. Prior to that, the hierarchy had only been concerned with whether or not the iconography corresponded to correct notions of worship and doctrine.[32] The question of taste had been left to the local parishes. The encyclical approved of the use of modern art within the church but deplored "recently introduced" contemporary images and forms that were a "distortion and perversion of true art" and which at times openly shocked "Christian taste, modesty, and devotion."[33] In 1952 the Vatican specifically directed criticism at *l'art Saint-Sulpice*. Bishops were told to forbid "second rate and stereotyped statues and effigies to be multiplied and improperly and absurdly exposed to the veneration of the faithful on the altars themselves or on the neighboring walls of the chapels."[34] Rome had given the green light to Catholic theologians, intellectuals, and artists to attack Catholic kitsch.

In general, Catholic art critics in America followed the conventions promoted by modernist architects like Walter Gropius, Le Corbusier, Mies van der Rohe, and Adolf Loos. Authenticity, functionalism, simplicity, honesty, essentialism were the values promoted by both Catholic and secular artists. "The Christian has only contempt for pious frauds which are passed off as art," explained Kilan McDonnell in 1957, "concrete used as though it were wood, steel used as if it were stone, false beams, simulated marble, imitation drapes. This is the heresy of Docetists in art. It is Christ seeming to be man, but not being man in reality."[35] Truth in art, however, should not be confused with realism. Promoters of modern

sacred art insisted that images should not trick people into thinking that representations were anything more than mere representations. Statues, paintings, stained glass should only *remind* Catholics of the existence of divine characters. Catholics trained in the tenets of modern art insisted that liturgical and sacred art go beyond the ornamental, and toward the "depth and heart of Christianity."[36] Catholic writers in the 1950s never questioned that they knew what the "depth and heart" of Christianity was. The heart of Catholic ritual life was the mass. Devotions to Mary and the saints that distracted the congregation from the centrality of the liturgy should be eliminated.

In 1957 *Liturgical Arts* published "before and after" renovation pictures of St. Donatus Catholic church in Brooten, Minnesota.[37] The original church interior was an excellent example of *l'art Saint-Sulpice* in a Midwestern American church. Plaster statues, for instance, were numerous and painted. A large statue of St. Donatus was placed at the center of the altar, flanked by statues of the Sacred Heart and the Immaculate Heart of Mary. Angels bowed before the statuary "Trinity." A small crucifix rested atop the tabernacle. Candles and flowers decorated the altar, which was made to look as if it had marble columns. At the base of the altar was a painted bas-relief of the Last Supper, reminding the congregation that through the mass they participate in that sacred event. Although it is difficult to tell from the black-and-white photograph, it looks like the sanctuary area was painted in at least two different colors. Given the modest size of the church, the pastor of St. Donatus and his congregation constructed an elaborate visual statement about the importance of the saints, angels, and the Eucharist. Their reliance on *l'art Saint-Sulpice* emphasized artifice, duplication, ornamentation, grandeur, and devotionalism.

The new St. Donatus sanctuary aptly reflected the new aesthetic promoted by magazines such as the *Catholic Art Quarterly* and the Benedictines of nearby St. John's Abbey, Minnesota. *L'art sacré* had replaced *l'art Saint-Sulpice*. Where decoration and artifice were once acceptable devices to promote the power of the sacred, now simplicity was preferred. The new renovation followed the convictions of an increasing number of liturgists in Europe and America that the mass had no connection with the cult of the saints.[38] Consequently, the plaster statues were removed and a carved "folk" style Virgin and child was placed in front of an open Bible. The literary realism of the biblical text replaced the visual realism of the saints. An abstract banner depicting the Lamb of Christ dominated the sanctuary. The symbol of the lamb now became a more "truthful" reminder of the sacrifice of Christ than the representation of the bleeding Sacred Heart. Since the mass itself was the re-enactment of the Last Supper, there was no need to duplicate the message in a painted bas-relief on the altar. The draped curtain along the sanctuary wall drew the parishioner's attention to the action going on at, not above, the altar. Such draping became popular in the 1930s but was removed from many churches when interiors were even more simplified in the 1960s. The bare altar, covered by a plain cloth, looked more like a table where a meal might be prepared. By painting the ceiling white, the embossed decorations became less evident. Only the flowers along the curtain lent a decorative air to the renovation. The changes at St. Donatus church reflected the triumph of *l'art sacré* over *l'art Saint-Sulpice*.

103. St. Donatus Church before its renovation.

104. St. Donatus Church after the renovations.

The Feminine Gender of Catholic Kitsch

On an aesthetic level, the stripping of Catholic sanctuaries followed trends in modern art toward abstraction and functionality. On a theological level, it asked Catholics to focus their devotional attention on what was most important in their churches, the sacrifice of the mass. However, when we look at the language critics used to promote this devotional change, other messages emerge. In 1958 a former member of the Board of Directors of the National Liturgical Conference wrote an article on religious art for the *Catholic World*. In it John Ryan echoed the common complaint that nothing should detract the worshipper from full participation in the mass. What distracted the Catholic was cheap, shoddy, uninspired, mass-produced, ornamental art. It was art that was fancy, sweet, and flamboyant. Although Ryan never used the term kitsch or *l'art Saint-Sulpice*, it is clear that distracting art was kitsch. "What is required," Ryan concluded, "are well-made, genuine things: things that are simple, manly, solid, chaste, honest, unsentimental, noble, hieratic."[39] It is my contention that Catholic art reformers employed a rhetoric that equated *l'art Saint-Sulpice* with feminine characteristics and *l'art sacré* with masculine ones. "Well-made" art could not be sweet or sentimental, attributes traditionally associated with femininity. "Fancy" or "flamboyant" art could not be "manly." What was at stake was not merely art or kitsch, the mass or devotions to the saints, but whether the church was to be masculine or feminine, a place for men or for women.

In spite of the feminine gender of the word *ecclesia* and the traditional understanding of the church as feminine in relation to Christ, Catholic critics in the 1950s and 1960s were uncomfortable with what they understood as a feminized church. For them, the church lost its spiritual power when it became too closely associated with women. "Gold gilt and meaningless frills are as becoming to Catholicism," wrote Virginia Cookston, "as rhinestones and pearls would be to a strong, young man."[40] Cookston associated ornamentation, wealth, and femininity together. All those traits were perceived as destructive forces in a modern, democratic, American church. Charles Blakeman, writing in the *Clergy Review*, used the traditional appellation "Mother Church," but he did not appreciate the "motherly" quality of the average church. He wondered if the lack of men in church was aggravated "by the excessively old-maidish character which is a feature of many sanctuaries." Blakeman had no affection for church furnishings that gave "that front parlour atmosphere: the altar dripping with lace and vases like an unused piano, and bearing no resemblance to the Altar of God; Altar of Sacrifice."[41] For the critics, ornamentation transformed the space into a domesticated, feminine space, redolent of either cheaply dressed hussies or powerless old women.

Catholic critics followed closely in the steps of architects like modernist Austrian Adolf Loos when they rejected ornamentation. For Loos, aesthetic simplicity was a form of creative rationality appropriate for the machine age. Ornamentation was a disease and a crime that weakened architecture. "Lack of ornament," he wrote in 1908, "is a sign of spiritual strength."[42] Playing on a frequently repeated dictum of architect Le Corbusier that a house is a machine to live in, artist Jean Charlot emphasized that "from God's point of view a church is *a machine to live in*, and from man's point of view, *a machine to pray in* [italics his]."[43] Following this line of thought a church, like a twentieth-century machine, should be sleek and plain. Like a man's body, it should be smooth, powerful, and strong. Art reformers perceived ornamentation as diminishing the power of the church by distracting the congregants.

When the ideal of a non-ornamental religious space was transposed into real churches, the results were buildings like St. Francis de Sales of Muskegon, Michigan. In 1961 the Michigan congregation accepted plans from the architectural firm of Marcel Breuer to construct a church that would seat twelve hundred people. Born in Pecs, Hungary, in 1902, Marcel Breuer studied in Germany with the Bauhaus group under Walter Gropius. He left Germany in 1935, became an American citizen in 1944, and by the 1960s was a well-known modernist designer. In 1962 his church for the Benedictine monks of Collegeville, Minnesota, set a standard for new changes in church design. Following contemporary trends, St. Francis de Sales was made of exposed concrete and had unmodulated curved walls towering to a height of seventy-five feet. No distracting statues or decorations cluttered the sanctuary. In 1967 the completed church cost $1,000,000.[44]

105. St. Francis de Sales of Muskegon, Michigan, reflects Adolf Loos' conviction that lack of ornamentation was a sign of spiritual strength.

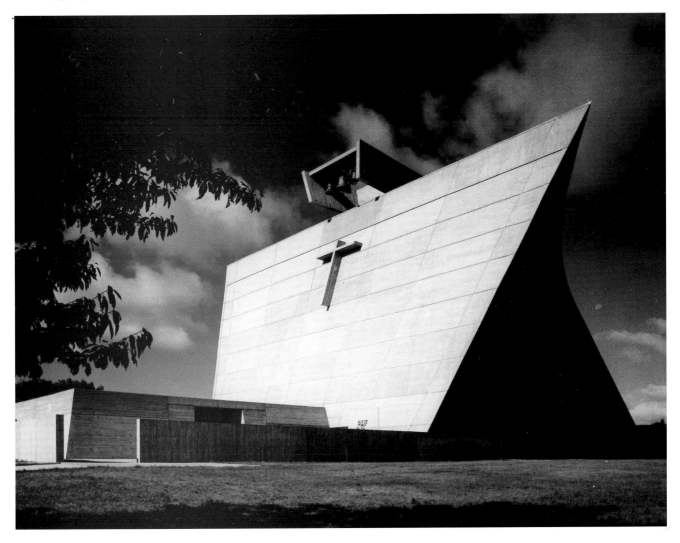

106.　The towering interior walls of St. Francis de Sales Church. Like a man's body, the modern church should be smooth, powerful, and strong.

107.　The Catholic art of mid-twentieth-century holy cards and statues tended to be realistic and intimate. In this case, prevailing standards of beauty were called upon to portray the Madonna and Child.

Catholic art reformers particularly distrusted ornamentation because it tended to be representational. For them, abstract art was more truthful and powerful than realistic art. Since *all* of the statuary of *l'art Saint-Sulpice* was realistic, one could imagine that writers might have varied their examples between condemning the realism of a statue of a female or of a male saint. Realism, however, was continuously associated with statues of the Virgin Mary. Virginia Cookston observed in "Sentiment Versus Simplicity in Catholic Art" that a "photographically perfect" statue of the Virgin Mary "has eyes, nose, fingers, and all other human features, perfect to the last detail . . . But the fact remains that it could be the statue of any beautiful woman."[45] Catholic critics joined modernist artists in arguing that realistic details could not create a bond with the divine world because they rooted the viewer too much in the mundane world. Good art was separated from mass culture and everyday life.

In bad art, the mundane world too easily slipped into a debased human world. Statues of Mary, according to Harriet Smith, too frequently looked like "a chorus girl with blonde flowing tresses."[46] A seminary professor was so disgusted by such

108. A holy card of "Mary Mediatrix" (Mary the Mediator), probably designed by Ade Bethune. The positioning of Christ over a sexually ambiguous Mary visually asserts the reformers' promotion of Christocentric devotions and masculinized art.

109. A holy card printed by a company from the famous rue Saint-Sulpice. Its depiction of the Sacred Heart was considered effeminate by Catholic art critics. Reformers saw in the representation the large eyes, curly hair, delicate mouth, and dainty hands of a woman.

110. Catholics feared that effeminate portrayals of Christ failed to convey his unconditional love, his cosmic nature, and his interest in the public sphere. In 1951 the *Catholic Art Quarterly* published this engraving by Clems Schmidt as an example of good devotional art. This Sacred Heart has short, straight hair, a well-defined masculine jaw, and large hands.

MARY MEDIATRIX

"realistic" representations that he facetiously suggested, "why not avoid all this bother" of making realistic statues "and simply hire Peggy McGillicuddy, the charming president of the young ladies' sodality, to make a suitable costume and stand on a pedestal over Our Lady's altar with her eyes cast up to heaven."[47] Details and realism rooted Catholics in a sensual, finite, feminine world. Women were in the realm of the body, the flesh, and the literal. For reformers, the church was to lift people out of the banalities of everyday life, not to reinforce them.

Catholic critics did not entirely embrace abstract art. They preferred religious art to be "hieratic." Hieratic art was an attempt to retain the representational quality of art while instilling in it an abstract formality. Hieratic art was solemn and majestic. It had a ritual stiffness to it that emphasized the characteristics of frontality, stasis, and severity.[48] The Catholic Art Association encouraged this type of art as a middle ground between *l'art Saint-Sulpice* and what they understood as the pretentious "aesthetic phariseeism" of abstract art.[49] Noted Catholic convert Thomas Merton preferred hieratic art because "of its power to convey the awesomeness of an invisible and divine reality, to strike the beholder with deep reverence and with the awareness of the divine presence, in mystery."[50] Merton sought a religious experience that was not rooted in the details of everyday life. Art should encourage the Catholic to move beyond the intimate and relational and toward the mystery of faith. Good art assisted in the masculine drive toward

MAY THE SACRED HEART OF JESUS
be loved everywhere. (100 Days Ind.)

transcendence.

By eliminating realistic details that were determined to be unauthentic, hieratic art was understood as promoting the *idea* of divinity rather than the *details* of divinity. For Catholic reformers, art expressed impressive and grand ideas. Virginia Cookston explained that a good statue had to convey the transcendental, universal character of the Virgin. "This Virgin is more than a woman," she reasoned, "she is the spirit of womanhood. She has no race and is no certain type of individual. She is more than human because her abstractness gives her a celestial quality."[51] Good art had to emphasize the ideal, abstract, divine, and transcendent aspects of Christ and the saints. Statues looking like women – with the distracting details of hair, fingers, noses, eyes – could not represent "woman." Critics did not want significance to be fixed on the trivial or everyday. Representations of Mary should resemble drawings by Catholic artists like Ade Bethune whose simple and angular figures eliminated feminine curves and sentimental gestures.[52]

In her study of the construction of femininity, Dorothy Smith concludes that "appearance constructs the woman who is desirable ... Appearance constructs the woman as object 'attractive' to man."[53] Ornamentation and realism are essential to feminine appearance. It is feminine appearance, I maintain, that both allures and frightens the men (and women assuming the male role) who view art.

For these Catholics, women could not represent woman because women were sexually arousing. David Freedberg constructs a persuasive argument for why a realistic Virgin might specifically be labeled kitsch and devalued as art. The Virgin is supposed to be a beautiful woman, and the only way to show her as beautiful is to use the prevailing standards of feminine beauty. At the same time she is supposed to be perfectly chaste. "How can we respond to her as such," Freedberg asks, "when she is made to look like those to whom we are prone to respond in the very opposite of ways?"[54] To have a realistic looking Virgin might evoke, elicit, and produce desire. Father Durand, who thought Peggy McGillicuddy could make a good statue, gives us a hint that perhaps the Virgin and Miss McGillicuddy might have too much in common. Throughout his article he argued that we must not favor art that "gratifies our senses," and we must wage war "against the flesh forces." When he wrote that "useless detail is always distracting and dulling," it is easy to imagine that he really meant the opposite, that details make the statue captivating and exciting. "Peggy on her pedestal" cannot represent the Virgin Mary because, according to Durand, "lovely images they may be, but their charm is altogether too physical." The argument is an old one – women and representations of the feminine seduce men away from spiritual things.

The problem for Catholic critics was not merely that female statues are too womanly to express womanhood. The most pressing problem with *l'art Saint-Sulpice* was that it was effeminate. Critics unrelentingly communicated their disgust that Christ and the male saints were portrayed with feminine characteristics. Father E. M. Catich, head of a Catholic college art department in Iowa and former president of the Catholic Art Association, attacked popular portrayals of the Sacred Heart by, in effect, saying they made Jesus look like a girl:

> What emerges is a young man in flowing gowns, with soft face, large eyes, small delicate mouth, slightly parted lips, small thin nose, downy beard, long curly hair parted in the middle and falling gracefully to the shoulders, slender dainty hands, narrow shoulders, long neck, [and] a slight tilt of the head and neck as if beseeching the viewer.

Representing Jesus with long hair was not only psychologically unwise "because it introduces the repugnancy of feminizing what should be a virile figure," it was historically inaccurate. According to Catich, first-century Jews, Greeks, and Romans wore their hair short.[55] Catholic women critics also decried the feminine Sacred Heart. Harriet Smith reminded her readers that in the mass, Christ sometimes was called "O Strong One." This Savior showed little resemblance to "the effeminate man gently drawing aside his garments in no recognizable fashion to demonstrate a pink painted valentine where his chest should be."[56] Writers did not suggest that the feminine characteristics be replaced with masculine ones but again reiterated their preference for abstract, hieratic representations.

Critics feared that a feminine Christ conveyed the idea that only women and femininity could be associated with the Christian concept of love. By portraying Christ as "a bearded young lady showing her heart," an Australian Jesuit explained in *Liturgical Arts*, it "fails to convey any inkling of the majesty of love incarnate; worse still, it succeeds in insinuating that the love of Christ is effeminate."[57] Feminine representations imply that virile men – like Jesus – might be incapable of showing unconditional love for humanity. The unspoken assumption is that the love of a woman is particular, limited to a specific lover or child. Feminized representations of love would lose their cosmic, universal nature and become subsumed under a partial, sentimental, domesticated love. Love had to be manly.

An important aspect of Catholic theological reform during this period was to encourage Catholics to become more involved with social issues in the modern world. Christianity, for liberal reformers, should have something to say in the public sphere and not merely be a source for private piety. Effeminate-looking Christs did not look like they would be capable of symbolizing a more active attitude toward societal problems. Although Daniel Berrigan consistently referred to the church as a "she" in his article on modern sacred art, it is clear that he preferred a "he" church, oriented toward the public sphere. "Since the late middle ages," Berrigan reflected, "religious art has been largely and progressively shunted to studio and drawing room; it has become the adjunct of prie-dieu, instead of the impassioned flowering of a public, virile and believing mind." In a few choice words, Berrigan conjures up an interior world of women mindlessly saying their rosaries in front of their home shrines. This picture evidently needed to be replaced with one of intelligent men shaping the political and business worlds based on Catholic civic-mindedness. "Men who live in the mind," Berrigan explained, "are beginning to produce and welcome an art of the mind."[58] Domesticity, femininity, and emotion – the world of women – is of the old order. In the new order, real art and real religion are manly.

Catholic art critics were one small part of a larger group of intellectuals who in the first half of the twentieth century condemned mass culture as the new opiate of the masses. Both conservative thinkers and neo-Marxists felt that popular art, music, literature, and entertainment had no intellectual content. Mass culture robbed people of genuine, authentic sensibilities and then turned them into unthinking robots. *L'art Saint-Sulpice* was condemned not only because it was sentimental and effeminate, it was ridiculed in the 1950s because it was mass produced in order to satisfy mindless tastes. As Andreas Huyssen discusses in his essay, "Mass Culture as Woman: Modernism's Other," the association of women with the unpredictable masses has a long history.[59] Huyssen shows that since the nineteenth century in philosophy, literature, and art the equation of women with the masses meant expressing contempt for both. Like women, the masses were capricious, irrational, passive, and conformist. Roland Marchand, in his work on the origin of modern forms of advertising, sees the same conflation of women and the unthinking consumer. "Despite occasional protests against this audience image," he writes, "advertisers of the 1920s became increasingly committed to a view of 'consumer citizen' as an emotional, feminized mass, characterized by mental lethargy, bad taste, and ignorance."[60] Catholic art reformers adapted this same rhetoric for their purposes. Catholic kitsch was coded feminine and said to appeal to the unschooled masses. True art was coded masculine and appealed to the thinking Catholic.

The desire to devalue *l'art Saint-Sulpice* was so persistent among Catholic reformers that they imagined every type of "old" art as having female characteristics. In 1960 Father Berrigan argued that the suffering Christ, as well as the pastoral Christ, is feminized. Writing in the journal *Worship*, he observed that in spite of the dead Christ's body being "anatomically rendered," it is done "often with a tendency toward the feminine in color and line."[61] It was not merely that the long-haired, robed Christ looked feminine to the critics of the 1950s and 1960s. Berrigan fails to elaborate on what specifically he perceived as feminine about the bloodied body of the dead Savior. Perhaps he sees the pink skin of young women, menstrual blood, or childbirth, or rape.

Twenty years after Berrigan wrote this provocative sentence, a professor at the University of Notre Dame again echoed the same sentiments. Writing in the influential Catholic magazine *Commonweal*, John Lyon first attacked what was left of *l'art Saint-Sulpice* in churches of the 1980s. He then fantasized a scenario to help his readers understand the "illusion" of the crucified Christ in "romantic church art." "The hip-to-one-side pose of the dead body of Christ seems to be anatomically akin to that pose so teasingly taken by seated women with short skirts who place their hands over their knees," Lyon wrote. "The immediate message conveyed by such a pose is 'Life is so boring. Come, violate me,' or 'Come, be violated with me'; but, upon reflection: 'I don't really mean it. I'm just playing. But the thought is alluring, isn't it? And, anyway, it relieves the boredom.'" Lyon emphasized his point by pausing in the essay and beginning a new section, but not a new thought. He now asked us to consider a reproduction of Hans Holbein's, *The Dead Body of Christ in the Tomb*. Here is the dead Savior without romance, "rather than that of a jaded 'gay' athlete posing for a Palestinian center-fold."[62] John Lyon does not want us to miss his point.

Lyon glaringly states that the kitsch Christ is female. Lyon's language, like much of the rhetoric condemning bad taste, is not subtle. He does not imagine the woman saying, "Come, play with me" or "Come, kiss me." Lyon imagines the woman/statue/Christ saying "Come, violate me." We return to Freedberg's analysis of statues coming alive. Statues can be feared because they may provoke emotion and impure thoughts. They might even come alive and make love with their creators. Or, in Lyon's darker fantasy, the woman/statue does not innocently come to the male viewer. Lyon plays on the longstanding association of kitsch with seduction and prostitution. People supposedly are tricked into buying kitsch because it tells them they will feel good without having to expend any effort. Kitsch, Clement Greenberg wrote, "pretends to demand nothing of its customers except their money – not even their time."[63] Robert Storr's paraphrase of Greenberg is even more revelatory: "Kitsch gratifies the demand for pleasure without making any demands of its own."[64] Even the corpse on the cross, a representation of Christ with no obvious nurturing, maternal, or sexual symbolism, can be read as a seductive woman who wants something she should not have.

It is not difficult to imagine the underlying sexual assumptions that Catholic art critics carry with them to the debate over aesthetics. Imagine a stereotypical male/female encounter. "Art" is distant and aloof. He stands in the corner, demanding those who want to approach him to think about who he is, what he represents. He is honest and he requires honest responses. Rationality and intelligence are prized. Kitsch, on the other hand, is the dizzy blond. She sends signals saying that she is easy and available. She is sensual and apparently simple minded. She is the type – extending Lyon's metaphor – who sits with her knees together but thinks with her legs apart. But kitsch is not honest and authentic. Kitsch lies, according to her critics, and so we are never sure of her intentions.

Critics who see kitsch as fundamentally an ethical and not an aesthetic problem, point an accusing finger not only at kitsch, but at the people who like kitsch. While their rhetoric is clearly misogynist it is simultaneously patronizing and elitist. "Our devotional drawings, paintings, and statues are degenerate because the imaginations of very nearly the whole Catholic population are degenerate," lamented the editor of *Catholic Art Quarterly*, "our imaginations are thoroughly corrupted."[65] Daniel Berrigan echoed the same generalization. Bad religious art was a symptom of a sick society because "since the fourteenth century, the western Christian community has been quite simply ill; not irrecoverably, but still seriously; and its religious art is the symptom of its illness."[66] The underlying assumptions of the lying nature of kitsch and the pathological nature of those who produce and use it is that people want to avoid true and authentic feelings and indulge in spurious ones. People lack authentic notions of divinity and are out of touch with the feelings that religion should generate. As Graham Carey put it, "it is futile to expect adequate representations of divinity from designers whose misfortune it is never to have entertained adequate notions of divinity."[67] Religious art could not be "art for art's sake" since it is intrinsically tied to the theological understanding of the producers and the users. For Catholic critics, kitsch in churches meant that people had the wrong idea about God and the world around them. Art, aesthetics, and faith were understood to be so inseparable that perceived defects in one reflected weakness in one of the others.

There has been little scholarly research done on how average Catholics in the 1950s and 1960s felt about the new philosophy of worship, the elimination of familiar devotions and art, or the new art that entered their churches. In spite of clerical paternalism, I suspect that no parish priest simply told his flock that they had never "entertained adequate notions of divinity" and bought new art for his church – without a battle. We can get a glimpse of what might have happened in many churches by looking at letters sent by the priests of Holy Family Church to the editor of *Liturgical Arts*, Maurice Lavanoux. A few years before the Second Vatican Council, a modern church was built by the architectural firm of Johnston and Campanella for Holy Family parish in Kirkland, Washington. Typical of American Catholic church building since the late nineteenth century, Holy Family parish built their school, convent, hall, gym, and priest's house all at the same time and all before the church. Their temporary church had been housed in the gym for twenty-five years.[68] In 1957 a church of pre-cast concrete was finished. Correspondence in 1958 indicated that new church furnishings were also being introduced.

Father John Domin enthusiastically wrote Maurice Lavanoux that "the work in the convent and church is all by Fitzgerald of Seattle, including the enamel and mosaic work." Del Lederle of San Francisco had made the Stations of the Cross and a statue of the Blessed Virgin Mary. A one-of-a-kind work of carved wood, the statue was intended for the convent. "Not a single item in [the] chapel for [the] sisters," he boasted, "nor [for the] church is from a catalogue." Domin had to prove to those who would donate money for the furnishings that handmade art cost less than statues purchased from catalogs.[69] He apparently needed their support for the purchase of any interior decorations. A letter from the pastor, Father Donald Conger, mentioned that since most of the parishioners of the suburban church were "young married couples with huge families. They have been most sympathetic with our use of contemporary design and materials."[70] Holy Family Church was one of the "new" breed of Catholic parishes. Its

111. In 1958 this statue of the
Virgin Mary, carved by Del
Lederle, was intended for the
convent of Holy Family Church
of Kirkland, Washington. Either
the archbishop of Seattle or the
sisters of the convent (or both)
did not like the statue, and it
was removed to the priest's
rectory.

parishioners most likely were well-educated Catholics not rooted in any urban ethnic religious culture. They probably appreciated both the open liturgy and the modern art.

However, the archbishop of Seattle, who had to approve the art purchased by the parish, did not like the statue of the Blessed Virgin. In keeping with modernist canons of art, the statue was devoid of feminine details or traditional Catholic iconography. Domin confided to Lavanoux that "the Archbishop asked that another sculpture replace it which would be more to the liking of the Sisters. I still think it is a good statue, and the pastor, Father Conger, will purchase it for his own home."[71] Conger wrote that "this statue has been the one point of controversy . . . and I am having some difficulty convincing our Archbishop that she should stay in the convent at all." It is unclear from the correspondence whether the archbishop was defending the sisters' right to have art that they liked in their convent, or if he himself just did not like the mahogany-carved Virgin Mary. There is also no information about where the statue eventually ended up.

I use this brief exchange of letters to suggest that when the ideology of good art versus bad art enters into the complicated world of parishioners, priests, nuns, and archbishops a simple binary logic can not always prevail. The exchange of letters hints that church renovations were complicated processes that were as much about gender and power as about aesthetics. Although this is just one anecdotal piece of evidence, it supports the general notion that *l'art sacré* belonged in a male, educated, and modern world. The archbishop's attitude either assumed or reflected the distaste of the religious women for the modern statue. The statue was deemed inappropriate (by the women or their "spokesman") for the convent – a private space for women. Rather than sending the statue back to its creator, Father Domin said it would be put in the home of the pastor. The old order, an order of women/nuns and aristocratic archbishops, could not appreciate the new art.

The liturgical changes that came about after the Second Vatican Council meant that the Catholic in the pew would finally be taught the "proper" theological understanding of the mass. On the surface, the artistic and liturgical changes were successful. Most American churches either threw out their "catalog" art or stuffed it in a small room set aside for private devotions somewhere in the back of the church. Altars were turned around and simplified. Catholic leaders promoted the reading and studying of the Bible. The cult of the saints was devalued and the mass correspondingly accentuated. While Catholics could still have their private devotions and statues at home, the official Catholicism of the 1960s and 1970s focused on the mass, the Bible, and social outreach. Devotionalism and *l'art Saint-Sulpice* slowly disappeared from public worship.

In the 1980s, however, a conservative pope and conservative American public demanded a re-evaluation of traditional Catholic activities. Some Catholic thinkers urged people to reinvigorate Catholic devotions, such as saying the rosary. Given that the intervening years had included the feminist movement and the integration of Catholic women into some areas of church leadership, we might suspect that the gendered rhetoric would have diminished. The reinterpretation of the rosary, however, reveals the same gendered binary logic that had been expressed a generation earlier. Interpreters of devotionalism, like critics of kitsch, continue to use a gendered rhetoric. To redeem rosary-saying as a legitimate Catholic act, it first had to be masculinized. If devotions were going to be reintroduced into Catholicism, then those devotions had to speak to "modern" Catholics. Given the gender of kitsch, "modern" meant masculine.

Writers who sought to promote devotionalism typically began their articles by describing the traditional association of rosary-saying and women. Steven Lanza began his essay, "Why I Started Saying the Rosary Again," by asserting that "I'm not one of your older, pious ladies in black who sit in church shadows addressing statues."[72] Franciscan Valentine Long asked rhetorically, "Do you still believe in these outmoded devotions for pious old women?"[73] The rosary, like *l'art Saint-Sulpice*, was presented as a symbol of the inward-looking devotionalism of an old, ethnic, feminized Catholicism. The proponents of a new devotionalism argued, however, that the rosary must no longer be a trinket fingered by marginal Catholics. Interpreters held that the rosary was not a series of mindless repetitions of Hail Marys but rather a series of meditations with a Christocentric focus. "While the rosary is related to Mary," Redemptorist Walter Halberstadt admitted, "it is really Christ-centered. It has its inspiration from the Scriptures and takes into account the saving events in Christ's life."[74] Even John Servis, a Protestant, wrote that he said the rosary because of its scriptural base.[75] While this emphasis on scripture goes along with Vatican II's promotion of the Bible, it also shifts the attention from a woman to a man. Christ must be the source of divinity, either in the mass or in a paraliturgical devotion like the rosary. Men could say the rosary because it was not a mindless prayer to Mary, it is a meditation on the Son of Man.

The masculinization of the rosary was vividly portrayed in a short article written for the lay-oriented magazine, *U.S. Catholic*. Steven Lanza connected his renewed interest in the rosary with the male experiences of his life. He told his readers that saying the rosary for him is "real prayer, raw prayer." He knows that he is praying because "I've got the prayer in my hands. It's tangible." Lanza explained that, "When the beads hang down at my side it helps. In fact, I *have* to let them hang down [italics his]." When the beads "hang down" they reminded him of going fishing with his dad on a remote lake in Canada. At some appointed time his father would decide to lower the anchor, "It would drop into those depths, blue-black, dark mirrors. . . . You could *feel* it down there, as you let the rope out, plunging deeper and deeper, weighted into secret kingdoms. The beads feel the same way." Lanza, most likely unintentionally, connects his own male sexuality with his experience with prayer. A few sentences later he contended that the "deepness called the Kingdom of God" can be reflected in prayer, "in the praise of the name of Jesus, the fruit of Mary's womb, her yielding to God." Even if the associations with male masturbation and intercourse are more in my imagination than Lanza's, he did admit that "the beads for me are not outdated. They symbolize physically and spiritually gospel realities – all those parables about seeds and planting and sowing; about birthing the Word unexpectedly into our lives like flowering mustard trees or olive branches."[76] For Lanza, saying the rosary linked gospel principles with the intimate aspects of his life as a man. Note that he did not write "giving birth" but rather the paternal act of "birthing." To renovate the rosary means to disassociate it from its roots in a feminine devotionalism while simultaneously clothing it in appropriate male symbols.

Pursuing the Manly Christ: Protestantism and Kitsch

I am not suggesting that Catholics produce a gendered rhetoric of kitsch and art because of priestly celibacy and lay sexual purity. It is not sexual repression that genders kitsch. Nor do I want to infer that Catholics are more misogynistic and patriarchal than other Christian groups. The problem of gender, art, and kitsch confronts both Catholics and Protestants. The problem is intrinsic to Christianity. It is easier to document the Catholic debate because churches with a liturgical orientation take seriously how the visual arts enhance or detract from worship. Catholics write about aesthetics and because of liturgical changes their views are influential. Protestants, on the other hand, deal with the arts in less explicitly theological ways. Since many denominations have a de-centralized church structure, greater independence in matters of taste occurs. In this section, I describe how the same debate over art and kitsch appears within liberal and conservative Protestantism.

The gendered division of the arts began during the eighteenth century with discussions of taste and aesthetics by noted philosophers who were Protestants. Edmund Burke and Immanuel Kant both wanted to challenge the classical focus on proportion (as the defining characteristic of good art) by shifting attention toward using feeling as a measure of aesthetics. They devised a system of aesthetics that divided visual expressions (natural and human-made) into two distinct categories: the beautiful and the sublime.[77] Beauty and sublimity were each generated by a separate set of emotions. The sublime could be produced through objects, sights, or art that reflected the characteristics of eternity, greatness, simplicity, depth, nobility, quiet wonder, power, vastness, and uniformity. The beautiful originated in the small, adorned, delicate, tender, and fragile. While the sublime evoked awe or astonishment without actual danger, the beautiful excited love without lust. "The sublime *moves*," Kant wrote, "the beautiful charms."[78]

Burke, who also made a distinction between the beautiful and the sublime, based his notion of beauty on the body of a woman. "Observe that part of the beautiful woman," he noted, "where she is perhaps the most beautiful, about the neck and breasts; the smoothness the softness; the easy and insensible swell."[79] A lesser known British philosopher of art, Sir Joshua Reynolds, held similar views. According to literary critic Naomi Schor, Reynolds associates details, ornamentation, and the particular with the feminine. For Schor, the focus on the sublime by eighteenth-century writers like Reynolds is an attempt by "a masculinist aesthetic designed to check the rise of a detailism which threatens to hasten the slide of art into femininity." Enlightenment critics found that since the Renaissance the decadence of art was "bound up with its loss of virility."[80] Protestants, especially from a Calvinist-influenced Britain, easily associated a decadent Catholicism with femininity, aristocracy, and sensuality.

The equation of morality with art accompanied a philosophical and theological preference for a non-utilitarian art that did not evoke sensual pleasure. Victorian writers like Rudolph Binder warned against enjoying the picture of a beautiful woman because "the beauty of the woman will arouse sensual desire."[81] Binder insisted that pleasure must be transformed into "the purer and more elevated atmosphere of the ideal." Art and religion were not supposed to kill the emotions but to "transform and control them."[82] Religious art, even more than secular art, has to be absolutely pure and unrelenting in its goal of moving the devout away from earthly sensualities and toward the immaterial divine.

In the twentieth century, German theologian Paul Tillich exerted the most influence on Protestant understanding of the arts. Tillich brought his fondness for abstract expressionism and philosophical idealism with him when he moved to America in 1934. Following modernist artists and art critics, Tillich separated authentic art from unauthentic art, just as he divided authentic religion from unauthentic religion. Unlike the limited influence of artists and art critics, Tillich's writings of the 1950s and early 1960s had tremendous impact, not only on Protestant and Catholic theologians but on ministers and their congregations. Although he criticized mass culture, his thoughts were widely read in popular magazines, and he wrote to influence the behavior of average Christians. Tillich expressed an ethical response to kitsch akin to fellow German Hermann Broch when he wrote that kitsch was not poor art but rather "a particular form of deteriorized idealism" or a "dishonest beautifying naturalism."[83] Such art was "the curse of the last hundred years of religious art."[84] Modern art, on the other hand, was an authentic aesthetic. Familiar with the fascist use of kitsch/art for propaganda, Tillich maintained in *The Courage to Be* that "modern art is not propaganda but revelation."[85] Unlike kitsch, that sugar-coated reality, art reflected the meaninglessness of modern existence while courageously presenting critical and revolutionary ideals. Honest art, like the real religion of Tillich's Ultimate Concern, expressed the depth of being, not the surface. Bad religious art with its "dishonest saccharine prettiness" could not represent religion in the modern age.[86]

Liberal Protestants warmly embraced Tillich's perspectives on art as they did his theology. What is surprising is that conservative Protestants when they spoke of art also sounded "Tillichean." In 1958 Robert Roth, writing in *Christianity Today*, perceived the same dualism between art and non-art as Catholics and liberal Protestants writing at the same time. Depending on whether art was in the service of Christ or Satan it was either "spiritual" or "demonic." This professor of the New Testament at a Lutheran seminary insisted that "art is never for art's sake."[87] Evangelical Frank E. Gaebelein brought this dualism into common parlance when he lamented that there were some people "who cannot distinguish a kind of religious calendar art from honest art."[88] He warned that "Evangelicals had better be concerned about the aesthetic problem," because "a tide of cheap and perverse artistic expression is constantly eroding the shoreline of noble standards and godly living."[89] If good art purified and uplifted Christians, he seemed to say, then bad art perverted and debased them. Writing in a Catholic journal, Lutheran artist Richard Muehlberger also connected bad art with bad faith. The faith expressed in the "common church art of the day" (1960) is not "the Christian faith." What has "touched the heart of Christianity" is the work of contemporary artists who have not yet been able to find their way into the service of the church.[90] Protestant art critics of all denominations insisted that religious art be taken seriously *not* solely because it might aid in devotion or education but because it revealed the inner state of the average Christian. Bad taste for them reflected not class differences or aesthetic ignorance but moral and spiritual weakness.

Protestants also used gendered language to discuss the art problem. In 1963 Clarence Simpson, a professor of English, created a character he dubbed "Peter Reborn." Peter was a "young Christian in the religious awakening" who was "not aloof from pleasure" or "insensitive to beauty." However, Peter failed to support art because of his lack of "taste" and "commitment." Peter overemphasized the utilitarian aspects of art, he enjoyed art that was imitative and decorative, and he was fearful of art's sensuality. Professor Simpson concluded that, "thus Peter Reborn, pious and practical Evangelical, associated with the arts pretty much as a respectable man might pay court to a somewhat darkly interesting woman."[91] When writers tried to translate their theories into images and common language, they turned art into women. As with Catholic critics, gendered language prevailed.

Peter Reborn, I would imagine, probably liked the art of Warner Sallman. By the 1960s, Sallman's *Head of Christ* was ubiquitous in Protestant culture. Critics, however, pointed an accusing finger at such mass-produced commercial art. When they became particularly annoyed, they noted its feminine characteristics. The chairman of the English department at Wheaton College wanted to know why Christians "make a fetish of Sallman's well-meant but pretty head of Christ, turning it into an evangelical icon?" Such art, for him, was as bad as "the cheap chromos of the most vulgar Roman Catholic devotion."[92] "In Sallman's *Head of Christ*," wrote Robert Roth, "we have a pretty picture of a woman with a curling beard who has just come from the beauty parlor with a Halo shampoo, but we do not have the Lord who died and rose again."[93] In another *Christianity Today* article, the chairman of the Music and Fine Arts department of an Indiana Bible college wanted to know if "the church of Christ shall indiscriminately be satisfied with the sentimental and effeminate art that for the most part adorns our walls, books, greeting cards, and educational helps."[94] Artist Richard Muehlberger, however, surpassed all of the colorful rhetoric of Protestant professors. Speaking to Catholics in his essay for *Liturgical Arts*, he repeated the refrain that catalog art had turned the Virgin into a "vapid-looking creature," the saints into "sugar-coated morons," and the Sacred Heart into "a biological Valentine." What really bothered him, however, was what Lutherans had done to Christ. The "Sons of the Reformation" had allowed the art of Heinrich Hofmann and Warner Sallman to make Christ into "a bearded woman with as much dignity as a movie-house billboard." According to the Protestant elite, evangelical or not, whatever art that Protestants had let into their churches or put into their homes was theologically suspect because it feminized the divine.

Warner Sallman never intended his art to be effeminate or his portraits of Christ to look like a "bearded woman." According to one story, Sallman was inspired to paint a manly Christ early in his career. In 1914 Sallman attended a Chicago Bible college where his artistic talents caught the eye of the school's dean. The dean told Sallman, "I hope you can give us your conception of Christ. And I hope it's a manly one. Most of our pictures today are too effeminate."[95] Kriebel and Bates, the company that held the copyright to Sallman's art, published the stories of this conversation. Their promotional material on Sallman's art advertised the *Head of Christ* as having been "acclaimed by artists, critics, and Christ-loving Christians as the most attractive masculine representation of the Savior."[96] In order to have Christians – the art was marketed to Catholics as well – replace their cherished pictures of Christ rendered by Hofmann with those of Sallman, Kriebel and Bates played on the concern for a "masculine" Christ found in Protestant men's organizations and in popular literature such as Bruce Barton's *The Man Nobody Knows* (1925).[97] As late as 1962, revisions requested on one of Sallman's versions of the *Head of Christ* (*Lord and Master*) read that the "top of the hair and the head looks too feminine" and needed to be "roughened."[98] To sell art meant to present your art as modern and masculine while tacitly criticizing the art of others as effeminate.

A similar situation occurred within the Church of Jesus Christ of Latter-day Saints. Warner Sallman's art, especially his *Head of Christ*, had been adopted by Mormons in the 1950s and 1960s for their chapels and Sunday schools. In the early 1970s, the hierarchy of the church began to regulate what art could and could not be placed in the ward buildings. Eventually, it was decided that images were unacceptable in the chapel but that art could be placed in the Sunday school and

112.   Warner Sallman's *Head of Christ* became a classic of post World War II Christianity (see Illustration 9). By the 1960s, however, it was losing some of its appeal. Sallman painted more contemporary versions, but marked on an early version of the 1962 painting *Lord and Master* was the comment "top of the hair & the head looks feminine."

113.   In 1983 Del Parson was commissioned by Latter-day Saint church authorities to paint a head of Christ. At one point he was told that the portrait needed to be more masculine. This painting is now the ''official'' depiction of Christ used by the LDS Church.

114. Del Parson's painting resembles this 1964 portrayal of Christ by Richard Hook. Copyrighted by a Lutheran publishing house, it was used extensively by the Jesus movement of the early 1970s and continues to be popular among evangelical Christians.

meeting areas. In 1983 Del Parson, a Utah artist, was commissioned by Latter-day Saint church authorities to paint a head of Christ. He submitted five sketches before one was chosen, and at one point was told that the portrait needed to be more masculine.[99] While it is not known whether church leaders wanted to replace the Sallman portrayal with something more masculine, they did seem concerned that the representation be masculine by prevailing cultural standards. Parsons's painting was then adopted as the "official" portrait of Christ used by the Latter-day Saint church. Warner Sallman's painting was removed from the list of acceptable ward art. While individual Mormons could still buy reproductions of Sallman's art for their homes, prints of Parson's painting were placed in the public spaces of the church. Parson's portrait resembled Richard Hook's portrait, copyrighted by a Lutheran publishing house in 1964. Protestants, like Catholics, did not want to represent Christianity by a feminized Christ.

Christianity and the Problem of Women

In 1986 *The New York Review of Books* published a review by J. M. Cameron in which he called a popular Protestant hymn kitsch. The *Review* later published a letter from Herbert McArthur who, while never admitting to liking "I Come To the Garden Alone," still wrote to defend his grandmother's favorite hymn. We can assume that McArthur loved his grandmother, but she, also, curiously resembled the feminized world of kitsch so distasteful to modern critics. "Grandmother" attended "more Baptist prayer meetings and sermons and revival services than I would care to imagine." She realized that the educated might find "her tastes too simple," but she tried to lead a life of "selfless devotion to other people's needs." Grandmother "never complained" and her "faith never wavered that Jesus, the son of God, would welcome her to heaven." McArthur's letter was published as a supposed rebuttle to Cameron but the letter's subtext contradicted its stated goal. What the letter did was to associate kitsch with religious old women who sacrificed themselves in order to achieve a personal relationship with Jesus and a place in heaven. Such people most likely would not be the typical reader of the *New York Review of Books*. J. M. Cameron then responded to McArthur's challenges. He basically said that one should love the sinner (grandmother) but hate the sin (kitsch hymnody). The hymn was not "authentic religious discourse." Lumping together such hymns, movie images of well-washed fat babies, and holy cards used by Catholic children, he condemned them all as presenting serious theological problems. "Kitsch is a form of lying," he concluded, "and religious kitsch lies about what is, for the believer, the deepest reality."[100] Kitsch, grandmothers, babies, holy cards, lies, and unauthentic discourse – they all were equally problematic.

Cameron repeats the same ethical response toward kitsch as Greenberg voiced in 1939 and Christian critics did in the 1950s and 1960s. His assumption is that art naturally divides between the authentic and the unauthentic, truth and lie, good and evil. Since religion is understood to engage the deepest recesses of the human soul, it is especially problematic when kitsch contaminates Christianity. The aesthetic theory developed in the eighteenth century and elaborated in the nineteenth and early twentieth centuries set up a binary logic of the arts that reflects cultural stereotypes of male and female. Since the human world splits between men and women, why not the visual world? This structural division parallels the Cartesian dualistic tendency to organize the world in pairs: mind/body; culture/nature; reason/emotion; objectivity/subjectivity; public/private.[101] The prevalence of Cartesian dualism in Western culture made it appear "natural" to Christian art critics that not only could there be good taste and bad taste but that taste could be described with gendered language. I am not saying that Catholics and Protestants consciously coded art and kitsch with gender. They did, however, work within a philosophical world that had a binary aesthetic system shaped by cultural constructions of masculinity and femininity.

Kitsch is gendered female because things that are feminized are devalued – and the converse – devalued things are feminized. Since art critics were promoting one type of art, they masculinized that art and feminized the rest. Anthropologists have noticed that when societies utilize a binary system of classification, whatever is defined as female – women, an activity done by women, or a trait ascribed to women – is less valued than the male constructs. Anthropologist Sherry Ortner contends in her classic article, "Is Female to Male as Nature Is to Culture?" that "woman is being identified with – or, if you will, seems to be a symbol of – something that every culture devalues, something that every culture defines as being of a lower order of existence than itself."[102] The intrinsic nature of the devalued thing has little relevance according to feminist anthropologists. Michelle Rosaldo reports that in parts of New Guinea, women grow sweet potatoes and men grow yams. Yams, not sweet potatoes, are the prestige foods distributed at tribal feasts. Or, in the Philippines, women grow rice and men hunt. While rice is the dietary mainstay, meat is considered more valuable and is shared by the community.[103] Ortner's explanations for such asymmetry center on women being ascribed the category of "nature" while men assume the higher category of "culture."

In the case of the controversy between art and kitsch, *l'art Saint-Sulpice* is no more essentially feminine than *l'art sacré*. As long as any cultural expression is perceived as positive, it is accorded either neutral or masculine characteristics. When something needs to be devalued, one rhetorical device available is to call it effeminate. Another device is to accuse it of contradicting "natural" boundaries. Feminine representations of Christ or the male saints cross the established lines between male and female. In a culture based on binary logic, blurring male and female categories is a dangerous activity. Things which do not "fit," like twins (for certain African societies) or a feminized male (for modern Americans), are rendered taboo. The feminized Christ statue challenges and destabilizes the binary symmetry. In the same way, when a supposedly chaste Virgin Mary looks like a "chorus girl", the established norms about sainthood and womanhood are challenged. Critics promoted one style over another by making Christians feel uneasy about viewing "wrong" art. They then presented their own modern art as true, honest, and moral. Art reformers did not necessarily do this consciously, but they used the philosophical and cultural tools available to them to create a strategy of devalorization and promotion.

In her book on cross-dressing and cultural anxiety, Marjorie Garber quotes a passage from *Lady Holland's Memoir* (1855) that highlights the problem of binary logic in Christianity: "As the French say, there are three sexes – men, women, and clergymen."[104] Critics of Christian art are uncomfortable with a feminine Sacred Heart or Head of Christ because "gender bending" has always been a part of Christianity. From the other worldliness of Jesus who refused to marry and have children, to medieval women saints who dressed as monks, to Victorian vicars represented as overly feminine, Christians have used theology and religious culture to transgress gender boundaries. In Western culture, the values of humility, purity, self-sacrifice, and love are associated with the world of women, but are taught as gender-neutral goals essential to the Christian message. Garber is correct in concluding that because religion in Western culture helps construct rigid gender roles, religion also "inevitably invites both gender parody and gender crossover."[105] Christian cultures are plagued with a double standard. On the one hand, Christianity advances maternal stereotypes as values for both men and women. On the other hand, it supports societal norms that encourage rigid and distinct gender roles.

Since in patriarchal cultures masculinity is prized and male behavior is defined as normative, the gender crossover is more threatening when the masculine is feminized. While some women who disguised themselves as monks were eventually canonized, there are no cases of male saints who hid out in convents and dressed like nuns.[106] A feminized statue of Christ is seen as perverse, but St. Joan of Arc dressed in battle gear is heroic. Likewise, nineteenth-century Protestants were not satisfied with churches filled with women, even those women who demonstrated the Christian values of self-sacrifice and cultivated feminine piety. By the late nineteenth century, the opinion among many ministers and theologians was that an environment of sentimental domesticity made the church an unwelcome place for men. Why else would men be flocking to fraternal societies like the Masons and the Improved Order of Red Men? Protestant reformers responded by setting up societies like the Men and Religion Forward Movement and promoted "muscular Christianity." The Social Gospel movement encouraged Protestants to become involved in social issues by promoting the "fatherhood of God and the Brotherhood of Man." Catholics pursued similar strategies to encourage male participation. Churches established social groups for men, set up parish missions so that men had their own services, taught their seminarians sports, and portrayed Protestant ministers as effeminate.[107] The masculinization of Christian arts is part of a subtle strategy, dating from the mid-nineteenth century, to continue Christianity's patriarchal nature by making the church a comfortable place for men (whether ministers and priests knew what made "men" "comfortable" is another question). Churches filled with women were not enough. "Honest" religion had to appeal to the normative human being: man.

The fear that women and women's values would drive men away from Christianity reappeared in postwar America. During World War II, women crossed the gender lines by working in factories and providing financial support for their families. In the 1950s, middle-class movement to the suburbs and the Baby Boom focused media attention on women and child rearing. Men imagined a double feminine threat: women could both take away their public sphere jobs and dominate their private sphere homes. Consequently, social criticism in the United States both promoted suburban domesticity while at the same time condemning women for exerting too much psychological control over the male world. Philip Wylie's *Generation of Vipers* and Edward Strecker's *Their Mother's Sons* popularized the threat that women posed to the masculinity of their sons. Originally published in the 1940s, these two books were reprinted again in the 1950s and early 1960s. While the men of the 1950s had firm control over business and politics, they feared the moral and nurturing power of their wives just as men had done in the previous century.

Postwar Catholics and Protestants faced similar circumstances. As Catholics moved from ethnic urban parishes out to the suburbs, their needs changed. Since 1880 Catholics had been commanded to send their children to parochial schools and by the 1950s they were doing so with enthusiasm. The family, particularly women and children, was increasingly highlighted in Catholic magazines and in parish life. At the same time, Catholic advice literature (often written by women) tried to reinforce gender roles by insisting that women stay out of the workplace and remain in the home. Far more than in the nineteenth century, when Catholic clergy realized that their churches were supported by the pennies of working Catholic women, clergy of the 1950s were unrelenting in their condemnation of the employed Catholic woman.[108] Rather than being merely a Catholic attempt to adopt modernist aesthetics, the attack on *l'art Saint-Sulpice* was another form of cultural criticism of the power of postwar women. Whether Catholic women really had more power, or any power at all, is not the issue. Women, European forms of "decadent" art, "Old World" private devotions, were all perceived as holding a virile American church back from moving into its rightful place in public life. Unlike the using of Lourdes water and building of replica shrines that cemented Catholics to a European past, art critics of the 1950s and 1960s tried to instill a sense of "forward-looking" Americanism unattached to feminine representations.

The Protestant circumstance, although less intense, follows the same pattern. Nineteenth-century liberal Protestantism already had strong associations with women and with domestic values. Suburbanization was merely the next historical step in a long line of feminizing tendencies in mainstream Protestantism. Protestant churches desperately wanted the suburban father involved with local congregations, while not insisting that he teach Sunday school or play the organ. For liberal churches, the fundamental question was: What was the role of the patriarch in a society where "father" had become "dad"?[109] One symbolic gesture that liberal clergy could make was to condemn Victorian "Sunday school" art as theologically suspect and morally degenerate. While they could not get rid of the Sunday school teacher, they could get rid of the art associated with her. Liberal Protestants attacked the feminization in their churches by attacking the art they equated with an effeminate nineteenth century. At the risk of oversimplifying, it seems they were saying: "One problem with our churches is that there are too many women and too much focus on children – all of which scare men away, Let us redefine ourselves and present a vision of a strong, virile church by making our image of Christ more masculine." Again, whether or not men *really* were scared by too many women and children is not the issue. The reality was that men were not at church and this was a problem.

For conservative Protestants, postwar evangelicalism was shedding its equation with rural, Southern, and poor America that it had acquired after the Scopes trial. As conservatives came more into contact with urban and suburban life in the twentieth century, they faced the same social changes as liberal Protestants. Evangelical and fundamentalist promotion of Victorian sex roles was also being undermined by elements within their own traditions. Women preachers like Aimee Simple McPherson took on ministerial roles, charismatic women prophesied, and women flocked to conservative churches partly because evangelicals insisted that men support their families rather than waste their time on wine, women, and song. Religious revivals historically have brought women and adolescents into the church, and the conservative movements of the postwar years were no exceptions. Perhaps even more than in liberal churches, conservatives both welcomed women's commitments to Christ and feared their influence.[110] For fundamentalists and evangelicals, if Christianity was a patriarchal religion based on the historic Jesus, then it was even more important to have powerful, masculine representations of the universal Savior.

Compared, however, to the enthusiasm with which Catholics attacked kitsch, the conservative response was mild. Conservative Protestants denounced kitsch because they were experiencing a shift in class rather than a shift in piety. It was professors at Bible colleges who took note of Warner Sallman's art in their churches. Even at the Bible colleges of the 1950s, professors writing on art would have been exposed to standards set by the secular academy and popular theologians such as Tillich. Pierre Bourdieu's research on taste is particularly useful here. For Bourdieu, "educational capital" provides the clearest determinate of "cultural practices."[111] While they might have also been influenced by Barthian neo-orthodoxy and fundamentalist patriarchy, I think that their distaste for calendar art had less to do with religion and more to do with education.[112] Evangelical professors did not reject the idea of a personal, historical Jesus; they were merely skeptical of the available representations.

At the same time evangelicals who took art seriously knew that aesthetic theory emphasizes detachment, disinterestedness, and indifference. Those character traits were difficult to integrate into a Christian system that emphasized personal commitment and involvement with a living Jesus. Conservatives continue to use Sallman's art in their churches and schools, in addition to more masculine portrayals of Christ, because their theology does not devalue the historical Jesus and promote a universal Christ. Conservatives emphasize the historic Jesus who interacts on a personal basis with Christians, and so their problem is not one of the bad taste of realistic art but rather the bad history of portraying Jesus as an effeminate male. Contemporary Christian artists like Marjorie Nordwall or Clive Upton could easily solve that problem by updating Jesus' portrait so that he looks more like an active male of the late twentieth century. On the other hand, Catholics and liberal Protestants can not so easily remedy their problem. They do not want to substitute a feminized art with a masculinized art. Catholics want a hieratic art that is not quite abstract but certainly not realistic. Liberal Protestants want art more in tune with contemporary secular art. Realistic art that might appeal to their congregations is deemed unable to represent an eternal, cosmic, somewhat detached Christ. For all three groups, having a feminine representation of Christ can not be tolerated.

The struggle over what type of art a church should have in its worship area, Sunday school classrooms, or meeting halls concerns the public "face" of Christianity. For both clergy and lay people, art is not merely the physical expression of personal taste. Artistic representations speak to their tradition's history and theology. While beliefs may be embodied in sermons and liturgies, the art that the church displays is the first sign to outsiders of the congregation's vision of the divine. Whether that vision is the vision of the pastor, the people in the pews, or a liturgical committee is not always clear. In this chapter I have examined the rhetoric of Christians whose artistic preferences were articulated in the public spaces of religious art magazines and theological journals. The aesthetics of this group of artists, teachers, and clergy was distinctly presented while the aesthetics of the people they frequently ridiculed remains unknown. In Chapter 7 I turn again to the spirituality of those who do not express themselves in journals or see themselves as religious professionals. I also move from public expressions of religious sentiments to intensely private ones. For members of the Church of Jesus Christ of Latter-day Saints, some sacred objects are too holy to be shared with those outside of the religious fellowship. How does an American-born Christian community establish religious meaning through sacred clothing given in secret rituals and seen only by members of their church?

7

Mormon Garments:
Sacred Clothing and the Body

"They're just a part of my life," Sarah explained to us. Wearing garments "was one of the things you did when you grew up."[1] In 1991 Sarah was a 45-year-old college professor with a husband and two children. She grew up in a Mormon family in southern Utah. When Sarah married, she started wearing a special type of undergarment as a symbol of her religious commitments. "It's an honoring of the promises I've made," she told us. "It connects me with my parents and grandparents." Garments provided her with a sense of spiritual protection and well-being. "The time I had surgery and was in the hospital," she recalled, "I always felt better when I had my garments on. Part of it is the return to normalcy; you're well enough to be back in your clothes. You had to be pretty sick not to have your garments on." At other times, wearing garments caused her embarrassment and anxiety. As a graduate student, she wore clothes that were not transparent because she "didn't want my being a garment-wearing Mormon to be an issue." Sarah feared that "people would think I wasn't very smart; just another dumb Mormon." Admitting that it is hard to feel sensual or sensuous "when you are wearing that much underwear," Sarah concluded that garments are not erotic or created to be erotic. However, when she does not wear them, "I feel strange." For Sarah, garments provide "one more layer between me and the world."

There are currently 8 million members of the Church of Jesus Christ of Latter-day Saints spread out across the globe. Sociologist of religion Rodney Stark vigorously defends his projections that in the year 2080 there will be 265 million Mormons.[2] He bases his calculations on the pattern of Mormon growth between 1930 and 1980. If the church grows by only 30 percent a decade, rather than 50 percent, then there would be 60 million Mormons in 2080. "Either way," this non-Mormon writes, "the Mormon Church would be a major world faith." Even if we ignore the demographic implications of Mormon growth, there can be no question that this native-born religion forms a significant part of American Christianity. Its theology is rich and complex, its ritual life diverse, and its history intricately interwoven with that of the United States. In recent years, institutional growth has transformed Mormonism from a religion of the inter-mountain West to a world religion with particular strength in Latin America. While their social attitudes on abortion, women's rights, and homosexuality align Mormons with evangelical Protestants and conservative Catholics, many fundamentalists do not consider Mormons Christian. Mormons, however, firmly assert that they are the church that Christ established "in the latter days."

In spite of the importance of Mormonism for American history and culture, the community is under-researched, misunderstood, and frequently maligned. From the very beginning of the church's history, anti-Mormon writers have sought to expose what they consider to be the follies and errors of Joseph Smith and the Book of Mormon.[3] As recently as 1993, ex-Mormon Deborah Laake's memoir of Mormon rituals and patriarchal misogyny zoomed to fourth place on the *New York Times*'s best-seller list.[4] Some of the blame for the continued misunderstanding of Mormonism must be placed squarely on church leaders' shoulders. Partially because of theological convictions, partially because of the history of anti-Mormonism, and partially in order to control information and members, the church does not support free-ranging scholarship. Latter-day Saint archival materials deemed too sensitive or sacred are not open to researchers. Information that might present the church in a negative light is left out of histories or biographies.[5] Theologians or historians who try to present alternative views to the church leadership are threatened with reprimands, disfellowshipment, or are excommunicated.[6] For non-Mormon and Mormon alike, conducting historical research on Latter-day Saint topics can be daunting.

Church leaders make pronouncements on doctrine, moral behavior, and the human condition but they do not discuss what they consider sacred. Matters considered by the elite to be private, confidential, or sacred are restricted for both Mormons and non-Mormons. Mormon leaders insist that the temple rituals are not secret, but that their sacred quality necessitates their set-apartness. Both scholarly analysis (well intentioned or not) and casual conversation would profane sacred subjects. Since garments are given during the private temple ceremony, there is almost no public discourse on their spiritual or social significance. Only a few sources exist that give some indication of the meaning and history of the temple.[7] Parents do not talk about garments, bishops (the equivalent of Protestant pastors) do not say much about them, missionary training courses do not present the theology behind wearing them, and even the temple ceremony only briefly discusses why Mormons wear garments.

In order to learn more about the meaning of garments in the religious lives of Mormons, while trying not to transgress the boundaries set out by church authorities, a student and I decided to ask Mormons themselves about the meanings of their garments. It was our conviction that church leaders are not the only ones who define the meaning of the sacred and set boundaries between the sacred and the profane. We felt that Mormons themselves would be best able to tell us about the role garments play in their lives. Since so little is set forth publicly, Mormons creatively imagine for themselves what garments are all about. They become silent theologians, thinking and feeling but not articulating these thoughts to family or friends. The silence about garments in the contemporary Latter-day Saint church is a form of theological, social, and individual control by an elite who understand themselves as being chosen by God to lead. At the same time, their silence leaves open the possibility that no single interpretation will be presented as the one, legitimate explanation. By insisting on silence, rather than conformity of thought, church authorities tacitly create an environment for a variety of personal interpretations. Ironically, church leaders naively assume that silence reflects uniformity of opinion.

Initially we worried that active Mormons would not speak to us at all. We found, however, that people did want to talk to us. The feelings, memories, and reflections that Mormons have about garments are varied and intense. Once we reassured them that they did not have to discuss anything that they thought compromised commitments they had made, they readily shared with us their ideas on the history and meaning of garments. Over a period of two years, Richard Ouellette and I conducted thirty-seven in-depth interviews.[8] We did not try to make our sample "representative." The people we talked to live in the Salt Lake City area, are educated, white, and middle-class. They consider themselves to be Mormon but do not accept without question all church teachings. To call them "liberal" Latter-day Saints would probably be just. We did not interview Mormon farmers from Idaho, members of the Quorum of the Seventy, Manhattan lawyers, recent converts from Ecuador, or polygamists from southern Utah. Future researchers can see how the various subcultures in Mormonism might find our results in harmony or disharmony with their own thinking.

Origins of the Priesthood Garment

The early history of garments is not easily determined. The archive department of the Church of Jesus Christ of Latter-day Saints withholds documents considered sacred, private, or confidential from scholars. Since garments are closely connected to the rituals conducted in the temple, church authorities restrict access to most materials that discuss garments. Existing nineteenth-century sources are often written by disgruntled ex-church members or anti-Mormons and must be dealt with judiciously. Historical documentation on garments is therefore limited. Mormon church leaders or theologians have not articulated an "origin myth" for garments that explains how it is that Latter-day Saints came to wear these clothes. We cannot search through theological interpretations for clues to historical development. Consequently, only fragments of history and myth are available to construct the specific historical circumstances in which garments first enter Mormon culture.

The priesthood garment makes up a part of the sacred clothing that Latter-day Saints wear when they receive their "endowments."[9] On May 4 and 5, 1842 a group of nine men gathered in the upper story of prophet Joseph Smith's store in Nauvoo (Commerce, Illinois) and participated in a ritual of instruction. We do not know exactly what this early endowment ceremony was like. Latter-day Saints, who were not members of the elite, first received their temple endowments on December 10, 1845 after Smith's death. In the mid-1840s the endowment ceremony included a washing and anointing with oil, the giving of the garment and a new name, and a dramatic recitation of the events of the Creation and the story of Adam and Eve. At the end of the ceremony, the Latter-day Saints stood before a curtain (referred to as a "veil") symbolizing the separation of humanity from the divine. What they had just learned and experienced permitted them to pass through the veil and enter into a room representing the heavenly kingdom or celestial realm. Latter-day Saints made promises called "covenants" to keep God's commandments, sustain and defend the Kingdom of God, and observe the law of chastity. According to Brigham Young, who assumed Mormon leadership in 1844, endowments enabled the faithful after death "to walk to the presence of the Father, passing the angels who stand as sentinels, being enabled to give them the key words, the signs and tokens, pertaining to the Holy Priesthood, and gain . . . exaltation in spite of earth and hell."[10] Latter-day Saints were told not to reveal what had been taught and to submit willingly to certain penalties if they did.

An early account of the endowment ceremony, written by someone who eventually left the church, described the garment Latter-day Saints were given as "a dress made of muslin or linen, and worn next to the skin, reaching from the neck to the ankles and wrists, and in shape like a little child's sleeping garments."[11] This description harmonizes well with autobiographical accounts that note that mothers made "union suits" (a type of long underwear) for children so that they "would be used to such a garment when [they] became eligible to wear it."[12] One 1842 exposé mentions that "a hole is cut in the bosom of [the] shirt" and another anti-Mormon source purports that during the 1846 Nauvoo Temple rite an undergarment was given that had two special markings, a square on the breast and a compass on the knee.[13]

Garments were only one piece of clothing that Mormons wore in the temple. Nineteenth-century sources mention initiates wearing a special robe, apron, cap, moccasins, and socks. This clothing initially was made inside the temple. On December 14, 1845 Brigham Young decided that all the cloth that was intended for temple clothing be "brought and either cut or made in this Temple under the superintendence of those who knew how to do it right."[14] The wives of the church leaders cut and sewed all the temple clothing, including garments, inside the temple.[15] Since early temple clothing did not leave the temple, women also washed and ironed previously worn clothing.[16] As the numbers of endowments increased, some women stayed up all night preparing temple clothing.[17]

In these early years, the surviving documentation reveals that Brigham Young struggled to make garments uniform in design. Apparently he was less interested in constructing a theology of sacred clothing and more interested in ensuring standardized production. "There are now scarcely two aprons alike nor two garments cut or marked right," he lamented.[18] On December 26, two weeks after stating garments must be made in the temple, Young conducted a general overhaul of temple activities. "We will have no more cooking and eating going on in those rooms," warned Young, "no person will be allowed to come in unless they are invited." Temple activities, that also included sleeping and dancing as well as prayer, were being limited. Young insisted that "I shall not have any more cutting and sewing of garments going on in the temple. I shall have houses selected where garments can be cut and made."[19] While sewing sacred clothing within the temple might ensure the greatest standardization, such continued production was both impractical and out of harmony with the increasingly sacral character of the temple space.

But why, we may ask, did Joseph Smith insist that garments be a part of the endowment ceremony? Latter-day Saints believe that their prophet received visions from God and various divine messengers. On September 21, 1823 a glorified and resurrected being (Moroni) appeared to Smith and instructed him to find and translate the record of God's dealings with the ancient inhabitants of the Americas. This translation, known as the Book of Mormon, is a volume of holy scripture comparable to the Bible. Joseph Smith continued to receive divine messages and many of these revelations are contained in the Doctrine and Covenants (D&C). Such revelations told the faithful to build a house for the baptism of the dead (D&C 124:33); informed them that angels have flesh and bones (D&C 129:1); and permitted men to take more than one wife (D&C 132:61f). However, nowhere in the texts that Mormons hold important for understanding their faith is there a discussion of the origins of garments or an explanation for why Mormons wear them. Latter-day Saints do not point to the writings of Joseph Smith or Brigham Young to support their understanding of priesthood garments. Unlike other religions that have elaborate creation myths to explain why they do what they do, Mormons do not have a narrative that reveals why they wear garments.

Diaries, autobiographies, memoirs, and letters of early Mormons that are not a part of the orthodox Mormon scriptures cite other visions that Joseph Smith received. Unlike some unofficial Latter-day Saint traditions, the visions regarding garments are not well known. "It was while they were living in Nauvoo that the Prophet came to my grandmother," reported a relative of James Allred, the bodyguard of Joseph Smith.[20] According to this account, Smith told local seamstress Elizabeth Warner Allred that "he had seen the angel Moroni with the garments on, and asked her to assist him in cutting out the garment." The seamstress and the prophet spread unbleached muslin out on a table, and Smith told her how to cut it. Only after a third pair was cut did Smith find the garments satisfactory. According to another memoir, the garment was presented to the whole community. Smith "held it up before them and said it was the exact pattern of the one the angel showed him, and was called 'the Garment of the Holy Priesthood,' and must be worn all through life, and would be a protection to them against all physical and spiritual dangers if they were always faithful to the covenants they made with the Lord."[21]

In these accounts we see hints of what early Mormons thought about garments – ideas which form the basis of current Latter-day Saint understanding. Garments, like the Book of Mormon, were of divine origin. The prophet Joseph Smith introduced them to the community as he did other revelations. Garments were to be worn not only during the temple ceremony but throughout one's life. They connected the faithful with the promises made in the temple, the "covenants," made with the Lord. If Latter-day Saints wore the garment and faithfully kept the promises made to God, then the clothing would protect them from "all physical and spiritual dangers."

The wearing of ritual clothing, while not a significant part of nineteenth-century Protestantism, was important for other groups that influenced the development of Mormon ritual and belief. Garments may have been easily integrated into early Mormon culture because ceremonial clothing played significant roles in Freemasonry, folk magic, and Judaism. While some Mormon historians see garments as a restoration of the ancient tradition of holy vestments, others argue that influences closer to Joseph Smith shaped attitudes toward garments.[22] If we set aside the possibility that an angel introduced the priesthood garment, what historical influences encouraged Mormons to wear special clothing?

The first endowment ceremony took place just over six weeks after Joseph Smith began his association with Freemasonry.[23] All nine men who participated in the first endowment ceremony were Freemasons. The room where the endowment occurred, the upper story of Smith's "Red Brick Store," also served as the meeting place for the Nauvoo lodge of Freemasons. Brigham Young belonged to a Masonic lodge in western New York in 1830. While the Protestant churches of Joseph Smith's day did not indulge in a complicated system of visual signs and symbols, Freemasonry did. Freemasonry became popular among American men in the eighteenth and nineteenth centuries, providing fraternal conviviality, ritual drama, and a unified system of religion and science. At each level of initiation, the initiate was instructed in morals and Masonic symbolism and was given secret signs, passwords, handshakes, and told of penalties that would befall him if he revealed any of this special information.[24] Mormon temple rituals also developed a series of secret signs, passwords, and penalties. Nineteenth-century Mormon iconography was replete with Masonic symbols: the beehive, the square and compass, the clasped hands, and the all-seeing eye. Masons and Mormons also both wear special clothing during their ceremonies.

The primary piece of Masonic ceremonial clothing is the apron.[25] Masons wore decorative aprons both during their temple rites and at public events such as parades and funerals. In 1793 Benjamin Latrobe sketched a group of Masons wearing aprons who were parading in celebration of the laying of the cornerstone for the nation's Capitol. Masons understood the apron to refer both to the protective garb of builders and to the leaves and skins that Adam and Eve wore after they left the Garden of Eden (Gen. 3:7; 32). They also cited the biblical injunction to wear fringed garments (Num. 15:37–40) and some aprons included fringes.[26] Mormon apostate John Hyde remembered an 1854 endowment ceremony where the "small square apron" worn over the temple robe looked "similar in size and shape to masonic aprons."[27] The Masonic apron also had characteristics similar to the priesthood garment worn by Mormons under clothing. Even though the white Masonic apron was often elaborately embroidered, it symbolized innocence, truth, integrity, and purity. In 1730 Mason William Hutchinson compared the apron with the white robes that early Christians put on after baptism: "Having put off the lusts of the flesh," he wrote about the Masonic initiate, "he had obliged himself to maintain a life of unspotted innocency." While Masons removed the apron after its ceremonial use, they were told that symbolically it should "ever be tied about you, and [so] to your dying day you can never remove the obligation which this garment symbolizes."[28] The apron, worn or imagined, was to be a reminder to the initiate of the commandments of God. In the nineteenth century, Mormon garments and Masonic aprons shared many of the same symbolic meanings.

Michael Quinn has cogently demonstrated that early Latter-day Saints, like many other Americans of that period, participated in occult beliefs and magical practices by which they sought to bring the divine in contact with their everyday lives. Nineteenth-century Mormons believed that physical objects could possess supernatural powers.[29] Joseph Smith used special stones to translate the Book of Mormon and to dictate the Doctrine and Covenants. Small, smooth stones called "seer stones" were also used by Mormons to peer into the future or locate lost livestock. Brigham Young owned a flat green stone with red streaks, mounted on a gold frame with eyelets that he carried with him for protection when going into unknown or dangerous places. Other Mormons possessed "mad-stones" to cure bites from rabid or venomous animals and pieces of parchment with magical words to protect houses from evil spirits. Given this acceptance of the magical power of objects, it is not surprising that garments were accorded special powers by the early church. Unlike seer stones and parchment charms, however, garments became integrated into official Mormon ritual practice and behavior. Sacred clothing, because of its acceptance in the temple, continued to be an important aspect of Mormon culture long after seer stones disappeared.

While some Mormons may have difficulty accepting the historian's judgment that early Mormonism was influenced by Freemasonry and folk magic, no Latter-day Saint would deny the connection between Mormonism and Judaism.[30] Latter-day Saints believe that the people recorded in the Book of Mormon were Israelites who journeyed to the Western Hemisphere from Jerusalem around 600 BCE. They were descended from Joseph of Egypt through his sons Manasseh and Ephraim. Latter-day Saints apply the name Israel to themselves, and they are expected to "seek out the other descendants of Israel [the Jews] and those who would become Israelites through adoption by baptism."[31] Non-Mormons, even Jews themselves, are called "gentiles" by Mormons.

Since Joseph Smith believed that Mormon temples parallel the ancient Jewish temple in function, it is not surprising that ritual clothing was introduced. According to Mormon historian Steven Epperson, the Nauvoo temple with its "sacred institutions and rites created a tradition connecting Mormonism with Hebrew scriptures and Israel's experience."[32] Joseph Smith could have read in his Bible that God instructed Moses to tell Aaron and his sons to make "holy garments" so that they could "minister unto me in the priest's office" (Ex. 28:1). Those garments included a breastplate, an ephod, a robe, an embroidered coat, a mitre, and a girdle (Ex. 28:4). To wear underneath this array of vestments, God commanded Aaron and his sons to make "linen breeches to cover their naked-ness; from the loins even unto the thighs they shall reach" (Ex. 28:42). This undergarment, that a later (New English Bible) translation calls "linen drawers," was to be worn whenever the priests came into the "Tent of the Presence or approach the altar to minister in the Holy Place" (Ex. 28:43). As I explained in Chapter 2, the activities and objects used by a clerical elite oftentimes are reduced and modified when adapted for use by all members of the community. By wearing special clothing in their temple ceremonies, early Mormons physically connected themselves with biblical Judaism.

In ancient Israel, the "linen breeches" were worn only by the priests who attended the temple. Once the temple was finally destroyed in 70 CE the tradition ended. Joseph Smith, however, may have acquired the idea of garments from the Judaism of the nineteenth century. Smith's 1836 Hebrew teacher, Joshua Seixas, may have worn a white garment called an *arba kanfot* ("four corners") under his clothes. Or, in 1842, when Orson Hyde returned from his visit to Palestine, he may have brought back information on this Jewish undergarment.[33] The *arba kanfot* evolved from the custom of Jewish men wearing fringes (*tzitzit*) on their clothes.[34] In the biblical book of Numbers (15:37–41), Israelites are commanded to wear fringes with a thread of blue so that they will remember God's commandments. In biblical times the fringes were worn by Jewish men on their clothing but eventually Jews adopted the garb of the Greeks and Romans. The *tzitzit* then were placed on a special four-cornered cloth called a *tallit* that was draped around the shoulders during prayer. While the origin of wearing fringes may have come from the ancient Assyrians and Babylonians, who believed they possessed talismanic power, the *tallit* was understood primarily to be a reminder of spiritual matters. Pious Jews who felt that they were in constant communication with God wore the *tallit* throughout the day. To facilitate the constant wearing of a *tallit*, it became reduced in size and strictly observant Jews wore it under their clothing. Also known as the *tallit katan* ("small tallit"), the *arba kanfot* evolved into a white undergarment with fringes worn during the day.

Freemasonry, folk magic, and Judaism all influenced the development of Mormon symbols, rituals, and beliefs. There are some important innovations, however, that set Mormon garments apart from these other traditions. Wearing *tzitzit* may have originally been designed as a way to distinguish male clothing from female clothing that were very similar during biblical times. Among Latter-day Saints, garments are worn by both sexes and there is little difference between the garments of men and those of women. Masonic initiation is only for men. In Mormonism, however, women were not excluded from temple ceremonies. Mormons are expected to wear their garments even when they sleep, but rabbis have interpreted the biblical passage on *tzitzit* to mean that the fringes must be seen, and so night wear is excluded. Masons marched in parades with their aprons on, but Mormons never willingly displayed their garments in public. Finally, since the *arba kanfot* must be treated reverently, it is not to be worn directly on the skin but over an undershirt. For Jews, proximity to the body would desecrate the garment rather than sacralize the body. Likewise Masonic aprons, even though they represent Edenic covering of the genitals, are worn over ceremonial robes. For Mormons, the garment must be worn continuously under any form of underwear. It must touch the body.

Historians can only speculate about whether or not Joseph Smith introduced garments because he read about priestly underclothes in his Bible or because he was influenced by Masonic rituals. Some believers assert that an angel passed on the original design and others believe that Joseph Smith received the temple ceremony as a revelation from God.[35] Let us move beyond the frustrating quest for origins and ask what contemporary Mormons think about the function of garments in their religious and social lives. What meanings do Latter-day Saints now ascribe to the garments they wear?

Community and Identity

Unlike liberal Protestantism that places a premium on faith, the Latter-day Saint church stresses the importance of appropriate behavior in defining the committed believer. The covenants that Latter-day Saints make with God are to be *acted out* in their lives. Merely attending Sunday services and being "good" is not enough. Food and beverage restrictions, pre-marital sexual abstinence, and tithing are ways that Mormons demonstrate their religious beliefs. Latter-day Saints are also expected to take part in social and religious activities that consume much of their leisure time and energy. Church projects, combined with the memories of their past theocratic society, foster the formation of a tight Latter-day Saint community. "Everything is the church," explained one older member.[36]

Consequently, when speaking of the promises they make to God, Latter-day Saints emphasize the need to *live* a certain way as opposed to merely *believing* in a certain way. Living out the proper divine/human relationship establishes community affiliation. *Wearing* garments demonstrates Latter-day Saint commitments to God and their community. "To me [garments] symbolize," summarized one man, "the religious goals in my life and the lifestyle I want to lead."[37] Because garments are uniquely Mormon, they are seen as an important means of asserting community identity. Garments define "the boundaries of our community," they "set you apart as an individual and a people."[38] Not only do garments serve as "an honoring of the promises I've made," they "connect me with my parents and grandparents."[39] Wearing garments separates Mormons from non-Mormons. Being a Mormon is demonstrated by what you do more than by what you think.

Latter-day Saints frequently told us that wearing clothing with religious significance is not unique to their religion. They emphasized that many other religious people wear symbols of their religious commitments. Jews wear yarmulkes (skull caps). Catholic priests sport Roman collars. Those we spoke to felt that the wearing of special clothing symbolizing one's religious commitments was not particularly unusual. The Latter-day Saint church does not have a professional clergy and sees all of its members as having religious responsibilities and obligations. Consequently, Latter-day Saints echoed sentiments voiced by church authority Boyd Packer who told military chaplains that "we draw something of the same benefits from this special clothing as you would draw from your clerical vestments."[40] Mormons use analogies with which other religious people might be familiar.

It is true that like many people, Mormons wear symbols of their religious commitments. Clothing can convey pious commitments, one's position in a religious hierarchy, or even one's status as a religious outsider.[41] It is not true that the way Mormons wear garments duplicates how sacred clothing is worn in other religious groups. Sacred clothing traditionally is worn to distinguish one group of people from another: lay from ordained, male from female, initiate from uninitiated. Clothing symbolizes powers, responsibilities, and duties that other people do not have. In order to make such distinctions clear, the clothing must be at least partially visible. Mormon garments do not serve to designate clerical status or to make *public* statements about a person's belief. Garments, while in the general category of religious clothing, are unique because they are unseen. They are more like a Catholic rosary tucked in the pocket than a nun's habit. Garments are private statements of communal affiliation, not public ones. Why, then, did the Latter-day Saints we interviewed frequently mention that their garment wearing was not unusual?

Mormons find themselves, like many minority communities in America, having a double consciousness.[42] On the one hand, they see themselves as being a "chosen" group of people who all share a common history and a particular set of religious commitments. Mormons believe they are different and non-Mormons usually agree. At the same time, Mormons act in ways indistinguishable from other middle-class Americans. They see themselves as valuing education, family life, hard work, economic independence, and authority as all good Americans should. Their attitudes toward garments – that they are both uniquely Mormon and yet have parallels in other religions – reflect this double consciousness. Garments represent a specific theology and history while at the same time they resemble the customs of other religious people. Saying that garments are like Roman collars or yarmulkes is like saying that a Mormon is like a Catholic or a Jew. Some Mormons want to be simultaneously inside and outside, the religious mainstream. They treasure their unique set of beliefs and practices but they also want to blend into middle-class America.

The desire to be simultaneously inside and outside appears in other instances in Latter-day Saint culture. On the one hand, Mormons we interviewed talked about the "church" as a "they" that had its own notions about spirituality, ritual activities, personal life styles, and sexual behavior. The church was spoken of as if it was one entity, an organized hierarchy, that speaks with a single voice. Individual Mormons, however, did not merely accept or reject this "they" church. Latter-day Saints believed that *they* were the church. Interacting on an emotional and intellectual level with the institutional church, Latter-day Saints tried to create for themselves a place to stand between the perceived church authority and their own views on religion. Since garments are considered too sacred to be discussed outside of the temple, church leaders have not articulated their meanings. Consequently, Mormons could more freely give meanings to their garments that reflect their own personal commitment to their church. That commitment may or may not always be in harmony with church leaders' understanding of what it means to be a Mormon in good standing.

Latter-day Saints can thus use their garments to signal their attitudes about the Mormon community and beliefs. Garments send messages out primarily, perhaps exclusively, to other Mormons. "It's an inward thing," one man reflected; "theoretically only God can see it."[43] However, other Latter-day Saints do notice each other's garments. One young man told us how he likes to take advantage of the nature of golf to surprise his playing partners by not wearing garments.[44] Mormons are not required to wear garments during sports, but since golf requires little physical exertion many Latter-day Saints wear their garments. This Mormon sees himself as somewhat "rebellious," and he wanted to get his partners to think about why they automatically wear their garments. On the other hand, a woman who considers herself liberal and perhaps a challenge to more conservative Mormons, proudly wears her garments. "Then those women and those people in that church cannot put me in any kind of weird category because obviously I'm a member," she concludes. She also wears her garments to the local university with the hopes of breaking down the stereotype that Mormons are "kind of stupid [and] conservative."[45] The people we interviewed frequently used the wearing or not wearing of garments as their own private, subtle, and significant statement on how they wanted to be viewed by the Latter-day Saint and non-Latter-day Saint community.

Latter-day Saints also are well aware that by wearing garments they demonstrate loyalty to their religion. Some Mormons have serious reservations about church doctrine and activities but still see themselves as part of the Latter-day Saint community. Wearing garments links them to the group, even if not to institutionalized beliefs. A woman who felt uncomfortable with the church at the same time felt compelled not to break with her religion. "I haven't really given up," she admitted, "it's my community. I grew up with those people. It's the only social life and friends I have, the community of Mormons."[46] Another man who has been wearing garments for thirty-five years does not feel involved with the church. He wears garments to prevent "friends, neighbors, and family from being unduly concerned and making comments." Like many Latter-day Saints, he does not want to "make waves" and upset the harmony of his family and community. As he put it, "You have to wear something," and so why cause unnecessary friction?[47] In a community that seeks to avoid disagreement, factionalism, and dissent, wearing garments diffuses conflicts by asserting the wearer's Mormon identity. By having such a strong symbol of "Mormonism," Latter-day Saints can privately question the tradition while at the same time indicating their obedience to its norms.

Ambiguous feelings about the church, both as an organization and a belief system, shape the ways Mormons perceive their garments. For Mormons who critically evaluate their faith and position within the church, garments become a multivocal symbol. Garments reminds them of their commitment to a higher order that they willingly accept while at the same time tying them to an organizational structure that some find oppressive. One wearer observed that garments are an expression of a spiritual life "of obedience, of doing the right thing, of wanting to please God." She wears her garments to church and parties because she is "not ready to be labeled inactive." In spite of her outward participation, her questioning conflicts with how she thinks she should feel about wearing garments. "At this point I feel phony in them. I don't feel obedient in them," she concluded. "I feel that I am in compliance, no questions asked."[48] Since garments are such a clear symbol of Latter-day Saint identity, wearing them while harboring doubts frequently causes guilt.

Mormons who decide to stop wearing garments make a strong statement to themselves, their family, and their community. Members may challenge doctrine, drink a beer or two, or stop going to services but when they stop wearing garments those around them know they have left the faith. For one woman, removing her garments signaled that she rejected her place within the religion. "I felt like it was another way of the church's power defining me, and it was the most sacred way, the most personal way," she recalled. "The blessing was coming from a controlling force, the patriarchy of the church."[49] Garments represented a church that excluded women from leadership positions, limited their spiritual activities, and promoted an unrealistic ideology of womanhood. "The garment is a symbol [of] everything divine and beautiful and life sustaining; all these great things" yet it "resonates with all the control that the male society [has] over women's bodies."[50] Another woman, who still wears garments, reflected that "part of them is on me."[51] The more women challenged Latter-day Saint doctrine and social practices, the less they accepted wearing garments. Garments became a symbol of the discipline and control forced on women by a patriarchal church.

The men we spoke to who had stopped wearing garments did not condemn the church for its patriarchal nature. For them not wearing garments was an act of defiance against a religion that had failed to deliver on its promises. After having grown up a good Mormon boy, gone on a mission, and married in the temple, one young man's marriage ended in a difficult divorce. As with several other men and women, he associated his garments with his marriage vows. "I've been terribly betrayed and rejected," he confided. "Why do I need God if this stuff is going to happen to me? I felt like I deserved better because of my previous actions. I felt that if it is not going to work then screw the whole system."[52] The blessings that his church promised him for righteous behavior and faith did not materialize. His garments became the sign of the failure of his God, his marriage, and, perhaps, himself. A father of six who stopped wearing garments told us, "I'm really angry with God now."[53]

The Temple Experience

In many ways, Mormonism in Utah is more like an ethnic group than a religion. People who have been raised Mormon but either leave the church or are expelled from it, still find that they think and act "Mormon." Their identity is defined less by theological concepts or ritual activities and more by a sense of collective history and sociological behaviors. Wearing garments, however, means more to Mormons than merely asserting community identity. Historically, theologically, and existentially, garments are the visible reminder of the temple experience. For the most part, Latter-day Saints live in a world devoid of powerful symbols. Their simple chapels do not contain elaborate religious art, their Sunday services are informal, and their preaching is done by those not trained in theology. Directness, plainness, and practicality are valued. Latter-day Saints will tell you that their meeting houses are not examples of sacred space. The temple, however, is different. It is the association of garments with the temple experience that makes garments different from Catholic scapulars or ministerial robes.

Temple activities were not a prominent part of Mormon life until the early twentieth century. While nineteenth-century Mormons spent considerable time and energy building their temples, by 1912 there were only four Utah temples that served almost half a million members.[54] Since many Mormons had never been to the temple, they had not received their endowments and were not wearing garments. By the 1920s, church authorities began to urge members to perform temple ceremonies not only for themselves but for the dead as well.[55] By building more temples and shortening the temple rituals, including the endowment ceremony, church authorities encouraged more people to perform more "ordinances." For the first time, temples and their rituals became central to Mormon life and regular attendance at the temple became the mark of a committed member. In 1995 there were 47 temples spread around the globe. Mormons could receive their endowments in Mesa, Arizona (1927), Washington, D.C. (1980), Nuku'alofa, Tonga (1983), or Frankfurt, Germany (1987).

For modern Americans who are used to informal living and church-going, temple ceremonies are arcane, symbolic, and highly ritualized. When arriving at the temple, Latter-day Saints remove their street clothes and wear special temple clothing. They move between elegantly decorated rooms. Sometimes they have parts of their bodies purified with water and anointed with oil. Special hand gestures and code words are used. The temple rituals involve both the intellect and the senses. "[It] was like a coronation," recalled one man, "preparing the body and the organs, all things, to become great."[56] Some members find the symbolism inspiring, others frightening. "I was shocked," summarized another church member.[57] Even for those who no longer are members of the church, memories of the temple ceremonies are powerful. Although some did not look forward to the ritual because they did not know what was going to happen to them, none left the temple feeling untouched by its symbolism.

The garment carries the memory of the temple experience because it is given during the endowment ceremony as a reminder of religious commitments. It also has special markings on it that replicate the markings on the temple veil. Before entering the celestial room (a place symbolic of heavenly life), Latter-day Saints move through a "veil," suggesting the separation between the abode of humans and the divine. On the veil are the same four marks as on the garment. Latter-day Saints are told during the endowment ceremony not to discuss the sacred matters of the ritual outside of the temple. Consequently, most Latter-day Saints we spoke with did not explain the details of the markings or their meanings. They spoke in general about the markings as reminding "us of direction, rightness, and shooting for the right direction. [The markings] remind us to nourish ourselves spiritually and physically, and to be worshipful, to praise God."[58] When we asked if they meditated on the markings or thought about them, the response typically was "no."

On the other hand, almost every Latter-day Saint we talked with knew that when garments grew old their markings should be cut out and either burned or shredded.[59] The old garments could then be used as rags, but the markings had to be ritually disposed of. Those who wore garments complied with this well-known regulation. Why? One reason is that the instructions on how to de-sacralize garments are clearly and consistently given prior to the endowment ceremony. Helpers in the temple describe how to take care of garments and how to treat them reverently. While the interpretation of the markings may be lost in the drama of the ritual, the instructions apparently remain. Another reason is that physical objects become holy not by what people say about them but by how they are manipulated and used. Cutting out markings and burning them is a ritual gesture that acknowledges the special nature of the garments. Utterly destroying the markings physically returns the garment to its status as profane underwear. It is not enough merely to "think" an object back to its profane state. The gesture recognizes that with the markings the garment is sacred and without them it is just a piece of cloth.

Latter-day Saints associate their garments with the drama of the temple and the sacred nature of the markings. The placement of the endowment ceremony within the life cycle of individual church members also intensifies the importance of wearing garments. Throughout childhood, Mormon boys are encouraged to prepare themselves spiritually and financially so that at the age of 19 they will be ready for a mission calling. Supported by family and their local church community, the young men spend two years proselytizing to non-Mormons. Before leaving for missionary training, they "take out" their endowments and begin wearing garments. Missionaries' days are filled with church activities and so personal freedom and privacy are often sacrificed for a greater good. After this time spent focusing on spiritual matters and refining religious commitments, men return home to marry. Having a mission calling, going through the temple, and wearing garments all cluster together as a rite of passage into spiritual manhood.

Until recently, most young women were not expected to go on a mission. When they took out their endowments it was in preparation for temple marriage. Wearing garments began within days of being married in the temple, for this life and for all eternity. All Mormon men are expected to go on missions, and now more and more young women are becoming "sister missionaries." At the age of 21, and for a slightly shorter period, women may leave their homes and serve their church in the United States and abroad. As with male missionaries, women also begin to wear garments just prior to going on their mission. Single men and women who choose not to go on missions or who find that marriage is slow in coming, may go through the temple anyway and receive their endowments. However, receiving one's endowments long before marriage or mission is the rare exception rather than the rule. Going on a mission and getting married are major rites of passage into adult Mormon culture. The wearing of garments physically marks that transition.

When missionaries return home, their garments can play a part in the next stage in the Mormon life cycle: courtship. Wearing garments communicates different messages to men and to women. "One friend of mine told me he was at a dance," a story was told to us, "and he had garments [on] and this girl came up and patted him on the leg ... and he said to her, 'Do you want to go to a bar or something?' And he just laughed in her face because he knew what she was trying to do."[60] By touching his leg, the girl learned whether or not the man wore garments. If he did not, he was not old enough to go on a mission and thus not at a point in his life when he would be serious about marriage. If he wore garments, then the girl knew that he had finished his two years on mission and would be looking for a bride. The boy, recognizing the unspoken code, decided playfully to tease the girl by acting like a non-Mormon and suggesting that they have a drink, something Mormons do not do. Another woman said her sister knew of "men who actually put tape around [their legs] to appear that they were wearing garments."[61] Garments on young men combined with the absence of a wedding ring send out the "availability" message to those women interested in hearing it. The man who has his endowments is thought to be more mature, spiritually minded, and ready to consider the next step in life after the mission: marriage.

If the wearing of garments by young men signals availability, the wearing of garments by young women frequently sends out different messages. Like returned male missionaries, female missionaries are also seen as older, more mature, serious, and spiritual. For women this can make them less desirable to the opposite sex. "A lot of men didn't like the fact that I had garments on," one women told us. "They knew that it was something that they had to respect. . . . This one man in particular said, 'Well, your garments are kind of a turn off.'"[62] This woman felt that men were unsure how to respond to women who had been through the mission experience. Since women traditionally received their endowments immediately prior to marriage, single women wearing garments were an anomaly. On the other hand, if men were looking for spiritually mature women, they could be attracted to those who had traveled, managed living without family, and made sacrifices for their religion. Garments on single women could be read as either threatening or attractive. For both men and women garments provided some help in the complicated negotiations of dating.

Marriage and mission are understood by Mormons as points of spiritual reflection and advancement into full adulthood. To begin to wear garments symbolizes the acceptance of more responsibility and of leaving childhood behind. Our interviewees told us that prior to taking out their endowments they felt fairly casual about how they dressed. Shorts and T-shirts, the summertime uniform of the young, symbolized their carefree life. More serious concerns were yet to come. However, once they began wearing garments they acquired a physical reminder of their changed spiritual and social status. A single woman who had yet to go through the temple explained that, "Maybe it shows my shallowness, but the temple is a commitment. The garments are a reminder [of that] all day long, every day."[63] Garments can be uncomfortable, especially for women because they are worn under their bras. A transformation of status is signaled by the very fact that garments are annoying and necessitate an alteration of one's clothing. "I had to consciously decide," recalled one woman, "that the mission was a more important thing than my vanity or my personal comfort."[64] Garments both recall the intensity of the temple as well as points of spiritual and emotional growth.

A Shield and a Protection

From the very beginning, garments were accorded a sacred character because they directly connected the wearer with the promises conveyed in the temple endowment. At the same time, nineteenth-century Mormons regarded the garment as a kind of spiritual amulet.[65] Like seer stones and magic parchments, the garments came to be perceived as having supernatural powers. William Jarman, who left the church in 1857, published his memories of the ceremony in 1869. He explained that it took nine hours and, after being washed and anointed with oil, an attendant helped put on the garment, an "undershirt and drawers combined in one."[66] Jarman was told during the ceremony that with the garment on, "it is impossible for the Devil to get into our body, for it extends high on the neck and covers the wrists and ankles. It is claimed to be a shield against fire, bullets, drowning and other physical danger." Because of its protective character, "the Saints are counselled to never be without this garment, that when changing a soiled one for a clean one, to remove but an arm or a leg at a time of the soiled garment, replacing it at once with the corresponding arm or leg of the clean one." Since the garment at that time was split up the middle, one could conceivably use the toilet, make love, and give birth without taking the garment off. Jarman, like other nineteenth-century Mormons, understood that the garment was more than a simple reminder of the temple covenants.

The notion that the garment affords physical as well as spiritual protection may have increased after the murder of Joseph Smith and his brother Hyrum. On June 27, 1844 a mob entered the Carthage, Illinois, jail where four Latter-day Saint leaders awaited trial. While trying to escape, three bullets fatally struck Joseph Smith and according to some accounts his "assailants who crowded around him . . . propped his body against a well curb and riddled it."[67] Latter-day Saints interpreted his death as sealing his prophetic mission in blood and thus paralleling Christ's sacrifice on the cross (D&C 135).[68] To emphasize that Smith, like Christ, willingly went to his death like an innocent lamb to the slaughter, stories circulated that he consciously removed his garments before going to Carthage. One Latter-day Saint recalled Smith stating that he would "lay down his life as a martyr to the testimony he bore but that his enemies could not take his life while he was wearing his garments."[69] Another account reported that the prophet took off his garments so they would not be exposed "to the sneers and jeers of his enemies."[70] By taking off his garments and allowing himself to be killed, Smith assumed responsibility for his own martyrdom. God, through the actions of his prophet, controlled events. The angry mob was merely an instrument of divine order. If taking off the garment makes one vulnerable then wearing it provides protection. Consequently, a contemporary report describing how "he had laid aside his garment on account of the hot weather" failed to become a part of Mormon tradition.[71]

Mormon folklore is rich with stories about garments protecting Latter-day Saints from attacking Indians and other dangers.[72] Faith-promoting stories told at church or at informal church gatherings at times describe how garments mysteriously protect their wearers. However, the Mormons we interviewed were skeptical about any claim that garments provided magical powers or supernatural physical protection from harm. They, like their leaders, see garments as giving spiritual not physical benefits. No one that we interviewed felt that wearing garments would really save them if their car were engulfed by flames or stop a boulder from crashing into them. "They're not going to penetrate to your heart and make you feel more strongly," predicted one woman. "They're not going to shoot electrodes to your brain to make you remember answers to a test. . . . They're just there to help you to remember what your commitment to the covenants that you took."[73] Some people commented that God would not be so arbitrary as to protect someone wearing garments while letting another be harmed. "If the Lord can't protect me without wearing a silly garment," said one exasperated man, "what good is it anyway?"[74] Some Mormons, like other contemporary Christians, stress the symbolic aspect of religious objects and reject the possibility that objects have supernatural powers.

And yet, almost everyone we talked with could tell at least one story demonstrating garments' protective role. While people were often unsure of the theological meanings of their garments, they could remember tales and folklore that stressed the supernatural powers of sacred clothing. Mormons explored the supernatural dimension of garments not through reflective thought but through telling stories. As with much of Latter-day Saint folk narrative, these stories often concern missionaries and are told in missionary circles.[75] In one story, a missionary in South Africa was attacked by a pack of dogs and bitten on his legs but not where his garments were.[76] Another told us a tale of a missionary who was in a jeep accident in Ecuador and whose life was saved by his garments.[77] As with other missionary tales, these stories function to instill proper behavior. Young men and women away from home for the first time are expected to abide by correct standards of conduct. Those who do not suffer the consequences. Garment protection stories are a form of social control. They tell about dire consequences that will befall those members who do not follow the codes laid down by church authorities.

The stories have another function. They illustrate the powerful and magical nature of the garments without indicating that the storyteller really believes garments save lives. Through storytelling we can say something that we might like to believe or feel but that our reason tells us is foolish. Telling stories of the protective nature of garments allows the exploration of the non-rational and the unexpected. These stories leave open the possibility that garments *are* powerful and provide their wearers with tangible benefits. The doctrines and traditions of the Mormon church assert that members will receive special blessings from God. Even if members question the veracity of garments' protective capacity, telling and listening to stories strengthens the belief that God is an active agent in their lives.

The most frequent garment narrative we heard was not a protection story. It was a story that combined two important themes in Latter-day Saint culture: power and secrecy. The basic story line is this: several missionaries are in a laundromat washing their clothes, including their garments. Then they decide to leave (one version says to get some hot chocolate). While they are gone, non-Mormons come into the laundromat, take the garments out of the machines, and display them for public ridicule. "Look at the Mormon monkey suits," they shout. But then the missionaries "dust their feet and the place burns down."[78] When I first heard this story I was confused. Why didn't the missionaries get punished when they were the ones who left their wash unguarded? However, the point of this story, as one woman told it, was "to be careful. I didn't feel like I wanted anyone to see my garments because I felt like they were sacred."[79] The story reinforces the notion that what is sacred is secret and reserved only for members of the community. "Things are sacred and not supposed to be displayed," noted one woman. "They're not supposed to be mocked."[80] The fear exists that the non-Mormon world is incapable of understanding the special nature of the garment and would inevitably desecrate it. Several people told us that they felt uncomfortable and embarrassed wearing their garments in non-Mormon settings such as a gym, hospital, or in the army. A long history of ridicule by non-Mormons of Latter-day Saint beliefs and activities can be cited to justify such feelings.

Modesty, Sex, and Bodies

The Mormons whom we interviewed see garments as being symbolic reminders of the covenants they have made with God. The clothing gains in spiritual significance because of its close association with the temple experience, going on a mission, and getting married. Wearing garments gives one a Mormon communal identity. Lingering nineteenth-century notions of its supernatural powers of protection make some Mormons wonder about other possible benefits accrued from garment wearing. Non-Mormons, however, rarely consider these aspects of garments. For them, garments must shape (probably for the worse) one's attitude toward the body and sexuality. Since the early twentieth century, garments have been associated with concepts of modesty and chastity. Contemporary Mormons also acknowledge that garments play a role in courting behavior and sexuality, although not to the extent that non-Mormons would assume.

Garments first became connected with changing notions of sexuality when some Utah Mormons stopped seeing themselves as a people struggling to survive in a hostile desert environment. As Mormons traded their frontier ethic for Victorian American culture, some people experienced a conflict between their desire for stylish clothing and their desire to be faithful garment wearers. In 1906 President Joseph F. Smith condemned the "foolish, vain, and indecent practices" of fashion and warned against any mutilation of the "garments of the holy priesthood." Evidently, Latter-day Saints were rolling up their garments' long sleeves and legs to make them fit under changing clothing styles. To emphasize the importance of not altering "that which should be held . . . the most sacred of all things in the world next to their own virtue," Smith declared that the garments were "unchanged and unaltered from the very pattern in which God gave them."[81] Still, Latter-day Saints continued to manipulate their garments. In 1918 Smith issued an "established and imperative rule" forbidding any deviation from the "approved pattern." "The pattern of endowment garments was revealed from Heaven," the president wrote, and "the blessings promised in connection with wearing them will not be realized if any unauthorized change is made in their form, or in the manner of wearing them."[82]

The struggle between a changing Utah society and church authorities trying to maintain religious standards was unavoidable. Mormon desire for simplicity and modesty conflicted with the ever-present American fascination with fashion. Sophisticated ladies wanted to wear dresses with short sleeves and more dramatic necklines. Although the "Gibson Girl" look of the early 1900s flattened the breasts and revealed no hint of cleavage, it did demand a show of the upper chest. Garments were looking less like standard underwear.[83] For President Smith, however, changing fashions did not dictate changes in the garments. Garments defined modesty by drawing lines around the body edges.

And yet, changing fashions had forced the president to make a critical theological statement that previously had not been articulated: the current garment style had divine origins and thus could not be changed. Latter-day Saints would not receive physical and spiritual protection if they altered the form of the garment. Changes introduced by humans to the material object would affect its power. In order to combat the influence of American society on the religious behavior of Latter-day Saints, church authorities articulated the special and sacred nature of garments. Previous to this time, there had been no reason to comment officially on the divine origin of the garment pattern. Properly worn garments served as a boundary that separated the believer from the non-believer, the faithful Mormon from the secular Mormon.

Rising skirt lengths and the increasingly informal nature of men's clothing continued to threaten the future of traditional garments. In 1913 Mary Phelps Jacob invented a soft, short brassière that separated the breasts and required no corset.[84] Brassières which flattened or supported the breasts became popular in the 1920s. After World War I, fashionable Americans no longer assumed that a layer of washable material must cover all the skin. Briefs had become brief and underwear, especially for women, no longer resembled men's long johns. By the early twentieth century, underwear had acquired erotic meaning.[85] "Drawers" were renamed "lingerie" or "panties," came in silk, muslin, and gauze, and were colorfully decorated with lace and ribbons.[86] What had once been a practical way of keeping clothes clean had become associated with the intimate parts and functions of the body. Especially for women, corsets and bras were supposed to heighten body contours and thus promote the appreciation of the female form. Although men's underwear did not reach the same sexualized level until the 1960s, it too followed the trend set by women's fashions.

If Mormon leaders had not changed the style of garments, their community would have been out of step with general American society. Mormons with their long dresses would have been like the Amish who wear the clothing of eighteenth-century rural Germany or Hasidic Jews who can trace their hats back to medieval Poland. To make that much of a statement against modern culture would not have been in keeping with the practical, and increasingly mainstream, nature of Mormonism. By the time that underwear was changing, Utah Mormons had given up trying to establish a separate nation, had outlawed plural marriages, and were eagerly pursuing the American Dream of private enterprise and personal freedom. Theological and ecclesiastical needs also necessitated the change in garments. When temple attendance was deemed to be essential to Mormon life, church leaders abbreviated and streamlined the ceremony. They also shortened and modified the garments.

In 1923 President Heber J. Grant permitted modifications to the garment. He approved: shortening the sleeve to the elbow and the leg to just below the knee; eliminating the collar; replacing the string ties with buttons; and closing up the crotch so that only the back would be open. The long-style garment still had to be worn in the temple, but the shorter garment became standard everyday wear. The connection between the rituals taking place in the temple and the sacred clothing on the body intensified. The theology surrounding the garment also was significantly modified. President Grant, to the consternation of some, proclaimed that "no fixed pattern of Temple garment has ever been given."[87] Revelation is a continuing process according to Mormon belief, and so such reversals are not seen as human adaptations to changing cultural standards. Change occurs when God communicates his will to those chosen to receive it.

The church leaders also followed the fashion trend of sexualizing underwear. A 1953 letter from church president David O. McKay approved of a ladies' garment with lace edging to be sold by church-owned department store, Z.C.M.I. The fact that women wore garments did not prevent them from adopting fashionable underwear (corsets, stockings, or bras) that accentuated the female contour. Gone were the days when Mormons made garments out of bleached flour sacks or sewed the markings on long johns.[88] In 1979 the church permitted the shorter garment in the temple, and the old-style garment was eventually discontinued. One reason that it can no longer be purchased is because orthodox Mormon authorities wanted to distance their garments from polygamist Mormons who still wore the old-style garment. Garments continued to undergo adjustments, the most obvious being the further shortening of sleeves and legs in the 1960s and the creation in 1983 of a two-piece garment.[89] The two-piece garment, which closely resembles men's boxer shorts (with legs to the knee) and T-shirt, is the current preferred style. Once the church leaders determined that design changes did not lessen the holiness or effectiveness of the garment, new fabrics and styles could be tried out.

Latter-day Saints are taught that the human body is a reflection of God. God gives his children bodies (tabernacles) so that they can be tested and perform those rituals (ordinances) that will enable them to achieve salvation. Possessing a body is a privilege and a blessing. Latter-day Saints also insist that God himself has a physical body (D&C 130:22; 131:7). The bodies of men and women are imperfect replicas of the bodies of the Heavenly Father and Mother. Since Latter-day Saints believe that all of humanity came into the world because of the reproduction of the Heavenly Father and Mother, bodies and sexuality have divine origin. "We came to this earth that we might have a body and present it pure before God in the celestial kingdom," wrote Joseph Smith, "the great principle of happiness consists in having a body."[90] Mormons do not have a concept of original sin or a tradition of asceticism. Sexuality is not the result of a fallen and corrupt human nature. God placed sexual feelings in men and women to achieve a joyful, emotional, and spiritual unity as well as to produce children.[91]

Following Christian tradition (John 2:19–22 and I Cor. 6:19–20), Latter-day Saints refer to the body as a fundamentally sacred space, a "temple of the Holy Spirit." Like the Mormon temple, the body is something that is not accessible to the uninitiated. Modesty and chastity limit the access to the body just as restrictions are placed on who can attend temple ceremonies. A man who had been wearing garments for twenty-seven years was shocked when his bishop told him that his nude modeling for a university art class must stop.[92] As with the garment, public exposure of the body is desecration. The Doctrine and Covenants is quite clear about the significance of defiling the body: "The elements are the tabernacle of God; yea, man is the tabernacle of God, even temples; and whatsoever temple is defiled, God shall destroy that temple" (93:35). In a 1968 pamphlet on chastity, Mark E. Peterson, a prominent church official, described the divine nature of sex: "Sex is so sacred, so divine, that when it is used in its proper way, those who participate in it become joint creators with God." Using the metaphor of body as temple, sex is described as a restricted space: "God has placed it way up on a high plane, so high that all right thinking people will regard it as being sacred."[93] Restrictions on sexual expression are not seen in official teaching as inhibitions but rather as ways to be in harmony with God's intention for the body.

The body has also been compared to a machine in official Mormon discourse. It must be cared for properly or else it can break down. In a classic 1976 statement by Boyd K. Packer discussing masturbation, a man's body is compared to a "little factory." The little factory must be "ruled," "kept under control," not "tamper[ed] with."[94] Whereas the metaphor of the temple leads us to imagine the body as a perfected, divine space which is in harmony with God, the metaphor of the factory brings to mind a human-constructed edifice that must be managed and regulated. The metaphor of body as factory echoes the Christian notion that the body tends toward sin and is in need of sexual restraint.[95] "All too often," writes John Durham Peters, "Mormons feel their bodies to be sinful, as sources of temptations, as secondary to the spirit, and in need of the spirit's discipline."[96] While sexual feelings are not evil, nevertheless like any appetite or passion, "physical desire can be distorted, overindulged, or misused."[97] Sexual expressions, according to Latter-day Saint doctrine, must be limited to one's heterosexual marriage partner. Certain sex acts conducted within marriage can be unnatural, impure, and unholy.[98] Masturbation also is a sin "because it is basically an act of self-debasement and abuse."[99] Because sexuality is God-given, homosexuality cannot be "natural" and Latter-day Saint leaders believe it can be overcome with prayer and counseling. Latter-day Saints see the body in both ways: as a sacred edifice and as a machine which must be controlled and regulated.

No one we interviewed spoke of the body or sexuality in the same richly metaphorical language as church leaders. No one spoke of their bodies as temples or factories. Some disagreed with the church's position on masturbation, pre-marital sex, and homosexuality. Others explained to us that garments shaped their body image or sexuality in a positive way. One man commented that he feels "more self-assured" and attractive wearing garments because he is thin and the extra clothing makes him feel "more solid."[100] Another felt more confident about his body when he had on the layer of the garment. Not liking being naked, the "garments are a relief."[101] One woman liked her garments because "they make you feel your entire body all the time."[102] For these people, garments were neither uncomfortable nor inhibiting. They gave them a sense of bodily security and modesty which enhanced their feelings about themselves. Bodies became a part of the cosmic order and assumed meaning that extended beyond the self. Just as Catholics focused on their sick bodies by using Lourdes water, garments enabled Mormons continuously to connect the physical self with the spiritual self.

On the other hand, others felt that garments contributed to a general Latter-day Saint phobia about the body and sexuality. Latter-day Saints critical of their church's position on sexuality argue that Mormons have adopted (perhaps unintentionally) traditional Christianity's antagonism toward bodily pleasure. They cited the church's negative attitude toward masturbation, oral sex, pre- and extra-marital sex, and same-sex relations, as evidence of an unhealthy fear of the body. Several of those who no longer wear garments commented that the church's emphasis on sexual control influenced their decision to become non-active. One man recalled that he could not accept the position that masturbation was sinful and that respecting his garments would stop this "self-abuse."[103] A woman admitted that while she felt spiritually beautiful she "never felt really sexy or very appealing with a garment on . . . physically I felt really ugly."[104] Even if the garment was physically comfortable, on a deeper level it shaped these people's perceptions of their bodies in a negative way. "Garments are anti-sensual," concluded a man who has been wearing them for thirty years. They "build a barrier between sensuality and spirituality. In my experience it damages both."[105] When people stopped wearing the garment and re-evaluated their attitudes toward the body and sexuality, they felt liberated. "I feel more connected to [my body] now," reflected another woman. "I feel like [my body] can be sexual. I'm a sexual person and not wearing the garments has helped me with that."[106]

Those Latter-day Saints who felt out of harmony with their church described garments as anti-sensual, awkward, and ugly. However, even regular church-goers felt garments had no part in their love lives. An active Mormon observed that wearing garments means "that there is a layer next to your skin and it's hard to be sensual or sensuous when you're wearing that much underwear. They're not erotic. They weren't created to be erotic."[107] Having worn garments for over forty years, one woman confided that garments were "sexually inhibiting." When she first married, it was unclear whether she and her husband could take them off at all while making love. They eventually agreed to put the garments back on immediately after sex. "I knew that there were lots of times that we would be closer, have more intimate sex, if we didn't have to have clothing on in bed," she disclosed. "It was inhibitive."[108] With only one exception, those we interviewed found nothing erotic about garments and wanted to take them off as quickly as possible when love-making began. "You are definitely more sexy without them," recalled one man.[109] "They are not very lovely things," remarked a woman.[110] For some, the removal of garments signaled that someone is interested in making love. If "I'm planning ahead of time that we're going to be together," a wife informed us, "I won't have them on. I'll have something prettier [on]." She also thought that people who sleep naked and don't wear garments "probably make love more often because your bodies are just together."[111] Couples removed their garments not because they felt that sexual activity would profane the garment but because garments did not make them feel sexy.

Since the early twentieth century, when Victorian standards of sexual morality gave way to more permissive perspectives on the body, Mormon discourse has stressed the importance of chastity and modesty. Early Mormons may have considered their garments a physical guard against harm, but contemporary Mormons are told that garments act as a shield and protection against impurity. Wearing such clothing should act to ensure modesty and proper sexual response. Contemporary Americans, however, are not used to understanding their underwear as promoting modesty rather than sexuality. Media and the advertising industry sell underwear by showing it as an accessory to sex. "All clothes are body fashions," writes Valerie Steele, "but the more intimate the connection between body and clothes, the sexier the clothes will be . . . the sexual power and charm of the body 'rub off' on to the clothes." Clothes are also seen as contributing an "additional stimulus of their own."[112] Given advertising's promotion of underwear as sexy and romantic, it is not surprising that some Mormons bridle at the thought of wearing garments. Although Mormon rhetoric sacralizes sex (the body as temple) it also seeks to control sexual activity (the body as factory). Garments effectively convey the importance of remembering covenants and dressing modestly, but they do not represent the positive side of the Mormon attitude toward sex.

The general notion is that wearing garments helps promote modesty and proper sexual behavior. When pressed, do contemporary Mormons believe that garments *really* protect moral purity as the church authorities hope? Does wearing garments keep unmarried Mormons from having sex? "It made me think twice," admitted one person interviewed, "but I don't think it ever stopped me."[113] When we asked if garments kept people from heavy petting or extra-marital sex the answer usually was no. One women related an account of a bishop who confessed to his congregation that he had committed adultery. When asked by a church member how he could do "this," he responded, "I just took them off." For the woman giving us the account, this was shocking. "I thought that taking off your garments would be embarrassing and that it would prevent you from even doing it," she reflected. "This was quite a revelation to me."[114] People knew that garments were supposed to help maintain physical purity but when asked if they really helped prevent sexual transgressions they were skeptical. Just as in the case of physical protection, the Mormons we spoke to devalued this aspect of garments.

However, a few told us stories reminiscent of garment protection stories. As with physical protection, there appears to be a hope that garments might stop or slow down the passionate. As with the folklore about supernatural physical protection, in tales of supernatural spiritual protection Mormons could explore the possibility that garments had this power without actually having to "believe" they did. In one story, a young man had returned from a mission and was courting a young woman. She invited him to her home, prepared him a nice meal, and afterwards they started to kiss and caress. According to the storyteller, "Things got out of hand and they were really going to have sex. She removed her clothes, and he was getting ready to remove his clothes, and he was down to his garments. When he looked down and saw his garments, his covenants came right back to him, and he put his clothes on and decided to leave."[115] That the temptress was an Eve-like woman not wearing garments who tried to seduce a virginal man who did, suggests the mythic character of the narrative. However, the moral of the story is clear. Garments provide an absolutely clear reminder of the body's boundaries. To remove the garments is to move immediately into the realm of "impure acts" and so is vigorously condemned. Garments again assert their ability to communicate messages to those within the Mormon community.

The Garment as (Flexible) Boundary

The early Mormon tradition of using seer stones, mad stones, and parchments with magical words is no longer an important part of Latter-day Saint culture. On the other hand, Mormons continue to use consecrated oil in healing rituals, and garments remain a vital part of Latter-day Saint spirituality. Unlike protective amulets, garments are associated with the ritual world of the temple. The endowment ceremony with its covenants forms a core aspect of Mormon belief. When a physical object is associated with core elements of belief, it then finds a secure place in religious culture. The garment connects two types of "temple" experience. It is first worn during a sacred temple ceremony in a restricted space where only Latter-day Saints in good standing may enter. The garment comes to symbolize temple promises and blessings. The garment also lies next to the body, which in official discourse is associated with a more generic "temple." The body is the temple of the Holy Spirit. The garment functions as the veil that separates the sacred, holy, and private space of the body from the public space of the environment. Garments locate the body within the realm of the sacred. The body, like the building of the temple, is owned by God and controlled by God's authorities on earth. Like the temple, the body is seen as secret, intense, and basic to the inner structure of Latter-day Saint religion. Garments, bodies, and temples are tightly interwoven.

The garment is a flexible boundary line. On the one hand, it creates a visible and tactile reminder of the boundaries between member and non-member, sacred and profane, appropriate behavior and inappropriate behavior, private and public, body and environment. One of the responsibilities assumed by religious leaders is to articulate the community's boundaries. Latter-day Saint leaders take this responsibility seriously and, perhaps more than in other American religions, intervene to correct the behavior of their church members. "The doctrines of the gospel are revealed through the Spirit to prophets," summarized Boyd Packer, "not through the intellect to scholars."[116] For some Latter-day Saints, garments cannot be understood by non-Mormons. The sacred should never be spoken about outside of the temple and so to discuss temple activities or garments in profane space is a form of desecration.[117] If we understand religion to be those ideals set forth by authoritative voices, then "Mormonism" or "Catholicism" or "Islam" is a fixed system of rituals, beliefs, and codes of behavior; a rigid set of boundaries. Discussing garments, even from a scholarly perspective, trespasses an established Latter-day Saint boundary.

On the other hand, ideal religious forms are fragile. People, including religious leaders, bend ideals to fit changing social and theological situations. Those we interviewed saw those boundaries as flexible, and they manipulated them to express their social and spiritual thoughts. Standards of modesty are slightly transgressed by pinning up the sleeves and legs of the garments to permit the wearing of summer shorts and shirts. Mormons wear garments to keep family and neighbors happy, even if they no longer believe in church teachings. Excommunicated Latter-day Saints wear their garments in defiance of efforts to isolate them from the Mormon community. This bending of boundaries does not merely make religion "easier" so that it harmonizes with conflicting social and psychological needs. People think about their religious situation and pray for divine guidance on difficult questions. Frequently they come up with answers different to those of their leaders. For the person who struggles with his or her faith, those answers are still religious answers.

Sociologist Georg Simmel, who wrote eloquently on the role of secrets and secrecy in societies, observed that our bodies are our primary property. To cut, scar, or in other ways remodel the body inscribes secrets on the person and thus dedicates that person to the elders and the dead.[118] To wear garments is to assent to the "secrets" of the ancestors and elders. By placing a cloth over the most intimate parts of the body and embroidering on it sacred signs, Mormons acknowledge the claim that their religion has over them. At the same time, they interpret the limits and meanings of that claim. That reflection brings tensions and ambiguities that are never easily resolved. In the same way, the hidden and concealed nature of the garment also provokes anxiety. Secrets empower and embolden the holder. Secrets provide special knowledge and protection. Secrets tell believers that you are "one of us."[119] At the same time, this set-apartness serves as a constant reminder of difference. The Mormons we interviewed frequently told us they were embarrassed when outsiders saw their garments and uncomfortable in situations where their garments might possibily be revealed. Mormons who want to "pass" in a society that is hostile, critical, or condescending toward them find that the unintentional display of garments weakens rather than strengthens the self. Just as some Mormons feel the conflict between accepting and not accepting the church's claim over their bodies, so they feel the strain of knowing the garment protects them and yet knowing that it symbolizes their strangeness. Secrecy places a burden as well as a privilege on the secret keeper.

Garments represent the intimate, concealed, secret parts of religion. When garments are exposed, the hidden elements of a faith are displaced. Within the Latter-day Saint community, however, clothing is also used publicly to assert faithfulness. For many Americans, when someone says the word "Mormon" the image conjured is of a pair of clean-cut young men, dressed in dark suits with white shirts and ties, trying to interest the unconcerned public in their religion. Throughout the world all Latter-day Saint missionaries (who can be male or female, married or unmarried, young or old, American or foreign) wear conservative American-style dress. The point of wearing a suit and tie in India is to facilitate the evangelizing process. Missionary clothing draws attention to the individual and projects an air of religious and social confidence. While garments are hidden and intimate, missionary garb is public. Garments speak to the community of fellow Mormons, while the "Sunday" dresses worn by sister missionaries in Argentina or Kenya capture the eye of potential converts. With both garments and missionary dress, clothing is used as a language to convey religious meanings and intentions without the use of traditional Christian iconography. In Chapter 8 I explore how other Christians who also take seriously Jesus' injunction to "Go ye, therefore, and teach all nations" (Matt. 29:19) make, market, and buy goods replete with Christian symbolism.

8

Christian Retailing

Jesus junk. Holy hardware. Christian kitsch. Perhaps only televangelists have been maligned as much as the material culture of contemporary Protestants. Walk into any Christian bookstore and you will be faced with T-shirts parodying advertising slogans, frilly covers for Bibles, and pewter miniatures of biblical scenes. While books and music are prominently displayed in the stores, it is the gifts, clothing, jewelry, art, and novelties that catch the eye. Critics blithely denounce the whole environment as indicative of how a commercial American mentality has invaded the inner sanctum of religion. They complain about how such products reduce Christianity to the trivial and reflect how profit directs piety. To hear how Christianity is going to hell in a hand basket, take a liberal Protestant or a media pundit to a Christian bookstore. If Christian exercise videos, cups inscribed with "Jesus ♥ Me," and rings with golden fish are symbols of a trivial, commercialized, and fundamentally unauthentic Christianity, then why do people buy them?

Christian retailing – the selling of Christian goods and services to a buyer for personal or household use – is a significant aspect of contemporary religious life in America. During the early 1990s, the sales of Christian products in bookstores exceeded $3 billion annually.[1] The trade show where Christian bookstore buyers come to order new books, necklaces, note pads, CDs, Bibles, and Bible paraphernalia ranks in the top 3 percent (in terms of square footage) of the almost 6000 annual trade shows in the United States. The number of Christian bookstores has exploded over the past thirty years. In 1965, 725 stores belonged to the Christian Booksellers Association (CBA). That number more than doubled in ten years to 1850, and by 1984 there were 3200 member stores. In 1995 the estimated total number of Christian bookstores, both CBA member and non-member stores, exceeded 7000. These bookstores buy their merchandise from over 880 suppliers. In the 1980s, Christian bookstore sales of $1 million or more were a rarity. By 1995, 105 stores boasted having $1 million plus sales. The success of Christian retailing is undeniable.

Scholars and the media have documented theological battles between conservative and liberal Protestants, the rise and fall of televangelists, and the political influence of the Religious Right. They have paid little attention, however, to the everyday lives of white, politically conservative, and fundamentalist Christians.[2] These Christians are no longer exclusively poor, rural and Southern. Instead, they are found throughout American society. To varying degrees, these Christians attempt to interact only with those who share their religious life styles while at the same time trying to "right" both American society and individual Americans. They send their children to private schools or, increasingly, teach them at home.[3] They live in the suburbs but their children do not watch television or go to popular movies. With their non-Christian neighbors they are friendly but rarely best friends. Churchgoing goes far beyond an hour on Sunday morning. Christian telephone books give them the names and numbers of Christian dentists, cruise companies, therapists, and plumbers. When they want to rent a video, learn how to cope with a divorce, or buy a wedding present, they go to a Christian bookstore.

For the segment of the population variously termed Born Again Christians, Evangelicals, Pentecostals, Fundamentalists, or just plain Christian, the Christian bookstore is an institution like the church, Sunday school, or missionary society. Its purpose is to minister to those who have developed a personal relationship with Christ and to witness to those who have not. For some Americans, Christian retailing reflects the positive intersection of faith, profit, and goods. Being Christian means to have a Christian life style that includes purchasing goods from a fellow Christian and using those goods. The stress that is placed on critically *thinking* about religion in liberal traditions holds less importance in conservative Christianity than *doing* religious activities and *identifying* oneself as Christian. Making, selling, marketing, and purchasing link Christians together. Religious objects, unlike ideas, can be given as gifts to cement friendship. Christian toys can be awarded for Sunday school attendance to children who cannot understand complicated beliefs. Teenagers can wear T-shirts to witness to Christianity's importance in their lives even if they can only awkwardly articulate their feelings. The visual, sensual, and tactile form of the object offers an immediacy that ideas do not always have. It is easy to laugh at the exotic quality of "Christian kitsch." It is more fruitful, however, to ask how this type of merchandise came into being, what trends can be seen in its production, and why Christians buy and use it.

Victorian Origins, 1840–1900

Recent scholarship refutes the notion that conservative Christianity hibernated after the Scopes trial only to emerge at the inauguration of Jimmy Carter. Likewise, Christian retailing and production have their origins before the Reagan years.[4] As we have seen in Chapter 5, Victorian domestic religion encouraged the production and use of religious objects. Christians of the nineteenth century could drink out of glasses etched with the Lord's Prayer or "Rock of Ages." On Sunday, children played with wooden Noah's Arks or Bible puzzles. Wax crosses were enshrined under glass. Ladies embroidered pious mottoes on bookmarks. Protestants did not invent "Jesus junk" during the twilight of the twentieth century. They carried it with them from the nineteenth. Cheaper production, more efficient distribution, and the willingness of Christians to integrate religion into every aspect of their lives caused the eventual explosion of Christian merchandise. What separates the nineteenth century from the twentieth century in terms of Protestant material culture is, first, the creation of a community of Christian producers and marketers; second, the exploitation of new advertising styles; and, third, the steady proliferation of goods.

Throughout the second half of the nineteenth century, religious goods were sold along with non-religious merchandise. Religious images were not perceived as being too sacred to market because people bought items with Christian references. A. H. Shipman included in his *The Amateur and Mechanics Manual and Catalogue*

115. and 116. The production of religious objects for the home has its origins in the nineteenth century. This late nineteenth-century glass etched with "My God Shall Supply All Your Need" has its echo in a child's plastic cup of contemporary vintage.

117. and 118. While nineteenth-century Christians frequently embroidered bookmarks on perforated cardboard, the modern trend is to purchase ready-made objects. In both instances, the point is to introduce religious sentiments into everyday activities such as reading.

119. Wax crosses frequently decorated the homes of Victorian Christians (see Illustration 77).

of Scroll Saws and Lathes (1881–2) the Lord's Prayer in fretwork. He concluded that this piece "should be in the house of everyone that has a Bracket Saw."[5] Gowans and Sons, from Buffalo, New York, was a premium company that gave people merchandise in return for soap wrappers. In 1898 forty wrappers could earn one a napkin ring, for fifty wrappers a watercolor reproduction of either Faith or Hope, and for 250 wrappers a razor.[6] Following in the footsteps of the better-known Currier and Ives, *Carter's Oil Chromos Catalogue* (1877) presented standard Victorian pictures of children, animals, and landscapes along with Easter crosses, the Sacred Heart of Jesus, and the Good Shepherd. Their knowledge of Christian imagery, however, was limited. A picture of Christ with a woman was labeled "Immaculate Conception."[7] Getting the labeling correct for the chromo was not terribly important. The purpose of the catalog was to sell people art, not to promote Christianity.

As I discussed in Chapter 3, companies marketed art or objects with religious themes only as long as this was fashionable. Victorian producers assumed a homogeneous buying public that saw Christian art and objects as an integral part of domesticity. By World War I, the eclectic and cluttered Victorian style was giving way to more simple and abstract styles. In 1911 Elsie de Wolfe's influential *The House in Good Taste* preached a gospel of simplicity, harmony, and unity in interior design. The Arts and Crafts movement, Colonial Revival, and the later

120.   Non-religious companies, such as the Gifted Line and Enesco, have marketed porcelain crosses that reflect once-again popular Victorian designs.

121.   During the nineteenth century, objects with religious themes were frequently to be found in secular catalogs and handicraft books. Men could show their woodworking skill and Christian commitments by carving the "Our Father" in fretwork.

122.   Since religious goods were not isolated from other merchandise, Christian images were used to sell commodities as prosaic as soap. In return for sending for fifty soap wrappers, consumers could pick either a water color reproduction of "Hope" or "Faith," or a gold-plated cuff link button.

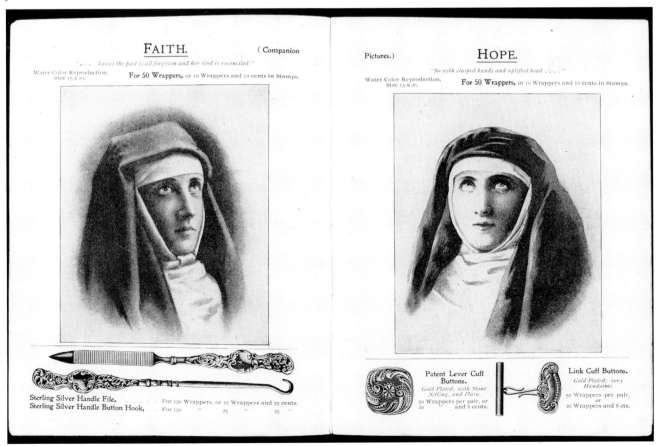

"modern" styles set the tone for fashionable Americans: clutter was out, restraint was in.[8] In particular, by presenting eighteenth-century America as the model of good taste, designers unconsciously promoted the Puritans' suspicious attitude toward religious art. While an antique sampler might be acceptable, brightly colored prints and mottoes of biblical scenes did not harmonize with Colonial Revival design. It was the change in aesthetics, more than any change in American religious life, that motivated secular producers to stop making goods with religious themes. Religious goods disappeared from ordinary stores and catalogs not because Christians rejected the commercialization of their beliefs but because religious art was no longer fashionable. The figurative image, whether sentimental or religious, was being replaced by the abstract form. By the 1920s, style-conscious Protestants might still go to church on Sunday but they did not display wax crosses in their living rooms. A child's bedroom might have a statuette of a praying Samuel but other religious knickknacks were relegated to the attic. Wherever the abstract was considered superior to the figurative, religious arts have had a difficult time finding a place in twentieth-century homes.

Not all Americans wanted a home free from "superficial application of ornament."[9] Not all Americans had the economic power to first collect and display, then reject and simplify. As historian Lizabeth Cohen points out, middle-class reformers failed to persuade immigrants and the working class to furnish their homes in the new modern style.[10] Working-class aesthetics had little in

123. In this comparative illustration from the 1930s, a Victorian home in England is transformed room by room into a modern interior. The simplicity of design and a preference for abstract form made the "modern" European or American home a hostile environment for Christian images.

124. While upper-middle class Americans were choosing more restrained styles of interior decorating, working-class and immigrant families continued the Victorian trend of floral wallpaper, curtained windows, plants, and religious mottoes. In 1937 FSA photographer Russell Lee took this picture of Mrs. Herman Perry in her Michigan home. According to the caption, Mrs. Perry "is the wife of an old-time iron miner who worked in the mines before they were abandoned." Note the motto to her right.

common with middle-class notions of taste. In the mid-1920s, Robert and Helen Lynd did not mention religious art in the "Middletown" homes of the very poor or the prosperous, but they did note pious mottoes in the home of "the working man."[11] Not only was "the working man" financially incapable of buying the latest Colonial Revival furniture, he was not willing to trade the figurative for the abstract. For some Protestants and Catholics, pictorial depictions of the scriptures or saints reflected the historical reality of the sacred and the personal nature of faith. This is not to say that they were not attuned to changing styles and fashions, but they did remain open to the possibilities that religious material culture could be used for decorative purposes. Consequently, secular companies that stopped selling religious arts and objects to Protestants left a vacuum that would be filled by explicitly religious companies with specific Christian commitments. Revivalism, tent camp meetings, Sunday schools, and sermons were not enough. Christian retailing and manufacturing developed in the late nineteenth century because certain Protestants needed physical reminders of their faith.

Christian Manufacturer: Gospel Trumpet Company

In 1877 Daniel Sydney Warner experienced sanctification, the realization that God had given him the gift of Christian perfection. From that point on, he understood that he would be free from all conscious or intentional sin. His desires and

125. In its early days, workers at Gospel Trumpet lived together and received no wages for their labor. Women did the repetitious handwork needed to assemble the motto cards while men undertook the printing.

motives would be utterly pure. Warner had been caught up in the Holiness movement of the 1870s. His enthusiastic proclamation of his sanctification led to him being expelled from his church. While Warner never wanted to establish yet another Holiness denomination, he did actively preach and publish. Slowly, an organization (which became known as the Church of God) emerged in Anderson, Indiana. Centered chiefly around Warner's activities as editor of a newspaper called *Gospel Trumpet* (1881), from the very beginning what would hold the "movement" together was not a set of doctrines and rituals but a publishing company. While many denominations have their own publishing houses, the Church of God is unique because its merchandising business formed the core of this movement's religious outreach. The publishing of *Gospel Trumpet*, along with the writings of Warner and his followers, eventually led to the marketing of tracts, stationery with scriptural sayings, mottoes, Christian postcards, and the distribution of other Christian merchandise. They first called their firm Gospel Trumpet Company, and in the 1960s renamed it Warner Press. Currently a company with net sales exceeding $24 million, the history of Warner Press illuminates how Christian retailing developed and evolved.

In contrast to companies that had no intention of shaping religious commitments, D. S. Warner intended Gospel Trumpet Company to be a Christian organization that reinforced authentic Christian truth. Between 1881 and 1915 company workers lived together and received no wages for their labor. "The entire force of workers," a leader of the community wrote, "were as one family in respect to their associations and manner of life. Until the size of the family would no longer permit, they all ate at one table, and participated in family worship together."[12] Men slept on one floor and women on another. They had their own library and reading-rooms. Striving to be self-sufficient, the group raised animals for food. Eventually the community constructed an old folks home and a cemetery. What held these people together were their commitments to particular religious principles and their willingness to work to produce a Christian newspaper and merchandise. While the communal life eventually died when the business expanded and workers married and had children, the faith commitments of the workers survived. Working for Gospel Trumpet was more than just a job.

The first Gospel Trumpet catalog produced by Church of God workers is dated 1895. It contains descriptions of books, tracts, Bibles, and song books along with the message that "We keep on hand an assortment of envelopes upon which are printed various mottoes and suitable scriptural texts with name and address."[13] To the best of its financial ability, Gospel Trumpet used efficient, rationalized, and technologically competent means to mass produce its products. Women were employed to do repetitive handwork while the men did the printing. After their experiment in communal living ended, employees earned salaries. Whatever profits Gospel Trumpet made went to fund Church of God operations rather than going back to the company. This continually drained Gospel Trumpet's profits and made it difficult for the company to achieve financial security.[14] The company, however, saw itself as a money-making business and so did not hesitate to fire employees during the hard years of the Depression. Faith, commerce, and technology were not understood to be in conflict.

While some products might have been sold through bookstores and at camp meetings, Gospel Trumpet distributed most products through independent agents. Not only was Gospel Trumpet a producer, it also ran a type of retail establishment through its traveling salesmen/women. Advertisements in Christian newspapers and in Gospel Trumpet catalogs explained that "the business can be handled successfully by both male and female." With only a small investment, anyone can make "a success of it . . . if you push the work with a determination to win, and follow our instructions."[15] Agents carried sample cases with Bibles, cards, books, mottoes, and other merchandise to show prospective customers. Once the goods were purchased, the agent could order more merchandise to sell, pocketing the profit. Church groups also sold Gospel Trumpet products and used the profits for their organizations.

Door-to-door selling continued the tradition of traveling Bible salesmen/women.[16] People accepted the selling of religious commodities because they received their Bibles that way, in addition to other secular goods. Protestant magazines advertised for readers to sell everything from religious merchandise to Comer's All-Weather coats.[17] During times of economic instability and unpredictability, such as the Depression, door-to-door selling provided work with a modicum of personal independence and control for the unemployed. While it was certainly possible that non-believers sold Gospel Trumpet products, advertisements for agents emphasized both the religious and financial nature of

126. In 1941 John
Vachon took this FSA
photograph of "the child
of a steel worker" in
Ambridge, Pennsylvania.
Vachon emphasized the
motto by positioning it on
a diagonal to the child.
The Biblical verse,
Heb.13:8, was popular in
Pentecostal circles.

the work. Mottoes and calendars appeared in the homes photographed by the
Farm Security Administration during the 1930s and 1940s, pointing to the success
of this type of distribution. For rural residents, the door-to-door agent functioned
somewhat like a walking Sears and Roebuck catalog for Christian merchandise.

An important item in the Gospel Trumpet agents' catalog was the Art Velvet
scripture motto. These paper mottoes were mass-produced versions of the
embroidered texts Victorian women had sewn on perforated cardboard in colorful
Berlin needlework.[18] Initially, however, Gospel Trumpet mottoes were simple in
design. Some mottoes had only a brief text. A floral design or nature scene (rarely
a figure) accompanied the motto. Of the twenty-four mottoes listed in the 1897/8
catalog, many texts sound a threatening note: "Behold, Now is the Day of

127. The motto in Vachon's photograph appeared in the 1933 Gospel Trumpet catalog and cost forty-five cents. It is one of several popular mottoes in the "art velvet" line.

Salvation," "Prepare to Meet thy God," "Ye must be Born Again," "Where will
you Spend Eternity?" A few show the leanings of the Church of God movement:
"Be ye All of One Mind" (anti-sectarianism); "Is any Afflicted? Let him Pray"
(faith healing); "Without Holiness no man shall see the Lord" (sanctification). By
1909 the harsh tones and sectarian sentiments had disappeared and the mottoes
contained words of consolation and faith in English, French, and German:
"Prayer Changes Things," "Jesus Never Fails," "Abide in Me." Gospel Trumpet
discovered that buyers wanted inspirational words and straightforward proclamations of belief. This language also supported the attitude of Church of God
leaders that sectarian division was un-Christian. Like their Victorian predecessors,
the paper mottoes preached a gentle Christianity that had no links to specific
doctrinal controversies.

The Gospel Trumpet company ignored theological subtleties, but it did not
ignore popular American proclivities. Religious goods producers have always been
keenly aware of what is in and out of style, and they follow cultural fads just as
other companies do. They are particularly concerned with following trends which
do not reflect specific class or ethnic tastes, fads that appeal to many Americans.
In 1901, for example, a picture postcard craze hit Europe. Four years later,
Americans were busily sending colorful cards through the mails. United States
Post Office officials counted over 667 million postcards sent in 1908 alone and by
1913, even when the fad was in decline, the numbers of cards mailed totaled
almost one billion.[19] Postcards illustrated every conceivable topic from animals to
politics, to advertising, to holiday greetings. While the types of illustrations on the
cards, and the ways the cards were used may reflect class differences, the fad itself
was part of turn-of-the-century popular mass culture.

Religious postcards were marketed by both secular and religious companies.
The Gospel Trumpet 1909 catalog reported that "we have about fifty different
designs of embossed post-cards with floral designs and beautiful landscapes. Some
of these cards are imported from Germany and are real works of art."[20] Americans
used religious postcards just like any other card. Christian images were not seen as
being too sacred to be sent through the mails or to be used as conveyors of
commonplace information. A postcard surviving in the Billy Graham Museum
shows a woman dressed in blue robes, looking piously upward with a cross in her
hands, and the text: "When I survey the wondrous cross." The note on the back
reads in broken English: "Hello Mary We are all right. We are plowing potatoes
and you can't see the ground for all pattoes it is two o'clock now and our cabbage
and meat is cooking nicely i will be in Saterday marning Good by seet heart from
W. Hafner."[21] When greeting cards replaced postcards as the fashionable means
of communication, Gospel Trumpet produced a line of cards for every occasion,
including ones for the newly created holiday of Mother's Day.[22] They soon
became the leading producer of religious greeting cards in the country.

Not only did Gospel Trumpet try to follow popular fads, it sought to present
products that were in style. Advertisements consistently emphasized that they sold
"new" merchandise in line with "good" taste. In 1925/6 copywriters hailed the
"Newart" hand-painted mottoes that "appeal to the taste of the tastiest. A motto
that shows class and refinement throughout. The dainty designs of flowers, sprigs
of blossoms, etc. are artistically arranged and show the taste of the artist. Much
delicate color work brings out the delightful appearance. The beautiful sentiments
and texts of Scripture will be appreciated by all."[23] Gospel Trumpet followed the

128. During the postcard craze of the early twentieth century, religious images were one genre among many. This postcard includes a photograph of a real woman posed to look like the images of "Faith" or "Hope" (see Illustration 122).

WHEN I SURVEY THE WONDROUS CROSS (No. 2)

Forbid it, Lord, that I should boast
  Save in the Cross of Christ my God;
All the vain things that charm me most,
  I sacrifice them to His Blood.

129. Religious postcards were used, as secular cards, to convey messages in the days before telephones. There is no indication that people felt such cards were too "sacred" for everyday sentiments.

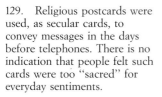

trends set by more sophisticated producers and advertisers in urban centers. As Roland Marchand points out, advertisers were "apostles of modernity" who combined an appeal to the new with a "buffer against the effects of modern impersonalities of scale."[24] By the 1920s, secular advertisers had introduced color into their copy in order to transform household objects into fashion goods. Gospel Trumpet also incorporated color in their catalogs and introduced new product designs. As with secular retailers, Gospel Trumpet embraced the advertising call of the 1920s to "cast off its sober, utilitarian outlook in favor of a new, more pleasure-minded, consumption ethic."[25] Christians, like other Americans, wanted new and stylish decorations in addition to reading uplifting and comforting messages.

In pursuit of the new and stylish, Gospel Trumpet developed an Art Deco motto: "Here is a beautiful combination of strong Christian verse and modern art. The soft, velvety backgrounds, as illustrated, are in different pleasing shades of grey, salmon, chestnut, black, green and beige." The mottoes reflected the geometrical "moderne" style that hit the American market between 1926 and the early 1930s. In 1929 Art Deco furniture and decorations were displayed in New York exhibitions and a few years later Gospel Trumpet advertised Art Deco mottoes in its 1930/31 catalog.[26] Company designers probably saw advertisements in *Ladies' Home Journal* and the *Saturday Evening Post* that used modern art to sell everything from Chryslers to Johnson's Baby Powder.[27] Even from Anderson, Indiana, designers could see that American tastes were changing. The mottoes were not cheap. During the 1920s and 1930s they cost fifty cents each. In 1930 fifty cents could buy a pound of sliced ham, two tubes of shaving cream, or five pounds of navy beans.[28] Given the cost of introducing new designs and making production changes, it is significant that Gospel Trumpet was willing to accommodate evolving taste in order to place its merchandise in people's homes. Thanks to advertising's promotion of the new and fashionable, even families of modest means wanted to feel that they had purchased modern, tasteful, and stylish religious goods.

Gospel Trumpet produced a steady line of religious paper products during the 1920s, but it was not until the 1930s that a full line of Christian products was marketed. Beginning in 1931, Gospel Trumpet experimented with combining a variety of objects with pious verses and pictures. Rather than make the items themselves, Gospel Trumpet contracted with other manufacturers to place religious sayings and pictures on their goods. Mottoes were put on thermometers. Plaques made of "mountain Rhododendron" displayed pictures of Jesus. A "Home Blessing" table set sold for a dollar: "Four beautiful heat-resisting and protecting mats – each with a Scripture text. This new item fills a definite need in the home. Hot dishes or pans can be safely rested now on table or buffet." The Good Shepherd and Jesus praying at Gethsemane decorated bookends. In 1935 Gospel Trumpet put Jesus' image on a lamp: "These lovely lamps with inspiring Scripture texts and beautiful pictures of the Savior will help to bring into your home that something so essential and yet so easily forgotten today. Nothing more quickly adds a touch of freshness and charm to a room than a new lamp." Texts from the scriptures and mottoes were etched on pencils, pencil-clips, rulers, and on the backs of mirrors. The catalogs advertised chromium-silver key chains with the head of Christ as "an ideal gift for Juniors or older boys."[29] Few objects seemed incapable of sporting a religious saying or figure.

130. The "art suede line" of mottoes advertised in the Gospel Trumpet 1931-2 catalog illustrates how the company followed design trends seen in popular magazines and newspapers.

New Religious Wall Mottoes

(THE ART SUEDE LINE)

HERE is a beautiful combination of strong Christian verse and modern art. The soft, velvety backgrounds, as illustrated, are in different pleasing shades of grey, salmon, chestnut, black, green and biege.

THE PERMANENTLY COLORED designs and artistically drawn texts are a part of the motto through a new process.

A silk ribbon loop is attached for hanging. Use Art Suede mottoes as Christmas and special occasion gifts.

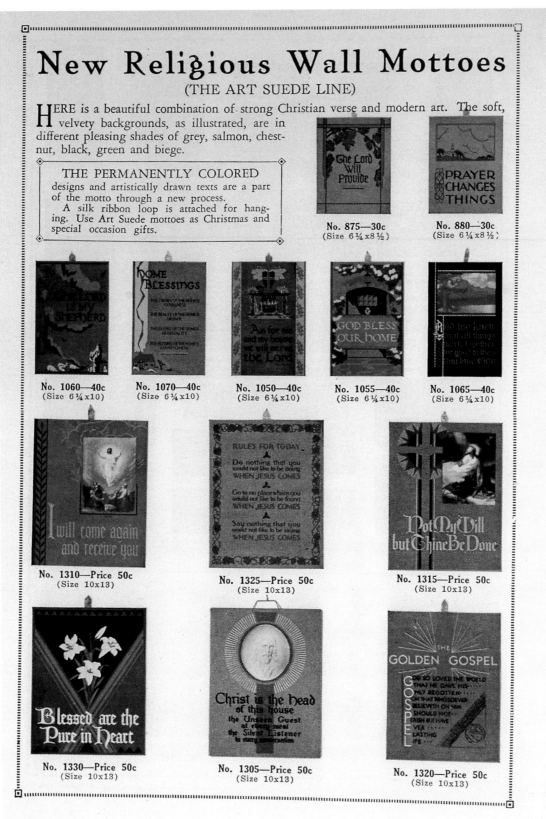

No. 875—30c
(Size 6¼ x 8½)

No. 880—30c
(Size 6¼ x 8½)

No. 1060—40c
(Size 6¼ x 10)

No. 1070—40c
(Size 6¼ x 10)

No. 1050—40c
(Size 6¼ x 10)

No. 1055—40c
(Size 6¼ x 10)

No. 1065—40c
(Size 6¼ x 10)

No. 1310—Price 50c
(Size 10x13)

No. 1325—Price 50c
(Size 10x13)

No. 1315—Price 50c
(Size 10x13)

No. 1330—Price 50c
(Size 10x13)

No. 1305—Price 50c
(Size 10x13)

No. 1320—Price 50c
(Size 10x13)

Artistic Non-Breakable Book Ends

Pictorial BOOK ENDS ARTISTIC POPULAR

No. 1   No. 2   No. 3

A practical and low-priced gift. You can't imagine their worth from this meager illustration. Made of best quality cold-rolled steel and given a trim appearance by deep-drawn embossing. The entire object is finished in a rich statuary bronze. Extreme outer edges are painted with a mixture of pale gold and copper bronzes giving it the finished touch.

50 cents a pair

In keeping with Cathedral architecture, these new Pictorial Book Ends are drawn to the true proportions of a Golden Section—a set of proportions discovered by the ancient Greeks and acclaimed by architects and designers alike throughout the ages as the most beautiful proportions of height and breadth.

The full-color pictures give a beautiful effect and lend additional religious influence wherever used. Light weight and sturdy. **Order by number.**

No. 1—**Christ in Gethsemane**   No. 3—**Old Dutch Mill**
No. 2—**The Good Shepherd**   No. 4—**The Boy Christ**

Worth Much More Than Our Low Price of—50 Cents a Pair Boxed

131. This Gospel Trumpet advertisement promotes these bookends as "in keeping with Cathedral architecture" since they have "the same proportions of height and breadth as that "discovered by the ancient Greeks and acclaimed by architects and designers alike throughout the ages."

Spread-the-Light Reading Lamps

These lovely lamps with inspiring Scripture texts and beautiful pictures of the Savior will help to bring into your home that something so essential and yet so easily forgotten today. Nothing more quickly adds a touch of freshness and charm to a room than a new lamp.

The delicately tinted bases are turned from finest grade steel and finished in "Woodtone" colors of ivory, amber, and mahogany enamels, thus blending well with any color scheme. Neatly gold striped. Each lamp stands 12 inches high. Shade is 10 inches wide at bottom. (Bulbs not included.) Has push button switch, non-breakable plug, and rayon cord.

Each dainty shade has a neat pattern in lacy lines of ivory and black. Hand-drawn text and border. Best lamp-shade parchment stock is used to give a glowing flood of soft light. The deep tones of the colored pictures are enhanced and protected by a sparkling coat of clear varnish. The entire shade may be wiped clean at any time.

Order by number.   Boxed complete $1.95

The "Ideal" Home Lamp A Testimony of Your Christian Faith

SHADE TILTS   SHADE TILTS

DESIGN No. 1030   **DESIGN No. 1031**

Scripture-text Post Card Packages

More and more of our beautiful Scripture-text post cards are being sold each year. Space does not permit our illustrating the many pretty designs. Choice verses and texts that are appropriate are used. May be mailed for only 1 cent each. Keep them on hand the year around. We offer five economical packages here.

No. 324—**Easter Assortment—15c**
(Ten choice cards that carry joy and hope)
No. 322—**Everyday Assortment—15c**
(Ten assorted post cards that please in every way)
No. 326—**Birthday Assortment—15c**
(Ten lovely cards to remember friends with)
No. 390—**Christian Fellowship Assortment—15c**
(Ten cards for Congratulation, Cheer, Get Well, etc.)
No. 323—**Christmas Assortment—15c**
(Ten colorful holiday designs. Choice texts)

Only 15c a package

132. The 1935 Gospel Trumpet catalog carried advertisements for lamps with pictures of Bernhard Plockhorst's "Good Shepherd" and Heinrich Hofmann's "Jesus in Gesthemene." The lamps were promoted as "a testimony of your Christian faith."

New "Utility" Pencils with Scripture Text

These handy pencils are just the thing for carrying in pocket or purse. The design and Scripture text are printed in two colors on white celluloid barrel. Complete with large red eraser and good quality lead.

No. 101—John 14:1
No. 102—John 3:16
No. 103—John 10:10

No. 104—Gal. 6:9
No. 105—The Golden Rule
No. 106—The Lord's Prayer

Size: closed, 4 inches; open, nearly 6 inches.

Sunday schools find them valuable as rewards. Refill with short, left-over ends of regular lead pencils.

Price only 10 cents

Eye hath not seen, nor ear heard, neither have entered into the heart of man, the things which God hath prepared for them that love him. But God hath revealed them un to us by his spirit
I Cor. 2:9-10

Use them as
Sunday-school awards.
Price 10 cents

Scripture-Text Mirrors

A useful and appreciated gift. Desirable for boys and girls as well as adults. Good quality mirror. Measures 2¼ inches in diameter. (Nearly twice the size of illustration.) Backs are covered with celluloid. Texts are in a pretty blue.

Carry a Scripture-text mirror in your purse or pocket. Give them to friends.

— Order by Number —

No. 1—I Cor. 2:9-10
No. 2—John 3:16

No. 3—Ps. 105:4-5
No. 4—Rom. 8:28

Our "Motto" Pencil Clips

Here is a useful article. Use this new method of testifying to others of your Christian faith. These attractive pencil clips are so sturdily made that they will last indefinitely. The celluloid covering neatly displays the texts in blue with red border. This is a splendid Sunday-school reward item. Illustration shows actual size.

— Order by Number —

No. 1—Jesus Never Fails
No. 2—God Is Love
No. 3—He Careth for You
No. 4—Prayer Changes Things

Price 5 cents each

PRAYER CHANGES THINGS

HE CARETH FOR YOU

have entered into the heart of man, the

THE LORD'S PRAYER
Our Father which art in heaven. Hallowed be thy name.
Thy Kingdom come. Thy will be done in earth.

Assorted colors and full sized eraser

Scripture-Text Pencils

— Order by Number —

No. 1—The Lord's Prayer
No. 2—John 3:16
No. 3—I Cor. 2:9-10
No. 4—Ps. 105:4-5
No. 5—Rom. 8:28
No. 6—10 Commandments
No. 7—The Golden Rule

Pencils are considered one of the best commercial advertising mediums. Why not spread the gospel through the use of Scripture-text pencils?

We offer here five choice texts on standard 7½ inch pencils. Miniature Bible on each pencil. The lead is medium soft and good quality.

Price 5 cents

Page 18

133. In this advertisement from a 1937 Gospel Trumpet catalog, scriptures were marked on small objects such as pencils and mirrors.

By the 1930s, Protestantism and secular advertising freely borrowed ideas from one another. Ad men tried to make their vacuum cleaners and refrigerators appear divine by visually emphasizing their size and numinous nature.[30] Churches tried to organize themselves around the principles of scientific management and even built "skyscraper churches."[31] Pastors devised sermons around advertising slogans.[32] Consequently, it is not surprising that Gospel Trumpet copied the gimmick of putting a company's name or logo on a pencil, calendar, or ruler where it would be frequently seen. "Pencils are considered one of the best commercial advertising mediums," announced one Gospel Trumpet caption in 1937. "Why not spread the Gospel through the use of Scripture-text pencils?"[33] Consumers of the 1930s could choose from a seemingly endless variety of goods and services. Gospel Trumpet joined the competition and followed the path cut by secular businesses.

In order to distinguish Gospel Trumpet goods from other goods, a limited number of Christian symbols were used on products. Designers could have used a multitude of images drawn from a long and rich tradition of Christian art. We have seen some of those symbols on graves in Laurel Hill Cemetery. Instead, producers used only a handful of illustrations, all contemporary to the period. In 1918/19 Gospel Trumpet first issued a series of illustrations on its art velvet mottoes based on paintings by the German artists Heinrich Hofmann (1824–1911) and Bernhard Plockhorst (1825–1907). Gospel Trumpet probably bought reproductions of the religious art of Hofmann and Plockhorst from print companies such as Perry Pictures of Malden, Massachusetts. Beginning in 1897, Perry Pictures issued a yearly retail catalog that contained a variety of pictures, including religious subjects. Small pictures cost one cent, larger ones two cents. Companies like Gospel Trumpet probably bought in large quantity for reduced prices. Perry Pictures advertised in Christian newspapers and their name became ubiquitous in Sunday school materials.[34] A select group of paintings and parts of paintings was placed on every conceivable novelty, embossed on stationery, printed on calendars, illustrated in stained glass, and reproduced in Bibles.

By the 1920s, Hofmann's *Christ in the Garden of Gethsemane*, a close-up of a head of Jesus from *Christ and the Rich Young Ruler*, and another from *Christ in the Temple* had become pervasive in Protestant visual culture.[35] As we saw in Chapter 2, companies made these close-ups of Jesus' face to emphasize the personal relationship one could have with the Savior. It also is possible that movie-going had influenced Christian producers just as it had advertising: "As an advertising technique," writes Marchand, "the close-up not only attracted attention, it also fostered the habit of intense self-scrutiny. . . . The movie-star phenomenon reminded advertisers of the popular hunger for personalities."[36] Plockhorst's *Good Shepherd*, *Entry into Jerusalem*, and *Christ Blessing Little Children* also were frequently reproduced. Two other pictures (the painters of which have not been identified) join this limited group of Protestant images: an elegantly winged, blond guardian angel guiding two children across a bridge and a seated Jesus watching the city of Jerusalem. In the early 1940s, Gospel Trumpet replaced the art of Heinrich Hofmann and Bernhard Plockhorst with the works of contemporary painter Warner Sallman. Small reproductions of Warner Sallman's *Head of Christ* were sent to U.S. troops serving overseas during World War II and his rendition quickly became the accepted likeness of Christ.

By using only a limited number of religious images, Gospel Trumpet and other companies established a small set of Protestant representations as a "brand name" for Christianity. They wanted people to feel unequivocally that the object they sold was not just a lamp, it was a Christian lamp. Christian companies followed secular producers who realized that when "selling in a market characterized by growing competition for consumer loyalty, brand names offered a relatively easy method to gain product differentiation, ensure customer loyalty, and even increase their share of the market."[37] A close-up of the face of Jesus, a guardian angel, or a Bible phrase marked the object as Christian and separated it from other, similar

135. The face of the adolescent Jesus became particularly popular as material for Sunday schools. During the war a trailer camp was set up for aircraft workers near Baltimore, Maryland. In 1943 FSA photographer John Collier captured this Bible class conducted for the workers' children where Hofmann's young Jesus figured prominently.

134. Heinrich Hofmann's *Christ in the Temple* follows the tradition of Protestant narrative paintings. As with his *Christ and the Rich Young Ruler* (Illustrations 7 and 8) printers excerpted and reproduced the head of the young Jesus. (From the 1937 Gospel Trumpet catalog.)

136. In 1938 FSA photographer Arthur Rothstein took this shot of a "farm-home interior" in Martin county, Indiana. The woman seated in the chair is not named. Above her is a Gospel Trumpet motto.

products. Since Protestants did not use halos (or other Catholic symbols) to signify saints or deities, they had to find other ways of efficiently conveying the message: "This is a sacred character." Through repeated exposure to a select group of illustrations, consumers quickly came to learn that a particular image was "Jesus."

As would be expected from such Protestant merchandise, religious goods were used for teaching, spiritual uplifting, and cementing bonds between people. The evangelizing function of Gospel Trumpet products is obvious but not exclusive. A 1922/3 catalog reveals that some Protestants may have used these goods in additional ways: "A short time ago a woman paralyzed from her waist down applied to her church for aid," read the citation under one art velvet motto advertisement. "It was refused. Not only to her own church people did she apply, but to others. In her room one day, sitting alone, tired out, discouraged, forsaken, her eyes by chance fell upon a motto. Through it her faith grasped the promises of God. She was instantly healed. Hundreds flocked to hear her tell her story." The

137. E. E. Byrum in the prayer room of the Gospel Trumpet company.

advertisement concluded: "See what a simple motto performed – just a little Scripture verse. Catch the vision of what God would have you do."[38] Here we have a glimpse of the function of religious goods as a means of channeling the power of God directly to the individual. It is important to note that the church, the institutional expression of religion, failed the invalid woman. God might have easily healed her without the intercession of the motto, but it was via the visual reminder that she "grasped the promises of God." The last sentences with their ambiguities heighten the sense of the power of the motto. The text does not say, "See what God performed through the motto." The copywriter insinuates that the "vision" of what God wants us to do is best "seen" on objects.

Faith healing, which frequently included anointing the sick with oil, was part of the tradition of the Church of God and many other conservative Protestant churches. A Church of God historian wrote that, in 1901, over six hundred anointed handkerchiefs were sent to those requesting prayers and healing.[39] Within the building where Gospel Trumpet manufactured its goods was a prayer room. In one photograph E. E. Byrum, an editor of the newspaper and important figure in the movement, is pictured in the prayer room surrounded by crutches, medicine bottles, his own writings, and Gospel Trumpet mottoes. The crutches and medicine bottles were given to him by people who had been healed through his mediation. The prayer room contained objects that proved that God healed those who came to him in faith. Even if Church of God members would deny that there was any "superstitious" power present in the room, visually the room functioned as a shrine to the healing power of God and E. E. Byrum. Just as Catholics place *ex votos* as thank yous for miraculous healing in holy places, so did some Protestants.

138. A large percentage of the goods that Gospel Trumpet sold was geared to children. These "Sacred Art Picture Puzzles" continued to present the Victorian art of Plockhorst and Hofmann to Protestant children well into the mid-twentieth century.

Gospel Trumpet did not typically promote the healing capacity of their merchandise. For the most part, Christian companies advertised that their products expressed personal piety and supported church activities. One church activity, the Sunday school, was especially important to companies like Gospel Trumpet.[40] Most denominational presses that produced Sunday school curriculum materials faced the problem of trying to sell their materials to churches other than their own. Written curricula also had to conform to prevailing educational philosophies. Non-print products, however, could be used by many different

139. While art was not always welcome in Protestant churches, it was an important part of Sunday school teaching. Photograph taken by Russell Lee, 1939, in San Augustine, Texas.

churches and were not as susceptible to changes in pedagogy. Gospel Trumpet sold fanciful cards where "each pupil is assigned a card and plays that she is Bo-Peep. Every Sunday she gets a new sheep, and at the end of the quarter, if she has a perfect record, she has a flock of thirteen sheep."[41] Students received cards with Biblical scenes when they correctly memorized a Bible verse, came to class on time, brought in a new visitor, or were particularly attentive. They then could trade in the cards for larger cards or even for books or gifts at the end of the year. Beginning in the 1920s, Gospel Trumpet sold sacred art picture puzzles, celluloid Sunday school pins, stickers, Bible games, and scripture mottoes. Teachers could buy cradle rolls (for enrolling babies), maps, art equipment, record books, diplomas, and wall rolls of biblical scenes.

During the first half of the twentieth century, the Sunday school was the main conduit for the movement of Protestant material culture into the home. Children made "art" in Sunday school, and they brought mass-produced products home. Both the reforming wing of the Sunday school movement and the more conservative forces made and used religious objects.[42] In some denominations, religious art and objects may have been limited in the space of the church but not in Sunday school rooms and the home. Consequently, the visual world that many Protestants were exposed to, and eventually would remember, had a child-like feel to it. While Gospel Trumpet tried to keep abreast of style changes for its mottoes and greeting cards, its Sunday school line barely changed over the years. The Victorian design of Sunday school materials remained steady because adults purchased the materials for children. Children were not supposed to be attuned to changing fashions, so why change the materials? Sunday school teachers assumed children liked bright colors, busy designs, and sentimental subjects. Victorian designs easily fulfilled these aesthetic criteria. When a Protestant critic condemned Christian merchandise as "very romantic Sunday School Art," she probably was remembering what she brought home as a child and what decorated her own households.[43] Victorian sentimentality was associated with Protestant material culture because of the proliferation of Sunday school materials and the importance of childhood memories in defining religious meaning.

Gospel Trumpet exploited, as did other advertisers and manufacturers of the 1920s and 1930s, the need for tradition, the numinous, self-sufficiency, and personal intimacy in a changing society. While Christian sentiments were eternal (a "buffer" against modernity), Christian products were mass produced in a business-like manner and reflected contemporary aesthetic taste. Gospel Trumpet saw no inconsistency in making a motto that was both a decoration and a sermon. It could, and it did, print mottoes with aesthetically pleasing flowers, a sorrowful Christ, and the text: "Even Christ Did Not Please Himself." The object both denied and affirmed pleasure. Kenneth Ames, in his analysis of nineteenth-century religious mottoes, calls the connection of fashion with faith an "uneasy union."[44] My sense is that by the 1920s this was a necessary union. Religious objects, like advertising, performed therapeutic functions. Americans were told, "they could enjoy every modern artifact and style without losing the reassuring emotional bonds of the village community."[45] The type of piety placed on wall plaques, key chains, and lamps expresses the religion of the imagined "village community." The style could be urbane but the sentiment had to be eternal. Objects with religious texts, from stationery to home blessings, reassured their users that even in a threatening world the old truths of the Bible remained constant.

Settling Down to Sell: The Christian Bookstore

After World War II social changes in the structure of American life made the door-to-door agent who sold religious merchandise obsolete. The number of people who lived on farms continued to decline and new subdivisions of affordable housing appeared around cities. As the population shifted, churches focused on the family living in the suburbs rather than in the city or on the farm. An expanded interstate highway system made transportation easier, and the postwar economic boom made it possible for rural people to drive their own cars into town for shopping. The GI Bill helped make it easier for men to get loans to begin their own small businesses. While traveling Bible salesmen and women would continue to sell in the South, typically only fundraisers peddled religious cards and novelties door-to-door. More enterprising Christians decided to set up their own stores to sell Bibles, books, stationery, and other merchandise to a growing middle class with more disposable income.

During the 1950s, independent Christian bookstores that were not associated with publishing houses began to be founded.[46] Between 1965 and 1975 the number more than doubled from 725 to 1850. Average store sales grew at an annual rate of 16 percent between 1975 and 1979, well above the national retail growth of 9.7 percent. The stores were independent, family-owned, with husband and wife making business decisions together. The money they earned was like that made by any family business, expenses and taxes were paid, and the modest profits went to buy houses and send children to college. At a store, larger and more fragile merchandise could be more efficiently sold to a population ever more able to buy expensive goods. CBA, a trade association begun in 1950, kept track of the burgeoning bookstores and suppliers. It intended to professionalize the business by providing guidance on how to set up stores, manage inventory and personnel, and educate consumers. Their annual national conventions drew suppliers and bookstore owners from around the world. In the late 1970s, bookstores and suppliers were joined by distributors who provided a link between the wholesale producer and the retail consumer. By the 1980s there were several ways that Christians could express their faith through retailing: as suppliers, distributors, bookstore personnel, or consumers.

Christian bookstores might have remained a minor aspect of American Protestant life if it had not been for the "Jesus movement" of the early 1970s. Bookstores would have continued to carry Bibles, Sunday school materials, and popular Christian art, but Protestants would have had little reason to purchase anything more. Scholars, who have been overly concerned with the impact on politics by the "New Religious Right" of the 1980s, have ignored the cultural impact of the earlier period of Protestant revivalism. A flurry of less-organized and more expressive evangelism in the late 1960s and 1970s imbued Christian merchandise with new meaning. Covered by news magazines, "Jesus freaks" and "Jesus people" achieved a media notoriety unique in postwar America.[47] More importantly, these evangelicals claimed that Christianity was not merely a belief system but a "life style."

Jesus people, who combined Protestant piety with the spirit of the 1960s counterculture, sought to experience the reality of Jesus outside of an institutionalized church structure. For them, the intense personal relationship that they had achieved with Christ motivated them to redirect their lives. Turning from drugs and a meaningless existence, they sought lives where every action would be shaped by faith and every question answered by the Bible. Like other counterculture people, they idealized a rural religious past, hoped to separate from mainstream society, and were suspicious of the claims made for science and technology. Jesus people felt that the End Time was near. Music became one way in which they experienced and expressed their new-found religious consciousness. For the youthful enthusiasts of the early 1970s, Christianity was not merely a private set of beliefs orchestrated by an institutional church. They understood their conversions to entail the total re-alignment of their lives. Following a general trend in postwar evangelism, Christians stressed the importance of living a holy life in accord with spiritual principles.[48]

The Jesus movement shifted the focus of conservative Christianity from the "Bible Belt" to the "Sun Belt." Those Christians who were expressing their faith commitments in public, and whom the media were following, were young people from California and the Northwest. These Christians fully exploited pop culture to express their new-found religious spirit. The Jesus movement involved more than transforming hippies into Christians. People not associated with the youth movement also began to show an interest in religion and looked for ways that Christianity could speak to their lives. As Protestants had done in the mid-nineteenth century, they looked to books to articulate their religious sensibility. The increase in the sales of religious goods came on the heels of a series of religious best sellers. Publishers saw that religious books would sell to more than ministers and seminarians. By combining current fashion with religious concerns, Christian publishers came up with best sellers. If a "best seller" is defined as a book reaching sales of 100,000 then in 1975 there were almost five hundred

national religious best sellers.[49] During the 1970s, three books in particular
signaled to Christian presses and bookstores that the wider American population
was ready to invest in religion.

The first book that drew people into Christian bookstores was written by a
Jesus movement leader who emphasized that God had chosen our times for a
special purpose. Author Hal Lindsey insisted that by deciphering the signs written
in contemporary events one could understand God's plans for the world. For him,
the current period was not merely a period of social unrest, it was the beginning of
the End of Time. *The Late Great Planet Earth* (1970) published by Zondervan
Press revitalized the connection between the cosmic order and the modern world.
The appeal of the book resided in its ability to show how the time *right now* was
eminently meaningful. In the first few months of its publication *The Late Great
Planet Earth* sold over 130,000 copies. By 1978, 9 million copies were in print.[50]
According to scholar Robert Ellwood, the book was "one of the few volumes
besides the Bible found in virtually every [Jesus] movement commune, home, and
church parlor. Next to the Scriptures, probably no other book is more read."[51]
The Late Great Planet Earth did not merely warn people that the end was near. It
functioned to make people think that *their* world held God's secrets.

In the same way that Christians saw their time made meaningful by the
proximity of the end of time, they had their contemporary language "sacralized"
by a new Bible. *The Living Bible* (1971) was a paraphrased Bible written in a
breezy, modern style.[52] While Christians continued to revere the King James
Version, they read *The Living Bible* for their own edification. Its first single print
order of 500,000 copies was the largest in the history of Bible publication. Over 3
million copies were sold during its first year of publication and by 1975 over 18
million had been sold. According to *Publisher's Weekly*, in 1972 it was the No. 1
best seller in the United States. It held that position into 1973, outselling the
popular *The Joy of Sex*. New Christians might admire the King James Version but
for everyday meditation many preferred a condensed Bible in everyday English.

In 1973 another book encouraged Christians to think that their everyday lives
could be sanctified. Marabel Morgan's *Total Woman* mixed evangelical Christianity with advice on sexual attractiveness. Like *The Living Bible* and *The Late
Great Planet Earth*, *Total Woman* made contemporary life the focus of attention.
During its first year and a half in print, *Total Woman* sold over a half a million
copies. By 1975 it was selling at a rate of between ten and twenty thousand copies
per week.[53] While American Christianity had frequently portrayed sex as a type of
innocent ecstasy, the widespread distribution of *Total Woman* encouraged
evangelicals to think of their bodies as God-given sites of pleasure.[54] In spite of its
anti-feminist stance that urged women to be obedient to their husbands, *Total
Woman* addressed women's concern of how to be sexual and Christian at the
same time.

All three of these exceedingly popular books emphasized that contemporary
time, language, and bodies could be the focus of divine concern. Their popularity
helped new Christians see themselves as part of a world filled with religious
meaning. Fashion and consumer goods also became an important medium for
telling the story of salvation and displaying Christian community. Jesus people did
not merely want to read about Christianity. Some of the Jesus people expressed
their sentiments by producing their own unique arts and handmade merchandise.[55] Previously established Christian presses, however, quickly adjusted

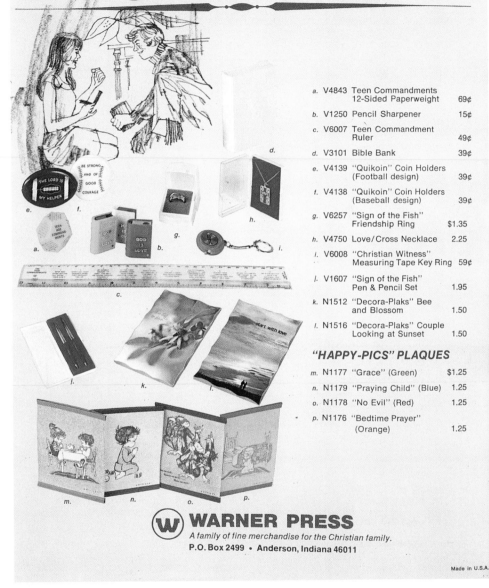

'With it' inspirational gifts for youth.

a.	V4843	Teen Commandments 12-Sided Paperweight	69¢
b.	V1250	Pencil Sharpener	15¢
c.	V6007	Teen Commandment Ruler	49¢
d.	V3101	Bible Bank	39¢
e.	V4139	"Quikoin" Coin Holders (Football design)	39¢
f.	V4138	"Quikoin" Coin Holders (Baseball design)	39¢
g.	V6257	"Sign of the Fish" Friendship Ring	$1.35
h.	V4750	Love/Cross Necklace	2.25
i.	V6008	"Christian Witness" Measuring Tape Key Ring	59¢
j.	V1607	"Sign of the Fish" Pen & Pencil Set	1.95
k.	N1512	"Decora-Plaks" Bee and Blossom	1.50
l.	N1516	"Decora-Plaks" Couple Looking at Sunset	1.50

"HAPPY-PICS" PLAQUES

m.	N1177	"Grace" (Green)	$1.25
n.	N1179	"Praying Child" (Blue)	1.25
o.	N1178	"No Evil" (Red)	1.25
p.	N1176	"Bedtime Prayer" (Orange)	1.25

WARNER PRESS
A family of fine merchandise for the Christian family.
P.O. Box 2499 • Anderson, Indiana 46011

Made in U.S.A.

140. Companies like Warner Press adapted their merchandise line to meet the needs of Jesus people and other evangelical Christians. From the *Bookstore Journal* June, 1973.

their goods to appeal to this new type of Christian. Companies realized that young people eagerly wore Christian symbols in order to publicize their new-found religious beliefs. At the same time, these "new" Christians – like generations of Christians before them – wanted symbols that harmonized with the fashion and mood of the times.

The former Gospel Trumpet Company, now called Warner Press, had already cultivated an appreciation for secular trends and the ability to adapt Christian ideas to current fashions. It ran advertisements heralding: "'With it' Inspirational

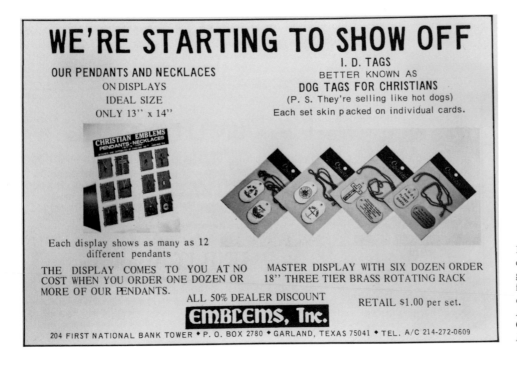

WE'RE STARTING TO SHOW OFF

OUR PENDANTS AND NECKLACES
ON DISPLAYS
IDEAL SIZE
ONLY 13" x 14"

I. D. TAGS
BETTER KNOWN AS
DOG TAGS FOR CHRISTIANS
(P. S. They're selling like hot dogs)
Each set skin packed on individual cards.

Each display shows as many as 12
different pendants

THE DISPLAY COMES TO YOU AT NO
COST WHEN YOU ORDER ONE DOZEN OR
MORE OF OUR PENDANTS.

MASTER DISPLAY WITH SIX DOZEN ORDER
18" THREE TIER BRASS ROTATING RACK

ALL 50% DEALER DISCOUNT

RETAIL $1.00 per set.

EMBLEMS, Inc.

204 FIRST NATIONAL BANK TOWER ◆ P. O. BOX 2780 ◆ GARLAND, TEXAS 75041 ◆ TEL. A/C 214-272-0609

142. Christian producers did not hesitate to use gimmicks like "Dog Tags for Christians" to catch consumer attention. Advertisement from the October 1973 issue of the *Bookstore Journal*.

gifts for youth." Warner Press was not alone; a Fleming G. Revell advertisement boasted that "Christ speaks to the NOW generation . . . in eye-catching, mind-bending, colorful capsule messages . . . sized for pocket and purse . . . shaped to command attention."[56] Companies translated the hippie battle cry of "Make Love Not War" into Christian terms. In 1973 World Wide Publications printed stickers saying: "I love you is that ok? Jesus C" and "Jesus = Peace." Emblems, Inc. made "dog tags for Christians (P. S. They're selling like hot dogs)." Bumper stickers made an enthusiastic appearance: "Jesus Gives Real Peace," "Smile, Jesus Loves You," "A Nice Day is Jesus." By the late 1970s producers also printed bumper sticker and poster slogans on T-shirts: "Keep on Trustin'" and "In case of RAPTURE This T-Shirt will be empty."[57] The "one-way sign" (an outstretched finger pointing upwards) was the most frequently duplicated symbol; appearing on posters, made into jewelry, and worn on clothing.[58] Plain wooden crosses and fish symbols were included on key chains and necklaces, reflecting an ethic of anti-materialism and simplicity. The Salt Company from Hollywood made a "Poverty Patch" to be sewn on jeans or framed. During the 1970s the market for Christian goods shifted from the Sunday school classroom and rural housewife to the under-30 evangelical.

Producers and bookstore owners proclaimed that a new era in Christian merchandising had begun. They disparaged previous generations of goods they felt were cheap, shoddy, and old-fashioned. "The young people are tired of an artificial world," reported the owner of a complex of artisan workshops and a bookstore in Orange County, California. "They are hungry to study the bible and share God's love in every possible way. In their disdain of a superficial society, they have rejected the plastic trinkets of the religious market and have begun creating witness items more relevant to their needs."[59] A manufacturer of jewelry recalled that "as 'holy hardware' glutted the market there was a concomitant downward swing in interest and sales. While the rest of America's great industrial machine shifted its emphases by stressing quality and innovation, the religious gift field slumped deeper into a morass of uninspired, unwanted trinkets."[60] Producers

141. Bumper stickers, clothing patches, buttons, and "witness notes" are some of the many items that companies adapted from the counterculture style of the 1960s to the Christian market of the 1970s. This advertisement appeared in the June 1973 issue of the *Bookstore Journal*.

If It's Worth Sharing, It's Worth Wearing.

Call us toll-free at 800-331-4670
or contact our order department at
P.O. Box 416, Sand Springs, OK 74063.
We also do custom work at
3915 N. 31st Avenue, Phoenix, AZ 85017,
(602) 274-1242.

the Idea Machine.
"The T-Shirt People"

143. While "Dog Tags for Christians" never became a part of evangelical clothing, T-shirts continue to be worn by Christians of all ages. Advertisement from the May 1978 issue of the *Bookstore Journal*.

144.   The "One-Way" sign quickly became the symbol of the Jesus movement, but it also could be seen on funeral sculpture and decorative religious arts of the Victorian period (see Illustrations 81 and 82). Advertisements from the November 1971 issue of the *Bookstore Journal*.

145. Both secular and Christian producers turned the anti-materialist sentiments of the youth movement into consumer goods. Advertisement from the February 1972 issue of the *Bookstore Journal*.

146. In this advertisement, directed at bookstore owners, Bob Siemon presents both himself and his goods as elite and high-quality. Advertisement published in the June 1990 issue of the *Bookstore Journal*.

of Christian art especially criticized established forms. "Christian art is cheap and worthless in comparison to the standards produced by the world. But it's not a matter of competing with the world," summarized a *Bookstore Journal* reporter, "it's a matter of *surpassing* the world's standards. We as Christians should be producing the finest paintings and the finest sculpture and the finest music anywhere."[61] Whereas the concern in the 1930s and 1940s was for inexpensive materials, the stated concern in the 1970s was for quality goods. Jesus movement artists and producers intended to establish a viable Christian alternative to the secular marketplace.

A variety of independent producers entered the marketplace hoping to meet the need for innovative, quality Christian goods. One company that flourished was the jewelry making firm of Bob Siemon. Siemon began his business after a college jewelry instructor said his "Jesus Saves" ring was "the most uncreative thing you've done." Other friends, however, liked it and were willing to buy copies. Siemon, who had drifted around in the 1960s, accepted Christ as his personal savior in 1970 after conversations held in a Christian bookstore. He decided to sell his jewelry through bookstores because "I became a Christian . . . because of the love and concern of one owner." "'Christian junk' makes me sick," complained Siemon in 1979. "I'm determined our jewelry will never be classified as cheap or gaudy. We hope to establish a standard that cannot be surpassed." The rose serves as his company's icon, "a symbol of purity, simplicity, and grace; of quality unsurpassed."[62] Artisans such as Siemon felt that their goods raised the aesthetic consciousness of Christians while at the same time expressing their own religious commitments.

Christian evangelical zeal, not profit or professional pride, continued to motivate those involved in the various aspects of Christian retailing. "While the profit angle has to be dealt with in order to stay in business," explained the producer of clocks shaped like fish, "our basic intention is to get products into as many homes and offices as possible where they will be used to draw attention to the Word of God and to the goodness of our living Lord."[63] During the 1970s

Serving A Hungry Industry

QUALITY.

Throughout our company, there is an absolute insistence on quality in every piece we make. From our beautiful 14K gold to our distinctive costume jewelry and gift products, quality is our main ingredient.

INNOVATIVE DESIGNS.

Never satisfied in following the pace of others, Bob Siemon sets the pace in innovation and creativity, and has earned recognition as a leading jewelry and giftware designer. You can always expect fresh, new designs to be introduced throughout the year.

MARKETING.

An essential part of moving product and generating business. From the smallest product card to our richly-finished oak Jewelry Center and compact, space-efficient Gifts of Joy, we work to market every item to stimulate your customers' appetites.

SERVICE.

We take pride in having one of the fastest and most complete fill-rates in the gifts industry. Our Customer Support staff will get you what you want, when you need it, and our Genesis Marketing representative will come to your store with the newest designs and proven best sellers.

BOB SIEMON DESIGNS. . .
dedicated to serving you!

BOB SIEMON DESIGNS, INC.

National: (800) 854-8358   CA: (800) 225-6401
Local: (714) 549-0678   FAX: (714) 979-2627

Christians showed their religious commitments by making and selling goods that both promoted the gospel and provided an alternative to secular goods. The diversity and quality of the goods far exceeded the merchandise of the prewar period. Some items, like T-shirts and bumper stickers, were meant to shock and appealed to an age group that likes to shock. Others, like the fine jewelry of Terra Sancta or Bob Siemon, encouraged Christians to realize that religion, aesthetics, and fashion were not mutually exclusive. Christian consumerism, born in the previous century, had been "born again" in the Jesus movement of the 1970s.

Contemporary Trends

By 1977 some of the merchandise that had some out of the Jesus movement had disappeared. Gone were the pendants in the shape of fish hooks, the poverty patches, and the bumper stickers. The 1980s and 1990s found the Christian consumer older and more conservative. Just as some of the hippies grew up to be yuppies, so Christians became more politically and socially conservative. They established their own private schools, hired lobbyists, and started their own Christian companies. They also continued to shop at Christian bookstores.

In 1992 the Christian Booksellers Association published a survey of 926 customers living in Georgia, Michigan, Wisconsin, Minnesota, Texas, Colorado, Washington, and Alaska.[64] They found that 75 percent of these customers were between the ages of 25 and 54. Three-fourths of the shoppers were women and a quarter men. Most were white (90 percent) while only 4 percent were African American. Bookstore customers typically were married with children. The survey showed that roughly an equal number of homemakers and white-collar working women (23 percent versus 21 percent) shopped at Christian bookstores. Of the men, 30 percent worked in some capacity for a church and 23 percent held white-collar positions. About half of those surveyed indicated having an annual household income of between $20,000 and $40,000 with the other half almost equally split between those with lower incomes (under $20,000) and higher incomes (over $40,000). Of those surveyed, 35 percent owned a personal computer and 86 percent had a VCR.

What separated these consumers from the rest of their age cohort was their churchgoing. Nearly 97 percent attended church once a week or more. Most say they are involved in church choirs, lay leadership, Sunday schools, or small study groups. Unfortunately, the study was not very careful in describing the types of churches to which they belong. Slightly over 33 percent said they go to a Baptist church; 18 percent checked off "Other Protestant" (e.g., Methodist, Presbyterian, Lutheran). Of the remainder, 20 percent described their affiliation as non-denominational, 10 percent charismatic, and 4 percent Roman Catholic. Christian consumers are church-going, middle-aged women and men, who have disposable income but not much time to spend it. They are concerned about their jobs and their children. While witnessing is important, they are more focused on creating a home and associating with others who share their religious beliefs and activities.

Successful Christian bookstores respond to the needs of this buying group. "It is our job to find out what our customers need, then seek to meet those needs," concluded one bookstore owner. "Our store's product mix is customer-driven. Any Christian bookstore that sets out to change the customer's desires is headed

147. Roman, Inc. began as a producer of Catholic statues but eventually branched out into the Protestant market. Their goods are expensive and high-quality. Advertisement from the February 1991 issue of the *Bookstore Journal.*

148. The youth market is still a large part of Christian retailing. Producers struggle to keep up with fashion trends in order to keep their merchandise selling. Advertisement from the May 1992 issue of the *Bookstore Journal*.

149. During the 1970s and 1980s many Christians set up their own companies but few survived into the 1990s. In 1983 World of Life Scriptures, Ltd. advertised its cookies with scriptural messages and tea bags with biblical texts, but the company went out of business by the end of the decade. From the *Bookstore Journal*, July 1983.

for bankruptcy. It's our job to serve the public by creating an outlet for the finest Christian products, not to tell customers what they should like."[65] Contemporary Christian bookstores cater to diverse tastes. They carry high-quality jewelry by Bob Siemon or religious statuary by Roman, Inc. and Enesco. At the same time, they have novelties for children (e.g., rulers with Bible scenes, "Jesus ♥ Me" plastic cups, skateboard pencil sharpeners saying "Jesus Keeps Me On My Toes") and T-shirts with clever slogans for teenagers. Standard pictures of Jesus or nature scenes compete with exotic products like scripture cookies or pendants containing the whole Bible on microchip. Music ranges from traditional hymns to Gospel to Christian Heavy Metal. Books also vary from the academic to the pop psychological. Most Christian bookstores provide their customers with a variety of goods, allowing them to purchase whatever meets their own stylistic and theological tastes.

While Christian bookstores are still stores with books, the number of books and the types of books they sell have been in flux. In 1978, 68 percent of store sales were for books, Bibles, and Sunday school curriculum items. By 1993 print materials had declined to 49 percent of total sales. Sales of Christian music had risen from 12 percent to 15 percent and the sales of non-print merchandise (jewelry, gifts, cards, films, games, toys, crafts, plaques, art) had doubled, from 20 percent to 36 percent. Publishers have increasingly made their books look less like books and more like merchandise. Books have bigger print, more white space, and are shorter. Book covers for Bibles, complete with handles, visually transform the

Gregg Biblecovers

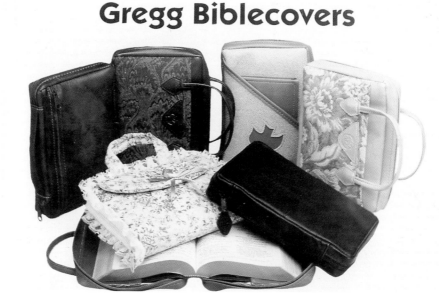

150. Bible covers preserve the scriptures from everyday wear-and-tear, emphasize the holy book's special nature, and present it as a fashion sport. Advertised in the June 1992 *Bookstore Journal*.

Holy Book into a fashionable object. In order to sell books to an increasingly pragmatic Christian population, publishers carefully follow secular trends. They know that the average book-buying Christian is focused on family life (especially raising elementary-age children), mid-life crisis, dying parents, and marital issues.[66] Political and social issues, while catching the eye of the media, do not sell as well as life-style and self-help books. "In my bookstore, I'm personally disappointed with pro-life books' slow sales," regretted one owner. "I can easily sell five times as many diet books. This proves to me that we're more interested in our own bodies than in the bodies of the innocent unborn. We hate fat more than murder."[67] Although many Christian bookstore shoppers would condemn abortion, such issues are not what they want to read about. They perceive themselves as not needing advice on the moral dilemmas of reproduction. Their concerns are the immediate problems of home, job, and their spiritual lives.

Theological discussions and denominational disputes also hold little interest. Christian bookstores survive because they are decidedly "Christian" and not denominational. Inspirational and self-help books connect biblical texts to everyday problems, but they rely less on theology and more on contemporary psychology. Gifts and music producers strive to appeal to a large number of Christians. Retailers have developed their own religious marketing niche by emphasizing a generalized Christianity. Christianity becomes, in effect, a type of brand name recognition. Since brand names have to be clear and distinct there must be no confusion as to whether something is or is not Christian. So it is not surprising that suppliers put unambiguous symbols on every item they sell. The name "Jesus," a biblical text, a cross or fish, these are the equivalent of Nike or Kellogg or Benetton. They clearly mark the product as "Christian" just as the art of Heinrich Hofmann or Warner Sallman did a generation earlier.

Retailers are aware of customer preference for a non-denominational, biblical-based Christianity. "Ten years ago, you could often tell a store's denominational stripe simply by looking at its inventory," recalled CBA president Bill Anderson, "but today's professional retailers recognize that their success hinges on their ability to serve the broadest sections of their communities possible, without violating personal conscience. As a result the yardstick being used to govern purchases is the fundamentals of the faith rather than personal preferences and denominational doctrines."[68] Baptist Book Stores, run by the Southern Baptist Sunday School Board, gave the name, "Life-Way Christian Stores" to their new stores in Denver, Albuquerque, and Fort Worth in order to downplay their denominational affiliation. They also plan to change management and training in order "to untrain our staff in old customer service paradigms, and retrain them in new paradigms."[69] Christian retailing downplays theological differences while stressing commitment to biblical principles, principles interpreted by the individual.

While theological differences are perceived as divisive and un-Christian, there is no notion that everyday life, including popular culture, taints religion. Christian retailing is possible because consumers refuse to separate the sacred from the profane, the extraordinary from the ordinary, the pious from the trivial. For these consumers, Christianity is intimately bound up in the day-to-day life of the family and its goods. Families who use Christian merchandise do not find it sacrilegious or in bad taste to wear baseball caps with "Jesus Christ, He's the Real Thing" stitched on them.[70] Nor do they think paper napkins decorated with blue ducks and the phrase "Praise the Lord" inappropriate for a ladies' luncheon. Children get combs imprinted with "Can't bear to be without Jesus" as party favors. When I point out to Christians that baseball caps get sweaty, napkins are thrown in the trash, and combs get coated with dandruff, their attitudes do not change. The objects – caps, napkins, combs – are good in themselves. The phrases are excellent Christian sentiments. Sweat or dirt or dandruff cannot profane either the object or the ideas. Holiness is achieved through proper behavior and not normally through the intrinsic meaning of an object. What is important is the promotion of the Bible. Fashion, advertising, popular culture, and style are merely the medium for the message.

Wearing T-shirts printed with "We are the fragrance of Christ" moves Christianity out of the space of the churches and into the everyday life of learning, family, and consumerism. However, there are important points of controversy about what constitutes "discernment" on the part of consumers and retailers. Christians who are attuned to the exact wording of the Bible are concerned with "discerning" what is good and what is evil. What is of God and what is of Satan? Is music that has rhythms just like modern rock music appropriate for Christians? Even if the lyrics praise the Lord, what if the beat makes one want to sway sensuously? Should a bookstore owner stock Oliver North's memoirs even if they contain swearing? What about children's Bible videos made by someone who is a Mormon? Should Christian bookstores carry Catholic rosaries? Such questions force suppliers, retailers, and consumers to consider not only what is good or evil but what exactly is Christian and non-Christian.

Each Christian bookstore has its own "mission statement" that helps decide what types of merchandise will be stocked to promote its religious goals. Some stores refuse to carry any books or merchandise that question the Virgin Birth, the infallibility of the scriptures, the Trinity, or the Second Coming.[71] Other stores have vague statements about promoting Christian principles. "We are a business whose ministry is in the product that we sell," remarks a store owner in Rancho Cucamonga, California. "We seek to provide Christian products to all people through Christian principles, sound business methods, and well-trained employees."[72] Store owners can decide for personal reasons not to carry Christian rock music or books that are too violent. For the most part, the trade association of Christian booksellers encourages its members to let the consumer decide what is appropriate merchandise.

As early as 1973 a writer for the *Bookstore Journal* urged readers to consider seriously the new ecumenical market of religious goods. After the changes of the Second Vatican Council, he explained, Catholic bookstores found that their clientele had dwindled. Liturgical changes encouraged Catholics to participate more fully at mass and to exchange their devotions to the saints for Bible study groups. The article correctly predicted the demise of the Catholic goods store and the preference of some Catholics to buy Bibles and inspirational books at Protestant-run bookstores.[73] Since the 1980s, however, Catholics have been rediscovering their material culture. Conservative trends in the church and new interpretations of traditional theology by liberals have reinvigorated paraliturgical devotions. Rosaries, statues, scapulars, medals, and holy cards have entered again into the worldview of some Catholics. Should Christian bookstores carry such goods? In the February 1992 issue of the *Bookstore Journal* two articles appeared on the Catholic consumer. One sought to straighten out common mis-understandings of Catholic doctrine in the hopes of making conservative Protestant bookstore owners more comfortable about carrying explicitly Catholic goods. The other presented practical hints on how to market merchandise to Catholics without offending Protestants.

In the following months, letters to the *Bookstore Journal* were evenly split between retailers who welcomed Catholics and their merchandise into the store and those who were still convinced that Catholics could not be Christians. While individual bookstore owners might still harbor anti-Catholic animosity, it was quite clear that the Christian Booksellers Association had few problems with Catholicism. *Bookstore Journal* articles on Hispanics, both Catholic and Protestant, recommended bookstores take demographic trends seriously in the United States: while liberal and moderate Protestants are on the decline, Catholics hold steady at about one quarter of the population.[74] For bookstore owners to continue long-standing hostility toward Catholics and ignore the Catholic community would be both unbusiness-like and un-evangelical.

While Christian retailers might be willing to change their attitudes toward Catholics, hostilities continue to be voiced about Mormons, Jehovah's Witnesses, and Seventh-Day Adventists. Many evangelicals consider these communities to be non-Christian "cults" and outside the boundaries of Christianity.[75] Mormons, Jehovah's Witnesses, and Seventh-Day Adventists buy general Christian merchandise, but Christian bookstores do not carry the material culture specific to these groups. Lapel pins of the angel Moroni or playing cards with the faces of the Latter-day Saint prophets can only be bought in a Mormon bookstore. While Latter-day Saints and Jehovah's Witnesses might be condemned by individual retailers, the CBA trade journal refrains from carrying stories discussing these religions. Federal trade regulations prohibit CBA from discriminating against companies on the basis of either their religious belief or product quality. Under law, they must allow any supplier who sells its product to at least ten Christian

151. In the past two decades, Latter-day Saints have followed the lead of evangelical Protestants and have begun to market merchandise specifically geared for Mormons. Since Mormon custom prohibits playing with standard face cards, Latter-day Saint companies have produced card games with the faces of church leaders.

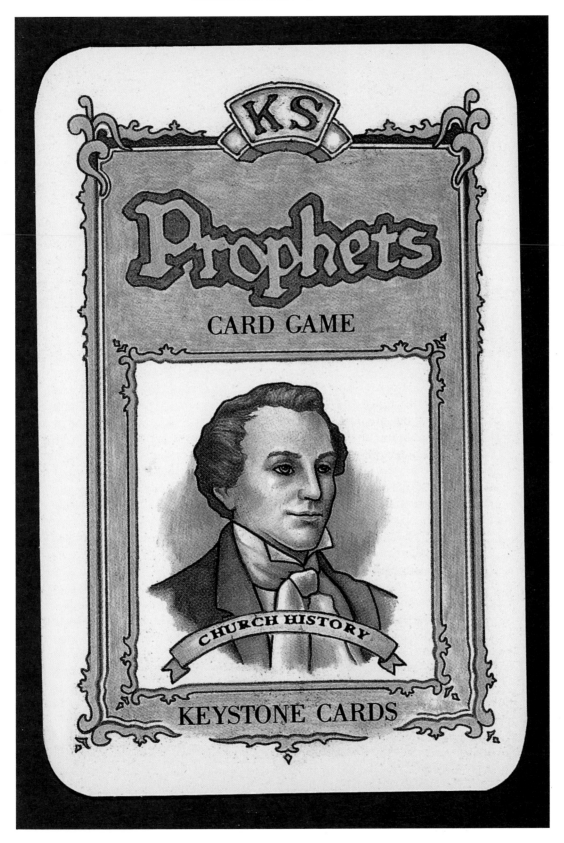

152. Crosses are not typically worn by Latter-day Saints. In recent years, the angel Moroni has become a favorite figure for decorating tie-clasps and ladies' pins.

bookstores to become a member of the association and to exhibit at their trade shows. By both law and inclination, CBA tends to be inclusive. Their editorial silence on these groups and their acceptance of Catholicism indicates a softening attitude toward non-evangelical Christianity.

In spite of this openness, there is no evidence that other world religions or humanistic philosophies are welcomed into the Christian bookstore movement. Non-Christian religions are ignored entirely or written about from a Christian perspective. The popular American movement of the New Age is explicitly condemned.[76] For many Christians, the New Age is a "pagan" religion combining the egocentric follies of secular humanism and the evil machinations of the devil. In a *Bookstore Journal* article entitled, "The New Age Goes Mainstream," not only is Shirley MacLaine and her penchant for channeling denounced but also Joseph Campbell, the popular writer on world mythology. According to Douglas Groothuis, author of the article and several anti-New Age books, Campbell "claims that humans are ultimately at one with an impersonal God, that morality is relative to the perceiver, that sin is an illusion, and that many paths lead to religious meaning."[77] For those like Groothuis, the main rival for the souls of Americans is not liberal Protestantism or Catholicism, it is a type of pantheistic humanism that rejects the need for a Bible-based Christianity.

Conservative Christians are so concerned with New Age influences that they do not participate in Halloween festivities. From their perspective, the autumn holiday actually glorifies the Evil One and his servants. Bookstores that promote every other popular American holiday have no displays for Halloween.[78] Children might dress up as Bible characters and have parties at their churches, but they do not pretend they are witches, ghosts, or super-heroes. "The hottest issue between now and 2001," predicted an industry spokesman, "will be the struggle between the New Age movement and Christianity to define what is spiritual."[79] Halloween, crystals, herbal medicines, tarot cards, Ouija boards, jewelry with pentacles – the material culture of the New Age – present a serious religious rival to the biblical orientation of conservative Christians. It is at this point that *Christian* becomes a meaningful term. Christian bookstores occupy a specialty marketing niche because they are not open to humanistic philosophies or other world religions.

Conservative Christians easily condemn New Agers for making pacts with the devil and ignoring biblical truth. What is more difficult to face is the harsh reality of the business side of Christian retailing. For example, just as independent grocery stores have been replaced by supermarket chains, so is the independent Christian bookstore owner threatened by bookstore chains. "Family Bookstores" is a chain of 130 Christian bookstores owned by Zondervan Publishing House. This chain (as well as others run by the Methodists and Baptists) provides stiff competition for the family-run bookstore. Chain bookstores order books and merchandise in bulk and then pass on their discounts to the consumer. A chain may allow one of their stores to run at a deficit for several years since other stores can make up the loss. Is such competition "Christian"? If we can take CBA's stance as an indication of general sentiments, the answer is yes. *Bookstore Journal* articles and letters to the editor encourage retailers to use the spur of competition to provide better service and products. Increased competition from chains and from other stores should motivate retailers to use the sophisticated techniques they learned in business school or at CBA conventions.[80] Rather than shrink from marketplace rivalries, CBA prods its members to see this as an important challenge and to act decisively. Competition is not un-Christian if it is expressed in a spirit of love and does not contradict biblical principles.

But what happens when a Christian company is purchased by a firm that does not care about biblical principles, however they are interpreted? The harsh reality of business sometimes leads Christian retailing away from its religious roots. Family Bookstores is owned by Zondervan Publishing House. In 1988 Zondervan was bought by Harper & Row for $57 million.[81] Harper & Row, now HarperCollins, is owned by the media magnate, Rupert Murdoch. "Two months ago HarperCollins published *The New Joy of Gay Sex*," complained a letter to the *Bookstore Journal*, "on one side, Murdoch is making money on sex technique manuals for homosexuals, and on the other side, he's making money on Zondervan NIV Bibles sold through Christian bookstores."[82] Christian music companies have been bought by Zondervan (Benson Music in 1980); ABC/Capital Cities (Word Records in 1986); and EMI (Sparrow Music in 1992). How should Christian musicians feel about recording with a company whose parent company (EMI) distributes the music of Sinèad O'Connor, infamous for ripping up the pope's picture on television? Perhaps the most successful Christian music company, Time Alliance, is owned by Time-Warner. When Time-Warner published *Sex*, Madonna's collection of erotica, a boycott of Time-Warner was seriously considered.[83] In another instance, the Christian magazine *Charisma* was criticized for running advertisements for the Christian books carried by Waldenbooks, "one of the largest distributors of pornographic materials in the United States," according to the American Family Association.[84] As Christian producers and retailers become successful, they also become attractive to non-Christian companies.[85] Can profit and mission be balanced if a company is not owned by Christians?

Those in Christian retailing are well aware of the conflict of interest created when non-Christian businesses buy Christian companies. For the most part, suppliers and retailers try not to look too deeply into the associations between

Christian and non-Christian businesses. Companies like Warner Press want to market their Christian products in discount stores like Wal-Mart and Kmart. General bookstores like Waldenbooks want to sell popular Christian novels. Warner Press and Waldenbooks both see market expansion as a natural extension of their missions: Christian retailers want to reach more people and secular companies want larger profits. Sparrow Music accepted its purchase by EMI by asserting that a wider audience would hear Christian music and so "further promote the gospel to the world."[86] In justifying including advertisements for Waldenbooks, the owner of *Charisma* and *Christian Retailing* explained that his decision is "based on my conviction that lighting a lamp in the darkness is more effective than screaming about the darkness."[87] When Christian retailers face the righteous indignation of fellow Christians, they can point to Jesus' interactions with sinners as justification for their involvement with those with whom they disagree. The pull of witnessing allows them to reject the voices of isolationists who insist on the creation of a pure, isolated Christian community. On the other hand, witnessing comes perilously close to assimilation.

In a curious way, the Christian bookstore "movement" that started in the 1950s mirrors the generational growth of the babies that were born during the same period. In the 1950s and early 1960s, bookstores were in their infancy. Their sales were low, their environments unprofessional. However, by the late 1960s, the bookstores were moving into early adulthood and they reflected the exuberance of the youth movements of the period. Merchandise changed as new suppliers responded to cultural and religious innovations. The number of stores increased and those already in existence enjoyed healthy sales. The growth and creativity of the late 1960s and 1970s was over by the early 1980s. The Baby Boomers – both stores and people – had matured. Merchandise became more conservative and of better quality. Fathers and mothers who started stores in the 1950s began to pass them on to their children who increasingly professionalize their businesses without relinquishing their Christianizing missions. Retailers face the more sophisticated problems of their "adult" profession: What does it mean to be a "Christian" bookstore? How do we relate to non-Christian businesses? When does success signal assimilation?

The Future of Christian Retailing

"Our ministry is really in the message of the products we sell," clarifies the owner of a store that conducts $2 million in annual sales. "Good Christian products change lives. So if we emphasize sales, getting as much product as possible into the hands of as many people as possible, we expand our ministry dramatically. We can't make one-on-one ministry our primary focus and be successful. We need to focus on reaching people with products and let the products minister to customers' needs."[88] For the consumer, the bookstore owner, and the supplier, Christian retailing is a religious activity. Over and over again these people insist that they express their Christian commitments through making, selling, and buying. The product becomes a sermon; the words of the preacher are replaced by the exchange of the visual object. Advertising and witnessing become inter-

153. The T-shirt craze which began in the United States in the 1960s has spread around the globe, and Christian producers worldwide adapt American sayings for their own consumers.

changeable. As the Atlanta bookstore owner cited above explains, "the products minister to customers' needs." A thing, not a word, gains the power to minister.

Christian retailing provides the visible and tactile images that help conservative Protestants create a Christian subculture. One of the effects of the minority rights movements of the 1960s and 1970s was to emphasize the importance of communities of like-minded individuals. Community was created not only by sharing ideas and goals but also by wearing T-shirts with political slogans, displaying appropriate art, and listening to certain kinds of music. Gays put lambda signs on their cars, feminists the symbol for woman, and Christians the fish. Christians – like gays, feminists, Chicanos – assert their special status as a community competing for social and cultural attention. By buying and displaying Christian art in their homes, giving gifts with biblical sayings, or wearing T-shirts, conservative Protestants translate their beliefs into visible messages. Christian retailing, like Christian schools and Christian therapists, is another part of the attempt to create a parallel religious culture to that of secular America.

According to retailing textbooks, half of all current retailers will be out of business by the end of the 1990s. The United States is "overstored," store owners are in debt, and consumers just are not buying as they did in the 1980s.[89] What chance do Christian retailers have to continue their merchandising mission? A good one. Conservative Christianity, both Protestant and sectarian (e.g., Mormons, Jehovah's Witnesses), continues to grow. Catholics are rediscovering their material culture. Christian bookstores have "positioned" themselves firmly in a particular specialty niche. "In a cluttered marketplace," advises one retail expert, "the well-positioned retailer is distinctive."[90] Like the pictures of Jesus in the 1930s and the biblical text as logo in the 1980s, Christian bookstores have themselves become a brand name within the general retailing market. They clearly communicate what they stand for and why they exist. Most importantly, they reflect the expectations and perceptions of their customers. They have established themselves in a narrowly focused market niche and, by downplaying denominational differences, are able to sell to people who consider themselves "Christian." Religious groups that historically have been excluded, such as the Mormons, set up their own stores and provide both explicitly Latter-day Saint and more general Christian merchandise. They, too, have benefited from the rise of Christian retailing.

The overall number of consuming Christians will also be expanding. For the first time in United States history, the number of Americans aged 35–59 is greater than those aged 18–34. By the year 2000 almost half of the population will be in the prime purchasing age group of 35–59.[91] This is also the age group that participates most vigorously in religion. Over the past forty years, Christian retailing has correctly shifted attention from Sunday school supplies and trinkets for children to the needs of the middle-aged woman consumer. The male pastor is no longer the sole reader of Christian books. In spite of efforts to lure men into Christian bookstores, CBA reports that women make up the majority of bookstore customers.[92] Women also both write and read most of the Christian literature.[93] While "feminism" might still be considered suspect, the power of women as consumers is deeply felt.

Christian retailing, American-style, also is being exported. Unlike the secular marketplace which is flooded with Japanese cars, French wine, and clothing made in practically every developing country, the expanding worldwide religious market is strictly American. While Victorian Protestants once exported Bibles, conservative American Protestants now send their missionaries to Europe, Asia, Latin America, and the former communist countries. Their promotion of a personal Jesus who should be brought into every aspect of life has combined with the foreign fascination for American consumer goods to produce a market for Christian merchandise. In Germany, the UlJö company produces gifts with Christian motifs and texts. Their product line reflects the long history of merchandise produced in the United States, from mottoes carved on slices of wood to needlepoint renditions of famous religious art to head sweatbands embroidered with *Jesus liebt Kinder.* Although gift merchandise is rarer in

India, one can buy posters of Warner Sallman's *Head of Christ*, plaques which say in Malayalam, "Christ is the Lord of this House," and magnets with the Immaculate Heart of Mary.[94] Hong Kong already has forty-eight Christian bookstores, Korea has 700 (fifty alone in Seoul), the CBA holds conventions in New Zealand and Australia and has chapters in South Africa, Canada, Nigeria, and Singapore.

Christian retailing appears to be following a pattern described thirty years ago by Harvard professor Malcolm P. McNair as the "wheel of retailing."[95] The wheel of retailing predicts that retail institutions evolve from low status, low price operations that have minimal services, poor facilities, and limited product offering. Eventually the institution develops its facilities, expands its services and products, and raises its prices. Quality becomes important. The mature retailer then must face the possibility of losing profit because the business has become conservative and top-heavy in goods and personnel. Up until the 1970s, both the agents who peddled Christian merchandise and the bookstores who sold to customers focused on low price products. Their overheads were minimal and their product offerings were of poor quality. Much of the material was geared toward children, rural clients, and the working class. Now, however, Christian bookstores rival secular retail establishments in product, selling environment, and price variety. Christian customers expect their local bookstore to be attuned to fashion, contemporary issues, and to provide high-quality items. More importantly, they assume that retailers are committed Christians. Christian retailing is a striking example of how lay men and women successfully integrate religious concerns, popular culture, and profit making.

Epilogue

It is only shallow people who do not judge by appearances. The true mystery of the world is the visible, not the invisible.

Oscar Wilde

Then saith [Jesus] to Thomas, Reach hither thy finger, and behold my hands; and reach hither thy hand, and thrust it into my side: and be not faithless, but believing.

John 20: 24–7

In the waning years of the 1980s, the American public became aware in a dramatic way of the political nature of desecration. Artist Andres Serrano's 1988 photograph *Piss Christ*, along with several other of Serrano's works, had won the Southeastern Center for Contemporary Art's annual fellowship competition. Serrano's art, along with that of the other winners of the competition, had been touring across the country. After the tour's end in January 1989, the American Family Association launched a letter-writing campaign to alert the sponsors of the competition to the fact that Serrano's photograph was offensive.[1] *Piss Christ* is a glossy, Cibachrome photograph of a crucifix submerged in urine. The photograph is five feet high, and a radiant yellow glow highlights the crucifix against a red background. Serrano, the son of a Cuban mother and a Honduran father, credited his Catholic upbringing for part of the inspiration for the work. Donald E. Wildmon, a Methodist minister who headed up the American Family Association, sent a letter with a reproduction of the Serrano photograph along with several other offending art pieces, to every member of Congress, catching the eyes of Senators Alfonse M. D'Amato and Jesse Helms. Shortly after, a series of photographs by Robert Mapplethorpe was kept from being exhibited at Washington's Corcoran Gallery of Art. In Chicago, conceptual artist Dread Scott's *What is the Proper Way to Display a U.S. Flag?* was causing a furor because it entailed laying a flag on the floor. Some Americans mourned the demise of Christian values while others lamented the end of artistic freedom in the United States.

Senator Helms eventually attached an amendment to an appropriations bill barring federal funds from being used to "promote, disseminate, or produce obscene or indecent materials including but not limited to depictions of sadomasochism, homoeroticism, the exploitation of children or individuals engaged in sex acts or materials which denigrate the objects or beliefs of the adherents of a particular religion or nonreligion."[2] That Helms, a conservative Republican from North Carolina, would seek to stop what he understood as degenerate art from being funded by taxpayers is not surprising. Eventually, however, the references to religion (and "nonreligion") were dropped from the proposed legislation. In the end, Congress told the National Endowment for the Arts not to fund obscene or indecent art, relying on the Supreme Court's 1973 decision on pornography to set the definition of obscenity. The "sanctity" of religious objects and beliefs had been forgotten in the political compromise. Mapplethorpe's photographs would be accused of being pornographic by a Cincinnati grand jury, but there was no easy parallel for what Serrano was doing with crucifixes.

During the same year of 1989, when Jesse Helms was trying to get his amendment passed, Senator Daniel K. Inouye from Hawaii successfully persuaded Congress to authorize the Smithsonian Institution to return approximately twenty thousand Native Americans' remains to those tribes that could identify their ancestors' bones. State legislatures in the late 1980s also passed codes restricting excavation of Indian burial grounds, stating that Native Americans should be "consulted" about archeological digs and that analysis of "scientifically significant remains" would be limited.[3] The Zuni tribe requested the return of their sacred objects and museums eventually complied.[4] From the perspective of Native Americans, the issue involved in the return of Indian goods and bones was not merely one of property rights. The desecration of the dead and of sacred objects was a spiritual concern.[5] Native Americans were offended that over the years thousands of skeletons had been placed on public display. The estimated three hundred thousand to six hundred thousand skeletons in American collections and countless number of grave goods were not perceived as neutral artifacts to be analyzed and used for educational purposes.

To various segments of the American population, crucifixes, bodies, flags, bones, and grave goods have religious meanings that overlay (and sometimes supersede) their status as artistic artifacts, scientific evidence, or educational information. The controversies over the funding of the National Endowment for the Arts, the meaning of the flag, and the dispute over who owns prehistoric bones are a complicated concoction of faith, political opportunism, and legal maneuvering. These controversies provoke a series of questions that cannot be answered in this book, but they accentuate the continuing importance of the material dimension of religion in American culture. Why would an evangelical Protestant care about a Catholic crucifix? Who thinks that artistic freedom should take precedence over religious freedom? Why is putting a flag on the floor desecration but sticking it on the bumper of a car patriotic? Without serious reflection on the meaning of objects in people's religious lives, we cannot adequately address the political and legal controversies that stem from conflicting views over objects and environments. The situation demands more than merely updating the Evolution debates of the 1920s by featuring creative East-coast artists pitted against media-sophisticated fundamentalists.[6] If we fail to see the power religion has over defining the meaning of the material, corporeal, and sensual world (and vice versa), then we will not understand why Native Americans are concerned about bones and evangelical Christians about bodies.

The case studies presented in this book reject the popular assumption that the material dimension of Christianity results from ignorance, superficial commercialism, status competition, and the desire of institutional churches and "The Culture Industry" to manipulate people. When we look carefully at the interaction between people and religious artifacts, architecture, and environments we see that the practice of Christianity is a subtle mixture of traditional beliefs and personal improvisations. Religions, as Robert Orsi points out, "are often inconsistent, even contradictory, and always include forbidden and outlawed beliefs and practices as well as those that are sanctioned."[7] By expanding our understanding of religion to include those activities that have been ignored as superficial or condemned as superstitious, we see that American Christianity has a distinct material dimension. These case studies demonstrate that "genuine" religion has always been expressed and made real with objects, architecture, art, and landscapes.

Artifacts become particularly important in the lives of average Christians because objects can be exchanged, gifted, reinterpreted, and manipulated. People need objects to help establish and maintain relationships with supernatural characters, family, and friends. Christians use goods and create religious landscapes to tell themselves and the world around them who they are. While some Christians accomplish the same thing through the exchange of ideas, many prefer to interact with visual and sensual symbols. Religious meaning is not merely inherited or simply accessed through the intellect. Orthodox statements of belief and formal rituals are only one part of the complicated structure of religion. Religious meaning must be constructed and reconstructed over and over. Amid the external practice of religion – a practice that utilizes artifacts, art, architecture, and landscapes – comes the inner experience of religion. We can no longer accept that the "appearance" of religion is inconsequential to the "experience" of religion. The sensual elements of Christianity are not merely decorations that mask serious belief; it is through the visible world that the invisible world becomes known and felt.

Religious goods and landscapes can tell Christians that they belong to a particular community or family, but material culture can also be used symbolically to exclude the "unworthy." When Mary Lee Bland Ewell converted to Mormonism, for instance, not only was her name erased from the family's Bible, her portrait was relegated to the attic. Anne Ellis resented the fact that her mother was too occupied with multiple childbirths to write Anne's name in the family Bible, although the insult was probably not intended. Laurel Hill Cemetery excluded from burial African American Philadelphians, and beggars were illustrated as sitting barely inside the grounds. Admission to Latter-day Saint temples is limited to Mormons with "temple recommends" and so not every church member may have access to that sacred environment. Laurel Hill Cemetery and Latter-day Saint temples teach not only the importance of inclusion but the reality of exclusion. When the Catholic church began revising its liturgy, parish priests removed certain ecclesiastical ornaments because the art supposedly distracted congregants from the centrality of the mass. The removal of statues of the saints was a visual statement that certain devotions were now "unworthy" of public attention. To embrace one style of art or theological orientation is often to reject or disparage others. We need to be aware not only of what the rules are of inclusion and exclusion but also of how a variety of Christians respond to them. Those excluded may resist their placement outside of the group. They, too, may use material culture to insist that they are a part of the community, and they may construct different religious meanings from the same objects and environments.

The material dimension of religion helps us to see how faith, fashion, and family are woven closely together. Quaker John Smith promoted Laurel Hill Cemetery as a Christian pilgrimage place because he thought attending to the dead was a sacred duty. Motivated both by the deaths of his children and by the financial prospects of a new business enterprise, Smith did not separate religion from commerce. When John McSorley imported Lourdes water for Fathers Sorin and Granger, he wrote that he also participated in the devotion to Our Lady. McSorley not only took the priests' payment for his import services, he asked them to pray for his wayward children. Consequently, we should not be surprised when Atlanta bookseller Jim Reimann understands his million-dollar retail business to be a Christian ministry. To assert that these people are participating in a false or unauthentic Christianity is to deny that they integrate material and spiritual elements in their lives. The practice of Christianity brings together the disparate elements of life that possess meaning; everything from our sense of style and social status to our trust in God. Sacred words become transformed into images. Physical feelings are objectified into religious language. The distinct categories of sacred and profane are inadequate to capture the complexity of Christian practice.

We must reject the facile assumption that Protestants (and Mormons) do not have a Christian material culture but that all Catholics do. Once we shift our attention from the church and seminary to the workplace, home, cemetery, and Sunday school, another side of Protestantism appears. In the nineteenth century, Methodists displayed statues of Wesley and Protestants in Philadelphia placed sculptures of angels at the graves of their loved ones. Children in contemporary Sunday schools bring home pencils printed with "I can't Bear to be without Jesus." Mormons may give prints of temples as wedding gifts and wear Angel Moroni tie-clasps. At times, denominational commitments are asserted through display and exchange of goods. At other times, the boundaries between one Christian group and another are deliberately weakened. An evangelical Baptist might not let her children play with Book of Mormon paper dolls but both she and her Latter-day Saint neighbor might cherish their Warner Sallman *Head of Christ* prints.

While many Catholics continue to utilize a rich Christian material culture, we should not assume that all Catholics have a consistent, positive attitude toward the religious material world. In the 1950s and 1960s, for instance, American church leaders criticized the Catholic reliance on paraliturgical devotions and the images that accompanied those devotions. Art and devotions that had been ubiquitous in Catholic parishes for one hundred years came under attack. While liturgists and theologians could justify their antagonism toward "catalog art" by referring to the documents of the Second Vatican Council, they also appealed to non-religious standards. Catholics, like Protestants and Mormons, are influenced by trends in art that set up categories of taste. Religious people and institutions are never immune from the social and cultural forces that structure American life. Christian communities do not have unchanging attitudes toward religious material culture. Attitudes toward the material dimension of Christianity ebb and flow as gender roles change, technology develops, fashions shift, and new theologies emerge.

We must be aware of how differences in taste limit our ability to understand how images and objects function. As we have seen, the dualism set up between mass-produced kitsch and autonomous art has as much to do with gender and class issues as with theology and aesthetics. We need to take seriously Roland Marchand's quip regarding the need for advertisers to know their audience: "It isn't the taste of the angler that determines the kind of bait to be used, but the taste of the fish."[8] We already know the "taste of the angler" regarding appropriate art and religion; it is now time to understand the "taste of the fish." Bright colors, realism, duplication, and sentimentality in Christian art may hold no spiritual appeal for those schooled to appreciate subtle shades, abstraction, singularity, and emotional distance. Those who define art (like religion) as something that challenges and provokes the spirit may find it difficult to understand those Christians who find comfort and reassurance in the familiar. If we define having a personal relationship with an image or object as superstitious anthropocentrism, then we will never understand how these things function in the religious lives of Christians. James Martin writes that "Art is about beauty and religion is about holiness."[9] But, we must ask, who defines the beauty of art and the holiness of religion?

The exchange of Christian goods and the construction of religious environments is not something that has appeared recently in American culture and it is not something that will disappear. While our American mythology stresses that newcomers sought "freedom of thought" in the New World, the struggle for "freedom from want" is a more realistic appraisal of immigrant goals. As Andrew Heinze shows in *Adapting To Abundance*, Eastern European Jews identified themselves as Americans through their consumption patterns. Jewish consumerism is not merely rote duplication of native patterns but a creative way to construct a meaningful life through a material world of clothing, pianos, and vacation resorts.[10] The construction of synagogues, churches, and eventually mosques and temples is a physical way for immigrants to leave their religious imprint on the American landscape. From the vast mega-churches in the suburbs to the image-laden homes of the urban poor, Americans signal their participation in a bountiful spiritual and economic order through religious expressions of abundance. Historical scholarship overstates the importance of Christian austerity and needs instead to recognize that excess – in religious devotion and visual display – is the more frequent expression of faith in the United States.

The emphasis in American religious scholarship on the mental, cognitive, and ethical dimensions of Christianity fails to take into account the close connection between spirituality and the body. Especially during the Romantic period, religious sentiments and feelings were stimulated through exciting the senses. Victorian writers do not deny the importance of the corporeal; often they seek its purification and refinement. Ministers, writers, and hymnists connect the Bible with mother's face, father's voice, and the tears shed by ancestors. The rhetoric surrounding Bible reading is as rich and sensual as the family Bible itself. Catholic art critics of the 1950s and 1960s also created rhetorical constructions of the female body to help them define what they understood as religious kitsch.

Not only is Christian language filled with bodily images and metaphors, Christian practice involves the body. The correspondence from people using Lourdes water indicates that the healing process entails recounting corporeal ills, describing the power of the supernatural, and recalling the miraculous cure that focused on the body. Faith healing reinforces the reality of the body as well as of the supernatural. Some Latter-day Saints explore the powers of garments by telling stories of protection; protection from physical and sexual harm. Mormons see garments as influencing (both positively and negatively) their attitudes toward their physical selves. Christian practice assumes an existential reality when it involves issues of health, healing, attitudes toward pain, sexuality, and the nature of the body. The dualism that associates the sacred with religion and the body with secular concerns inadequately describes how Christians have used the body as the primary mediator to express and appropriate religious experiences. Even though Christian theology may deny that the body is more significant than the spirit, Christian practice accentuates the relevance of the physical self.

Although this book focuses on Christianity in the United States, we must acknowledge the importance of European social and technological innovations for the material world of American Christians. The sentimentality and romanticism cultivated in eighteenth- and nineteenth-century Europe encouraged Christians to see their faith as closely bound to their emotions and feelings. Printing technology and even advertising techniques initially traveled across the Atlantic to the United States. Nineteenth-century guides to Laurel Hill Cemetery compared the Philadelphia burial ground to those of Père Lachaise in Paris and Highgate in London. From the wilds of the Midwest, a French priest mailed blessed water from southern France to Irish Catholics. Catholics not only maintained and maintain ethnic ties through their churches, they participate in devotions that originated in Europe, imported (or copied) *l'art Saint-Sulpice*, and duplicated Old World pilgrimage shrines. Masonic iconography developed in eighteenth-century Europe continues to be used by Mormons as symbols of their sacred covenants. Even the aesthetic taste of educated Catholic and Protestant art critics depended (and still depends) on the artistic insights of modernist architects in Germany, Holland, France, and Britain. By the 1980s, chic Americans were also borrowing freely from the religious images of Mexico. As evangelical Protestants sell Christian T-shirts and bumper stickers around the globe, we must remind ourselves that the current outpouring of American images remains small compared to the extensive importation of European cultural values, iconography, design styles, and technological innovations.

The material dimension of Christian practice in America far exceeds the few case studies discussed here. Christians in the southern United States, for instance, have a rich heritage of faith healing that entails anointing with blessed oils and focusing on bodily ills. In the upper Midwest, Lutheran ethnic communities have developed traditions of church suppers where food becomes a means of maintaining solidarity and asserting attitudes about spiritual and economic abundance. Latter-day Saints are not the only Christian community that has a tradition of special clothing. Some African American churches define appropriate dress for their members and prescribe uniform clothing for church ushers, elders, and other attendants. Why do such traditions endure? Altar making – not only in Mexican American homes but in the homes of ethnic Italians, Poles, Portuguese, Irish, and even Protestants – is a vital part of domestic Christianity. Sunday schools also need to be examined as places where religious artistic sensibilities are developed. Children in general are greatly neglected in American religious history. How do children use toys creatively to express and experience Christianity? What role do objects play in developing religious imagination? At the other end of the life cycle, we can ask how religious objects function in the memories of the elderly.

Does the material world of Christianity lose or gain in intensity as we age? Finally, we can extend the whole question of materiality to other religious groups and pose similar queries to American Jews, Muslims, Buddhists, and Native Americans. This study has focused on a heretofore neglected way that American Christians live their religion. It has ranged broadly over many expressions of material Christianity. As we turn our attention to this essential, if neglected, way of being religious, a richer and more varied understanding of religious practice will unfold.

Notes

1 Material Christianity

1 The Farm Security Administration (FSA) was an outgrowth of the Resettlement Administration created in 1935. Established in 1937, the FSA was a New Deal response to rural poverty. It provided loans, grants, and advice to tenant farmers and sharecroppers. Within the Information Division of the FSA was a photographic unit directed by Roy Stryker. The main purpose of the photographic unit was to make an accurate record of the various phases of the Resettlement Administration and later Farm Security Administration. Government-paid photographers were sent out to shoot objects useful for promoting the agency (e.g., land-clearing projects, activities in resettlement communities, migrant labor camps, and loan recipients on improved farms). Stryker, however, gave his photographers a free hand and many produced detailed representations of rural and urban life. The photographs were used to gain congressional support for FSA programs and to educate the public. The photographic unit supplied images to major American magazines and newspapers, set up exhibits at art museums, and organized book projects using their photographs. The goals of many of the photographers were to document America's poverty in the hopes of provoking community awareness and social change. Ansel Adams wrote to Roy Stryker that "what you've got are not photographers. They're a bunch of sociologists with cameras" (Levine, p. 25). After the American entrance into World War II, the FSA was brought under the auspices of the Office of War Information and charged with producing domestic propaganda. It ceased operation in 1943 when its almost 77,000 images were placed in the Library of Congress. On FSA photography, see Lawrence W. Levine, "The Historian and the Icon," in *Documenting America, 1935–1943*, eds., Carl Fleischhauer and Beverly W. Brannan (Berkeley: Univ. of California Press, 1988); Nicholas Natanson, *The Black Image in the New Deal: the Politics of FSA Photography* (Knoxville: Univ. of Tennessee Press, 1992); James Curtis, *Mind's Eye, Mind's Truth: FSA Photography Reconsidered* (Philadelphia: Temple Univ. Press, 1989); Andrea Fisher, *Let Us Now Praise Famous Women: Women Photographers for the U.S. Government, 1935–44* (London: Pandora Press, 1987); Pete Daniel *et al.*, *Official Images: New Deal Photography* (Washington, D.C.: Smithsonian Institution Press, 1987).

2 See George A. Lindbeck in *The Nature of Doctrine: Religion and Theology in a Postliberal Age* (Philadelphia: Westminster Press, 1984), pp. 32–41.

3 John Michael Vlach, "Morality as Folk Aesthetic," Robert E. Walls and George H. Schoemaker, *The Old Traditional Way of Life* (Bloomington, IN: Trickster Press, 1989), pp. 28–37.

4 See my article, "Interpreting Things: Material Culture Studies and American Religion," *Religion* 21 (1991), pp. 371–87.

5 Diane M. Douglas, "The Machine in the Parlor: A Dialectical Analysis of the Sewing Machine," *Journal of American Culture* 5 (1982), pp. 20–9; and James Deetz, "Remember Me as You Pass By," *In Small Things Forgotten: The Archeology of Early American Life* (Garden City, NY: Anchor, 1977), pp. 64–90.

6 Daniel D. Arreola, "Fences as Landscape Taste: Tuscon's Barrios," *Journal of Cultural Geography* 2 (1981), pp. 96–105; John Stilgoe, *Common Landscape of America: 1580 to 1845* (New Haven and London: Yale Univ. Press, 1982); Grady Clay, *Close-up: How to Read the American City* (1973; Chicago: Univ. of Chicago Press, 1980).

7 Thomas C. O'Guinn and Russell W. Belk, "Heaven on Earth: Consumption at Heritage Village, USA," *Journal of Consumer Research* 16 (1989), pp. 227–37; Paul Venable Turner, *Campus, An American Planning Tradition* (Cambridge: MIT Press, 1984), pp. 89–128; and Roger Robins, "Vernacular American Landscape: Methodists, Camp Meetings, and Social Respectability," *Religion and American Culture* 4 (1994), pp. 165–92.

8 David Chidester and Edward Tabor Linenthal, ed. *American Sacred Space* (Bloomington: Indiana Univ. Press, forthcoming).

9 Dell Upton, *Holy Things and Profane: Anglican Parish Churches in Colonial Virginia* (Cambridge: MIT Press, 1986); Barbara G. Lane, *The Altar and the Altarpiece: Sacramental Themes in Early Netherlandish Painting* (New York: Harper & Row, 1984); Leo Steinberg, *The Sexuality of Christ in Renaissance Art and in Modern Oblivion* (New York: Pantheon Books, 1983); Margaret R. Miles, *Carnal Knowing: Female Nakedness and Religious Meaning in the Christian West* (Boston: Beacon Press, 1989).

10 James Clifford, "Histories of the Tribal and the Modern" and "On Collecting Art and Culture" in *Predicament of Culture: Twentieth-Century Ethnography, Literature and Art* (Cambridge: Harvard Univ. Press, 1988), pp. 189–214; 215–51; and Donna Haraway, "Teddy Bear Patriarchy: Taxidermy in the Garden of Eden, New York City, 1908–1936" in *Culture/Power/History*, Nicholas B. Dirks *et al.*, eds. (Princeton: Princeton Univ. Press), pp. 49–95; David Halle, *Inside Culture: Art and Class in the American Home* (Chicago: Univ. of Chicago Press, 1993); Henry Glassie, *Folk Housing in Middle Virginia: A Structural Analysis of Historic Artifacts* (Knoxville: Univ. of Tennessee Press, 1975).

11 See, for example, Dell Upton, *Holy Things and Profane*; Dolores Hayden, *Seven American Utopias: The Architecture of Communitarian Socialism, 1790–1975* (Cambridge: MIT Press, 1978); and Peter Williams, *American Church Architecture* (Chicago: Univ. of Chicago Press, forthcoming). On elite arts, see Doug Adams and Diane Apostolos-Cappadona, eds., *Art as Religious Studies* (New York: Crossroad, 1987) and John Dillenberger, *The Visual Arts and Christianity in America: The Colonial Period through the Nineteenth Century* (Chico, CA: Scholars Press, 1989). On folk arts, C. Kurt Dewhurst, Betty MacDowell, and Marsha MacDowell, *Religious Folk Art in America* (New York: E. P. Dutton, Inc., 1983).

12 Gregg, Finley, review of *Material Culture: A Research Guide* by Thomas J. Schlereth, *Winterthur Portfolio* 21 (1986), p. 334.

13 Emile Durkheim, *The Elementary Forms of the Religious Life* trans., Joseph Ward Swain (New York: Free Press, 1915), p. 55.

14 Ibid., p. 347.

15 Elaine Scarry, *The Body in Pain: The Making and Unmaking of the World* (New York: Oxford Univ. Press, 1985), pp. 181–243; David Freedberg, *The Power of Images: Studies in the History and Theory of Response* (New York: Columbia Univ. Press, 1989), p. 61f.

16 *Ioannis Calvini Opera Omnia*, ed. W. Baum, vol. 26, pp. 150f as quoted in Sergiusz Michalski, *The Reformation and the Visual Arts* (London: Routledge, 1993), p. 62.

17 Sarah Beckwith, *Christ's Body: Identity, Culture and Society in Late Medieval Writings* (London: Routledge, 1993).

18 John of Damascus, *De imaginibus orationes*, Migne *PG* 94 as quoted in Ewa Kuryluk, *Veronica and Her Cloth: History, Symbolism, and Structure of a "True" Image* (Oxford: Basil Blackwell, 1991), p. 53.

19 Jon Butler, "Historiographical Heresy: Catholicism as a Model for American Religious History," in Thomas Kselman, ed., *Belief in History: Innovative Approaches to European and American Religion* (Notre Dame, IN: Univ. of Notre Dame Press, 1991), pp. 286–309.

20 David D. Hall, *Worlds of Wonder, Days of Judgment: Popular Religious Belief in Early New England* (Cambridge: Harvard Univ. Press, 1990). An example of traditional approaches to Puritanism can be found in Perry Miller's works on the "New England Mind": *The Seventeenth Century* (Boston: Beacon, 1939) and *From Colony to Province* (Boston: Beacon, 1953).

21 Secularization has been the dominant sociological theory for explaining religious evolution until recently and can be found in Bryan Wilson, *Religion in Secular Society* (London: C. A. Watts, 1966); Anthony F. C. Wallace, *Religion: An Anthropological View* (New York: Random House, 1966); Peter Berger, *The Sacred Canopy* (Garden City, NY: Doubleday, 1967); Robert N. Bellah, *Beyond Belief: Essays on Religion in a Post-Traditional World* (New York: Harper & Row, 1970); and Karel Dobbelaere, "Some Trends in European Sociology of Religion: The Secularization Debate," *Sociological Analysis* 48 (1987), pp. 107–37.

22 Karl Marx, *Capital* vol. 1 trans. Ben Fowkes (Harmondsworth: Penguin, 1976), p. 125.

23 Sut Jhally, "Advertising as Religion: The Dialectic of Technology and Magic," in *Cultural Politics in Contemporary America*, eds. Ian Angus and Sut Jhally (New York: Routledge, 1989), p. 218.

24 Ray B. Browne and Marshal Fishwick, eds., *Icons of America* (Bowling Green, OH: Popular Press, 1978) and Ray Browne, ed., *Objects of Special Devotion: Fetishism in Popular Culture* (Bowling Green, OH: Popular Press, 1982).

25 Jim Pollman, "CB Radio as Icon," in Browne and Fishwick, pp. 161–76.

26 Recent revisions include: Eileen Barker, *et al.*, *Secularization, Rationalism, and Sectarianism: Essays in Honour of Bryan R. Wilson* (New York: Oxford Univ. Press, 1993); Roger Finke and Rodney Stark, *The Churching of America, 1776–1990: Winners and Losers in our Religious Economy* (New Brunswick: Rutgers Univ. Press, 1992); Wade Clark Roof and William McKinney, *American Mainline Religion: Its Changing Shape and Future* (New Brunswick: Rutgers Univ. Press, 1987); Rodney Stark and William S. Bainbridge. *The Future of Religion: Secularization, Revival, and Cult Formation* (Berkeley: Univ. of California Press, 1985); and Stephen Warner, "Work in Progress toward a New Paradigm for the Sociological Study of Religion in the United States," *American Journal of Sociology* 98 (1993), pp. 1044–93.

27 Susan Harding, "The Born-Again Telescandals," in *Culture/Power/History*, p. 555.

28 Freedberg, p. 63.

29 Hans Belting, *Likeness and Presence: A History of the Image Before the Era of Art* (Chicago: Univ. of Chicago Press, 1994), p. 132.

30 *The Confessions of Augustine* Book IX, Chapter 10.

31 Gregory the Great (600CE) in response to Serenus, *Ad Sevenum Episcopum Massiliensem, PL* 77, col. 1027f. See Freedberg, p. 163 for other theologians who based their ideas about images on this argument.

32 Judith Herrin, "Women and the Faith in Icons in Early Christianity," in Raphael Samuel and Gareth Stedman Jones, eds., *Culture, Ideology and Politics* (London: Routledge & Kegan Paul, 1982), pp. 56–83 and "Women and Icons," in Kuryluk, pp. 65–87.

33 See J. M. Bernstein's introduction to Theodor W. Adorno, *The Culture Industry: Selected Essays on Mass Culture* (London: Routledge, 1991), pp. 1–25; Patrick Brantlinger, *Bread and Circuses: Theories of Mass Culture as Social Decay* (Ithaca, NY: Cornell Univ. Press, 1983), pp. 222–48; and Eugene Lunn, "The Frankfurt School in the Development of the Mass Culture Debate," in *The Aesthetics of the Critical Theorists: Studies on Benjamin, Adorno, Marcuse, and Habermas*, ed., Ronald Roblin (Lewiston, NY: E. Mellen Press, 1990), pp. 26–84.

34 Dwight Macdonald, "A Theory of Popular Culture," *Politics* 1 (1944), p. 20.

35 Paul Tillich, *The Religious Situation* trans. H. Richard Niebuhr (1932; New York: Meridian, 1956), p. 88f. Tillich is referring to Fritz von Uhde, a late nineteenth-century German painter.

36 Ortega y Gasset, *The Revolt of the Masses* (New York: New American Library, 1950), p. 12.

37 An impressionistic discussion of folk religions can be found in Simon J. Bronner, *Grasping Things: Folk Material Culture and Mass Society in America* (Lexington: Univ. Press of Kentucky, 1986), pp. 143–59. "Morality as Folk Aesthetic," by John Michael Vlach in *The Old Traditional Way of Life* uses only vague definitions of religion and morality. On the folklore aspects of Christian denominations, see Kurt Dewhurst *et al.*, *Religious Folk Art in America*; "The Handclasp Motif in Mormon Folk Burial" in Richard C. Poulsen, *The Pure Experience of Order: Essays on the Symbolic in the Folk Material Culture of Western America* (Albuquerque: Univ. of New Mexico Press, 1982), pp. 45–55; and the whole issue of *New York Folklore* 8 (1982). On religious utopias, see Dolores Hayden, *Seven American Utopias* and the citations on Shakerism in note 38. The fascination with New England graveyards also reflects the modern interest in abstraction, simplicity, and purity of line; see Thomas Schlereth, *Material Culture Studies in America* (Nashville, TN: American Association for State and Local History, 1982), p. 61.

38 Stephen Stein, unpublished paper presented at the 1987 American Studies Association meeting, New York City. The works by Edward Deming Andrews and Faith Andrews on Shaker life display this "material culture" orientation. See *Shaker Furniture* (1937; New York: Dover, 1964) and *Religion in Wood* (Bloomington: Indiana Univ. Press, 1966). See also Mary Lynn Ray, "A Reappraisal of Shaker Furniture and Society," *Winterthur Portfolio* 8 (1973), pp. 107–32. For a more critical appraisal of Shaker life, see Stephen J. Stein, *The Shaker Experience in America: A History of the United Society of Believers* (New Haven and London: Yale University Press, 1992) and for an alternative version of their artistic vision, Sally M. Promey, *Spiritual Spectacles: Vision and Image in Mid-Nineteenth-Century Shakerism* (Bloomington: Indiana Univ. Press, 1993).

39 Although neither of these books focuses exclusively on Catholic material culture, both provide discussions of Catholic use of objects, images, and spaces: Paula M. Kane, *Separatism and Subculture: Boston Catholicism, 1900–1920* (Chapel Hill: Univ. of North Carolina Press, 1994) and Robert Anthony Orsi, *The Madonna of 115th Street: Faith and Community in Italian Harlem, 1880–1950* (New Haven and London: Yale Univ. Press, 1985).

40 C. W. E. Bigsby, ed., *Approaches to Popular Culture* (London: Edward Arnold, 1976), p. 17. For a discussion of the development of cultural studies, see Patrick Bratlinger, *Crusoe's Footprints: Cultural Studies in Britain and America* (New York: Routledge, 1990). Examples of the Birmingham School's concern with subcultures are: Dick Hebdige, *Subculture, The Meaning of Style* (London: Meuthen, 1979) and Stuart Hall and Tony Jefferson, *Resistance through Rituals: Youth Subcultures in Post-war Britain* (London: Hutchinson, 1976).

41 Ernest B. Gilman, *Iconoclasm and Poetry in the English Reformation* (Chicago: Univ. of Chicago Press, 1986), p. 34.

42 Sergiusz Michalski, *The Reformation and the Visual Arts* (London: Routledge, 1993), pp. 56, 90.

43 Tessa Watt, *Cheap Print and Popular Piety, 1550–1640* (Cambridge: Cambridge Univ. Press, 1991), p. 135.

44 Keith Thomas, *Religion and the Decline of Magic* (New York: Scribner, 1971); David D. Hall, *Worlds of Wonder, Days of Judgment* (New York: Alfred A. Knopf, 1989), pp. 71–116; Jon Butler, *Awash in a Sea of Faith: Christianizing the American People* (Cambridge: Harvard Univ. Press, 1990), pp. 7–97; Charles E. Hambrick-Stowe, *The Practice of Piety: Puritan Devotional Discipline in Seventeenth-Century New England* (Chapel Hill: Univ. of North Carolina Press, 1982), pp. 23–53.

45 Chandra Mukerji, *From Graven Images: Patterns of Modern Materialism* (New York: Columbia Univ. Press, 1983), p. 2.

46 This thesis also underpins the articles collected in John Brewer and Roy Porter, eds., *Consumption and the World of Goods* (London: Routledge, 1993). Economic support for an early consumer revolution is argued by Joan Thirsk, *Economic Policy and Projects: The Development of a Consumer Society in Early Modern England* (Oxford: Oxford Univ. Press, 1978) and Neil McKendrick, John Brewer, and J. J. H. Plumb, eds., *The Birth of a Consumer Society: The Commercialization of Eighteenth-Century England* (Bloomington: Indiana Univ. Press, 1982).

47 Colin Campbell, *The Romantic Ethic and the Spirit of a Modern Consumerism* (Oxford: Basil Blackwell, 1987).

48 Freedberg, p. 437.

49 Martin Luther, *Works* vol. 19 ed. Hilton C. Oswald (St. Louis, MO: Concordia Publishing House, 1962), p. 90 as quoted in David Chidester, *Word and Light: Seeing, Hearing, and Religious Discourse* (Urbana: Univ. of Illinois Press, 1992), p. 122.

50 Martha Grau, *Calvins Stellung zur Kunst*, unpublished dissertation, University of Munich, 1917, p. 18f as cited in Michalski, p. 64.

51 Michalski, p. 51.

52 *Huldreich Zwinglis Sämtlich Werke* vol. 4 (Berlin: C. A. Schwetschke und Sohn, 1905–), p. 145f as quoted by Michalski, p. 55.

53 Gilman, p. 41.

54 Notable exceptions are Peter Gardella, *Innocent Ecstasy: How Christianity Gave America an Ethic of Sexual Pleasure* (New York: Oxford Univ. Press, 1985); Catherine Albanese, "Physical Religion: Natural Sin and Healing Grace in the Nineteenth Century," in *Nature Religion in America* (Chicago: Univ. of Chicago Press, 1990); and the discussion of dead bodies in David Chidester, *Salvation and Suicide: An Interpretation of Jim Jones, the Peoples Temple, and Jonestown* (Bloomington: Indiana Univ. Press, 1988).

55 Michel Foucault, *The Birth of the Clinic: An Archaeology of Medical Perception*, trans. A. M. Sheridan Smith (New York: Pantheon Books 1973) and *The History of Sexuality*, trans. Robert Hurley (New York: Pantheon Books, 1978). The following gives a sample of the diversity of recent "body" books: Angela Zito and Tani

E. Barlow, eds., *Body, Subject, and Power in China* (Chicago: Univ. of Chicago Press, 1994); Steven Shaviro, *The Cinematic Body* (Minneapolis: Univ. of Minnesota Press, 1993); E. Jane Burns, *Bodytalk: When Women Speak in Old French Literature* (Philadelphia: Univ. of Pennsylvania Press, 1993); and Peter Lehman *Running Scared: Masculinity and the Representation of the Male Body* (Philadelphia: Temple Univ. Press, 1993).

Historians of Europe and the ancient world discuss more frequently the religious meaning of the body: see Elaine Pagels, *Adam, Eve, and the Serpent* (New York: Vintage, 1989); Peter Brown, *The Body and Society: Men, Women, and Sexual Renunciation in Early Christianity* (New York: Columbia Univ. Press, 1988); Caroline Walker Bynum, *Holy Feast and Holy Fast: The Religious Significance of Food to Medieval Women* (Berkeley: Univ. of California Press, 1987) and Sarah Beckwith, *Christ's Body: Identity, Culture and Society in Late Medieval Writings* (London: Routledge, 1993); Naomi R. Goldenberg, *Resurrecting the Body: Feminism, Religion, and Psychotherapy* (New York: Crossroad, 1993).

56 Peter Burke, "Overture: The New History, its Past and its Future," in *New Perspectives on Historical Writing* (University Park: The Pennsylvania State Univ. Press, 1992), p. 14.

57 See E. Mclung Fleming, "Artifact Study: A Proposed Model," *Winterthur Portfolio* 9 (1974), pp. 153–61 and Jules D. Prown, "Style as Evidence," *Winterthur Portfolio* 15 (1980), pp. 197–210 and "Mind in Matter," *Winterthur Portfolio* 17 (1982), pp. 1–17; Philip D. Zimmerman, "Workmanship as Evidence: A Model for Object Study," *Winterthur Portfolio* 16 (1981), pp. 283–307; and Henry Glassie, "Structure and Function, Folklore and the Artifact," *Semiotica* 7 (1973), pp. 3132–51.

58 Michel Vovell, *Ideologies and Mentalities* (Chicago: Univ. of Chicago Press, 1990), p. 99.

59 Kenneth L. Ames, *Death in the Dining Room and other Tales of Victorian Culture* (Philadelphia: Temple Univ. Press, 1992), pp. 150–84.

2 Piety, Art, Fashion: The Religious Object

1 Casey Perez's story is discussed in Kay Turner's dissertation, "Mexican-American Women's Home Altars: The Art of Relationship," University of Texas, Austin, 1990, p. 134. Press release on *Reassemblages*, August 18, 1992. Interview with Patrick Knight March 15, 1992. The boutique is "Eclec-tic" in Austin, Texas.

2 Toril Moi, *Sexual/Textual Politics: Feminist Literary Theory* (London: Routledge, 1985), p. 160.

3 Robert Plant Armstrong, *The Powers of Presence: Consciousness, Myth, and Affecting Presence* (Philadelphia: Univ. of Pennsylvania Press, 1981), p. 3.

4 James Alfred Martin, *Beauty and Holiness: The Dialogue Between Aesthetics and Religion* (Princeton: Princeton Univ. Press, 1990), p. 27.

5 *Constitution of the Sacred Liturgy*, Chapter III, "Of the Other Sacraments and the Sacramental," No. 59.

6 Paul Tillich, *A History of Christian Thought* (New York: Harper & Row, 1967), p. 156.

7 "Of the Other Sacraments and the Sacramentals," No. 61.

8 H. A. Reinhold, "The Hallowing of All Life," *Commonweal* 38 (1943), p. 608.

9 Bob Scribner, "Ritual and Popular Religion in Catholic Germany at the Time of the Reformation," *Journal of Ecclesiastical History* 35 (1984), p. 69.

10 Ibid., p. 70. On the ability of sacramentals to remit venial sins see Aegidius Doolan, "Is 'Holy Water' Holy? The Theology of Sacramentals," *Irish Ecclesiastical Record* 93 (1960), p. 178 and Valerian Flynn, "The Sacramentals of the Church," *American Ecclesiastical Review* 141 (1959), p. 297. Both authors base their arguments on Thomas Aquinas.

11 John F. Sullivan, *The Externals of the Catholic Church* (New York: P. J. Kennedy & Sons, 1959), pp. 262–71. See also "The Scapular," *Ave Maria* 1 (1865), pp. 132–3, 147–8 continued in vol. 2, pp. 264–83; "Scapular of the Immaculate Conception of the Blessed Virgin," *Ave Maria* 8 (1872), pp. 73–4. For a discussion of how Italian Catholics use scapulars, see Robert A. Orsi, *The Madonna of 115th Street: Faith and Community in Italian Harlem, 1880–1950* (New Haven and London: Yale Univ. Press, 1985), p. 173f.

12 Sullivan, p. 265.

13 Ibid., p. 266.

14 The apostolic constitution, *Indulgentiarum doctrina* (1967) explained what an indulgence is and announced a detailed reform of traditional practice and norms regulating it. In 1968 the Apostolic Plenipotentiary issued the reform document "Enchiridion indulgentiarum." It was revised in 1986 so as to be in accord with the 1983 revisions in Canon Law, *Enchiridion Indulgentiarum: normae et concessiones* (Rome: Libreria Editrice Vaticana, 1986). In spite of this, indulgences have never recaptured the position they held in pre-Vatican II Catholicism. *The New Dictionary of Catholic Worship* ed. Peter E. Fink (Collegeville, MN: Liturgical Press, 1990) has no mention of them. Michael P. Morissey comments in *The New Dictionary of Catholic Spirituality* (Collegeville, MN: Liturgical Press, 1993) that "the diminishing theological interest in indulgences today is due to an increasing emphasis on the sacraments, the prayer life of Catholics, and an active engagement in the world as constitutive of the spiritual life" (p. 28).

15 On indulgences see Henry Charles Lea, *A History of Auricular Confession and Indulgences in the Latin Church*, 3 vols. (Philadelphia: Lea Brothers & Co., 1896), esp. vol. 3. A Catholic response is Alexis Lepicier, *Indulgences, Their Origin, Nature and Development* (London: K. Paul, Trench, Trübner, 1895). The official list of indulgences is contained in Joseph Christopher, ed., *The Raccolta, or a Manual of Indulgences* (New York: Benziger, 1952).

16 Michel Foucault, *Discipline and Punish: The Birth of the Prison*, trans. Alan Sheridan (New York: Vintage Books, 1979), p. 139f.

17 The term "universe of pious objects" is from Jean Pirotte, "The Universe of Pious Objects: Use and Evolution of the Pious Object from the 16th to the 20th Century," *Lumen Vitae* 41 (1986), pp. 410–25. "Arsenal" comes from Paul Parfait, *L'Arsénal de la dévotion: Notes pour servir à l'histoire des superstitions* (Paris: Decaux,

1876). Historians of Catholicism have only begun to explore the role that the sacraments and sacramentals have played in social control; see John Bossy, "The Social History of Confession in the Age of the Reformation," *Transactions of the Royal Historical Society* 5 ser. 25 (1975), pp. 21–38.

18 On women giving blessings and healing with consecrated oil see D. Michael Quinn, "Latter-day Saint Prayer Circles," *Brigham Young University Studies* 19 (1978), pp. 79–105 and Margaret and Paul Toscano, *Strangers in Paradox: Explorations in Mormon Theology* (Salt Lake City, UT: Signature Press, 1990) p. 186.

19 For theories of images and meditation see David Freedberg, *The Power of Images: Studies in the History and Theory of Response* (Chicago: Univ. of Chicago Press, 1989), pp. 161–91 and Hans Belting, *Likeness and Presence: A History of the Image before the Era of Art* trans. Edmund Jephcott (Chicago: Univ. of Chicago Press, 1994), esp. pp. 362–76; 409–25.

20 In addition to David Freedberg's work on the role of images in devotions see Sixten Ringbom, "Devotional Images and Imaginative Devotions," *Gazette des Beaux-Arts* 73 ser. 6 (1969), pp. 159–70; Patrick Gaery, "Sacred Commodities: The Circulation of Medieval Relics," in Arjun Appadurai, *The Social Life of Things: Commodities in Cultural Perspective* (Cambridge: Cambridge Univ. Press, 1986), pp. 169–88; and William A. Christian, *Apparitions in Late Medieval and Renaissance Spain* (Princeton: Princeton Univ. Press, 1981), p. 38. On eating images see J. P. Donovan, "Novenas and Devotional Tastes," *Homiletics and Pastoral Review* 43 (1943), p. 643f and S. Woywod, "A Peculiar Use of Images of the Blessed Virgin and Other Saints," *Homiletics and Pastoral Review* 39 (1939), p. 1216f. The peasant's cloak revealed the image that would be known as Our Lady of Guadalupe and the Virgin appeared to St. Catharine Labouré showing her the design for the Miraculous Medal. For an example of a contemporary enlivened picture see "Saint's Weeping Portrait Draws Many," *New York Times*, November 5, 1990.

21 Peter Burke, *Popular Culture in Early Modern Europe* (New York: Harper Torchbook, 1977); Keith Thomas, *Religion and the Decline of Magic* (New York: Scribner, 1971); R. C. Scribner, *For the Sake of Simple Folk: Popular Propaganda for the German Reformation* (Cambridge: Cambridge Univ. Press, 1981) and *Popular Culture and Popular Movements in Reformation Germany* (Ronceverte, WV: Hambledon Press, 1988). And for similar changes in the American colonies see David D. Hall, *Worlds of Wonder, Days of Judgment: Popular Religious Belief in Early New England* (Cambridge: Harvard Univ. Press, 1990), pp. 1–20; 71–116 and Jon Butler, *Awash in a Sea of Faith: Christianizing the American People* (Cambridge: Harvard Univ. Press, 1990), pp. 1–97.

22 Tessa Watt, *Cheap Print and Popular Piety, 1550–1640* (Cambridge: Cambridge Univ. Press, 1991), p. 135.

23 John Calvin, *Institutes* Book I, ch. 11, sec. 12.

24 Watt, p. 159.

25 Victorian John Tyrwhitt did not approve of religious statues and paintings, since "the beauty of St. Sebastian or St. John [may] be used to awaken the sentiment of women, or hot-blooded men be invited to look at the unwasted forms of voluptuous Magdalens." He did see a difference between "pictures of saints doing something, and saints standing alone, as it were, to be adored." He felt that congregations could see this difference, as "historical paintings of this kind are educational and instructive – not devotional." *Contemporary Review* 3 (1866), p. 197.

26 Margaret Swain, *Historical Needlework* (New York: Charles Scribner's Sons, 1970), p. 40; N. G. Cabot, "Pattern Sources of Scriptual Subjects in Tudor and Stuart Embroideries," *Bulletin of the Needle and Bobbin Club* 30 (1946), pp. 3–54; and Rozsika Parker, *Subversive Stitch: Embroidery and the Making of the Feminine* (London: The Woman's Press, 1984), pp. 97–103; 161–4.

27 Helene Weis, "Those Old, Familiar Faces," *Stained Glass* 86 (1991), pp. 204–18. On popular art in Baptist churches, see Josephine Sellers, "Art in Southern Baptist Churches," *Baptist History and Heritage* 4 (1969), pp. 8–17; 65.

28 The director of the study, David Morgan of Valparaiso University, placed the advertisement in twenty publications of diverse denominational affiliation. A total of 495 responses were received, 56 respondents expressed a negative opinion of Sallman's work, which is 12.3 percent of the those who expressed an opinion.

29 The original copies of the correspondence are at the Wilson Galleries, Anderson College. I will cite the letters by number, keeping the writers anonymous. Respondent No. 28.

30 Respondent No. 3.

31 Respondent No. 214.

32 Freedberg, p. 191.

33 Respondent No. 39.

34 Respondents Nos. 288 and 322.

35 Freedberg, p. 220.

36 Respondent No. 4.

37 Respondent No. 123.

38 Respondent No. 214.

39 Respondent No. 259.

40 Respondent No. 254.

41 Respondent No. 10.

42 Yvonne J. Milspaw, "Protestant Home Shrines: Icon and Image," *New York Folklore* 12 (1986), pp. 119–36.

43 Turner, p. 188; "Mexican American Home Altars: Towards Their Interpretation," *Azlán: International Journal of Chicano Studies Research* 13 (1982), pp. 309–26; and "'Giving an Altar' The Ideology of Reproduction in a St. Joseph's Day Feast," *Journal of American Folklore* 100 (1987), pp. 446–60.

44 Jane Tompkins, *Sensational Designs: The Cultural Work of American Fiction, 1790–1860* (New York: Oxford Univ. Press, 1985), p. 170.

45 The following discussion is based on Turner, pp. 163–220.

46 As yet, there are no studies that analyze the role religious objects play in the expression of domestic authority. For a discussion of the darker side of family and religion see Orsi, pp. 107–49.

47 David G. Orr, "Roman Domestic Religion: The Evidence of the Household Shrines," in *Aufstieg und Niedergang der römischen Welt*, Wolfgang Haase, ed., vol. 16 part II second series (Berlin: Walter de Gruyter, 1978), pp. 1559–91; James Mellaart, *Catal Hüyük, A Neolithic Town in Anatolia* (London: Thames & Hudson, 1967).

48 Arlene Raven, "The Art of the

Altar," *Lady-Unique-Inclination-of-the-Night* (Spring 1983), p. 31.

49 Barbara Ellmann, "Altars-II," *Lady-Unique-Inclination-of-the-Night* (Spring 1983), p. 44.

50 Interview on March 15, 1992, Austin, Texas.

51 (Salt Lake City) *Art Center Newsletter* 4 (Summer/Fall 1992), p. 3.

52 Celeste Olalquiaga, *Megalopolis: Contemporary Cultural Sensibilities* (Minneapolis: Univ. of Minnesota Press, 1992), p. 42.

53 See Carol Gilligan, *In a Different Voice: Psychological Theory and Women's Development* (Cambridge: Harvard Univ. Press, 1982); Mary Field Belenky, *et al., Women's Ways of Knowing: The Development of Self, Voice, and Mind* (New York: Basic Books, 1986); Jennifer Coates and Deborah Cameron, *Women in their Speech Communities: New Perspectives on Language and Sex* (London: Longman, 1989); Ellyn Kaschak, *Engendered Lives: A New Psychology of Women's Experience* (New York: Basic Books, 1992).

54 Of the writers of 495 letters, 329 correspondents (67 percent) were identifiable as women, 155 (31 percent) as men and 2 percent could not be attributed to either sex conclusively.

55 Orsi, pp. 86; 105 and Colleen McDannell, "Catholic Domesticity, 1860–1960," in Karen Kennelly, ed., *American Catholic Women: a Historical Exploration* (New York: Macmillan, 1989), pp. 48–80.

56 Turner, "Mexican American Home Altars," p. 173.

57 Susanne Küchler and Walter Melion, eds., *Images of Memory, On Remembering and Representation* (Washington: Smithsonian Press, 1991), esp. pp. 1–7; 74–86; David Thelen, ed., *Memory and American History* (Bloomington: Indiana Univ. Press, 1990) and John Bodnar, *Remaking America: Public Memory, Commemoration, and Patriotism in the Twentieth Century* (Princeton: Princeton Univ. Press, 1992), pp. 13–20. On memory and objects, see Russell W. Belk, ed. "Possessions and the Sense of the Past," *Highways and Buyways: Naturalistic Research from the Consumer Behavior Odyssey* (Provo, UT: Association for Consumer Research, 1991) pp. 114–30.

58 Pierre Nora, "Between Memory and History: *Les Lieux de Mémoire,*" *Representations* 26 (1989), p. 8f.

59 Respondent No. 152.

60 See Nigel Llewllyn, *The Art of Death: Visual Culture in English Death Ritual, 1500–1800* (London: Reaktion Books, 1991); Anita Schorsh, "A Key to the Kingdom: The Iconography of a Mourning Picture," *Winterthur Portfolio* 14 (1979), pp. 41–71; Martha Pike, "In Memory Of: Artifacts Relating to Mourning in Nineteenth Century America," in Ray B. Browne, ed., *Rituals and Ceremonies in Popular Culture* (Bowling Green, OH: Bowling Green Univ. Popular Press, 1980), pp. 296–315.

61 James VanDerZee, *The Harlem Book of the Dead* (NY: Morgan and Morgan, 1978) and Deborah Willis-Braithwaite, *VanDerZee, Photographer 1886–1983* (New York: Harry N. Abrams, Inc., 1993), pp. 148–53.

62 Susan Stewart, *On Longing: Narratives of the Miniature, the Gigantic, the Souvenir, the Collection* (Baltimore: Johns Hopkins Univ. Press, 1984), p. 23.

63 Ibid., pp. 140; 136.

64 Respondent No. 298.

65 Respondent No. 170.

66 On the Catholic use of relics see Francis J. Weber, "The Relics of Christ," *Review for Religious* 21 (1962), pp. 79–89; "Care of Relics," *American Ecclesiastical Review* 147 (1963), pp. 387–8; "Veneration of Relics of the Saints," *Clergy Review* 48 (1963), pp. 252–4 and Paul R. Coyle, "Authenticity of Relics," *The Priest* 15 (1959), pp. 148–50.

67 Robert E. Clay, Jr., "Memorialization and Enshrinement: George Whitefield and Popular Religious Culture, 1770–1850," *Journal of the Early Republic* 10 (1990), pp. 339–60. Jon Butler, *Awash in a Sea of Faith: Christianizing the American People* (Cambridge: Harvard Univ. Press, 1990), p. 188.

68 Wilbur E. Schoonhoven (Long Island City, NY) to Ezra Tipple, February 1, 1932. Methodist Archives, Drew University.

69 Arthur D. Cummings, *A Portrait in Pottery* (London: Epworth Press, 1962), p. 42f. See also Roger Lee, *Wesleyana and Methodist Pottery: A Short Guide* (n.p., n.d.).

70 Mary Douglas, "Goods as a System of Communication," *In The Active Voice* (London: Routledge & Kegan Paul, 1982), p. 24.

71 Raymond Brennan, "Everybody Needs Devotion Devices!" *The Liguorian* 50 (1962), p. 9f.

72 Deborah Laake, *Secret Ceremonies: A Mormon Woman's Intimate Diary of Marriage and Beyond* (New York: William Morrow, 1993), pp. 144–8.

73 Turner, pp. 352–7; James R. Curtis, "Miami's Little Havana: Yard Shrines, Cult Religion and Landscape," *Journal of Cultural Geography* 1 (1980), pp. 1–15; and James R. Curtis, "Santeria: Persistence and Change in an Afro-Cuban Cult," in *Objects of Special Devotion: Fetishism in Popular Culture*, ed., Ray B. Browne (Bowling Green, OH: Bowling Green Univ. Popular Press, 1982), pp. 336–51.

74 Respondent No. 251.

75 Kenneth L. Ames, "Words to Live By," *Death in the Dining Room and Other Tales of Victorian Culture* (Philadelphia: Temple Univ. Press, 1992), pp. 97–149.

76 Interview conducted August 13, 1993. One of eighteen interviews conducted during the 1993 Sunstone Symposium.

77 David Cheal, *The Gift Economy* (London: Routledge, 1988), p. 15. See also Russell W. Belk and Gregory S. Coon, "Can't Buy Me Love: Dating, Money, and Gifts," *Advances in Consumer Research* 18 (1991), pp. 1–7.

78 I'd like to thank Sister Ellen Joyce from the College of St. Elizabeth, Morristown, New Jersey, for this observation. The use of Protestant material culture to provoke memories and laughter is exploited in Patricia Klein, *et al., Growing Up Born Again: A Whimsical Look at the Blessings and Tribulations of Growing up Born Again* (Old Tappan, NJ: Fleming H. Revell Co., 1987).

79 Wholesale Catalog, 1943–4, Foley & Dugan, Providence, Rhode Island. Strong Museum, Rochester, New York.

80 *The Sign* 36 (1957), p. 70. Protestant children also played preacher with clerical props. William Augustus Muhlenberg, raised a Lutheran, gave sermons and "he would always have a crimson shawl placed over a piece of furniture for a pulpit, and never forgot to take up a collection, the man-servant being usually present with a plate for the purpose." Anne Ayres, *The Life and Work of William Augustus Muhlenberg* (New York: Harper & Bros., 1880), p. 11.

81   See Colleen McDannell, *The Christian Home in Victorian America, 1840–1900* (Bloomington: Indiana Univ. Press, 1986), pp. 20–51.

82   On the antebellum American production of Protestant statues see Richard Carter Barret, *Bennington Pottery and Porcelain* (NY: Crown Publishers, 1958), pp. 20f; 256–79.

83   In addition to C. Hennecke's Florentine Statuary catalog, the Strong Museum in Rochester, New York, has other catalogs with mixed religious and secular statuary. See the catalogs of Fritz Krug (1913); Kölner Kunst Figuren-Fabrik (1895); H. J. Bing & Sons (1850); Copeland's Porcelain Statuary (1853).

84   Henry T. Williams and Mrs. C. S. Jones, *Beautiful Homes; or, Hints in House Furnishing* (New York: Henry T. Williams, 1878), p. 85.

85   For other examples of household paintings and prints of the Virgin Mary, see William Seale, *The Tasteful Interlude: American Interiors through the Camera's Eye, 1860–1917* 2nd edn. (Nashville, TN: American Association for State and Local History), plate 58: parlor, 2 Park Street, Boston, *c.*1885; plate 149: parlor, Boston suburb, 1900; plate 209: home of Martin Luther, Beaumont, TX, 1909–12. In 1876 Mary Nealy wrote about the edifying role of art on children: "When we received our chromo of Murillo's 'Madonna,' two years ago, from Prang, and it was properly framed and hung in a good light in our sitting-room, I noticed Arthur looking at it often in the pauses between his lessons." *Ladies Repository* 36 (1866), p. 76.

86   Pierre Bourdieu, *Distinction: A Social Critique of the Judgement of Taste* trans., Richard Nice (Cambridge: Harvard Univ. Press, 1984), pp. 34 and 53.

87   John Fiske, "Cultural Studies and the Culture of Everyday Life," in Lawrence Grossberg, *et al.*, *Cultural Studies* (New York: Routledge, 1992), pp. 154–71; Brett Williams, *Upscaling Downtown: Stalled Gentrification in Washington, D.C.* (Ithaca, NY: Cornell Univ. Press, 1988), p. 102; and

Odina Fachel Leal, "Popular Taste and Erudite Repertoire: The Place and Space of Television in Brazil," *Cultural Studies* 4 (1988), pp. 19–29.

88   On the Protestant appropriation of Catholic art see McDannell, *The Christian Home*, pp. 34–45.

89   Francine Parnes, "Simply Divine," *Denver Post*, December 3, 1993.

90   R. Laurence Moore, *Selling God: American Religion in the Marketplace of Culture* (New York: Oxford Univ. Press, 1994), p. 11.

91   Olalquiaga, p. 50.

92   Susan Sontag in "Notes on Camp" writes, "Thus the Camp sensibility is one that is alive to a double sense in which some things can be taken. But this is not the familiar split-level construction of a literal meaning, on the one hand, and a symbolic meaning on the other. It is the difference, rather, between the thing as meaning something, anything, and the thing as pure artifice" (p. 281); *Against Interpretation and Other Essays* (New York: Octagon Books, 1978), pp. 275–92. See also Moe Meyer, ed., *The Politics and Poetics of Camp* (New York: Routledge, 1994).

93   Peter Gardella, *Innocent Ecstasy* (New York: Oxford Univ. Press, 1985).

94   Madonna reportedly explained, "I have always carried around a few rosaries with me. One day I decided to wear [one] as a necklace. Everything I do is sort of tongue in cheek. It's a strong blend – a beautiful sort of symbolism, the idea of someone suffering, which is what Jesus on a crucifix stands for, and then not taking it seriously. Seeing it as an icon with no religiousness attached. It isn't sacrilegious for me." Quoted in John Fiske, "British Cultural Studies and Television," in *Channels of Discourse*, ed. Robert C. Allen (Chapel Hill: Univ. of North Carolina Press), p. 275f.

95   Freedberg, p. 332.

96   James Agee and Walker Evans, *Let Us Now Praise Famous Men* (Boston: Houghton Mifflin Company, 1939; reprint 1980), p. 164.

97   Mihaly Csikszentmihalyi and Eugene Rochberg-Halton, *The Meaning of Things: Domestic Symbols and the Self* (Cambridge: Cambridge Univ. Press, 1981), p. 17.

3   The Bible in the Victorian Home

1   Anne Ellis, *The Life of an Ordinary Woman* (Boston: Houghton Mifflin Co., 1929), pp. 104–6; 79. Anne Ellis's mother came to Colorado from Tennessee after divorcing her husband. She supported her family by taking in laundry and sewing. She eventually remarried but the family depended on the income of all members to survive. Anne Ellis recalled reading to her mother when she was 14 in 1890.

2   Ellis remembers buying "The Yellow Back" and the "Ten-Cent Novel" as well as borrowing books (pp. 122–6). As the family became more financially stable they bought books including an old and leather-bound volume of Plutarch's *Lives*.

3   A series of books on the cultural history of the Bible in America was published in the 1980s. Nathan O. Hatch and Mark A. Noll, eds., *The Bible in America: Essays in Cultural History* (New York: Oxford Univ. Press, 1982) included essays presented at a conference at Wheaton College in 1979. The Society of Biblical Literature sponsored a series of books under the general editorship of Edwin S. Gaustand and Walter Harrelson. Each had their own editor and contained a series of articles on specific topics. All were published by Fortress Press and Scholars Press; see David L. Barr, *The Bible in American Education* (1982); Ernest R. Sandeen, *The Bible and Social Reform* (1982); Giles Gunn, *The Bible and American Arts and Letters* (1983); Allene Stuart Phy, *The Bible and Popular Culture in America* (1985); James Turner Johnson, *The Bible in American Law, Politics, and Political Rhetoric* (1985) and Ernest S. Frerichs, *The Bible and Bibles in America* (1988).

4   Patricia Anderson, *The Printed Image and the Transformation of Popular Culture, 1790–1860* (Oxford: Clarendon Press, 1991), p. 33.

5   David D. Hall, *Worlds of Wonder, Days of Judgment: Popular Religious Belief in Early New England* (Cambridge: Harvard Univ. Press, 1990), p. 51.

6   On the Catholic use of the Bible in domestic worship, see Colleen McDannell, *The Christian Home in*

Victorian America, 1840–1900 (Bloomington: Indiana Univ. Press, 1986), pp. 70f, 89f.

7 Ronald J. Zboray, *A Fictive People: Antebellum Economic Development and the American Reading Public* (New York: Oxford Univ. Press, 1993), p. 12–14 and Margaret T. Hills, *The English Bible in America: A Bibliography of Editions of the Bible and New Testament Published in America 1777–1957* (New York: American Bible Society and the New York Public Library, 1962), pp. xviii–xx.

8 ABS distribution statistics come from Creighton Lacy, *The Word Carrying Giant: The Growth of the American Bible Society* (South Pasadena: William Carey Library, 1977), pp. 56, 104, 152. On British Bible societies, see Leslie Howsam, *Cheap Bibles: Nineteenth-Century Publishing and the British and Foreign Bible Society* (Cambridge: Cambridge Univ. Press, 1991) and for the history of the American Bible Society, Peter J. Wosh, *Spreading the Word: The Bible Business in Nineteenth-Century America* (Ithaca, NY: Cornell Univ. Press, 1994).

9 These statistics are based on editions cited in Hills. We must recognize that many Americans, especially immigrants, bought Bibles imported from European countries or printed in foreign languages leading to an even higher number of editions sold in the United States. Hills explains that "there is no complete list of printings, and certainly not of the number of copies printed . . . commercial publishers do not often issue their statistics [of Bibles published]" (p. xxi).

10 William J. Gilmore, *Reading Becomes a Necessity of Life: Material and Cultural Life in Rural New England, 1780–1835* (Knoxville: Univ. of Tennessee Press, 1989), p. 323f.

11 Ibid., p. 192.

12 Based on my survey of probate records at the Family History Library, Salt Lake City, Utah on Adams County, Illinois; Allegheny and Philadelphia Counties, Pennsylvania; Glen County, California.

13 Probate records from Hartford County, Connecticut, and Adams County, Illinois, on record at the Family History Library, Salt Lake City, Utah.

14 Gilmore, p. 295.

15 Steven Mailloux, "Misreading as a Historical Act: Cultural Rhetoric, Bible Politics, and Fuller's 1845 Review of Douglass's *Narrative*," in James L. Machor, ed., *Readers in History: Nineteenth-Century American Literature and the Contexts of Response* (Baltimore: The Johns Hopkins Univ. Press, 1993), p. 20.

16 Albert J. Raboteau, *Slave Religion: The "Invisible Institution" in the Antebellum South* (New York: Oxford Univ. Press, 1978), pp. 239–43.

17 Richard D. Brown, *Knowledge is Power: The Diffusion of Information in Early America, 1700–1865* (New York: Oxford Univ. Press, 1989), pp. 273, 282.

18 Michael Fried, *Absorption and Theatricality: Painting and Beholder in the Age of Diderot* (Berkeley: Univ. of California Press, 1980), p. 9.

19 Isabel Rivers, *Reason, Grace, and Sentiment: A Study of the Language of Religion and Ethics in England, 1660–1780* (Cambridge: Cambridge Univ. Press, 1991), pp. 164–204.

20 Ibid., p. 185.

21 The following summary of patriarchal authority is derived from: Steven Ozment, *When Fathers Ruled: Family Life in Reformation Europe* (Cambridge: Harvard Univ. Press, 1983), pp. 50–99, 132–77; Edmund S. Morgan, *The Puritan Family* (New York: Harper & Row, 1944), pp. 29–86; Nancy Cott, *The Bonds of Womanhood* (New Haven and London: Yale Univ. Press, 1977), pp. 126–159; Philip Greven, *The Protestant Temperament: Patterns of Child-Rearing, Religious Experience, and the Self in Early America* (New York: Meridian Books, 1977), pp. 21–178; and Steven Mintz and Susan Kellogg, *Domestic Revolutions: A Social History of American Family Life* (New York: Free Press, 1988), pp. 1–42.

22 Jonathan Edwards, *The Great Awakening*, ed. C. C. Goen (New Haven and London: Yale Univ. Press, 1972), p. 394 as cited in Greven, p. 31.

23 Roger Chartier, *The Cultural Uses of Print in Early Modern France* trans. Lydia G. Cochrane (Princeton: Princeton Univ. Press, 1987), p. 226 quoting D. Diderot, *Salons de 1759, 1761, 1763*, ed. Jean Seznec (Paris, 1976), p. 164.

24 Fried, pp. 55, 11.

25 Erastus Hopkins, *The Family, A Religious Institution: or, Heaven Its Model* (Troy, NY: Elias Gates, 1840), p. 52.

26 McDannell, pp. 108–26.

27 Sarah Hale, "Evening Devotions," *Godey's Lady's Book* 24 (1842), p. 241.

28 A. Gregory Schneider, *The Way of the Cross Leads Home: The Domestication of American Methodism* (Bloomington: Indiana Univ. Press, 1993), pp. 136–43.

29 Fanny Lamson to John Bocker (?) June 12, 1827. Schlessinger Library, Radcliff College.

30 Annie Wright Ussery, *The Story of Kathleen Mallory* (Nashville: Broadman Press, 1956), p. 1.

31 Robert Richardson, *Memoirs of Alexander Campbell* (Philadelphia: J. B. Lippincott, 1868), p. 34.

32 Alexander V. G. Allen, *Life and Letters of Phillips Brooks* vol. 1 (New York: E. P. Dutton, 1901), p. 33.

33 Published in *Millenial Star* (Manchester, England) and reprinted in David Sylvester Tuttle, *Missionary to the Mountain West, Reminiscences of Bishop Daniel S. Tuttle* (Salt Lake City: Univ. of Utah Press, 1987), p. 336.

34 See, for example, Chartier, pp. 225–33; Robert Darnton, "History of Reading" in Peter Burke, ed., *New Perspectives on Historical Writing* (University Park: Pennsylvania State University Press, 1991), pp. 148–51; Gilmore, p. 88; Rhys Isaac, "Books and the Social Authority of Learning: The Case of Mid-Eighteenth-Century Virginia," in William L. Joyce *et al.*, *Printing and Society in Early America* (Worcester, MA: American Antiquarian Society, 1983), p. 233.

35 Zboray, p. 88.

36 Rivers, p. 189 quoting E. Parsons, ed., *The Works of the Rev. Isaac Watts* vol. 2 (Leeds, 1800), p. 272.

37 Barbara Welter, "The Cult of True Womanhood, 1820–1860" in *Dimity Convictions*, pp. 21–41 and Ann Douglas, *The Feminization of American Culture* (New York: Knopf, 1977).

38 Goodrich, p. 124.

39 Jane Tompkins, "Sentimental Power: *Uncle Tom's Cabin* and the Politics of Literary History," in *Sensational Designs: The Cultural Work of*

American Fiction, 1790–1860 (New York: Oxford Univ. Press, 1985), pp. 122–46 and Pam Hardman, "Elsie Dinsmore and the Training of a Victorian Child," *American Studies Association* 29 (1988), pp. 69–91.

40 Davis F. Newton, *Apples of Gold in Pictures of Silver* (New York: Published by the Author, 1869), p. 38. The earliest catechism printed in New England, John Cotton's *Spiritual Milk for Boston Babes in either England, Drawn out the Breasts of both Testaments for their Souls' Nourishment,* equated the biblical truths communicated to children with mother's milk. On female imagery in Puritan culture, see David Leverenz, *The Language of Puritan Feeling: An Exploration in Literature, Psychology, and Social History* (New Brunswick: Rutgers Univ. Press, 1980) and Amanda Porterfield, *Female Piety in Puritan New England: The Emergence of Religious Humanism* (New York: Oxford Univ. Press, 1992), pp. 80–115.

41 Ernest B. Gordon, *Adoniram Judson Gordon* (New York: Fleming H. Revell Co., 1896), p. 17.

42 David Coulter, *Memoir of David Coulter, D. D.* (St. Louis: Presbyterian Publishing Company, 1878?), p. 14.

43 Alexander C. Zabriske, *Arthur Selden Lloyd, Missionary-Statesman and Pastor* (New York: Morehouse-Gorham Co., 1942), p. 13.

44 Sara C. Palmer, *Dad Hall, "Bishop of Wall Street"* (Chicago: Moody Press, 1954), p. 18.

45 Joseph Howard, *Life of Henry Ward Beecher* (Philadelphia: Hubbard Brothers, 1887), p. 33.

46 Chartier, p. 219.

47 Ibid., p. 220.

48 Cathy N. Davidson, "The Novel as Subversive Activity," in Alfred Young, *Beyond the American Revolution* (DeKalb: Northern Illinois Univ. Press, 1993), pp. 283–316.

49 Michael Kammen, *Mystic Chords of Memory: The Transformation of Tradition in American Culture* (New York: Alfred A. Knopf, 1991), p. 12.

50 Charles Wolfe, "Bible Country: The Good Book in Country Music," in Allene Stuart Phy, *The Bible and Popular Culture in America*, p. 86f. For instance, see J. S. Mills, *A Manual of Family Worship* (Dayton: W. R. Funk, 1900) and H. Mattison, *Sacred Melodies for Social Worship* (New York: Mason Brothers, 1859). I would like to thank Mary De Jong for bringing these Bible hymns to my attention.

51 Wolfe, p. 89f.

52 As printed in *Graham's Magazine* 19 (1841), p. 51.

53 French E. Oliver, *Oliver's Songs of Deliverance* (Kansas City: F. E. Oliver, 1908), no. 113.

54 On the transformation of commodities to possessions in Victorian literature, see Gillian Brown, *Domestic Individualism: Imagining Self in Nineteenth-Century America* (Berkeley: Univ. of California Press, 1990), p. 47 and Jane Tompkins, p. 144.

55 McDannell, pp. 78, 144.

56 Lori Merish, "'The Hand of Refined Taste' in the Frontier Landscape: Caroline Kirland's *A New Home, Who'll Follow?* and the Feminization of American Consumerism," *American Quarterly* 45 (1993), p. 487. See also Colin Campbell, *The Romantic Ethic and the Spirit of Modern Consumerism* (New York: Basil Blackwell, 1987), pp. 156ff and David Watkin, *Morality and Architecture* (New York: Oxford Univ. Press, 1977).

57 *The Holy Bible* (Worcester, MA: Isaiah Thomas, 1791).

58 Wosh, pp. 19; 23f. On Harper's *Illuminated Bible*, see Eugene Exman, *The Brothers Harper* (New York: Harper & Row, 1965), pp. 163–5, 172, 190, 244.

59 The 1849 diary of Mary Lee Bland Ewell reprinted in Kate B. Carter, *Our Pioneer Heritage* (Salt Lake City: Daughters of the Utah Pioneers, 1965).

60 Ralph W. Hyde, "The Traveling Bible Salesman: The Good Buck from the Good Book," in Phy, p. 143.

61 *Dr. Scott's Family Bible* (New York: Dodge and Sayer, 1816). This Bible is not listed in Hill's catalog but exists in fascicles at the American Bible Society archives in New York City.

62 *Christian Advocate*, April 4, 1878, p. 223.

63 For examples of highly illustrated secular books, see John Harthan, *The History of the Illustrated Book: The Western Tradition* (New York: Thames & Hudson, 1981).

64 Hill, p. 25.

65 *The Holy Bible* (New York: Collins, Perkins and Co., 1807). The Gothic-style family records were found in the copy owned by the Logan Library, Philadelphia.

66 *The Holy Bible* (Philadelphia: A. J. Holman, 1882).

67 Henry T. Williams and Mrs C. S. Jones, *Household Elegancies: Suggestions in Household Art and Tasteful Home Decorations* (New York: Henry T. Williams, 1875), p. 96.

68 Helen E. Chapman, *Jennie Prindle's Home* (Philadelphia: Presbyterian Board of Publication, 1875), p. 96.

69 Elizabeth Fox-Genovese, *Within the Plantation Household: Black and White Women of the Old South* (Chapel Hill: Univ. of North Carolina Press, 1988), p. 231.

70 Kenneth Ames, *Death in the Dining Room and Other Tales of Victorian Culture* (Philadelphia: Temple Univ. Press, 1992).

71 Peter C. Marzio, *Pictures for a Nineteenth-Century America, The Democratic Art: Chromolithography, 1840–1900* (Boston: David R. Godine, 1979).

72 R. K. Hennywood, *Relief Molded Jugs, 1820–1900* (Woodbridge, England: Antique Collectors' Club, 1984), pp. 27–31, 51, 108, 159, 184–8, 196.

73 All of these goods are at the Philadelphia Archidocesan Historical Research Center.

74 Katherine C. Grier, "The Decline of the Memory Palace: The Parlor after 1890," in Foy and Schlereth, *American Home Life*, p. 58f.

75 On Susan Warner, see Nina Baym, *Woman's Fiction: A Guide to Novels by and about Women in America, 1820–1870* (Ithaca, NY: Cornell Univ. Press, 1978), pp. 140–174 and Jane Tompkins, pp. 147–185.

76 Susan Warner, *The Wide, Wide, World* (New York: A. L. Burt Co., 1851), pp. 28–33. I would like to thank Jenny Francot for her suggestions on interpreting this scene.

77 Stanley Coben, *Rebellion Against Victorianism: The Impetus for Cultural Change in 1920s America* (New York: Oxford Univ. Press, 1991), p. 35.

78 Grier, p. 68 quoting Hazel Adler, *The New Interior: Modern Decoration for the Modern Home* (New York: Century, 1916), p. 38.

79   Kammen, p. 12.
80   Grier, p. 63.
81   Roland Marchand, *Advertising the American Dream* (Berkeley: Univ. of California Press, 1985), p. 273.

4   The Religious Symbolism of Laurel Hill Cemetery

An earlier version of this chapter was published in the *Pennsylvania Magazine of History and Biography* 111 (1987), pp. 275–303.

1   Smith's comments on Philadelphia's poor soil are mentioned in "Laurel Hill," *Godey's Lady's Book* 28 (1844), p. 107 and in John Watson, *Annals of Philadelphia, and Pennsylvania* (Philadelphia: Edwin S. Stuart, 1887), p. 138. The loss of his daughter's grave was cited in Smith's memoranda book (November 8, 1835) which is now lost. Reporter Jim Quinn in his article for the *Philadelphia Magazine*, "The Resurrection of Laurel Hill" 69 (September 1978) pp. 174–6, 224–30 mentions the memoranda book and the problem of the lost grave. In 1978 the memoranda book was owned by Drayton and Jane Smith. According to Laurel Hill caretakers, they were killed in a car accident and the memoranda book cannot be located. Quaker burial practices are discussed in J. William Frost, *The Quaker Family in Colonial America* (New York: St. Martin's Press, 1973), pp. 41–4 and in J. Thomas Scharf and Thomas Westcoff, *History of Philadelphia, 1609–1884* (Philadelphia: L. H. Everts and Company, 1884), VIII, p. 2360.
2   John Jay Smith, *The Recollections of John Jay Smith* (Philadelphia: J. B. Lippincott, 1892), vol. 2, p. 268.
3   Ibid., p. 267.
4   "Laurel Hill," *Godey's Lady's Book* 28 (1844), p. 108.
5   Jon Butler, *Awash in a Sea of Faith: Christianizing the American People* (Cambridge: Harvard Univ. Press, 1990), p. 4.
6   In addition to the historians mentioned, see also Randall H. McGuire, "Dialogues with the Dead: Ideology and the Cemetery," in *The Recovery of Meaning: Historical Archeology in the Eastern United States* eds. Mark P. Leone and Parker B. Potter, Jr.

(Washington: Smithsonian Institution Press, 1988); Peggy McDowell, "Influences on 19th-Century Funerary Architecture," in *New Orleans Architecture* vol. 3 "The Cemeteries," ed. Mary Louise Christovich (Getna, LA: Pelican Publishing Co., 1974), pp. 71–133; and Jack G. Voller, "The Textuality of Death: Notes on the Reading of Cemeteries," *Journal of American Culture* 14 (1991), pp. 1–10.
7   Kenneth L. Ames, "Ideologies in Stone: Meanings in Victorian Gravestones," *Journal of Popular Culture* 14 (1980/1), p. 654.
8   Stanley French, "The Cemetery as Cultural Institution," in David E. Stannard ed., *Death in America* (Philadelphia: Univ. of Pennsylvania Press, 1975), p. 82.
9   John F. Sears, *Sacred Places: American Tourist Attractions in the Nineteenth Century* (New York: Oxford Univ. Press, 1989), p. 115.
10   Jon Butler, "Historiographical Heresy: Catholicism as a Model for American Religious History" in *Belief in History*, ed. Thomas Kselman (Notre Dame, IN: Univ. of Notre Dame Press, 1991), p. 296.
11   John F. Sears discusses the cemetery as a sacred place, "places which might serve as national monuments or where the divine might appear to enter the world," but he shies away from its Christian character (pp. 99–115).
12   The following discussion of the history of Christian burial practices is derived from: Philippe Ariès, *Western Attitudes towards Death*, trans. Patricia M. Ranum (Baltimore, MD: The Johns Hopkins Univ. Press, 1974) and *The Hour of Our Death*, trans. Helen Weaver (New York: Knopf, 1981).
13   Howard Colvin, *Architecture and the After-Life* (New Haven and London: Yale Univ. Press, 1991), p. 137.
14   Historian Emma Disley writes that "The notion that we can earn any reward, either eternal life itself, or rewards within eternal life, was absolutely rejected by orthodox Protestants" (p. 79). However, she does point out that Protestants did believe that there could be gradations in heaven and hell but that entrance to such states was strictly coordinated by God. "Degrees of Glory: Protestant Doctrine and the Concept of Rewards

Hereafter," *Journal of Theological Studies* 42 (1991), pp. 76–105.
15   On the Englightenment cemetery, see Richard A. Etlin, *The Architecture of Death: The Transformation of the Cemetery in Eighteenth-Century Paris* (Cambridge: MIT Press, 1984); Colvin, pp. 327–63; and Thomas A. Kselman, *Death and Afterlife in Modern France* (Princeton: Princeton Univ. Press, 1993), pp. 165–221.
16   Article 10 of the law of 23 Prairial as cited in Kselman, p. 183.
17   The history of American cemeteries is discussed in James Deetz and Edwin Dethlefsen, "Death's Head, Cherub, Urn and Willow," *Natural History* 76 (1967), pp. 28–37; David E. Stannard, ed., *Death in America* (Philadelphia: Univ. of Pennsylvania Press, 1975); Charles O. Jackson, ed., *Passing: The Vision of Death in America* (Westport, CT: Greenwood Press, 1977), pp. 102–11; James J. Farrel, *Inventing the American Way of Death, 1830–1920* (Philadelphia: Temple Univ. Press, 1980); Michel Vovelle, "A Century and One-half of American Epitaphs (1660–1813): Toward the Study of Collective Attitudes about Death," *Comparative Studies in Society and History* 22 (1980), pp. 534–47; Blanche Linden-Ward, *Silent City on a Hill: Landscapes of Memory and Boston's Mount Auburn Cemetery* (Columbus: Ohio State Univ. Press, 1988); Camilo Jose Vergara and Kenneth T. Jackson, eds., *Silent Cities: The Evolution of the American Cemetery* (New York: Princeton Architectural Press, 1989); Richard E. Meyer, *Ethnicity and the American Cemetery* (Bowling Green, OH: Popular Press, 1993).
18   French, p. 91.
19   Throughout the nineteenth century, the Laurel Hill Cemetery Company published and sold guidebooks to the cemetery. The guides included the history of the cemetery, comments on who was buried there, lists of the types of trees, evocative poetry and anecdotes, rules and regulations, and illustrative engravings. The first edition of the guidebook (1844) was large, artistically designed, and contained illustrations. Smaller, less elaborate guides that contained basically the same text were published in 1846, 1847, 1851, 1853, and 1854.

The last edition was published in 1858. In 1865 the *Rules and Regulations of Laurel Hill Cemetery* included the text of the *Guide* with only minor changes. The 1872 *Rules and Regulations* contained the *Guide* text, but with no illustrations. The *Rules and Regulations* from 1879, 1885, and 1892 have only a very abbreviated description of Laurel Hill.

20   John Watson, *Annals of Philadelphia and Pennsylvania* (Philadelphia: Edwin S. Stuart, 1887), p. 138.

21   Lori Merish, "'The Hand of Refined Taste' in the Frontier Landscape: Caroline Kirland's *A New Home, Who'll Follow?* and the Feminization of American Consumerism," *American Quarterly* 45 (1993), pp. 485–523.

22   Mrs. Z. Barton Stout, "Thoughts in Laurel Hill Cemetery," in *Guide to Laurel Hill Cemetery Near Philadelphia* (Philadelphia: n.p. 1844), p. 153. To simplify documentation I cite pages only from the 1844 *Guide* although the same text can be found in the other editions and in the *Rules and Regulations*.

23   *Rules and Regulations of the Laurel Hill Cemetery of Philadelphia* (Philadelphia: Office of the Company, 1892), p. 2.

24   *Godey's*, p. 107.

25   *Guide*, p. 18.

26   Ibid., p. 14.

27   In 1849 Lebanon Cemetery was established for African Americans. It was outside the center of the city at Passyunk and Broad Streets. Catholics also built a cemetery in West Philadelphia that year. In the nineteenth century, Catholics were not permitted by their church to be buried in Protestant cemeteries because they could only be buried in "hallowed" grounds sanctified by a priest. Neither the African American nor Catholic cemeteries were as elaborate or large as Laurel Hill.

28   *Guide*, p. 47. I have not been able to find the cost of cemetery plots during this period. At the end of the list of plot-holders cited in the *Regulations of the Laurel Hill Cemetery* (1846) at the University of Pennsylvania Library there is the following penciled in:

Single grave $20
5 by 8 feet with
a deed 38

10 by 8 [illegible] 66
10 by 8 [illegible] 46

It is unclear if the higher amounts included maintenance or when the prices were current.

29   *Guide*, pp. 42–3. Smith could not have initially expected picnickers because the stipulation "No refreshments, and no party carrying refreshments, will be permitted to come within the grounds of Laurel Hill" was not in the first rules and regulations book, *Regulations of the Laurel Hill Cemetery* (Philadelphia: A. Waldie, 1837).

30   R. A. Smith, *Smith's Illustrated Guide to and Through Laurel Hill Cemetery* (Philadelphia: Willis P. Hazard, 1852), p. 38. The need to obtain tickets from the company for weekday admission arose sometime between 1844 and 1852.

31   *Guide*, p. 25.

32   Scharf and Westcoff, III, p. 1880.

33   "Cemeteries," *New Englander* 85 (1863), p. 606.

34   See Karen Halttunen, "Mourning the Dead: A Study in Sentimental Ritual," in *Confidence Men and Painted Women: A Study of Middle-Class Culture in America, 1830–1870* (New Haven and London: Yale Univ. Press, 1982), pp. 124–52; Martha V. Pike, ed., *A Time to Mourn: Expressions of Grief in Nineteenth-Century America* (Stony Brook, NY: The Museum of Stony Brook, 1980); and Ellen Marie Snyder, "At Rest, Victorian Death Furniture," in *Perspectives on American Furniture*, ed. G. W. Ward (New York: W. W. Norton, 1988), pp. 241–72.

35   *Smith's Illustrated Guide*, p. 52.

36   *Guide*, p. 13. On the role of nature in the rural cemetery movement, see Thomas Bender, "The 'Rural' Cemetery Movement: Urban Travail and the Appeal of Nature," *New England Quarterly* 47 (1974), pp. 196–211.

37   Catherine L. Albanese, *Nature Religion in America* (Chicago: Univ. of Chicago Press, 1990).

38   Andrew Jackson Downing, "Public Cemeteries and Public Gardens," *Horticulturist* 4 (1849), p. 10.

39   *Smith's Illustrated Guide*, p. 66.

40   Ibid., p. 35.

41   Colleen McDannell and Bernhard Lang, *Heaven: A History* (New

Haven and London: Yale Univ. Press, 1988), pp. 276–306.

42   Andrew Jackson Downing, "A Talk About Public Parks and Gardens," *Horticulturist*, 4 (1849), p. 157.

43   "American Architecture: Architecture of Philadelphia and New York," *New Englander* 43 (1836), p. 360.

44   *Guide*, p. 14.

45   R. A. Smith, *Philadelphia As It Is* (Philadelphia: Lindsay and Blakiston, 1852), p. 341. The same entry on Laurel Hill was contained in R. A. Smith's, *The Stranger's Guide in Philadelphia* (Philadelphia: Lindsay and Blakiston, 1860).

46   *Guide*, p. 22.

47   Ibid., p. 40–41.

48   *Smith's Illustrated Guide*, p. 39.

49   Ibid., p. 41.

50   *Guide*, p. 68.

51   A copy of this book which is now in the Library Company, Philadelphia, was owned in 1857 by Mary Rebecca D. Smith (not known if related to John Jay Smith).

52   On businessmen's prayer meetings, see Marion Bell, *Crusade in the City: Revivalism in Nineteenth-Century Philadelphia* (Lewisburg, PA: Bucknell Univ. Press, 1977); John Jenkins, *Plain Thoughts on the Present Great Awakening* (Philadelphia: n.p. 1858); and William Conant, *Narratives of Remarkable Conversions and Revival Incidents* (Philadelphia: n.p. 1858).

53   Sydney E. Ahlstrom, *A Religious History of the American People* (New Haven and London: Yale Univ. Press, 1972), p. 744.

54   On the Protestant adaptation of the Gothic, see Colleen McDannell, *The Christian Home in Victorian America* (Bloomington: Indiana Univ. Press, 1986), pp. 28–31.

55   *Reminiscence of Gideon Burton* (Cincinnati: George P. Houston, 1895), p. 98.

56   *Godey's Lady's Book* 90 (1875), p. 560; 95 (1872), p. 457; 78 (1869), p. 451.

57   *Smith's Illustrated Guide*, p. 100f.

58   Henry T. Williams and Mrs C. S. Jones, *Household Elegancies: Suggestions in Household Art and Tasteful Home Decorations* (New York: H. T. Williams, 1875), pp. 83f; 180–82.

59   An example of a wooden cross

wall bracket is located at the Philadelphian Archdiocesan Historical Research Center, Overbrook, PA. *Household Elegancies*, p. 83.

60   An example of this cross is located at Philadelphia Archdiocesan Historical Research Center, Overbrook, PA. For an illustration of the pattern, see Frances Lichten, *Decorative Art of Victoria's Era* (New York: Charles Scribner's Sons, 1950), p. 187.

61   The following discussion is based on: Edmund Lorenz, *Practical Hymn Studies* (New York: Fleming H. Revell Co., 1937), pp. 26–32; Duncan Morrison, *The Great Hymns of the Church* (Toronto: Hard & Co., 1890), pp. 92–3; George Pentecost, *Song Victories of "The Bliss and Sankey Hymns"* (Boston: D. Lathrop & Co., 1877), pp. 88–91; Louis Banks, *Immortal Hymns & Their Story* (Cleveland: The Burrows Brothers, 1898), p. 58; Jeremiah Reeves, *The Hymn in History and Literature* (New York: The Century Co., 1924), pp. 200–201; Erik Routley, *Hymn and Human Life* (London: John Murray, 1952), pp. 105–9; Louis Benson, *Studies of Familiar Hymns* (Philadelphia: Westminster Press, 1923), pp. 108–18; Nicholas Smith, *Hymns Historically Famous* (Chicago: Advance Publishing Co., 1901), p. 114–17.

62   Currier and Ives lithographs (ones printed in 1868 and 1874), bookmarks, and postcards are at the Billy Graham Center Museum, Wheaton, IL. The bread dish and an etched drinking glass are at the Philadelphia Archdiocesan Historical Research Center, Overbrook, PA.

63   Richard Carter Barret, *Bennington Pottery and Porcelain* (New York: Crown Pub., 1958), p. 257 and C. Hennecke and Company catalog (1887), Strong Museum, Rochester, NY.

64   *Smith's Illustrated Guide*, p. 76.

65   McDannell and Lang, p. 184 quoting Calvin, *Psychopannychia* in *Tracts and Treatises in Defense of the Reformed Faith* (Grand Rapids, MI: Eerdmans, 1958), p. 432.

66   McDannell and Lang, p. 184f referring to Thomas Burnet, *A Treatise Concerning the State of Departed Souls Before, and at, and·after the Resurrection* (London: Bettesworth & Hitch, 1733).

67   Ibid. From Watt's hymn, "A

Prospect of Heaven Makes Death Easy" in *The Norton Anthology of Poetry*, ed. Arthur M. Eastman, *et al.*, (New York: Norton, 1970), p. 427.

68   See McDannell and Lang, pp. 257–75.

69   For a more pessimistic appraisal of the bed imagery in cemeteries, see Snyder, pp. 241–72.

70   R. Laurence Moore, *Selling God: American Religion in the Marketplace of Culture* (New York: Oxford Univ. Press, 1994), p. 38.

71   *Guide*, p. 18.

5   Lourdes Water and American Catholicism

1   Mary Hayes to Alexis Granger, November 17, 1879. Unless otherwise noted, all letters are held by the University of Notre Dame Archives in the Granger letters collection. Spelling mistakes in the original letters have been corrected unless they show a consistent pattern of error reflecting the educational level of the correspondent.

2   The Lourdes Center run by the Marist fathers in Boston was established around 1955. It produces a magazine called *Lourdes Echo*. Between 1956 and 1961 when the devotion went out of favor, Notre Dame clergy distributed fifty thousand bottles of Lourdes water. Current distribution of the water is approximately seventy gallons per year.

3   Henri Lasserre, *Our Lady of Lourdes*, abridged and translated (St. Paul, MN: Catechetical Guild, 1943), p. 57. The bibliography on the Lourdes apparitions is voluminous and mostly of a hagiographic nature. The primary reference work that contemporary scholars utilize is the multi-volume set of documents compiled by René Laurentine, ed., *Lourdes: dossier des documents authentiques* 2 vols. (Paris: Lethielleux, 1962) and *Lourdes: Historie authentique* 4 vols. (Paris: Lethielleux, 1962). My summary is based on critical discussions included in: Sandra L. Zimdars-Swartz, *Encountering Mary: From La Salette to Medjugorje* (Princeton: Princeton Univ. Press, 1991), pp. 43–67; Thomas A. Kselman, *Miracles and Prophecies in Nineteenth-Century France* (New Brunswick: Rutgers

Univ. Press, 1983) and Victor Turner and Edith Turner, *Image and Pilgrimage in Christian Culture: Anthropological Perspectives* (Oxford: Basil Blackwell, 1978), pp. 226–32. See also Mary Lee Nolan and Sidney Nolan, *Christian Pilgrimage in Modern Western Europe* (Chapel Hill: Univ. of North Carolina Press, 1989). For a contemporary analysis of Lourdes pilgrimages see John Eade and Michael J. Sallnow, *Contesting the Sacred: The Anthropology of Christian Pilgrimage* (London: Routledge, 1991), pp. 30–76.

4   Visitor (tourists and pilgrims) statistics were cited during a 20 June, 1990 interview with Père Joulia, Director of the Lourdes Press Bureau and included in Lourdes publicity materials. Water production cited in Turner, p. 227.

5   s.v. Holy Water, *New Catholic Encyclopedia*. Thomas Aquinas, *Summa Theologica, Qu. disp. De Mal.* Q. 7 a. 12. Lasserre, pp. 19–20.

6   Mircea Eliade, *The Sacred and the Profane* (New York: Harcourt, Brace & World, Inc., 1957), pp. 129–38; *Images and Symbols* (London: Harvill Press, 1961), pp. 151–60; *Patterns in Comparative Religion* (New York: Sheed & Ward, 1958), pp. 188–215. In *Patterns of Comparative Religion*, Eliade writes: "Living water, the fountain of youth, the Water of Life, and the rest, are all mythological formulae for the same metaphysical and religious reality: life, strength, and eternity are contained in water." On holy wells see Patrick Logan, *The Holy Wells of Ireland* (Gerrards Cross: Colin Smythe, Ltd., 1980).

The grotto also may have held importance in the development of the cult. Throughout the Mediterranean, grottoes were pre-Christian places of the sacred.

7   Maggie Duncan-Flowers, "An Ampulla from the Shrine of St. John," in Robert Ousterhout, ed., *The Blessings of Pilgrimage* (Urbana: Univ. of Illinois Press, 1990), p. 129f citing Photius quoting Ephraim of Antioch, *PG* pp. 103; 986–7.

8   The mobility of relics and other holy objects is explored in William A. Christian, Jr., *Apparitions in Late Medieval and Renaissance Spain* (Princeton: Princeton Univ. Press, 1981).

9   For an excellent analysis of how

visions become institutionalized by the church or fall into disrepute, see William A. Christian, Jr., *Moving Crucifixes in Modern Spain* (Princeton: Princeton Univ. Press, 1992).

10 Barbara Corrodo Pope, "Immaculate and Powerful: The Marian Revival in the Nineteenth Century," in *Immaculate and Powerful: The Female in Sacred Image and Social Reality* ed. C. W. Atkinson, Constance H. Buchanan, and Margaret Miles (Boston: Beacon Press, 1985), pp. 173–200.

11 Michael Carroll, *The Cult of the Virgin Mary: Psychological Origins* (Princeton: Princeton Univ. Press, 1986), pp. 49–74; 96–100. See also Kselman.

12 Ibid., pp. 113–40.

13 *Ave Maria* 1 (1865), p. 1.

14 For a discussion of some of the women who published essays and fiction in *Ave Maria*, see Colleen McDannell, "Catholic Women Fiction Writers, 1840–1920," *Women's Studies* 19 (1991), pp. 385–405.

15 William Lucey, "Catholic Magazines 1865–1880," *Records of the American Catholic Historical Society of Philadelphia* 63 (1952), p. 25.

16 Our Lady of the Miraculous Medal appeared three times in 1830 to a French nun, Catherine Labouré, in the chapel of her Parisian convent. The Virgin requested a medal be struck with her image as the Immaculate Conception. On one side was the Virgin with her arms outstretched and pointing down, her feet stepping on a serpent's head. Around the figure was the text: "O Mary conceived without sin, pray for us who have recourse to thee." On the back were twelve stars, two hearts (one of Mary pierced with a sword and the other of Jesus entwined with thorns), and a cross resting on a large "M." The vision of Catherine Labouré encouraged the development of the dogma of the Immaculate Conception of Mary.

Devotion to the Sacred Heart of Jesus was encouraged by the Jesuits. In 1675 the Sacred Heart appeared to Margaret Mary Alocoque, a French nun. Christ promised to send peace, comfort, and other blessings to those who devoted themselves to his heart and who placed a picture of it in their homes. Typically the Sacred Heart is portrayed by depicting Christ with one hand pointing to his inflamed

heart, surrounding by a string of thorns, and topped with a cross. His other hand is stretched out in a gesture of encouragement.

The Infant Jesus has been portrayed in medieval art as a baby in his mother's arms and in baroque art as a richly clothed toddler. Devotion both to the Holy Family and to the Infant Jesus was promoted by Teresa of Avilà, John of the Cross, and the Carmelite Order.

17 *Ave Maria* 3 (1867), p. 763.

18 *Ave Maria* 2 (1866), p. 323.

19 Alexis Granger to bishop of Fort Wayne, June 11, 1869. Congregation of Holy Cross Indiana Provincial Archives, Notre Dame University (hereafter HCPA).

20 *Ave Maria* 5 (1869), p. 648.

21 Joseph P. Chinnici, *Living Stones: The History and Structure of Catholic Spiritual Life in the United States* (New York: Macmillan, 1989), p. 64.

22 Ann Taves, *Household of Faith: Roman Catholic Devotions in Mid-Nineteenth-Century America* (Notre Dame, IN: Univ. of Notre Dame Press, 1986), p. viii. On the family as devotional model, see also Robert A. Orsi, *The Madonna of 115th Street: Faith and Community in Italian Harlem, 1880–1950* (New Haven and London: Yale Univ. Press, 1985), pp. 219–31; Kay Turner, "Mexican-American Women's Home Altars: The Art of Relationship," unpublished dissertation, University of Texas at Austin (1990), pp. 163–229.

23 Turner and Turner, p. 206.

24 *Ave Maria* 4 (1868), p. 732.

25 Ibid., p. 716.

26 *Ave Maria* 6 (1870), p. 138.

27 Ibid., p. 12.

28 "In 1870–71 an extension known as Lourdes Hall was added to the north of Music Hall and was used as the convent until 1889." *Our Provinces: Centenary Chronicles of the Sisters of the Holy Cross, 1841–1941*, vol. 5 (Notre Dame, IN: Saint Mary's of the Immaculate Conception, 1941), p. 8.

29 Kselman, pp. 118–25 and Pope, p. 187.

30 *Ave Maria* 8 (1872), p. 500.

31 Ibid., p. 516.

32 Philip A. Kemper to Alexis Granger, February 19, 1873.

33 *Ave Maria* 9 (1873), p. 425. Also

Edward Sorin to Alexis Granger, May 26, 1873 (HCPA): "In a few days I expect to receive a supply of water from Lourdes, all our letters relative to it had been lost or forgotten."

34 On shipping Lourdes water, see John A. McSorley to Edward Sorin, July 19, 1877; J. Daniel to unknown, July 12, 1878 (HCPA); John A. McSorley to Alexis Granger, February 13, 1889 (HCPA). For a discussion of the cost and amounts shipped, see John A. McSorley to Edward Sorin, November 19, 1881; John A. McSorley to Edward Sorin, June 2, 1880 (HCPA); John A. McSorley to Alexis Granger, May 23, 1889.

35 On donations to the church and prayers for McSorley's brother and infant daughter, see John A. McSorley to Alexis Granger, March 25, 1879 (HCPA). On death of eldest son, see John A. McSorley to Edward Sorin, November 19, 1881 (HCPA). For mention of statue and rose, see John A. McSorley to Edward Sorin, February 21, 1877 (HCPA).

36 *Ave Maria* 8 (1872) p. 8.

37 Because of the duplication of Irish names and the lack of addresses for many of the correspondents, I could not find useful census information. In the rare case that a letter writer could be identified, I include that information in the appropriate endnote citation.

38 Robert A. Orsi, "The Cult of the Saints and the Reimagination of the Space and Time of Sickness in Twentieth-Century American Catholicism," *Literature and Medicine* 8 (1989) pp. 63–77 at p. 70 and p. 75.

39 Mary Sullivan to Alexis Granger, August 22, 1873.

40 Elaine Scarry, *The Body in Pain* (New York: Oxford Univ. Press, 1985), p. 35.

41 Ibid., p. 16.

42 John Kirmane to Alexis Granger, February 7, 1874, and James Easley to Alexis Granger, February 19, 1877.

43 Harman Griese to Alexis Granger, April 28, 1873.

44 C. A. Korby to Alexis Granger, August 2, 1873. Korby was one of the few names that appeared in the 1880 (incomplete) census. It states he was born in Kentucky, was 38 years old, married to Mary Korby (age 33), and had four children (ages 10, 9, 7, 5).

45 John S. Haller, Jr., *American Medicine in Transition 1840–1910* (Urbana: Univ. of Illinois Press, 1981), p. 106. Haller writes that homeopathy was significant "in its faddish popularity among the upper classes, it also represented the last of the major medical systems to flourish before the onrush of extensive advances in germ theory, treatment of infection, pathology and pharmaco-therapeutics." Raymond J. Cunningham, "From Holiness to Healing: The Faith Cure in America, 1872–1892," *Church History* 43 (1974), pp. 499–513.

46 Susan E. Cayleff, *Wash and be Healed: The Water-Cure Movement and Women's Health* (Philadelphia: Temple Univ. Press, 1987), p. 5.

47 On water cures, see Kathryn Kish Sklar, "All Hail to Pure Cold Water!" in *Women and Health in America: Historical Readings*, ed. Judith Walzer Leavitt (Maidson: Univ. of Wisconsin Press, 1984), pp. 246–54 at p. 246, and Catherine L. Albanese, *Nature Religion in America* (Chicago: Univ. of Chicago Press, 1990), pp. 117–52.

48 Henry F. Maguire to Alexis Granger, n.d. 1879. (HCPA).

49 Cayleff, p. 12, and Haller, pp. 105–29.

50 Mary Garrigan to Alexis Granger, October 12, 1872.

51 C. A. Korby to Alexis Granger, August 2, 1873.

52 Gertrude Sevey to Alexis Granger, July 15, 1877. Mrs James Cody wrote to Granger on Feburary 28, 1878 that "the Little Sisters of the Poor made a novena and we gave him [her husband] some of the blessed water every day on the ninth day the doctor said the fever left him and he began to get better."

53 Rev. H. Delbaere to Alexis Granger, July 8, 1875.

54 B. B. Kelly to Alexis Granger, March 11, 1873.

55 Jos. V. A. Mukawtz [?], October 27, 1874.

56 Mich[ae]l White to Alexis Granger, n.d.

57 Orsi, "The Cult of the Saints," pp. 69–70.

58 John Nalsh to Alexis Granger, August 28, 1873.

59 B. B. Kelly to Alexis Granger, March 11, 1873.

60 Alice Kessler-Harris, *Out to Work: A History of Wage-Earning Women in the United States* (New York: Oxford Univ. Press, 1982), p. 148, and Stephen Thernstron, *Poverty and Progress: Social Mobility in a Nineteenth Century City* (Cambridge: Harvard Univ. Press, 1964), p. 93.

61 Martha Conaty to Alexis Granger, June 1, 1874.

62 Mrs. C. Lancaster to Alexis Granger, June 16, 1873.

63 Emma Gorman to Alexis Granger, June 30, 1873.

64 Michael McDonnell to Alexis Granger, November 17, 1873. Census information from 1870 says that McDonnell was 29, born in Ireland, had a wife Bridget (age 28), and four children (ages 5, 3, 2, and an infant).

65 Peter Brown, *The Cult of the Saints: Its Rise and Function in Latin Christianity* (Chicago: Univ. of Chicago Press, 1981), p. 89. During the Middle Ages, relics were not always freely given away; see Patrick J. Geary, *Furta Sacra: Thefts of Relics in the Central Middle Ages* (Princeton: Princeton Univ. Press, 1978).

66 Robert A. Orsi, "'He Keeps Me Going': Women's Devotion to Saint Jude Thaddeus and the Dialectics of Gender in American Catholicism, 1929–1965" in *Belief and History: Innovative Approaches to European and American Religion*, ed. Thomas Kselman (Notre Dame, IN: Univ. of Notre Dame Press, 1991), pp. 137–69 at p. 147. See also Orsi, "What Did Women Think They Were Doing When They Prayed to Saint Jude?," *U. S. Catholic Historian* 8 (1989), pp. 67–79.

67 John Healey (on behalf of Mary and James Dougherty) to Alexis Granger, July 23, 1873.

68 John M. Sullivan to Alexis Granger, November 29, 1873. According to the 1870 census, Sullivan was born in Ireland, he was 43, he had a wife Ellen (41), and one child (age 2, born in New York).

69 Rev. G. C. Thilban to Alexis Granger, March 7, 1875.

70 James McGeogh to Alexis Granger, May 25, 1873.

71 Patrick Early to Alexis Granger, n.d. September 1873. According to the 1870 census, Early was born in Ireland, was age 42, had a wife Mary (age 42), and four children (ages 15, 13, 10, 8).

72 John Nalsh to Alexis Granger, August 28, 1873.

73 Mark M. Foote to Alexis Granger, August 21, 1876 (HCPA).

74 John Kirmane to Alexis Granger, February 7, 1874.

75 A typical letter of the eight clergy or brothers is that of Rev. E. J. Brien to Alexis Granger, May 28, 1874: "The water has done great benefits to many in my parish by curing them when the doctors could do nothing for them."

76 Research on "feminized" religion has been research on Protestantism. See Ann Douglas, *The Feminization of American Culture* (New York: Knopf, 1977), and Barbara Welter, "The Feminization of American Religion: 1800–1860" in *Dimity Convictions* (Athens, OH: Ohio Univ. Press, 1976), pp. 83–102. On possible feminization in Catholicism, see Colleen McDannell, "Catholic Domesticity, 1860–1960" in Karen Kennelly, ed., *American Catholic Women: A Historical Exploration* (New York: Macmillan, 1989), pp. 48–80. On men's roles, see Colleen McDannell, "'True Men as We Need Them': Catholicism and the Irish-American Male," *American Studies* 27 (1986), pp. 19–35.

77 There have been no studies of why men participate in certain religious devotions and not in others. Michael Carroll in *The Cult of the Virgin Mary* analyzes the Marian traditions from a psychoanalytic viewpoint and concludes, "If, then, excessive Marian devotion on the part of males derives from a strong but strongly repressed sexual desire for the mother, then these same males should exhibit a masochistic need for punishment. In other words, we would expect to find an association between excessive Marian devotions and masochism. Though the evidence is sketchy, I think that evidence of such association does exist" (p. 62). He then goes on to link Marian devotions to what he calls the "father-ineffective family common in proletarian settings in southern Italy and Spain" (p. 73). That devotion to Our Lady of Lourdes is evidenced among American, Irish American, and German American men who were active in trying to relieve the suffering of their families tends to contradict Carroll's argument.

78 Louise Ifams to "Director of the

Confraternity," September 2, 1883 (HCPA). The letter is filed in the "letters to Sorin" file.

79 Edward N. Robinson to Alexis Granger, November 16, 1878 (HCPA).

80 Laurence Corcoran to Alexis Granger, May 6, 1879. Corcoran wrote: "Thomas Robinson, Ella Robinson and Elizabeth McLaughlin all Protestants, or non-Catholics rather, and esteemed friends of mine. The latter received a Catholic education but is married to a bigoted Protestant and has lost faith in Christianity altogether."

81 James Neil to Alexis Granger, December 17, 1879.

82 Sister Eusebia to Alexis Granger, May 7, 1873.

83 Sara Trainer Smith to Daniel Hudson (editor of *Ave Maria*), April 24, 1893.

84 David Freedberg, *The Power of Images: Studies in the History and Theory of Response* (Chicago: Univ. of Chicago Press, 1989), p. 157. See also Michael Carroll, *Madonnas That Maim: Popular Catholicism in Italy Since the Fifteenth Century* (Baltimore: The John Hopkins Univ. Press, 1992), pp. 82–7.

85 Freedberg, p. 153.

86 Catharine Cassidy to Alexis Granger, May 25, 1875.

87 Turner and Turner, *Image and Pilgrimage*, p. 205.

88 Sisters of the Holy Cross, *Our Mother House: Centenary Chronicles of the Sisters of the Holy Cross, 1841–1941* vol. 4 (Notre Dame, IN: Saint Mary's of the Immaculate Conception, 1941), p. 83.

89 s.v. "Santa Casa," *Catholic Encyclopedia* (1911), p. 455. In 1906 Canon Chevalier published a refutation of the authenticity of Sacra Casa which convinced the author of the encyclopaedia article, Herbert Thurston. While the chapel may not have been the Nazareth house, Thurston still accepted the possibility of the miraculous: "On the other hand, even if the Loreto tradition be rejected, there is no reason to doubt that the simple faith of those who in all confidence have sought help at this shrine of the Mother of God may often have been rewarded, even miraculously" (p. 455).

90 Edward Sorin to Archbishop

Purcell of Cincinnati, February 11, 1862: "For this chapel I obtained the indulgences of the famous sanctuary of Assisium and since, the Holy Father has been willing to declare it a regular pilgrimage of devotion to the B. V. Mary." See also, Edward Sorin, *Chronicles of Notre Dame du Lac*, trans. John M. Toohey, edited and annotated by James T. Connelly (Notre Dame, IN: Univ. of Notre Dame Press, 1992) p. 273f. I would like to thank Jaime Vidal for his help in understanding the Portiuncula Indulgence.

91 *Notre Dame Scholastic* 7 (August 30, 1873), p. 6.

92 *Notre Dame Scholastic*, 9 (October 2, 1875), p. 73, and (October 9, 1875), p. 91.

93 *Ave Maria* began to be published in a German translation in 1874 (vol. 10, p. 234) indicating that German Catholics, not only those near Notre Dame, were interested in Marian devotions.

94 Sorin and others discussed the first American pilgrimage to European sacred sites in *Ave Maria* 10 (1874), pp. 101–2; 235; 250; 347–8; 365–8; 424–6; and 458–60. Eventually 108 Americans left New York in May to visit Rome, Paris, Chartres, Lourdes, Loreto, and Assisi.

95 "There are already three miniature representations of the Grotto in the United States, one at the House of the Sisters of Notre Dame in St. Aloysius parish in Washington, D.C., one at the House of the Sisters of Charity at Yonkers, on the Hudson, and one at St. Mary's at Notre Dame, Ind." On October 13, 1877, the *Scholastic* included a story about St. Mary's shrines that indicates their grotto was a close replica to the one at Lourdes:

The entrance [to the grotto] is in the shape of a crooked arch; the rock sloping back from the entrance becomes narrower on either side; above, to the right is a niche-like orifice . . . in the niche is the statue [of the Immaculate Conception]. . . . Kneeling at the base of the rock is a life-size statue of Bernadette in peasant costume. . . . To the right of the altar, and nearer to the front, is a small receptacle to represent the fountain from which the miraculous water flows (p. 99f).

The *Scholastic* reported on August 22,

1878, that a visitor, Miss Mary Regina Jamison of Wheeling, West Virginia, "says the facsimile of the Grotto of Lourdes at St. Mary's Academy comes nearer the original than any that she has seen in either this country or in Europe" (p. 16).

96 *Notre Dame Scholastic* 11 (September 29, 1877), p. 75.

97 *Notre Dame Scholastic*, 30 (August 20, 1896), p. 14.

98 *Notre Dame Scholastic*, 13 (October 11, 1879), p. 90f.

99 *Notre Dame Scholastic*, 21 (August 27, 1887), p. 9.

100 William Corby to Thomas Carroll, June 8, 1896 (HCPA).

101 Born in Ireland in 1836, Carroll went to Notre Dame and was ordained a Holy Cross priest in 1856. Carroll served as a chaplain in the Union Army during the Civil War but left the Holy Cross Order in 1864 to join the staff at the Catholic cathedral in Cleveland, Ohio. In 1871 he became pastor of St. Joseph's Church in Oil City, Pennsylvania, where he remained until his death in 1898. Carroll evidently made some wise investments in the oil industry because at his death his real and personal property was valued at $177,000. The first person mentioned in his will was his "faithful friend" Susan Gallagher of Oil City to whom he left $20,000, approximately $5000 more than he left his sister. Money was also left to fund students from his native parish in Clougesh, County Longsford, to attend Maynooth Seminary. The $2000 which Carroll gave to Notre Dame two years before his death was an important contribution to the college but a small amount of his total wealth (Carroll file, University of Notre Dame Archives).

102 In order to promote devotion to Our Lady of Lourdes during the Marian year of 1953, the Department of Public Information of the university issued a press release about the grotto. Their text was a romantic account of the origin of the grotto that confused the construction of the first grotto with the second. On December 14, 1953, Joseph Maguire, C.S.C. sent a corrective to Notre Dame archivist Thomas McAvoy. At that time Maguire was the last person to have actually known Edward Sorin. Maguire explained that the grotto was not built in a "beautiful dell" but in the old dump and that the water did not mysteriously disappear but was stopped ("Grotto of Our Lady of Lourdes" file, University of Notre Dame Archives).

103   The Lourdes grotto continues to be an important site on the Notre Dame campus. In 1940 a plenary indulgence was granted to those who visited the shrine in a state of grace.

104   For examples of replica shrines built in the United States, see Walter Thomas Murphy, *Famous American Churches and Shrines* (Bloomfield Hills, MI: Walmur Publishing Co., 1968); Francis Beauchesne Thornton, *Catholic Shrines in the United States and Canada* (New York: W. Funk, 1954); and Thomas A. Kselman and Steven Avella, "Marian Piety and the Cold War in the United States," *Catholic Historical Review* 72 (1986), pp. 403–24.

105   Freedberg, p. 200.

106   Miles Orvell, *The Real Thing: Imitation and Authenticity in American Culture, 1880–1940* (Chapel Hill: The Univ. of North Carolina Press, 1989), p. 48.

107   Ibid., p. 55; xxiii.

6   Christian Kitsch and the Rhetoric of Bad Taste

1   Fred Orton and Griselda Pollock, "Avant-Gardes and Partisans Reviewed," in Francis Frascina, ed., *Pollock and After: The Critical Debate* (New York: Harper & Row, 1985), p. 169. On Greenberg, see T. J. Clark, "Clement Greenberg's Theory of Art," and "How Modernism Works: a Response to T. J. Clark," both in the same volume; Robert Storr, "No Joy in Mudville," in *Modern Art and Popular Culture*, ed. Mark Greenberg (New York: Museum of Modern Art, 1990), pp. 161–90; Saul Ostrow, "Avant-Garde and Kitsch, Fifty Years Later," *Arts Magazine* 64 (1989), pp. 56–7 and Joshua Decter, "The Greenberg Effect," same volume, pp. 58–9; Mark C. Taylor, *Disfiguring: Art, Architecture, Religion* (Chicago: Univ. of Chicago Press, 1992), pp. 165–8.

2   Clement Greenberg, "Avant-Garde and Kitsch," in Frascina, p. 24. All subsequent quotes from Greenberg come from "Avant-Garde and Kitsch," pp. 21–33.

3   The best discussion of the historical emergence of high and low culture is Lawrence W. Levine, *Highbrow/Lowbrow: The Emergence of Cultural Hierarchy in America* (Cambridge: Harvard Univ. Press, 1988).

4   See, for example, the essays in Hilde Hein and Carolyn Korsmeyer, eds., *Aesthetics in Feminist Perspective* (Bloomington: Indiana Univ. Press, 1993); Arthur Danto, *The Transfiguration of the Commonplace* (Princeton: Princeton Univ. Press, 1980); and George Dickie, *Evaluating Art* (Philadelphia: Temple Univ. Press, 1988).

5   Joan Wallach Scott, *Gender and the Politics of History* (New York: Columbia Univ. Press, 1988), p. 49.

6   Matei Calinescu, *Faces of Modernity: Avant-Garde Decadence Kitsch* (Bloomington: Indiana Univ. Press, 1977), p. 234. See also Harry Pross, "Die große Versöhnung: Kitsch als soziales Produkt," *Merkur: Deutsche Zeitschrift für europäisches Denken* 38 (1984), pp. 834–8.

7   Gilbert Highet, "Kitsch," in William Hammell, ed., *The Popular Arts in America* (New York: Harcourt Brace Jovanovich, Inc., 1977), p. 48.

8   Examples of the cultural approach are varied. The classic theoretical discussion is Herbert J. Gans, *Popular Culture and High Culture: Analysis and Evaluation of Taste* (New York: Basic Books, 1974). For specific examples of the approach in material culture studies, see Peter Lloyd Jones, *Taste Today: The Role of Appreciation in Consumerism and Design* (Oxford: Pergamon Press, 1991) and Mihaly Csikszentmihalyi and Eugene Rochberg-Halton, *The Meaning of Things: Domestic Symbols and the Self* (Cambridge: Cambridge Univ. Press, 1981); in "trivial" literature, Janice A. Radway, *Reading the Romance: Women, Patriarchy, and Popular Literature* (Chapel Hill: Univ. of North Carolina Press, 1984); in design, Thomas Hine, *Populuxe* (New York: Knopf, 1986); and in community studies, Dick Hebdige, *Subculture, The Meaning of Style* (London: Methuen, 1979).

9   Pierre Bourdieu, *Distinction: A Social Critique of the Judgement of Taste* trans. Richard Nice (Cambridge: Harvard Univ. Press, 1984), p. 7.

10   Jean Pirotte, "The Universe of Pious Objects," *Lumen Vitae* 41 (1986), p. 423.

11   Other examples of the aesthetic approach include Matei Calinescu's writings, especially "Modernity and Popular Culture: Kitsch as Aesthetic Deception," in *Sensus Communis*, ed. János Riesz, *et al.* (Tübingen: Günter Narr, 1986), pp. 221–6; Abraham Moles, *Le Kitsch: l'art du bonheur* (Paris: Mame, 1971); Jochen Schulte-Sasse, *Literarische Wertung*, 2nd edn. (Stuttgart: Metzler, 1976); and most of the discussion in "On Kitsch: A Symposium," *Salmagundi* No. 85–6 (1990), pp. 198–312.

12   Stuart Ewen, *All Consuming Images: The Politics of Style in Contemporary Culture* (New York: Basic Books, 1988), p. 64.

13   Greenberg, p. 25.

14   Ibid., p. 26.

15   Hermann Broch, "Evil in the Value System of Art," in Gillo Dorfles, ed., *Kitsch: The World of Bad Taste* (New York: Bell Pub. Co., 1968), p. 76.

16   Other ethical responses include Richard Egenter, *The Desecration of Christ* trans. Edward Quinn (Chicago: Franciscan Herald Press, 1967) originally published as *Kitsch und Christenleben* (1950); the essays in Dorfles, *Kitsch*; and Ludwig Giesz, *Phänomenologie des Kitsches* 2nd edn. (Münich: Wilhelm Fink Verlag, 1971).

17   Immanuel Kant, *Critique of Judgment* trans. Werner S. Pluhar (Indianapolis: Hackett Pub. Co., 1987).

18   James Lindsay, "Theology and Art," *Bibliotheca Sacra* 62 (1905), pp. 476; 479.

19   Kant actually separated the morally good from the judgment of taste. See Jane Kneller, "Discipline and Silence: Women and Imagination in Kant's Theory of Taste," in Hein and Korsmeyer. On the development of the morality of art in the nineteenth century, see David Watkin, *Morality and Architecture* (Chicago: Univ. of Chicago Press, 1977), pp. 17–31.

20   Broch, "Evil in the Value System of Art," p. 76.

21   Broch, "Notes on the Problem of Kitsch," in Dorfles, *Kitsch*, p. 63.

22   Avishai Margalit, "The Kitsch of Israel," *New York Review of Books* 35 (November 24, 1988), pp. 20–4.

23   Yve-Alain Bois, "Fontana's Base Materialism," *Art in America* (April 1989), p. 241. Also see Eva

Sperling Cockcroft, "Kitsch in Cuba," *Art Forum* 23 (1985), pp. 772–3; John P. Sisk, "Art, Kitsch & Politics," *Design for Art in Education* (Sept./Oct. 1988), pp. 11–16; and Ellen Lee Klein, "Toby Buonagurio: More Optical Bounce to the Ounce," *Arts Magazine* 60 (1986), pp. 55–7. On the transformation of kitsch into camp, see Susan Sontag, "Notes on 'Camp'" in *Against Interpretation and Other Essays* (New York: Octagon Books, 1978), pp. 275–92.

24   "A Concept, A Picture, A Sculpture, A Lawsuit," *New York Times*, September 20, 1991. On Jeff Koons, see Roberta Smith, "Rituals of Consumption," *Art in America* (1988), pp. 164–71 and "Jeff Koons," *Art News* (February 1989), p. 139.

25   Pirotte, p. 421 quoting *Assemblée générale des catholiques en Belgique. Première session à Malines* (Brussels, 1864), p. 121.

26   Claude Savart, "A la Recherche de l' 'art' dit de Saint-Sulpice," *Revue d'Histoire de la Spiritualité* 52 (1976), p. 269. While *l'art Saint-Sulpice* is what Catholics saw in their churches for over one hundred years, almost no historical research has been done on its origins, development, or impact. Polemical pieces condemning the art appeared in French Catholic art magazines: "Soldes a Saint-Sulpice," *L'Art d'Eglise* 22 (1954), p. 268; "La Réprobation de 'Saint-Sulpice'" *L'Art Sacré* (May– June 1952); and "Deux Mondes," *L'Art Sacré* (Sept–Oct. 1953), pp. 7–12. A theological discussion is Alain Vircondelet, "La Dérive du Sacré dans l'Imagerie Saint-Sulpicienne," *Revue de l'Institute Catholique de Paris* 30 (1989), pp. 57–72. French scholars have been more interested in the evolution of holy cards. See Catherine Rosenbaum-Dondaine, "L'Imagerie de Piété du XIXe siècle au Département des Estampes de la Bibliothèque Nationale," in *L'Image de Piété en France, 1814–1914* (Paris: Musée-Galerie de la Seita, 1984) and Alain Vircondelet, *Le Monde Merveilleux de Images Pieuses* (Paris: Editions Hermé, 1988). For a journalistic description of turn-of-the-century production, see Thiébault-Sisson, "Les Paradis," *L'illustration* 104 (1894), pp. 526–9.

27   David Freedberg, "Verisimilitude and Resemblance: From Sacred Mountain to Waxworks," *The Power of Images* (Chicago: Univ. of Chicago Press, 1989), pp. 192–245.

28   On the impact that mass-produced European lithographs had on indigenous New Mexican, Mexican, and Puerto Rican arts, see Yvonne Lange, "Lithography, an Agent of Technological Change in Religious Folk Art: a Thesis," *Western Folklore* 33 (1974), pp. 51–64. Devotional prints also influenced European folk arts such as glass painting, see Helena Waddy Lepovitz, "Paintings for the *Herrgottswinkel*: The Popular Market in Religious Art," in *Images of Faith: Expressionism, Catholic Folk Art, and the Industrial Revolution* (Athens: Univ. of Georgia Press, 1991), pp. 93–115.

29   John Tebbel, *A History of Book Publishing in the United States* vol. 3 (New York: R. R. Bowker Company, 1978), pp. 241 and 243.

30   John A. McSorley to Edward Sorin, March 17, 1883, Holy Cross Provincial Archives, Notre Dame University.

31   Irish American Catholicism has been portrayed as not stressing liturgical aesthetics. The question of taste notwithstanding, the Irish did produce highly decorative churches. See my article, "'Going to the Ladies' Fair: New York Irish Catholics" in Ronald Baylor and Timothy Meagher, eds., *The New York Irish* (Baltimore: The Johns Hopkins Univ. Press, forthcoming).

32   Cyril Barrett, "Art and the Council," *Council* 31 (1964), p. 15.

33   "Mediator Dei" (On the Sacred Liturgy) reprinted in James J. Megivern, *Worship & Liturgy* (Wilmington, NC: McGrath, 1978), p. 124 (sec. B. No. 195).

34   "Instructions to Ordinaries on Sacred Art," No. 51 from Sacred Congregation of the Holy Office, June 30, 1952.

35   Kilan McDonnell, "Art and the Sacramental Principle," *Liturgical Arts* 25 (1957), p. 92.

36   Richard Charles Muehlberger, "Sacred Art – A Critique on the Contemporary Situation," *Liturgical Arts* 28 (1960), p. 69.

37   The original church was built in 1911. Father Henry Fehrenbacher, who was pastor between 1953 and 1960, renovated the church and built a new rectory. It is unclear when the church was actually altered, the "before and after" pictures were published in November 1957 in *Liturgical Arts*. The rectory cost a pricey $22,000 in 1954 and eventually had to be rebuilt because its flat roofs and shingles could not take the Minnesota snow. Remembered as "way ahead of his time," Fehrenbacher eventually left for the East coast where he contributed essays to Catholic newspapers. In 1964 Father Maurice Landwehr became pastor and decided to build an entirely new church. The old church was moved to another part of town and became a warehouse. In the new church, built sometime between 1964 and 1967, the statue of St. Donatus was painted white and placed at the back of the church. None of the other statues, including the folk-style Virgin Mary, survived. I would like to thank Marcie Reimer and Sister Mary Weidner of St. Donatus parish for their help in reconstructing this history.

38   Anton Henze and Theodor Filhaut, *Contemporary Church Art*, trans. Cecily Hastings (New York: Sheed and Ward, 1956), p. 48. For a concise summary of the history of the Catholic liturgical movement, see the Sacerdotal Communities of Saint-Severin of Paris and Saint-Joseph of Nice, *The Liturgical Movement* (New York: Hawthorn Books, 1964), pp. 9–48. Pages 86–120 discuss how changes in the 1950s and 1960s affected the Divine Office and the sacraments. On art, see Susan White, *Art, Architecture and Liturgical Reform* (New York: Pueblo Publishing Co., 1990).

39   John Julian Ryan, "Toward a Sound Religious Art," *Catholic World* 187 (1958), p. 11.

40   Virginia Cookston, "Sentiment Versus Simplicity in Catholic Art," *Catholic World* 181 (1955), p. 100.

41   Charles Blakeman, "The Problem of Church Art," *Clergy Review* 48 (1955), p. 27.

42   Adolf Loos, "Ornament and Crime," in Ludwig Münz and Gustav Künstler, eds., *Adolf Loos: Pioneer of Modern Architecture* (London: Thames & Hudson, 1966), p. 231.

43   Jean Charlot, "Catholic Art in America: Debits and Credits," *Liturgical Arts* 27 (1958), p. 21.

44   St. Francis de Sales Church,

Liturgical Arts Society Collection, Notre Dame University Archives.

45   Cookston, p. 101.

46   Harriet Rex Smith, "Let's Not Call it Art at All," *Catholic World* 166 (1948), p. 349.

47   Anthony Durand, "'Church-Good' Statues and Good Church Statues," *American Ecclesiastical Review* 124 (1951), p. 192.

48   Michael Paul Driskel, *Representing Belief: Religion, Art, and Society in Nineteenth-Century France* (University Park: Pennsylvania State Univ. Press, 1992), p. 5.

49   "Extremes and the Mean," *Catholic Art Quarterly* 22 (1958), p. 11.

50   Thomas Merton, "Seven Qualities of the Sacred," *Good Work* 27 (1964), p. 15.

51   Cookston, p. 102.

52   See Judith Stoughton, *Proud Donkey of Schaerbeek: Ade Bethune, Catholic Worker Artist* (St. Cloud, MN: North Star Press, 1988).

53   Dorothy E. Smith, *Texts, Facts, and Femininity: Exploring the Relations of Ruling* (London: Routledge, 1990), p. 175.

54   Freedberg, p. 322f.

55   E. M. Catich, "Sentimentality in Christian Art," *The Furrow* 10 (1959), p. 514.

56   Smith, p. 350.

57   J. P. Kenny, "Towards an Esthetic of Sacred Art: Four Canons," *Liturgical Arts* 35 (1967), p. 147.

58   Daniel Berrigan, "The New Spirit of Modern Sacred Art," *The Critic* 20 (1961–2), p. 30.

59   Andreas Huyssen, *After the Great Divide: Modernism, Mass Culture, Postmodernism* (Bloomington: Indiana Univ. Press, 1986), pp. 44–62.

60   Roland Marchand, *Advertising the American Dream* (Berkeley: Univ. of California Press, 1985), p. 69.

61   Daniel Berrigan, "The Catholic Dream World and the Sacred Image," *Worship* 35 (1960–61), p. 549.

62   John Lyon, "Of Plaster Statues and Romantic Heresy," *Commonweal* 110 (1983), p. 172. The fear that the kitsch Christ is not merely feminized but actually presents Christ as a homosexual also occurred to Protestants. In two letters (No. 2 and No. 331) that were sent to David Morgan concerning Sallman's *Head of Christ*, writers voiced such fears. French artists Pierre and Gilles have claimed the effeminate

and masochistic Christ and the saints rejected by modern Christians and have transformed them into camp icons popular in gay culture. Bleeding Sacred Hearts and tearful saints are sold in photographic picture books and mailed as postcards. See *Pierre et Gilles* (Köln: Benedict Taschen, 1993). I would like to thank Jean-François Kerneis for bringing these artists to my attention.

63   Greenberg, p. 25.

64   Storr, p. 162.

65   Graham Carey, "Lo! The Poor Indian . . .," *Catholic Art Quarterly* 17 (1954), p. 48.

66   Daniel Berrigan, "The New Spirit of Modern Sacred Art," *The Critic* 20 (1961–2), p. 30.

67   Graham Carey, "Figures of the Sacred Heart," *Catholic Art Quarterly* 15 (1951), p. 5.

68   John Domin to Maurice Lavanoux, February 8, 1958. Correspondence between Holy Family Parish and Maurice Lavanoux is located at Notre Dame University Archives, Liturgical Arts Society Collection.

69   Ibid.

70   Donald Conger to Maurice Lavanoux, July 26, 1958.

71   John Domin to Maurice Lavanoux, March 17, 1958.

72   Steven M. Lanza, "Why I Started Saying the Rosary Again," *U. S. Catholic* 45 (1980), p. 31.

73   Valentine Long, "The Rosary," *Homiletic and Pastoral Review* 88 (1988), p. 20.

74   Walter Halberstadt, "How to Make the Rosary a Family Affair," *Liguorian* 69 (1981), p. 11.

75   John R. Servis, "A Protestant Prays With Mary," *Liguorian* 73 (1985), pp. 24–6.

76   Lanza, p. 31f.

77   Edmund Burke, *A Philosophical Enquiry into the Origins of our Ideas of the Sublime and the Beautiful* ed. with introduction by James T. Boulton (Oxford: Basil Blackwell, 1987) and Immanuel Kant, *Observations on the Feeling of the Beautiful and the Sublime* trans. John T. Goldthwait (Berkeley: Univ. of California Press, 1960).

78   Kant, p. 47.

79   Burke, p. 115.

80   Naomi Schor, *Reading in Detail: Aesthetics and the Feminine* (New York: Methuen, 1987), p. 22. Sir

Joshua Reynolds (1723–92) is perhaps better known for his portrait painting although his lectures to the Royal Academy published as *Discourses on Art* are recognized "as one of the most considerable and representative bodies of Academic aesthetics produced in Europe in the latter half of the eighteenth century (Schor, p. 11). An example of a nineteenth-century author attributing feminine decadence to post-Renaissance painters is Jules Michelet who "assaulted" Guido Reni's *Annunciation* as being agreeable, delicate, pretty, gracious, and seductive. Michael Driskel, *Representing Belief*, p. 141.

81   Rudolph M. Binder, "Art, Religion, and the Emotions," *American Journal of Theology* 8 (1904), p. 643.

82   Ibid., p. 644.

83   Paul Tillich, as quoted in Sydney and Beatrice Rome, eds., *Philosophical Interrogations* (New York: Holt, Rhinehart & Winston, 1964), p. 407 reprinted in Paul Tillich, *On Art and Architecture*, ed. John Dillenberger; trans. Robert P. Scharlemann (New York: Crossroad, 1987), p. 132f. See also Kelton Cobb, 'Reconsidering the Status of Popular Culture in Tillich's Theology of Culture,' *Journal of the American Academy of Religion* LXIII (1995), pp. 53–8.

84   Paul Tillich, "Contemporary Visual Arts and the Revelatory Character of Style," (1958) in *On Art and Architecture*, p. 131.

85   Paul Tillich, *The Courage to Be* (New Haven and London: Yale Univ. Press, 1952), p. 147f.

86   Paul Tillich, "Authentic Religious Art" (1954) in *On Art and Architecture*, p. 233. For a fuller discussion of Tillich's place in the Protestant discussion of art and kitsch, see Sally M. Promey, "Interchangeable Art: Warner Sallman and the Critics of Mass Culture," a paper presented at the symposium, "Icons of American Protestantism: The Art of Warner Sallman," held at the University of Chicago, March 4, 1994.

87   Robert Paul Roth, "Christ and the Muses," *Christianity Today* (March 3, 1958), p. 8.

88   Frank E. Gaebelein, "The Aesthetic Problem: Some Evangelical Answers," *Christianity Today* 9 (1965), p. 543.

89   Ibid., p. 544.

90 Muehlberger, p. 71.

91 Clarence Simpson, "Or Why Evangelicals Have Failed the Arts," *Eternity* 14 (1963), pp. 10–11, 28–31.

92 Clyde S. Kilby, "The Artistic Poverty of Evangelicalism," *Eternity* 16 (1965), p. 17.

93 Roth, p. 9.

94 Rene Frank, "The Christian and the Arts," *Christianity Today* 7 (1963), p. 25.

95 This story was first published in 1943 in an interview with Sallman; see T. Otto Nall, "He Preaches As He Paints," *Classmate* 50 (December 1943), p. 7. Another version was cited by Sylvia E. Peterson, "The Ministry of Christian Art," *Lutheran Companion* 55 (April 2, 1947), p. 11 and Dorothy Haskin, "The Man Who Painted a Manly Head of Christ," *Contact* (February 1, 1959), p. 1 reprinted in Dorothy Haskin, *Christians You Would Like to Know* (Grand Rapids, MI: Zondervan, 1954).

96 For instance, in their advertisements in *Our Home* (Sept. 1947), end page.

97 Gail Bederman, "'The Women Have Had Charge of the Church Work Long Enough': The Men and Religion Forward Movement of 1911–1912 and the Masculinization of Middle-class Protestantism," *American Quarterly* 41 (1989), pp. 432–65; Margaret Lamberts Bendroth, *Fundamentalism and Gender* (New Haven and London: Yale Univ. Press, 1993), pp. 64–8. Bruce Barton, *The Man Nobody Knows: A Discovery of the Real Jesus* (Indianapolis: Bobbs-Merrill, 1925). On Barton, see T. J. Jackson Lears, "From Salvation to Self-Realization," in *Culture of Consumption* (New York: Pantheon Books, 1983), pp. 29–37.

98 The revisions to this portrait are at Anderson College with the Warner E. Sallman collection. The words "too feminine" are written on a plastic over-lay on a Sallman drawing.

99 Steven Moser, "Alumnus," *Ricks College Summit Magazine* (Spring 1993), p. 8.

100 J. M. Cameron, "Christian Kitsch," *New York Review of Books*, May 29, 1986, p. 56.

101 Carol H. Cantrell, "Analogy as Destiny: Cartesian Man and Woman Reader," in Hein and Korsmeyer, p. 218.

102 Sherry B. Ortner, "Is Female to Male as Nature is to Culture?," in Michelle Zimbalist Rosaldo and Louise Lamphere, eds., *Woman, Culture, and Society* (Stanford: Stanford Univ. Press, 1974), p. 72.

103 Michelle Zimbalist Rosaldo, "A Theoretical Overview," in ibid., p. 19.

104 Marjorie Garber, *Vested Interests: Cross-Dressing and Cultural Anxiety* (New York: Routledge, 1992), p. 210.

105 Ibid., p. 213.

106 Garber cites Saints Pelagia, Eugenia, Anna, and Wilgefortis as women who dressed as men and who were eventually canonized (pp. 213–17).

107 The discussion of the male role in American religions is only beginning to be explored. See Mark Carnes, *Secret Ritual and Manhood in Victorian America* (New Haven and London: Yale Univ. Press, 1989); Janet Forsythe Fishburn, *The Fatherhood of God and the Victorian Family* (Philadelphia: Fortress, 1981); Colleen McDannell, "True Men as We Need Them: Catholicism and the Irish Male," *American Studies* 27 (1986), pp. 19–36; and Leslie Woodcock Tentler, "Priest and People: Revisiting the History of the Parish Clergy," unpublished paper given at Princeton University, June 18, 1994. An evocative description of a contemporary African-American minister's attempt to strengthen male participation in his church and community is Samuel G. Freedman, *Upon This Rock: The Miracles of a Black Church* (New York: HarperCollins, 1993).

108 It is not a coincidence that Mary J. Oates's article on "Catholic Laywomen in the Labor Force" spans the years 1850 to 1950, in *American Catholic Women*, ed. Karen Kennelly (New York: Macmillan, 1989), pp. 81–124. Paula Kane in *Separatism and Subculture: Boston Catholicism, 1900–1920* (Chapel Hill: Univ. of North Carolina Press, 1994), pp. 244–8 indicates that attacks on working women in Boston began in the early twentieth century. Examples of magazine stories that extolled home and family above a woman's outside employment include: Florence Christian, "Dinner at Joe's," *Ave Maria Catholic Home Weekly* 77 (1953), pp.

52–6; Anna-Margaret Record, "Working Mothers – Elsewhere and at Home," *Ave Maria Catholic Home Weekly* 82 (1955), pp. 12–14; and Kay Sullivan, "From Suburbs to Saints: Phyllis McGinley," *Catholic World* 185 (1957), pp. 420–25.

109 The transformation of the role of the father in liberal Protestantism has not been fully explored; for an introduction, see Colleen McDannell, "Parlor Piety: The Home as a Sacred Space in Protestant America," in *American Home Life, 1880–1930* ed. Jessica Foy and Thomas J. Schlereth (Knoxville: Univ. of Tennessee Press, 1992), pp. 176–80.

110 On conservative Christianity in the postwar years, see David Harrington Watt, *A Transforming Faith: Explorations of Twentieth-Century American Evangelicalism* (New Brunswick: Rutgers Univ. Press, 1991), pp. 93–136 for a discussion of women's issues. See also Bendroth, *Fundamentalism and Gender* and Betty A. DeBerg, *Ungodly Women: Gender and the First Wave of American Fundamentalism* (Minneapolis: Fortress Press, 1990). For examples of conservative Protestant women preachers, see Edith Waldvogel Blumhofer, *Aimee Semple McPherson: Everybody's Sister* (Grand Rapids, MI: Eerdmans, 1993); Susie Cunningham Stanley, *Feminist Pillar of Fire: The Life of Alma White* (Cleveland: The Pilgrim Press, 1993); Elaine J. Lawless, *Handmaidens of the Lord: Pentecostal Women Preachers and Traditional Religion* (Philadelphia: Univ. of Pennsylvania Press, 1988); and Charles H. Barfoot and Gerald T. Sheppard, "Prophetic vs. Priestly Religion: The Changing Role of Women Clergy in Classical Pentecostal Churches," *Review of Religious Research* 22 (1980), pp. 2–17. On reasons why women are attracted to conservative churches, see Nancy Tatom Ammerman, *Bible Believers: Fundamentalism in the Modern World* (New Brunswick: Rutgers Univ. Press, 1987), pp. 134–46; Lesley Gill, "'Like a Veil to Cover Them': Women and the Pentecostal Movement in La Paz," *American Ethnologist* 17 (1990), pp. 708–21.

111 Bourdieu, p. 13.

112 In contrast with this conclusion, David Morgan argues for a theological explanation for the gendered rhetoric of discourse on Warner Sallman's art in "'Would Jesus have sat for a portrait?' The Likeness of Christ in the Popular Reception of Sallman's Art," a paper presented at the symposium, "Icons of American Protestantism: The Art of Warner Sallman" held at the University of Chicago, March 4, 1994.

7 Mormon Garments: Sacred Clothing and the Body

1   SX, 45 (FW). See note 8 for explanation of interviewing procedures.

2   Rodney Stark, "Modernization and Mormon Growth: The Secularization Thesis Revisited," in *Contemporary Mormonism: Social Science Perspectives* eds. Marie Cornwall, Tim B. Heaton, and Lawrence A. Young (Urbana: University of Illinois Press, 1994), p. 1.

3   Such exposés are numerous and include: Mrs G. S. R., *Mysteries of the Endowment House* (n.p., 188?); John C. Bennett, *The History of the Saints; or an Exposé of Joe Smith and Mormonism* (Boston: Leland & Whiting, 1842); Increase McGee and Maria Van Dusen, *The Mormon Endowment; A Secret Drama, or Conspiracy, in the Nauvoo Temple, in 1846* (Syracuse, NY: N. M. D. Lathrop, 1847); William Jarman, *Uncle Sam's Abscess, or Hell Upon Earth* (Exeter, England: Leduc's Steam Printing Works, 1884); J. H. Beadle, *Life in Utah; or, the Mysteries and Crimes of Mormonism* (Philadelphia: National Pub. Co., 1870); Stuart Martin, *The Mysteries of Mormonism* (London: Odhams Press Ltd., 1920); n.a., *Temple Mormonism: Its Evolution, Ritual and Meaning* (New York: A. J. Montgomery, 1931); Andrew Husberg, "Temple Garments" (1936, typescript, Utah State Historical Society); John L. Smith, *I Visited the Temple* (Little Rock, AK: Challenge Press, 1966) reprinted with other anti-Mormon texts in J. Gordon Melton, ed., *Cults and New Religions* (New York: Garland Publishing, 1990); Max B. Skousen, "The Temple Endowment" (1971 typescript, Utah State Historical Society); Jerald and Sandra Tanner, *The Changing World of Mormonism* (Chicago: Moody Press, 1980), esp. pp. 524–9 and *Evolution of the Mormon Temple Ceremony: 1842–1990* (Salt Lake City: Utah Lighthouse Ministry, 1990).

4   Deborah Laake, *Sacred Ceremonies: A Mormon Woman's Intimate Diary of Marriage and Beyond* (New York: William Morrow and Co., 1993). Kenneth L. Woodward with Jeanne Gordon, "The Latter-day Secret Sharer," *Newsweek* (June 28, 1993), p. 59.

5   On the question of how history should or should not be written by believers, see George D. Smith, ed., *Faithful History: Essays on Writing Mormon History* (Salt Lake City: Signature Books, 1992) and Leonard J. Arrington, "The Search for Truth and Meaning in Mormon History," in *The New Mormon History: Revisionist Essays on the Past* ed. D. Michael Quinn (Salt Lake City: Signature Books, 1992).

6   In the early 1980s, Mormon leaders began their recent harassment of Latter-day Saints who published controversial historical or theological views. Plural marriages, God the Mother, women in the priesthood, and ecclesiastical authority were the topics most apt to be censored. In 1988 D. Michael Quinn, a Mormon historian, resigned from his position at Brigham Young University, accusing the institution of failing to support academic freedom. Three years later in 1991, the First Presidency condemned attendance at Sunstone Symposia (see note 117). At an All-Church Coordinating Council Meeting in May 1993 Boyd K. Packer warned members of the church against being dangerously "caught up and led away" by intellectuals, feminists, and homosexuals. During the fall of 1993 and winter of 1994 Paul Toscano, Lynne Whitesides, Maxine Hanks, Michael Quinn, David Wright, Michael Barrett, and Lavina Fielding Anderson – all well-known historians and theologians – were brought to church trials and either disfellowshiped or excommunicated. Margaret Toscano was asked to cease publishing her ideas. That same year of 1993 David Knowlton and Cecilia Conchar Farr were dismissed from their faculty positions at Brigham Young University because of their controversial writings and activities. In 1995 theologian Janice Allred was excommunicated. Lavina Fielding Anderson, "The LDS Intellectual Community and Church Leadership: A Contemporary Chronology," *Dialogue: A Journal of Mormon Thought* 26 (Sprint, 1993), pp. 7–64 and George D. Smith, *Religion, Feminism, and Freedom of Conscience* (Salt Lake City: Signature Books, 1994).

7   The most complete discussion by a church authority is Boyd K. Packer, *The Holy Temple* (Salt Lake City: Bookcraft, 1980). For other in-house views, see John K. Edmunds, *Through Temple Doors* (Salt Lake City: Bookcraft, 1978); N.B. Lundwall, *Temples of the Most High* (Salt Lake City: Bookcraft, various editions) and the entry in the *Encyclopedia of Mormonism* (New York: Macmillan, 1992). For scholarly accounts, see Carol Cornwall Madsen, "Mormon Women and the Temple: Toward a New Understanding," in Maureen Ursenbach Beecher and Lavina Fielding Anderson, eds., *Sisters in Spirit: Mormon Women in Historical and Cultural Perspective* (Urbana: Univ. of Illinois Press, 1987) and Mark P. Leone, "The Mormon Temple Experience," *Sunstone* 10 (1985), pp. 4–7.

8   The interviews were conducted between 1991 and 1992. We located people we thought would speak about garments through friends and the Sunstone Foundation. Each interview lasted approximately two hours. While we had a set of questions to ask and topics to raise, we often followed the lead given by those interviewed. We interviewed seventeen men and twenty women who ranged in age from 24 to 73. The average age was 40. Twenty-four of those interviewed were married, eleven were single, one was widowed, and one was divorced. Of those married, all but two had children. The smallest family had two children, the largest six. Most families had at least three children. All those we talked with were white and middle-class. Six were converts (three from the Episcopal church, one Lutheran, and one Catholic). Twenty-two told us that they wear their garments all the time. The average amount of time that full-time wearers wore their garments was twenty years. Five said they wear their garments on and off. The average amount of time that garments were worn by mixed-wearers was eighteen years. Nine no longer wear garments.

The average amount of time that they wore their garments before stopping was eight years. One woman had not yet received her endowment and so does not wear garments.

Interviews are cited by coded initials, age, and if the garments are worn full time (FW), mixed (MW), or currently not worn at all (NW). An approximation of how long a person has worn the garment can be ascertained by subtracting 20 from the age.

9 Because the endowment rituals are considered too sacred to discuss, scholarship on the evolution of the ceremonies is limited; see David John Buerger, "The Development of the Mormon Temple Endowment Ceremony," *Dialogue: A Journal of Mormon Thought* 20 (1987), pp. 33–76 and the sources on the temple in note 7.

10 Brigham Young, *Journal of Discourses* 2:31.

11 John Hyde, *Mormonism: Its Leaders and Designs* (New York: W. D. Fetridge & Company, 1857), p. 92 recalling an 1854 endowment ceremony in the Council House in Salt Lake City.

12 Benjamin F. LeBaron, "How We Obtained Our Garments," 1940 typescript, Church of Jesus Christ of Latter-day Saints Historical Department Archives, Salt Lake City, (hereafter cited as LDS Archives or LDS Library). A similar statement is published in "Autobiography of Benjamin Franklin LeBaron," pp. 1–3, 1946 typescript, Brigham Young University Library Archives (hereafter cited as BYU Archives).

13 John C. Bennet, *The History of the Saints: or An Exposé of Joe Smith and Mormonism* (Boston: Leland & Whiting, 1842), p. 277. This exposé is probably the earliest description of the temple "garments" and was published before the December 10, 1845 endowments. The text reads:

One of the most curious and ludicrous ceremonies, connected with the initiation into Order Lodge, is this: After the precious ointment has been poured upon the candidate, a hole is cut in the bosom of his shirt. This shirt must never, on any account, be worn again, but must be sacredly preserved, to keep the Destroying Angel from them and their families. The shirts are committed to the care of the wives of the members, and none but them must touch them, or know of their existence. They believe that these shirts will preserve them from death, and secure them an earthly immortality; but Bishop Vinson Knight, one of the members, has recently died, so that it is evident the hole in his shirt could not save him. Joe will probably; however, say that a spiritual immortality only was promised.

The 1846 ritual was summarized in Increase McGee Van Dusen and Maria Van Duseun, *Startling Disclosures of the Wonderful Ceremonies of the Mormon Spiritual-Wife System . . .* (NY: np, 1852), np.

Another account of early garments from the 1870s explained that "the 'garment' had cuts, worked around in button-hole stitch, a right angle on the right breast, a heart on the left breast, a straight line at the navel, and a straight line at the right knee. The significance of these symbols I do not remember." David Sylvester Tuttle, *Missionary to the Mountain West, Reminiscence of Bishop Daniel S. Tuttle* (Salt Lake City: Univ. of Utah Press, 1987), p. 316.

14 This early account does not mention the sash worn in contemporary endowment rituals and "socks" are no longer a part of temple clothing. George D. Smith, ed., *An Intimate Chronicle: The Journals of William Clayton* (Salt Lake City: Signature Books, 1991), p. 243 (December 30, 1845) and p. 212 (December 14, 1845). Heber C. Kimball, an early Mormon leader, began keeping a journal of the activities of the Nauvoo, Illinois, temple on November 21, 1845. Because he was not a learned man and writing was difficult for him, he turned this record over to William Clayton on December 10. Clayton frequently functioned as scribe for the early community. Clayton kept this record until January 7, 1846. It is this portion of the Clayton journal, "Journal 3, Nauvoo Temple," 1845–6, which contains early descriptions of the endowment ceremony that is cited here. On the relationship between Kimball and Clayton, see Stanley B. Kimball, *On The Potter's Wheel: The Diaries of Heber C. Kimball* (Salt Lake City: Signature Books, 1987), pp. xiii–xiv; and Smith, *An Intimate Chronicle*, p. 199. On Kimball's role in temple work, see Stanley B. Kimball,

"The Nauvoo Years," *Brigham Young University Studies*, vol. 14, no. 4 (Summer 1975), p. 276.

15 Smith, *Journals of William Clayton*, p. 217 (December 16, 1845).

16 Ibid., p. 237 (December 27, 1845).

17 Ibid., p. 219 (December 18, 1845).

18 Ibid., p. 212 (December 14, 1845).

19 Ibid., p. 234 (December 26, 1845). Five days earlier, on December 21, Kimball himself evidently also told people to stop making their garments in the temple: "We dont [*sic*] want you to come here and take up the time to cut your garments. Go to a good faithful sister, and secrete yourself, and make your garments. We have been crowded too much and we have got to stop it. And if you have cloth, and come here to get your cloth cut, we shall keep it here to make use of till we get through." Smith, *Journals of William Clayton*, p. 228.

20 The complete text reads:

It was while they were living in Nauvoo that the Prophet came to my grandmother, who was a seamstress by trade, and told her that he had seen the angel Moroni with the garments on, and asked her to assist him in cutting out the garment. They spread unbleached muslin out on the table and he told her how to cut it out. She had to cut the third pair, however, before he said it was satisfactory. She told the Prophet that there would be sufficient cloth from the knee to the ankle to make a pair of sleeves, but he told her he wanted as few seams as possible and that there would be sufficient whole cloth to cut the sleeves without piecing. The first garments were made out of unbleached muslin and bound with turkey red and were without collars. Later on the Prophet decided he would rather have them bound with white. Sister Emma Smith, the Prophet's wife, proposed that they have a collar on as she thought they would look more finished, but at first the Prophet did not have the collars on them. After Emma Smith had made the little collars, which were not visible from the outside, then Eliza R. Snow introduced a wider collar of finer material to be worn on the outside of the dress. The garment was to reach to the ankle and the sleeves to the wrist. The marks were always the same.

This text was found in the LDS Archives and was marked: "Early Pioneer History, related by Eliza M. A. Munson. [Note: Practically all of this information was taken from a diary which was kept by James T. S. Allred, father of Mrs Munson]" However, at the top of the document in green pencil is the note: "This article is not to be accepted as authentic JFB." I have not been able to locate any copy of "Early Pioneer History," James Allred's diary, neither do I know who JFB is. For a similar summary, see Elizabeth Elmira Allred Aiken, "Brief Sketch of James Allred" in "Biographical Sketches" located at the Utah State Historical Society.

21 "Autobiography of Benjamin Franklin LeBaron," pp. 1–3.

22 For garments as a continuation of ancient themes, see Hugh W. Nibley, "Sacred Vestments: Preliminary Report," (Provo, UT: Foundation for Ancient Research and Mormon Studies, 1975) and John A. Tvedtnes, "The Temple Ceremony in Ancient Times," Part I Temple Clothing, 1973 typescript, Utah Historical Society. David Buerger writes, "Although there is much to be said about ancient parallels, it seems more reasonable to explore a source much closer to Joseph Smith: Freemasonry," in "The Development of the Mormon Temple Endowment Ceremony," p. 39.

23 See B. H. Roberts, comp., *Comprehensive History of the Church of Jesus Christ of Latter-day Saints*, vol. 2 (Salt Lake City: Church of Jesus Christ of Latter-day Saints, 1930), pp. 135–6; E. Cecil McGavin, *Mormonism and Masonry* (Salt Lake City: Stevens & Wallis, Inc., 1947); D. Michael Quinn, "Latter-day Saint Prayer Circles," *Brigham Young University Studies* 19 (1978), pp. 79–105; Jack Anderson, "The Treasure of the Widow's Son," in David C. Martin, ed., *No Help for the Widow's Son: Joseph Smith and Masonry* (Nauvoo, IL: Martin Publishing Co., 1980), pp. 1–12; Mark Carnes, *Sacred Rituals and Manhood in Victorian America* (New Haven and London: Yale Univ. Press, 1989), pp. 6 and 173. On October 15, 1911 the Latter-day Saint First Presidency acknowledged this association by explain-

ing that, "because of their Masonic characters, the ceremonies of the temple are sacred and not for the public." James R. Clark, ed., *Messages of the First Presidency of the Church of Jesus Christ of Latter-day Saints* vol. 4 (Salt Lake City: Bookcraft, 1965–75), p. 250. However, that same year church leaders reiterated the position held since the presidency of Wilford Woodruff that those who joined secret societies debarred themselves from the temple. The reason given was not the ritual similarities between Mormonism and Masonry but that the church required "their undivided devotion and fealty." *Messages of the First Presidency*, July 25, 1911, p. 251f.

24 Buerger, p. 41.

25 *Bespangled, Painted, and Embroidered: Decorated Masonic Aprons in America 1790–1850* (Lexington, MA: Scottish Rite Masonic Museum of Our National Heritage, 1976).

26 Colin Dyer, *Symbolism in Craft Freemasonry* (London: Lewis Masonic, 1976), p. 48. See the illustrations in *Bespangled, Painted, and Embroidered* for fringed aprons.

27 Hyde, p. 92.

28 Dyer, p. 146 quoting *Leaves from Georgia Masonry* (no other information given).

29 D. Michael Quinn, *Early Mormonism and the Magic World View* (Salt Lake City: Signature Books, 1987), pp. 27–111; 192–213.

30 See Steven Epperson, *Mormons and Jews: Early Mormon Theologies of Israel* (Salt Lake City: Signature Press, 1992).

31 *Encyclopedia of Mormonism* s.v. "Israel," p. 705.

32 Epperson, p. 129.

33 We can only speculate about early Mormon knowledge of the *arba kanfot*. Joshua Seixas taught Hebrew to Joseph Smith, Mormon leaders, and other Mormons for seven weeks. Seixas was born into a Sephardic family, the son of Gershom Mendes Seixas who led the Shearith Israel synagogue in New York City beginning in 1768 and was a regent at Columbia University. He was not a rabbi (there were no rabbis in the colonial and early federal periods) but a lay "reverend." According to Howard M. Sachar, in *A History of the Jews in America* (New York: Knopf, 1992), "years passed before Mendes Seixas

mastered even the rudiments of Jewish ritual practice," (p. 36). Seixas probably did preside over marriages and funerals, carry out kosher butchering, and ritual circumcisions. Joshua Seixas came from an aristocratic Sephardic family who, if the men did wear *arba kanfot*, most likely did not let the fringes hang down over their pants like the Ashkenazim. Because of the persecutions of the Jews in Spain and Portugal, Sephardim learned to hide many Jewish practices. On the other hand, Palestinian Jews of the period were considered the most pious of all Jews. Jewish men definitely would have been wearing *arba kanfot*. Orson Hyde spent some three weeks in Palestine and had stopped to meet with European Jews on his way. He would have encountered Jews whose fringes could be seen hanging from under their outer clothes. I would like to thank Dianne Ashton for her research into these matters.

34 This discussion on *tallit, tzitzit,* and *arba kanfot* is based on information in: *The Universal Jewish Encyclopedia, Jewish Encyclopedia, The Jewish Encyclopedia,* and *Encyclopaedia Judaica*. Another Christian group, the Russian "Old Believers," also wear fringes as a sign of obedience to God's commandments. The Old Believers are the descendants of seventeenth-century Russians who rebelled against reforms of the Orthodox Church. They settled in Oregon in the 1960s and wear a woven fringed belt from the day of baptism as an infant.

35 Contemporary Mormon polygamists insist that they wear the original garments patterned after the one shown by an angel to Joseph Smith. In 1890 church president Wilford Woodruff declared that Latter-day Saints should no longer sanction plural marriages. Those Mormons who did not agree with this change broke away from what they considered an errant church and continued to practice polygamy. There are an estimated forty thousand men, women, and children living in polygamous households in the inter-mountain West and practicing what they see as authentic Mormonism. Just prior to the official end of polygamy, John Taylor was Latter-day Saint President (1880–87). Polygamous Mormons argue that September 27, 1886 in his home in Centerville,

Utah, Taylor had a revelation that upheld the continuation of plural marriages. Latter-day Saint church officials have never recognized the revelation's authenticity. At this same time, Taylor is said to have given an eight-hour sermon that included a discussion of the garments. According to Daniel R. Bateman, who was present, "Part of the time [Taylor] stood mid-air with a halo of light around him. President Taylor told us the time would come when changes in the Garment would be made and it was necessary for the brethren to have the correct understanding of the pattern and meaning of the marks so as to be able to teach the Saints at the time. He told us it was the pattern of the garments given Adam and Eve in the Garden of Eden and it all had a sacred meaning." Polygamous Mormons publish descriptions of nineteenth-century garments to support their claim that the design of the garment, like the design of marriage, has been changed by human will and not by God's. "Temple Ordinances and Garments," *Truth* 2 (January 1937), pp. 33–6 at p. 35; Ken Driggs, "Twentieth-Century Polygamy and Fundamentalist Mormons in Southern Utah," *Dialogue: Journal of Mormon Thought* 24 (Winter 1991), pp. 44–58. On the polygamist view on garments, see B. Harvey Allred, *A Leaf in Review of the Words and Arts of God and Men Relative to the Fullness of the Gospel* (Caldwell, ID: Claxton Printers, Ltd., 1933); Francis M. Darter, "The Holy Priesthood, Temple, 'Marriage Garment' Read and Weep"; 1961 typescript, University of Utah Library Rare Books Department; Ogden Kraut, "The Priesthood Garment," 1971 typescript; Robert R. Openshaw, ed., *The Notes or Selected References or the Fullness of the Gospel for Saints and Other Interested Students* (Pinesdale, MT: Bitterroot Publishing Co., 1980).

36 FP, 73 (FW).
37 LC, 24 (FW).
38 PE, 37 (MW).
39 SX, 45 (FW).
40 Packer, *The Holy Temple*, p. 77f. Boyd K. Packer is a member of the Council of the Twelve which, after the First Presidency, is the highest level of Latter-day Saint leadership.
41 There are only a few sources on the meaning of religious clothing, see

Leigh Eric Schmidt, "'A Church Going People are a Dress Loving People': Clothes, Communication, and Religious Culture in Early America," *Church History* 58 (1989), pp. 36–51; Gerilyn Tandberg, "Clothing for Conformity: A Study of the Brethren Sect," *Costume* 20 (1986), pp. 63–71; John Hostetler, *Amish Society* (Baltimore: Johns Hopkins Univ. Press. 1980), pp. 232–4; and Ewa Kuryluk, *Veronica and Her Cloth* (Oxford: Basil Blackwell, 1991).

For general discussions of the ability of clothing to communicate, see Grant McCracken, "Clothing as Language: An Object Lesson in the Study of the Expressive Properties of Material Culture," in *Material Anthropology: Contemporary Approaches to Material Culture*, ed. Barrie Reynolds and Margaret A. Stott (Lanham, MD: Univ. Press of America, 1987), pp. 103–28; Valerie Steele, *Fashion and Eroticism: The Ideals of Feminine Beauty from the Victorian Era to the Jazz Age* (New York: Oxford Univ. Press, 1985) and *Men and Women: Dressing the Part* (Washington, D.C.: Smithsonian Institution Press, 1989); and Alison Lurie, *The Language of Clothes* (New York: Random House, 1981).

42 W. E. B. DuBois eloquently described "double-consciousness" in *The Souls of Black Folks* (1903) as "this sense of always looking at one's self through the eyes of others, of measuring one's soul by the tape of a world that looks on in amused contempt and pity. One ever feels his twoness. . . ." In John Franklin Hope, *Three Negro Classics* (New York: Avon Books, 1965), p. 215.
43 RD, 35 (FW).
44 BR, 26 (FW).
45 WL, 47 (FW).
46 PR, 64 (FW).
47 SF, 55 (FW).
48 CC, 40 (MW).
49 SK, 29 (NW).
50 Ibid.
51 AS, 42 (FW).
52 OJ, 25 (NW).
53 CR, 38 (NW).
54 The first two temples at Kirtland, Ohio and Nauvoo, Illinois, are no longer active. In 1912 there were four temples in Utah: St. George (1877), Logan (1884), Manti (1883), and Salt Lake (1893). Buerger, p. 57.

55 Thomas G. Alexander, *Mormonism in Transition: A History of the Latter-day Saints, 1890–1930* (Urbana: Univ. of Illinois Press, 1986), p. 299.
56 BD, 34 (FW).
57 CC, 40 (MW).
58 BK, 31 (FW).
59 Although there does not seem to be any formal legislation on the matter, Catholics also burn old clerical vestments to make sure that they are not put to any profane use. See Joseph Braun, S. J. *Handbuch der Paramentik* (Freiberg: Herder, 1912), pp. 71–2.
60 SK, 29 (NW).
61 BR, 27 (NW).
62 SK, 29 (NW).
63 MD, 34; not yet received endowments.
64 BR, 27 (NW).
65 Quinn, *Early Mormonism*, p. 213.
66 William Jarman, "Temple Endowment Ritual and Ceremonies," edited with commentary by Wesley M. Jones, 1965, typescript University of Utah Marriott Library Archives, p. 1. A similar description is found in William Jarman, *U.S.A. Uncle Sam's Abscess, or Hell Upon Earth* (Exeter, England: Leduc's Steam Printing Works, 1884), p. 69.
67 Thomas F. O'Dea, *The Mormons* (Chicago: Univ. of Chicago Press, 1957), p. 69.
68 On December 21, 1845 George Miller explained that his garments protected him from being shot. In explaining the design and purpose of the garment's symbols, he said: "Paul said he bore in his body the marks of the Lord Jesus Christ, which was as plainly as he dare allude to these things in writing. But the marks Paul alluded to were just such as we now have on our garments." Smith, *Journals of William Clayton*, p. 223. Contemporary Latter-day Saint theologians, Margaret and Paul Toscano make a direct connection between the garments and the sacrifice of Jesus Christ, by-passing Joseph Smith's role as martyr. They understand the garment markings to represent Christ's wounds. *Strangers in Paradox: Explorations in Mormon Theology* (Salt Lake City: Signature Books, 1990), p. 286.
69 Linda King Newell and Valleen Tippets Avery, *Mormon Enigma: Emma Hale Smith* (Garden City, NY: Doubleday & Co., Inc., 1984), pp.

189–90 citing statement of Sarah Louise Dalton Elder, Church Manuscripts collection compiled by Alan H. Gerber, BYU Archives.

70 Newell and Avery, p. 189 citing Oliver B. Huntington, "History of the Life of Oliver B. Huntington," p. 406, LDS Archives.

71 On December 21, 1845 Mormon leader William Wines Phelps recalled before a congregation of seventy-five persons how the prophet Joseph Smith had left off his garment because of the weather. In the next paragraph, however, Clayton describes how Heber C. Kimball explained that "word came to him and to all the Twelve about that time to lay aside their garments, and take them to pieces, or cut them up so that they could not be found." Smith, *Journals of William Clayton*, p. 224.

72 On examples of the magical qualities of garments, see Anthon S. Cannon, *Popular Beliefs and Superstitions from Utah* (Salt Lake City: Univ. of Utah Press, 1984), entries 3106, 9228, and 3542. Entry 9929 implies that at least some oral tradition indicated that the garments did not entirely protect their wearers: "The Indians killed these people, and when they unbuttoned their shirts and saw the garments they had on, they didn't even scalp them" (recorded in 1944). James Moody believed that the shirt the Ghost Dancers (participants in a Native American revival movement) wore may have been suggested by Mormon garments. Because the Mormons argue that Native Americans are the "Lamanites" discussed in the Book of Mormon, considerable efforts were made in evangelizing neighboring tribes of the Ute, Paiute, Bannock, and Shoshoni. Native American converts might have been invested with garments and may have understood their protective ability. Since the Ghost Dancers believed that their shirts had protective powers, Moody suggests they might have been adapted from Mormon contact. *The Ghost-Dance Religion and the Sioux Outbreak of 1890* abridged by Anthony F. C. Wallace (Chicago: Univ. of Chicago Press, 1965), p. 34.

73 LH, 25 (FW).

74 SG, 48 (FW).

75 William A. Wilson, "The Folklore of Mormon Missionaries," *Sunstone* 7 (1982), pp. 32–40.

76 JB, 39 (FW).

77 CM, 25 (MW).

78 OJ, 25 (NW). Shaking the dust from the feet as a symbol of contempt is found in Luke 10:11 and Acts 13:51.

79 SK, 29 (NW).

80 LH, 25 (FW).

81 Joseph F. Smith, *The Improvement Era*, 9 (1906), p. 813.

82 *Messages of the First Presidency*, 5 (1918), p. 110. A flyer in the LDS Library indicates that this dictum was distributed among Latter-day Saints.

83 Prior to 1877, most Euro-American men and women wore two-piece undergarments. The bottoms, called "drawers," consisted of almost two separate sections, one for each leg, joined just below the waist; a "chemise," looking like a shirt, comprised the top. A one-piece undergarment became fashionable during the late 1870s when a smooth, slim look prevailed in clothing design. One-piece garments, with long sleeves, legs, and slits would not have been considered unusual during the nineteenth-century. Women could have easily worn garments under corsets and petticoats. Elizabeth Ewing, *Underwear: A History* (New York: Theater Arts Books, 1981), p. 60.

84 C. Willet Cunnington, *The History of Underclothes* (London: Faber & Faber, 1981), p. 86.

85 Jennifer Craik, "States of Undress: Lingerie to Swimwear," *The Face of Fashion* (London: Routledge, 1994), pp. 115–52.

86 Cunnington, p. 129.

87 Letter of the First Presidency, June 14, 1923. On June 4, 1924 the *Salt Lake Tribune* printed an article on the garment style changes. They quoted "one good woman of long membership in the church" as uttering her "fervid objection" to the changes: "I shall not alter my garments, even if President Grant has ordered me to do so. My garments are made as they were when I was married in the endowment house long before the temple was built. The pattern was revealed to the Prophet Joseph and Brother Grant has no right to change it."

88 An oral history, Rose Marie Reid (1973). LDS Archives.

89 Rose Marie Reid, a well-known swim suit designer in the 1940s, made the pattern changes in the 1960s. See Rose Marie Reid. Approval of the two-piece item is mentioned in a letter from Barbara B. Smith to Stake and District Relief Society Presidents and Ward/Branch Garment Representatives, January 23, 1980, LDS Archives. In the interview "LW trans 15" Barbara Smith is accredited with pushing through the change to the two-piece garment.

90 I Cor. 3:16–17. *Teachings of the Prophet Joseph Smith*, p. 181. See also *Encyclopedia of Mormonism*, s.v. "Physical Body," p. 1080f.

91 The classic, but severe, statement on sexuality written by a modern church authority is Spencer W. Kimball, *The Miracle of Forgiveness* (Salt Lake City: Bookcraft, Inc., 1969). A more recent and open discussion is Joana B. Bennett, *et al.*, *Between Ring and Temple: A Handbook for Engaged L.D.S. Couples (and others who need a review)* (Salt Lake City: Olympus Publishing Company, 1981). See especially, Richard M. Herbertson, "Sexuality in the LDS Marriage," (pp. 83–107).

92 SG, 48 (FW).

93 Mark E. Peterson, "Chastity" (pamphlet, Provo, UT: Brigham Young Univ. Press, 1968).

94 Boyd K. Packer, *To Young Men Only* (Salt Lake City: Corporation of the President of the Church of Jesus Christ of Latter-day Saints, 1976), n.p.

95 On pessimistic Christian attitudes toward the body, see Peter Brown, *The Body and Society: Men, Women, and Sexual Renunciation in Early Christianity* (New York: Columbia Univ. Press, 1988), pp. 213–338 and Frank Bottomley, *Attitudes to the Body in Western Christendom* (London: Lepus Books, 1979).

96 John Durham Peters, "Reflections on Mormon Materialism," *Sunstone* 17 (March 1993), p. 48. See also David Knowlton, "On Mormon Masculinity," *Sunstone* 16 (August 1992), p. 25 and the articles in Brent Corcoran, ed., *Multiply and Replenish: Mormon Essays on Sex and Family* (Salt Lake City: Signature Books, 1994).

97 *Encyclopedia of Mormonism*, s.v. "Sexuality," p. 1306.

98 On January 5, 1982 a letter from the First Presidency was sent to all Stake, Mission, and District Presidents; Bishops; and Branch Presidents. The letter outlined what should

be asked of people being interviewed for "positions of responsibility" and "temple recommends." One sentence of the two-page document became immediately controversial: "The First Presidency has interpreted oral sex as constituting an unnatural, impure, or unholy practice." By April of the same year, another directive was sent out indicating that interviewers should avoid indelicate inquiries about intimate matters and that couples should "determine by themselves their standing before the Lord." The directive, however, did not withdraw the previous statement on oral sex. *Sunstone Review* (April 1982), p. 6.

99 *Welfare Service Packet: Homosexuality* (Salt Lake City: The Church of Jesus Christ of Latter-day Saints, 1973), p. 16.

100 FB, 28 (FW).
101 CM, 25 (MW).
102 LH, 25 (FW).
103 OR, 24 (NW).
104 BR, 27 (NW).
105 SG, 48 (FW).
106 SK, 29 (FW).
107 SX, 45 (FW).
108 PR, 64 (FW).
109 CM, 25 (MW).
110 JB, 39 (FW).
111 SJ, 30 (FW).
112 Craik, p. 116 citing Valerie Steele, "Clothing and Sexuality," in *Men and Women: Dressing the Part*, p. 55f.
113 PE, 37 (MW).
114 PR, 64 (FW).
115 SG, 48 (FW).
116 Boyd K. Packer, All-Church Coordinating Council Meeting (May 18, 1993); unpublished manuscript, LDS Library.
117 On August 23, 1991, the *Deseret News*, a church-owned newspaper, published a "Statement" on the front page of its metropolitan section. The statement was signed by the Council of the First Presidency and the Quorum of the Twelve Apostles, the highest authorities of the church. The point of the statement was to discourage Mormons from attending conferences sponsored by a liberal Mormon organization called "Sunstone." At a recent conference were "some presentations relating to the House of the Lord, the holy temples, that are offensive. We deplore the bad taste and insensitivity of these public discussions

of things we hold sacred." In a follow-up article in the *Salt Lake Tribune* (August 24) reporter Peggy Fletcher Stack cited an earlier draft of this chapter as one of the offending presentations.

118 *The Sociology of Georg Simmel* trans. Kurt H. Wolf (Glencoe, IL: The Free Press, 1950), p. 322.

119 In addition to Simmel's writings, see Sissela Bok, *Secrets: On the Ethics of Concealment and Revelation* (New York: Pantheon Books, 1982); Mary H. Nooter, *Secrecy: African Art that Conceals and Reveals* (New York: Museum for African Art, 1993); and Colleen McDannell, "Sacred, Secret, and the Non-Mormon," *Sunstone* (forthcoming).

8 Christian Retailing

1 All statistical information on Christian retailing comes from the trade association, Christian Bookseller's Association, Colorado Springs, Colorado, unless otherwise noted. While $3 billion is a substantial amount of money, we must keep in mind that in the 1980s retail sales of books were $11 billion and merchandise in convenience stores $50 billion. J. Barry Mason *et al.*, *Modern Retailing*, 6th edn. (Homewood, IL: Irwin, 1993).

2 On televangelism, see Janice Peck, *The Gods of Televangelism: The Crisis of Meaning and the Appeal of Religious Television* (Cresskill, NJ: Hampton Press, 1992); Jeffrey K. Hadden, *Televangelism, Power, and Politics on God's Frontier* (New York: H. Holt, 1988) and Razelle Frankl, *Televangelism: The Marketing of Popular Religion* (Carbondale: Southern Illinois Univ. Press, 1987).

Recent works on political activities include, Walter H. Capps, *The New Religious Right: Piety, Patriotism, and Politics* (Columbia: Univ. of South Carolina Press, 1990); Steve Bruce, *The Rise and Fall of the New Christian Right: Conservative Protestant Politics in America, 1978–1988* (New York: Oxford Univ. Press, 1988), and Samuel Hill, *The New Religious-Political Right in America* (Nashville: Abingdon, 1982).

On theological and institutional struggles, see George M. Marsden,

Reforming Fundamentalism: Fuller Seminary and the New Evangelicalism (Grand Rapids, MI: William B. Eerdmans Pub. Co., 1987); Nancy Ammerman, *Baptist Battles: Social Change and Religious Conflict in the Southern Baptist Convention* (New Brunswick: Rutgers Univ. Press, 1990) and *Southern Baptists Observed: Multiple Perspectives on a Changing Denomination* (Knoxville: Univ. of Tennessee Press, 1993).

The notable exceptions to the lack of critical scholarship on Christian culture is Nancy Tatom Ammerman's ethnographic study of fundamentalists in a middle-class, Northeast suburb, *Bible Believers: Fundamentalists in the Modern World* (New Brunswick: Rutgers Univ. Press, 1987) and Judith Stacey, *Brave New Families: Stories of Domestic Upheaval in Late Twentieth Century America* (New York: Basic Books, 1990) about a family in the Silicon Valley of California.

3 On Christian private schools, see Alan Peshkin, *God's Choice: The Total World of a Fundamentalist Christian School* (Chicago: Univ. of Chicago Press, 1986); Paul F. Parson, *Inside America's Christian Schools* (Macon, GA: Mercer Univ. Press, 1987); Susan D. Rose, *Keeping them Out of the Hands of Satan: Evangelical Schooling in America* (New York: Routledge, 1988); and Melinda Bollar Wagner, *God's Schools: Choice and Compromise in American Society* (New Brunswick: Rutgers Univ. Press, 1990). On home schooling and Christianity, see Colleen McDannell, "Creating the Christian Home: Home Schooling in Contemporary America," in David Chidester and Edward Linenthal, eds., *Sacred Space in America* (Bloomington: Indiana Univ. Press, forthcoming).

4 See Betty A. DeBerg, *Ungodly Women: Gender and the First Wave of American Fundamentalism* (Minneapolis: Fortress Press, 1990) and David Harrington Watt, *A Transforming Faith: Explorations of Twentieth-Century American Evangelicalism* (New Brunswick: Rutgers Univ. Press, 1991).

5 A. H. Shipman, *The Amateur and Mechanics Manual and Catalogue of Scroll Saws and Lathes (1881–1882)*, p. 30. Strong Museum, Rochester, New York.

6 *List of Gowans & Sons Premiums,*

Surprises for 1898, Strong Museum. One could also get reproductions of biblical scenes by sending in R. Buckles Coffee wrappers.

7   *Carter's Oil Chromos Catalogue* (1877), no. 20. Strong Museum.

8   Elsie de Wolfe, *The House in Good Taste* (1911; New York: Century Company, 1913). For an excellent discussion of twentieth-century design, see Lisa Phillips, *et al.*, *High Styles: Twentieth-Century American Design* (New York: Whitney Museum of American Art, 1985). On the realization of such designs in middle-class housing, see Candace M. Volz, "The Modern Look of the Early Twentieth-Century House: A Mirror of Changing Lifestyles," and Katherine C. Grier, "The Decline of the Memory Palace: The Parlor after 1890," in Jessica H. Foy and Thomas J. Schlereth, eds., *American Home Life, 1880–1930: A Social History of Spaces and Services* (Knoxville: Univ. of Tennessee Press, 1992), pp. 25–74; Gwendolyn Wright, *Building the Dream: A Social History of Housing in America* (Cambridge: MIT Press, 1981) pp. 158–76; and Margaret Marsh, *Suburban Lives* (New Brunswick: Rutgers Univ. Press, 1990), pp. 90–155.

9   Ogden Codman, *The Decoration of Houses* (New York: Charles Scribner's Sons, 1897), p. xix.

10   Lizabeth A. Cohen, "Embellishing a Life of Labor: An Interpretation of the Material Culture of American Working-Class Homes, 1885–1915" in Thomas J. Schlereth, ed., *Material Culture Studies in America* (Nashville, TN: American Association for State and Local History, 1982), pp. 289–305.

11   Robert S. Lynd and Helen Merrell Lynd, *Middletown: A Study in Contemporary American Culture* (New York: Harcourt, Brace and Company, 1929), p. 100; "'Knickknacks' of all sorts are about – easeled portraits on piano or phonograph, a paper knife brought by some traveled relative from Yellowstone Park, pictures that the small daughter has drawn in school, or if the family is of a religious bent, colored mottoes: 'What will you be doing when Jesus comes?' or 'Prepare to meet thy God.'"

12   N. H. Byrum, *Familiar Names and Faces* (Moundsville, WV: Gospel Trumpet Publishing Co., 1902), p. 140.

13   *1895 Descriptive Catalogue of Books and Tracts, etc.* All Gospel Trumpet/Warner Press catalogs are located at the Warner Press headquarters in Anderson, Indiana. I would like to thank Charles Harrington for so graciously sharing with me his materials and insights into the company.

14   Harold L. Phillips, *Miracle of Survival* (Anderson, IN: Warner Press, 1979), pp. 173–255 discusses the struggles of the company to become financially stable and to cope with the "excess baggage" (p. 226) of church organizations.

15   *1900 Catalogue of Holiness Literature*, n.p.

16   See Ralph W. Hyde, "The Traveling Bible Salesman: The Good Buck from the Good Book," in *The Bible and Popular Culture in America*, ed. Allene Stuart Phy (Philadelphia: Fortress Press, 1985), pp. 137–64 and for selling in general, Timothy B. Spears, "'All Things to All men': The Commercial Traveler and the Rise of Modern Salesmanship," *American Quarterly* 45 (1993), pp. 524–57.

17   The advertisement for coats was in *King's Business* 15 (1924), p. 258. Typical advertisements for religious merchandise to be sold by agents include one for the Christian Light Press of Elizabethtown, PA, in *Christian Life* (1946), p. 6; The Christian Company, Chicago, IL, in *Christian Life* (1948), p. 53; Judson Press, Philadelphia, PA, in *King's Business* (1924), p. 830; Church Service, New York, in *Christian Advocate* (1920), p. 251.

18   On the social significance of mottoes, see Ken Ames, "Words to Live By," in *Death in the Dining Room and Other Tales of Victorian Culture* (Philadelphia: Temple Univ. Press, 1992), pp. 97–149.

19   Dorothy B. Ryan, *Picture Postcards in the United States, 1893–1918* (New York: Clarkson N. Potter, Inc., 1982), p. 22. According to Ryan, the "earliest commercially produced picture postcards began with the souvenir issues sold at the 1893 World Columbian Exposition in Chicago. In 1898 the government permitted privately printed postcards to be mailed at the same rate as government issues, one cent instead of two."

20   *1909 Catalogue of Books, Tracts, Papers, Bibles, Mottoes, & c.* n.p.

21   Postcard 83.395, Billy Graham Center Museum, Wheaton, IL.

22   On the creation of Mother's Day by florists, ministers, and promoters of domesticity, see Leigh Eric Schmidt, "The Commercialization of the Calendar: American Holidays and the Culture of Consumption, 1870–1930," *Journal of American History* 78 (1991), pp. 887–916. On religious motifs in greeting cards, see George Bunday, *The History of the Christmas Card* (London: Rockliff, 1954) and C. R. Hill, "Christmas Card Selections as Unobtrusive Measures," *Journalism Quarterly* 46 (1969), pp. 511–14.

23   *1925–1926 Trade Catalog*, n.p.

24   Roland Marchand, *Advertising the American Dream: Making Way for Modernity 1920–1940* (Berkeley: Univ. of California Press, 1985), p. 9.

25   Ibid., p. 118.

26   Exhibitions in 1929 of French-influenced Art Deco Moderne furniture includes the Eleventh Annual Exhibition of American Industrial Art at the Metropolitan Museum and one organized by R. H. Macy and Company at Designer's Gallery, Phillips *et al.*; *High Style*, p. 64. *1931–32 Catalog*.

27   Marchand, p. 140.

28   Scott Derks, *The Value of a Dollar, 1860–1989* (Detroit: Gale Research, Inc., 1994), pp. 236, 252, 234.

29   *1937–1938 Gospel Trumpet Company Catalog*, n.p.

30   Marchand, pp. 264–84. The intermingling of advertising and religion started earlier. Leigh Eric Schmidt in "The Commercialization of the Calendar," included a 1906 example of a window display which used a cross and lilies to sell hats during Easter (p. 896). See also his "The Easter Parade: Piety, Fashion, and Display," *Religion and American Culture* 4 (1994), pp. 135–64.

31   Rolf Lundén, *Business and Religion in the American 1920s*, (New York: Greenwood Press, 1988), pp. 56–88. See also Robert Handy, "The America Religious Depression 1925–1935," *Church History* 24 (1960), pp. 3–16 quoting Charles Fiske in 1929, "America has become almost hopelessly enamored of a religion that is little more than a sanctified commercialism" (p. 8) and Thomas K. Pritchett, *et al.*, "The Marketing of Religion: 1900–1930," *Essays in Economic and Business History* 8 (1990), pp. 147–57.

32 "Sermons in Slogans," *Literary Digest* 73 (April 29, 1922), pp. 31–2. See also R. Laurence Moore, "Religious Advertising and Progressive Protestant Approaches to Mass Media," *Selling God: American Religion in the Marketplace of Culture* (New York: Oxford Univ. Press, 1994), pp. 204–37.

33 *1937–1938 Gospel Trumpet Company Catalog*, n.p.

34 Helene Weis, "Those Old Familiar Faces," *Stained Glass* 86 (1991), pp. 204–7; 217–18. Perry Pictures Inc. was established by Eugene Ashton Perry who at the time was Master of the Center Grammar School in Malden, MA. He made and distributed half-tone reproductions of paintings, sculpture, and architecture. Perry Pictures apparently reproduced paintings that a museum or an artist would allow to be photographed. Little is known about the company. Perry died in 1948. In 1968 the company became a department of Franklin Watts, Inc. which later became a subsidiary of Grolier, Inc.

35 These three paintings: *Christ in the Garden of Gethsemane, Christ and the Rich Young Man*, and *Jesus in the Temple* are at Riverside Church in New York City.

36 Marchand, p. 62.

37 James D. Norris, *Advertising and the Transformation of American Society, 1865–1920* (New York: Greenwood Press, 1990), p. 98.

38 *1922–23 Religious Books for the Home Church Study*, n.p.

39 Byrum, *Familiar Names and Faces*, p. 176. In early America, lay men and women wrote requests for healing on pieces of paper and posted them in church or gave them to a minister. According to David Hall, these notes were seen as "possessing special efficacy." *Worlds of Wonder, Days of Judgment: Popular Religious Belief in Early New England* (Cambridge: Harvard Univ. Press, 1989), p. 200. For other examples of faith healing using material objects, see David Edwin Harrell, *All Things are Possible: the Healing and Charismatic Revivals in Modern America* (Bloomington: Indiana Univ. Press, 1975); Melvin Easterday Dieter, *The Holiness Revival of the Nineteenth Century* (Metuchen, NJ: Scarecrow Press, 1980); and Edith Waldvogel Blumhofer, *Restor-ing the Faith: The Assemblies of God, Pentecostalism, and American Culture* (Urbana: Univ. of Illinois Press, 1993).

40 The role of the Sunday school in disseminating and shaping Protestant visual sensibility has not been explored. For the early history of Sunday schools, see Anne M. Boylan, *Sunday School: The Formation of an American Institution, 1790–1880* (New Haven and London: Yale Univ. Press, 1988).

41 *1922–23 Religious Books for the Home Church Study*.

42 Robert W. Lynn and Elliott Wright, *The Big Little School* (New York: Harper & Row, 1971), pp. 76–99.

43 Frances Schaeffer, *Art and the Bible* (Downers Grove, IL: Inter-Varsity Press, 1973), p. 9.

44 Ames, p. 144.

45 Marchand, p. 360.

46 Such stores include: Newton's Christian Bookstore, Palo Alto, CA (1954); The Christian Light Bookstore, Upland, CA (1955); The Green Centre Bookstore, Kalona, IA (1950); Jack's Religious Gift Shop, Salisbury, MD (1959), Intermountain Bookstore, Salt Lake City, UT (1952).

47 *Time* (June 21, 1971), pp. 56–63; *Newsweek* (March 22, 1971), p. 97; *Life* (May 28, 1971) pp. 80–85.

48 Robert Ellwood, *One Way: The Jesus Movement and its Meaning* (Englewood Cliffs, NJ: Prentice-Hall, Inc., 1973), pp. 18–20. On "life-style Christianity," see Watt, *A Transforming Faith*, pp. 24–5; Quebedeaux, *The Young Evangelicals: Revolution in Orthodoxy* (New York: Harper & Row, 1974), p. 40.

49 "Trends in Christian Bookselling," p. 81. On religious publishing, see Moore, pp. 252–5 and John Tebbel, *A History of Book Publishing in the United States* vol. 4 (The Great Change, 1940–1980), pp. 589–626.

50 Paul Boyer, *When Time Shall Be No More: Prophecy Belief in Modern American Culture* (Cambridge: Harvard Univ. Press, 1992), p. 5.

51 Ellwood, p. 89.

52 Kenneth Nathaniel Taylor, *The Living Bible: Paraphrased* (Wheaton, IL: Tyndale House, 1971). Originally distributed by Doubleday the text is a compilation of the previously published Scripture paraphrases: *Living Letters* (1962); *Living Prophecies* (1965); *Living Gospels* (1966); *Living Psalms and Proverbs* (1967); *Living Lessons of Life and Love* (1968); *Living Books of Moses* (1969); *Living History of Israel* (1970).

53 "Recent Trends in Christian Bookselling," *Bookstore Journal* (October 1975), p. 79.

54 Peter Gardella, *Innocent Ecstasy: How Christianity Gave America an Ethic of Sexual Pleasure* (New York: Oxford Univ. Press, 1985), pp. 80–94; Quebedeaux, *The Young Evangelicals*, pp. 102–9.

55 Little has been written on the "folk" arts that evolved out of the Jesus movement. For a discussion of one group's arts, see David T. Stewart, "A Survey of Shiloh Arts," *Communal Societies* 12 (1992), pp. 43–67.

56 *Bookstore Journal* (June 1973), n.p. Fleming H. Revell was founded in 1920. *Bookstore Journal* (January 1972), p. 91.

57 Stickers: *Bookstore Journal* (June 1973), n.p.; dog tags: *Bookstore Journal* (October 1973), p. 80; bumper stickers: *Bookstore Journal* (April 1971), np; T-shirts: *Bookstore Journal* (March 1977), p. 136 and (June 1979), p. 61; fish and crosses: *Bookstore Journal* (Nov.–Dec. 1971), n.p.; patches: *Bookstore Journal* (February 1972), p. 70; happy face: *Bookstore Journal* (Nov.–Dec. 1971), p. 50.

58 According to sociologist Robert Ellwood, it was "the Jesus people's answer to the clenched fist of the activists and the two fingers of the peace sign" (p. 63), and originated with a movement leader Lance Bowen who had "confusing experiences with all sorts of oriental gods, psychedelic visions, the faces on the Tarot cards, the powers contacted with witchcraft and magic." The one-way sign symbolized "the attraction of a single path, of one sure and strong helping hand leading out of that psychic vortex." The up-raised finger, however, was not invented by the Jesus people. In the mid-nineteenth century, Christians used the up-raised finger as a symbol of hope and heaven. It appeared in both their funerary and domestic sculpture where angels and allegories of Hope pointed their fingers skyward. For the Victorians, who still harbored fears of fiery damnation, the gesture reminded them of God's mercy and their eventual home in heaven. For post–1960s Christians, the symbol reassured them that they had chosen the correct set of beliefs and life style out of a myriad of possibilities. It was not an angel or allegorical figure who guided the soul upward, it was the Christian who forcefully demonstrated his or her own commitment.

59 Stan Jantz, "Maranatha Village," *Bookstore Journal* (July–Aug. 1974), p. 119.

60 I. A. Scott, "The Terra Sancta Story," *Bookstore Journal* (Nov.–Dec. 1972), p. 54.

61 Jantz, p. 120.

62 "People in Progress: Suppliers Share their Stories," *Bookstore Journal* (September 1979), p. 109. For discussions of Christian jewelry, see Lesley Hull, "Jewelry in a Christian Bookstore? Why Not?" *Bookstore Journal* (June 1975), pp. 9–10; Danny DeVeny, "How to Merchandise and Sell Jewelry," *Bookstore Journal* (Nov.–Dec. 1978), p. 13f.

63 "California Preferred Products Becomes a House of Praise," *Bookstore Journal* (July–Aug. 1975), p. 212. See also Daniel Gottry, "The Proper Balance: Establishing Your Identity as a Ministry/Business," *Bookstore Journal* (February 1985), pp. 77–9; Frances E. Gardner, "The Witnessing," *Bookstore Journal* (Nov.–Dec. 1969), p. 10f.

64 Thomas W. Gruen *et al.*, *1992 CBA Christian Bookstore Customer Profile Expanded Statistics* (Colorado Springs: CBA Center for Research and Information, 1991).

65 "Open Forum," *Bookstore Journal* (August 1991), p. 10.

66 *1991 CBA Customer Profile* n.p.

67 "Open Forum," *Bookstore Journal* (August 1991), p. 10.

68 Bill Anderson, "Focus," *Bookstore Journal* (November 1991), p. 27.

69 "Industry Watch," *Bookstore Journal* (July 1993), p. 12.

70 Discussions of the use of Christian merchandise were conducted with five conservative Christian families from Austin, Texas, in 1992. See Colleen McDannell, "Creating the Christian Home: Home Schooling in Contemporary America," in *Sacred Space in America*.

71 Christian Supply Service, Tueplo, Mississippi and Christian's Family Book Store, Anniston, Alabama, will not even special order non-fundamentalist literature.

72 Long's Christian Bookstore, Rancho Cucamonga, California.

73 "The Catholic bookseller has already taken the initiative. With business suffering because of the church's Americanization program and the resulting loss of sales in liturgical ware, church ornamentation, missals, and medals, the Catholic church goods dealer has been forced to concentrate on its one bright hope. The Catholic laity as well as their major Protestant denomination counterparts have become avid readers and a surging new market." Gary Wharton, "Reaching Out into the New Ecumenical Market," *Bookstore Journal* (April 1973), pp. 88–9. See also Eileen E. Freeman, "Catholic Market," *Bookstore Journal* (July–Aug. 1979), pp. 64–6.

74 Meg Gullar, "Hispanics in the '90s," *Bookstore Journal* (May 1991), pp. 29–34 and Joel Ceballos, "The Hispanic Market: 'Viva La Oportunidad,'" *Bookstore Journal* (August 1993), pp. 53–64.

75 The attitude toward these groups, however, may be changing. Hansen, a Latter-day Saint maker of statuary, became a member of CBA and exhibits her goods at the annual CBA trade shows. Her white statues are primarily of family scenes so it is not surprising that non-Latter-day Saint bookstores might carry the product. A statue of a praying woman may be understood as reflecting only pious sentiments and thus may be acceptable to more bookstore owners.

76 Anti-New Ages books advertised in the *Bookstore Journal* include: Will Baron, *Deceived by the New Age* (Boise, ID: Pacific Press, 1990); Terry Ann Modica, *The Power of the Occult* (Avon, NJ: Magnificat Press, 1990); David K Clarg and Norman L. Geisler, *Apologetics in the New Age* (Grand Rapids, MI: Baker Book House, 1990) and Russ Parker, *Battling the Occult* (Downers Grover, IL: InterVarsity Press, 1990).

77 Douglas Groothuis, "The New Age Goes Mainstream," *Bookstore Journal* (October 1990), pp. 25–6.

78 On the social significance of Halloween for contemporary Americans, see Russell W. Belk, "Halloween: An Evolving American Consumption Ritual," in *Advances in Consumer Research*, Richard Pollay,

Jerry Gorn, and Marvin Golderby, eds., v. 17 (Provo, UT: Association for Consumer Research, 1990), pp. 508–17 and "Carnival, Control, and Corporate Culture in Contemporary Halloween Celebrations," in *Halloween and Other Festivals of Life and Death*, ed. Jack Santino (Knoxville: Univ. of Tennessee Press, 1994), pp. 132–50. A series of videos by Jeremiah Films, of Hemet, CA on Satan and devil worship includes: *Halloween: Trick or Treat*. The advertisement promoting the video calls it "A highly informative video that traces the pagan origins and history of New Age, sorcery, witchcraft, and satanism that masquerades for social acceptance behind Halloween – the second largest holiday celebration in the U.S.!"

79 "Industry Watch," *Bookstore Journal* (May 1992), p. 16.

80 Some of these techniques include: forming "buying groups" where stores get together and either buy large amounts of product or produce cooperative advertising (a buying group called "Parable" has 250 members and carefully screens prospective members); following their customers farther and farther out into the suburbs, with Christian bookstores in shopping malls becoming quite common; remodelling stores to keep them "new" and enlarging them to hold more and more merchandise; selling more gifts and less books since gifts take up less space and garner more profit.

81 Boyer, p. 7.

82 "Open Forum," *Bookstore Journal* (February 1993), p. 13.

83 Steve Camp, "What Do We Do With Madonna? A Guest Editorial," *Bookstore Journal* (January 1993), pp. 37–9.

84 "Open Forum," *Bookstore Journal* (February 1993), p. 11.

85 There is some evidence that non-Christian companies purchased successful Christian businesses during the boom time of the 1980s when acquisitions flourished and now they want to divest. In 1992 Thomas Nelson Publishers purchased Word, Inc. (mostly books and music) from Capital Cities/ABC. Thomas Nelson was the world's largest Bible producer with sales revenues prior to their purchase of Word, Inc. of $93.1 million. The purchase of Word, Inc. made

Thomas Nelson the largest distributor of Christian products. "Word's mission statement was the key factor in the decision to sell the company," said a spokesperson from Word, Inc. "Capital Cities/ABC did what every other company in the country is doing. . . . The managers looked at their portfolio and decided that a religious communications company didn't fit." *Bookstore Journal* (June 1992), p. 17. In 1993 Zondervan made it known that they would be open to selling Benson Music. It is unclear whether companies merely over-extended themselves and are now are paring back or if they envision a decline in the Christian marketplace.

86 "Industry Watch," *Bookstore Journal* (November 1992), p. 13.
87 "Open Forum" *Bookstore Journal* (February 1993), p. 12.
88 Jim Reimann and Carolyn Linn, "Retail Principles That Work, Part I" *Bookstore Journal* (March 1993), p. 24.
89 Joseph Mason *et al.*, *Modern Retailing: Theory and Practice* 6th edn. (Homewood, IL: Irwin, 1993), p. 6.
90 Leonard L. Berry, "Retail Positioning Strategies for the 1980s" *Business Horizons* (Nov.–Dec. 1982), p. 45.
91 Mason *et al.*, p. 732.
92 Articles that try to encourage men to buy at Christian bookstores include, Phil Landrum, "Capturing The Male Market," *Bookstore Journal* (April 1981), pp. 32–3; "How to Sell to Men," *Bookstore Journal* (October 1977), pp. 10–12; Newt Heisely, "Men's Display Ideas," *Bookstore Journal* (October 1977), n.p.
93 Carolyn Linn, "Fiction 1991: Jetting to New Prominence," *Bookstore Journal* (June 1991), p. 41.
94 Serge Schmemann, "Religion Returns to Russia, With a Vengeance," *New York Times* (July 28, 1993). The article mentions along with Bibles, "Americans handing out ballpoint pens to puzzled Russian children." UlJö exhibits at the Frankfurt Book Fair and the Indian items were collected in 1991. A reproduction of

Warner Sallman's art was placed on the study wall of a Chinese Christian pastor in LuShan, China (LuAnn Van Fossen to David Morgan, March, 1993) and in Methodist churches in Korea (Thomas E. Frank to David Morgan, March 15, 1993). Letters at Anderson College Art Museum, Warner Sallman Collection.
95 A summary of this theory is in Mason, pp. 29–32. See also Stephen Brown, "The Wheel of Retailing," *International Journal of Retailing* 3 (1988), pp. 16–40.

Epilogue

1 The Southeastern Center for Contemporary Arts (SCCA) made ten awards to artists from ten geographical areas. Each received $15,000. In addition to *Piss Christ*, Serrano displayed seven other works in the "Awards in the Visual Arts" exhibition. The SCCA was funded in 1988 by the Equitable [Life Insurance] Foundation, the Rockerfeller Foundation, and the National Endowment for the Arts. The American Family Association (AFA) was established in 1987 as a reorganization of the National Federation for Decency founded in 1977 by Donald E. Wildmon. The Association is a watch-dog group that monitors television, movies, and bookstores. It initiates boycotts and letter-writing campaigns against advertisers that sponsor programs that transgress AFA's standards on sexuality, violence, and profanity. On Serrano and the AFA, see Steven C. Dubin, *Arresting Images: Impolitic Art and Uncivil Actions* (London: Routledge, 1992), pp. 96–101.
2 Ibid., p. 180.
3 J. E. Peterson, "A Conflict of Values: Legal and Ethical Treatment of American Indian Remains," *Death Studies* 14 (1990), p. 553. See for instance, North Carolina Rev. Stat. 227-C: 8 (1988); Florida St. 872.05 (1988); and Maine Rev. St. 194.400 to

194.410 (1988). See also Chris Raymond, "Reburial of Indian Remains Stimulates Studies, Friction Among Scholars," *Chronicle for Higher Education* (October 3, 1990).
4 Steve Talbot, "Desecration and American Indian Religious Freedom," *Journal of Ethnic Studies* (1985), p. 10. The Zuni people had asked the Denver Art Museum to return its twin war gods in 1978 and, according to the Zuni Governor's Office, the gods were returned "in late 1980." See also Roberto Suro, "Quiet Effort to Regain Idols May Alter Views of Indian Art," *New York Times* (August 13, 1990).
5 Glen Davidson, "Human Remains: Contemporary Issues," *Death Studies* 14 (1990), p. 495.
6 An excellent example of the refusal to take seriously the religious dimension of the debate is the *New York Times Magazine* article, "Reverend Wildmon's War on the Arts" by Bruce Selcraig (described as former United States Senate investigator). Selcraig continually presents Wildmon as a southern hick (" a balding, pink-faced father of four . . . [who] relishes quiet weekends in Tupelo [Mississippi] riding his lawn mower") even though he has a graduate divinity degree from Emory University and has managed a successful campaign against the NEA.
7 Robert Orsi, "The Smell of God: Ethnicity and Religion in the United States," unpublished paper given at the University of Utah, October 1990.
8 Roland Marchand, *Advertising the American Dream: Making Way for Modernity 1920–1940* (Berkeley: Univ. of California Press, 1986), p. 70.
9 James A. Martin, *Beauty and Holiness: The Dialogue Between Aesthetics and Religion* (Princeton: Princeton Univ. Press, 1990), p. 3.
10 Andrew R. Heinze, *Adapting to Abundance: Jewish Immigrants, Mass Consumption, and the Search for American Identity* (New York: Columbia Univ. Press, 1990),

Index